The
Death of The Master

The Death of The Master

patrickkyle.com

Published by Koyama Press
koyamapress.com

First edition: October 2019
ISBN: 978-1-927668-71-9
Printed in Canada

Koyama Press gratefully acknowledges the Canada Council
for the Arts and the Ontario Arts Council for their support of
our publishing program.

Patrick Kyle would like to acknowledge funding support from
the Ontario Arts Council, an agency of the Government of
Ontario.

ONTARIO ARTS COUNCIL
CONSEIL DES ARTS DE L'ONTARIO

an Ontario government agency
un organisme du gouvernement de l'Ontario

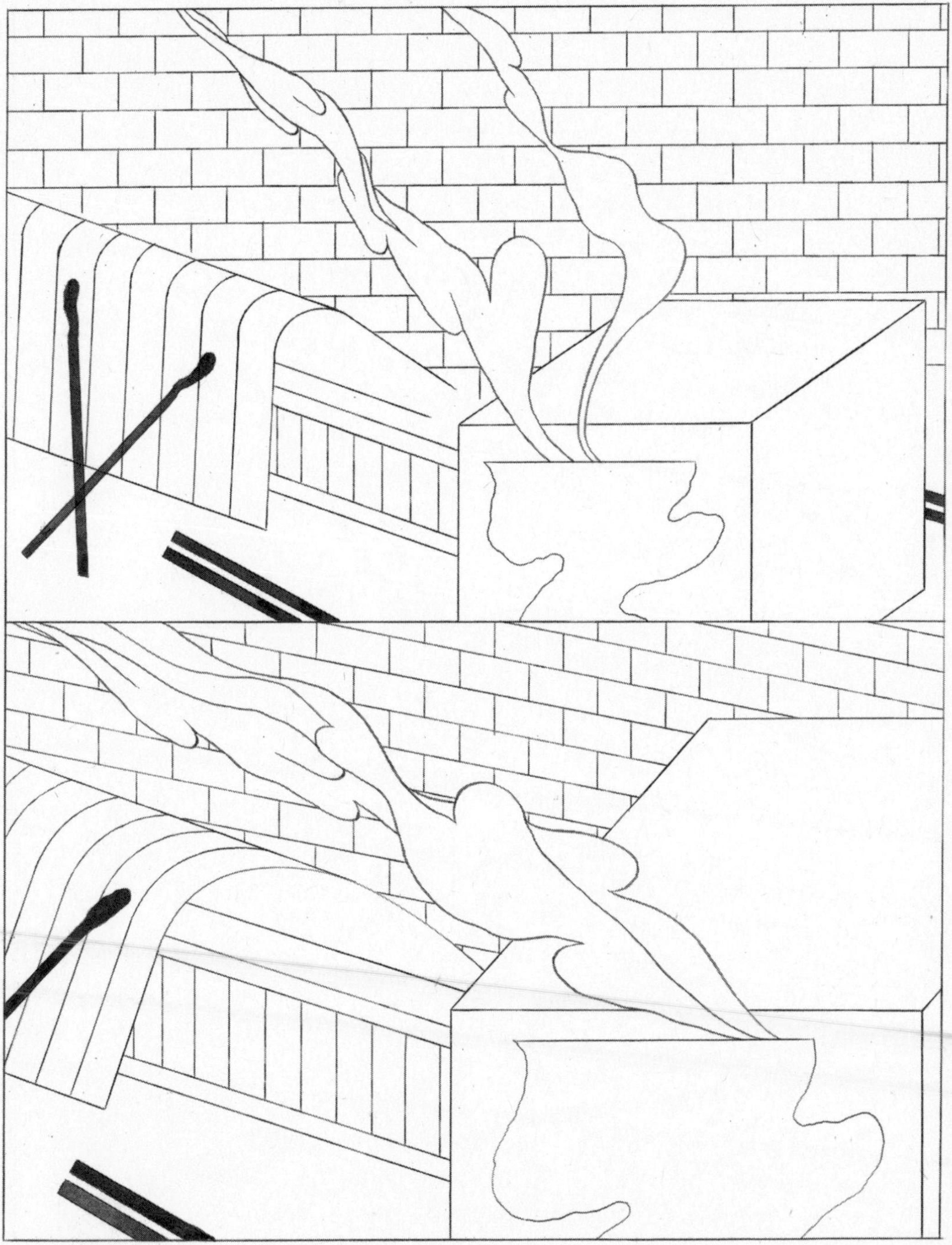

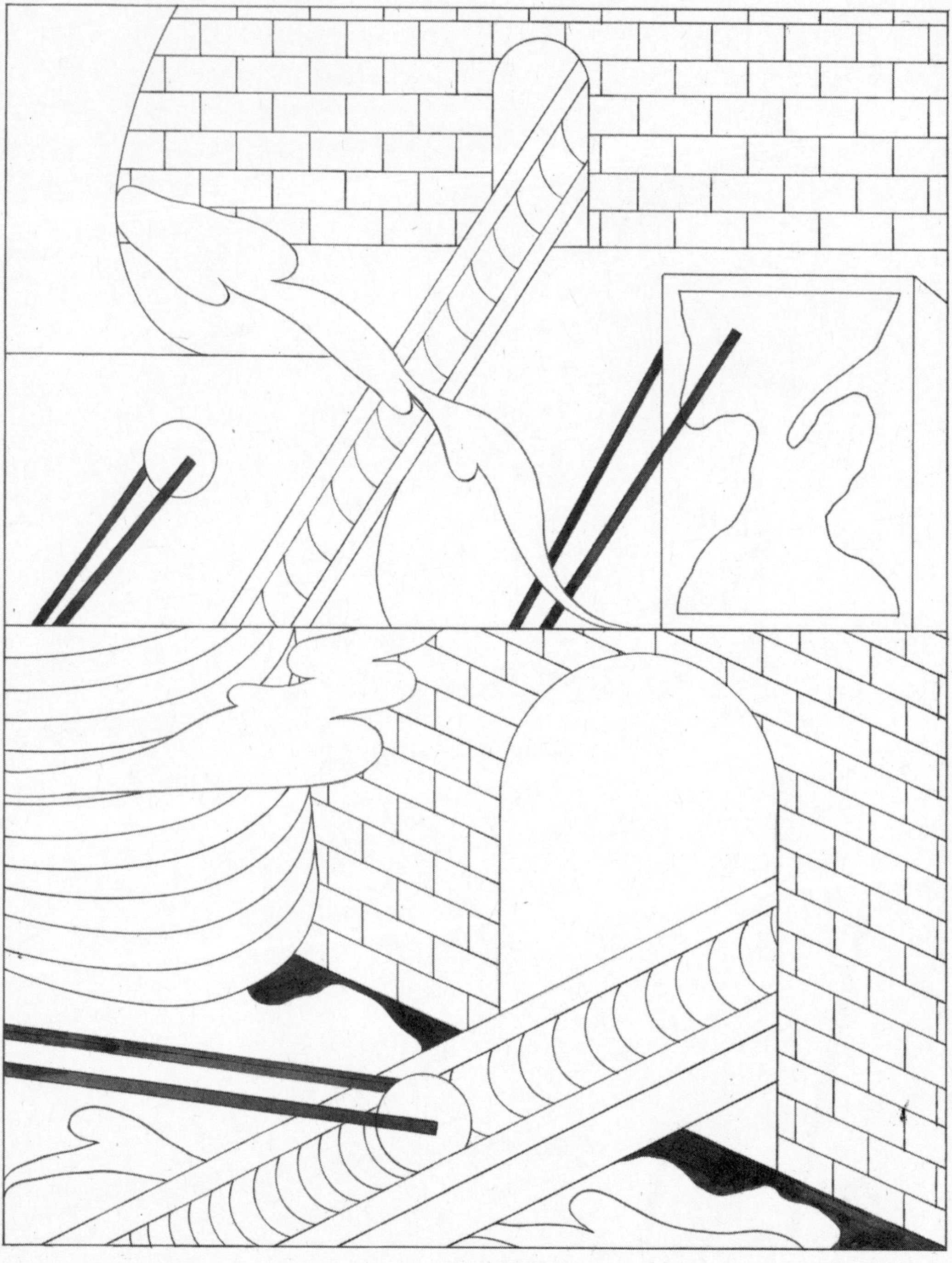

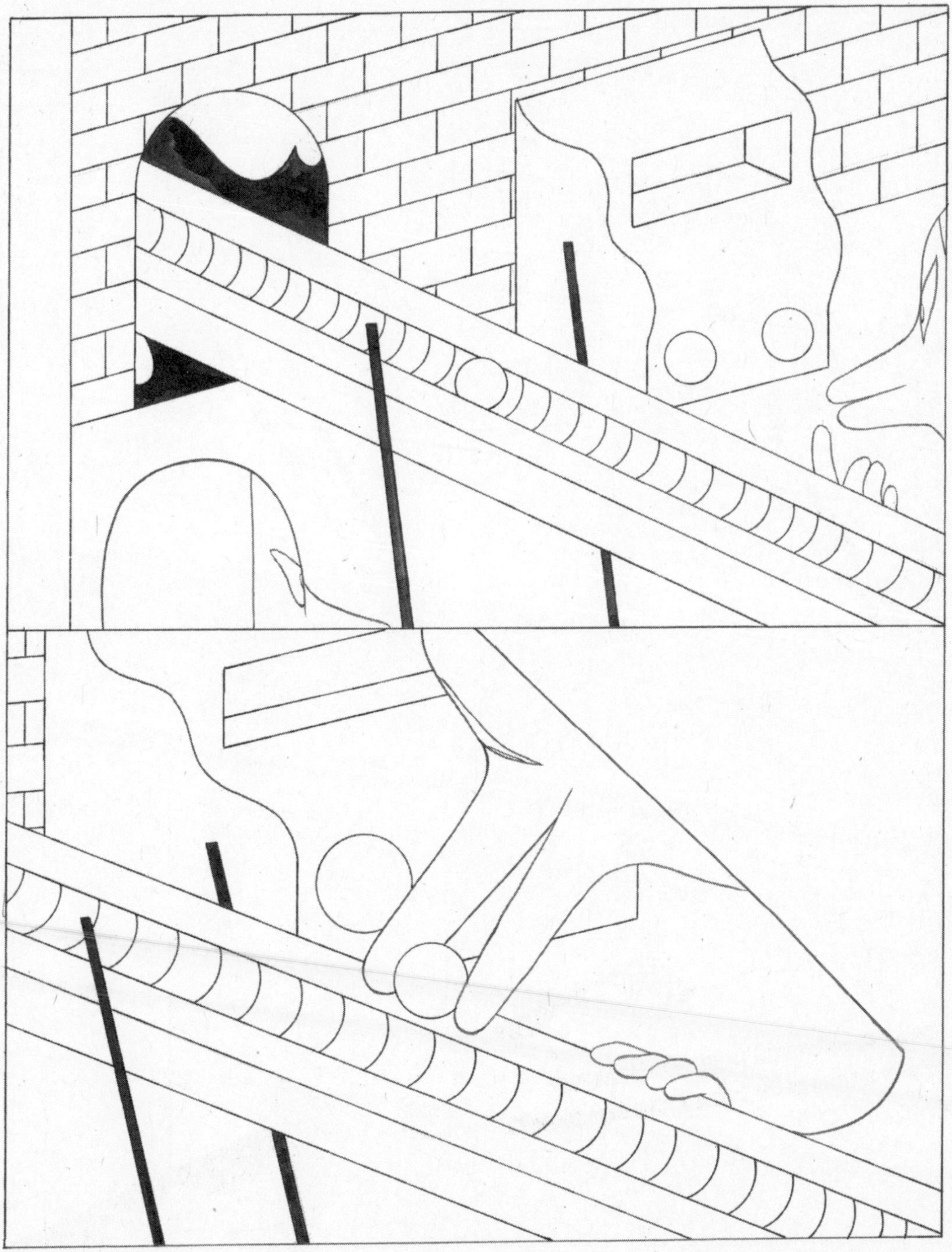

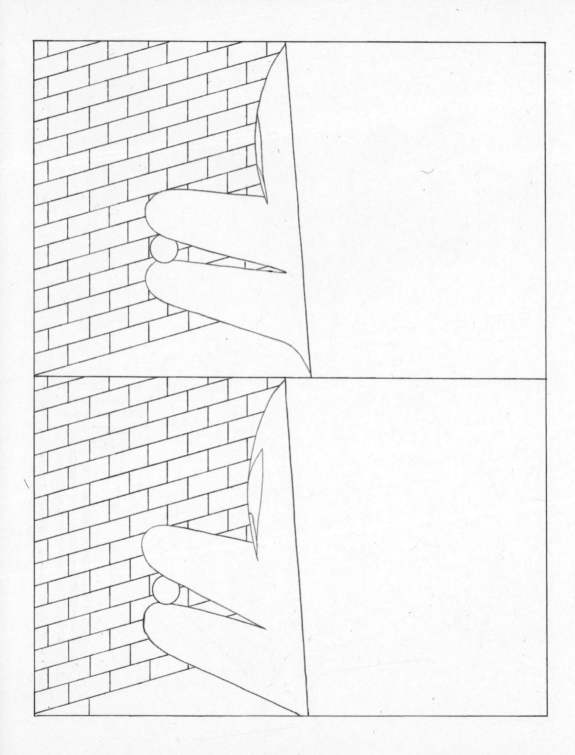

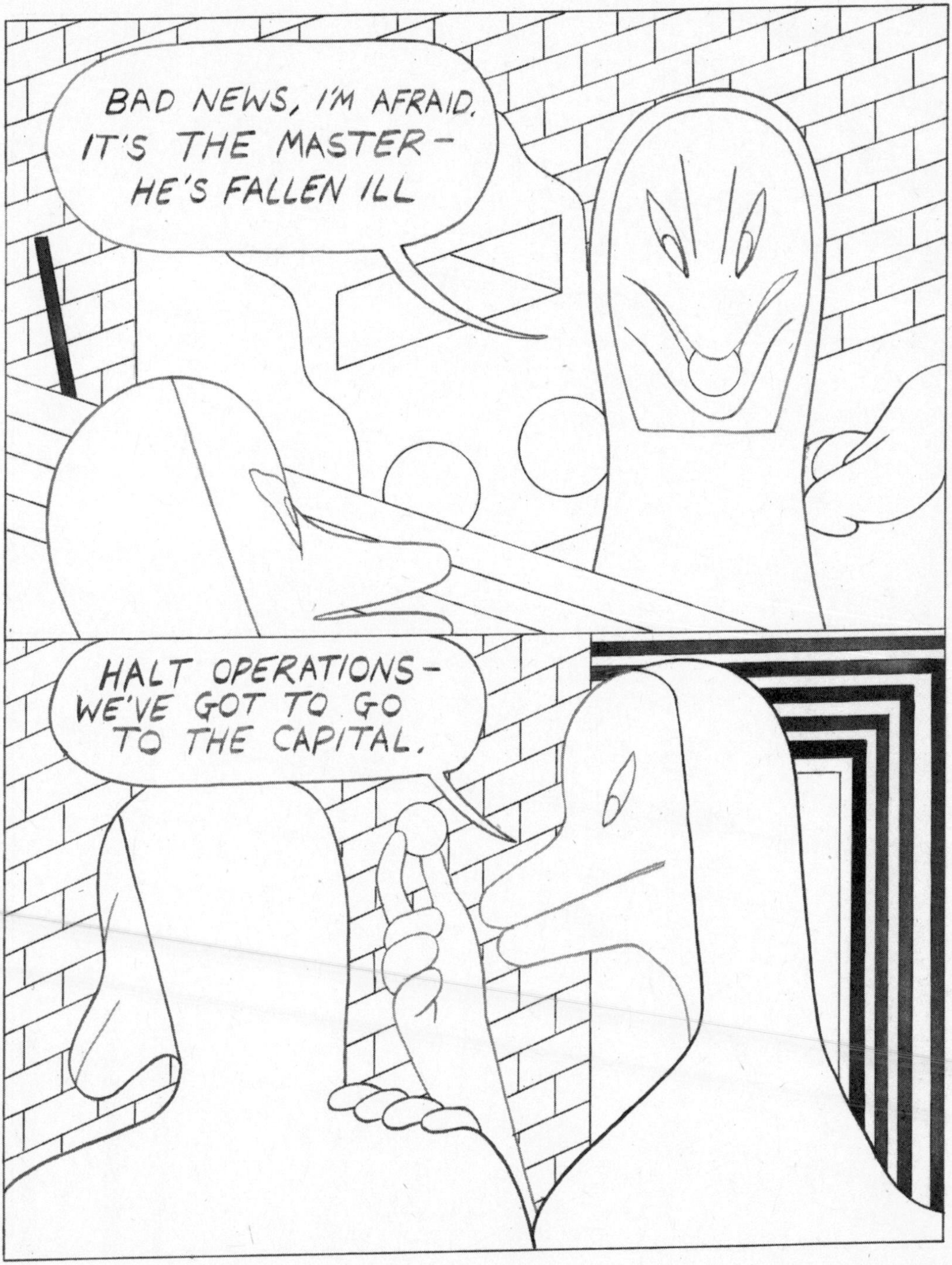
BAD NEWS, I'M AFRAID. IT'S THE MASTER- HE'S FALLEN ILL
HALT OPERATIONS- WE'VE GOT TO GO TO THE CAPITAL.

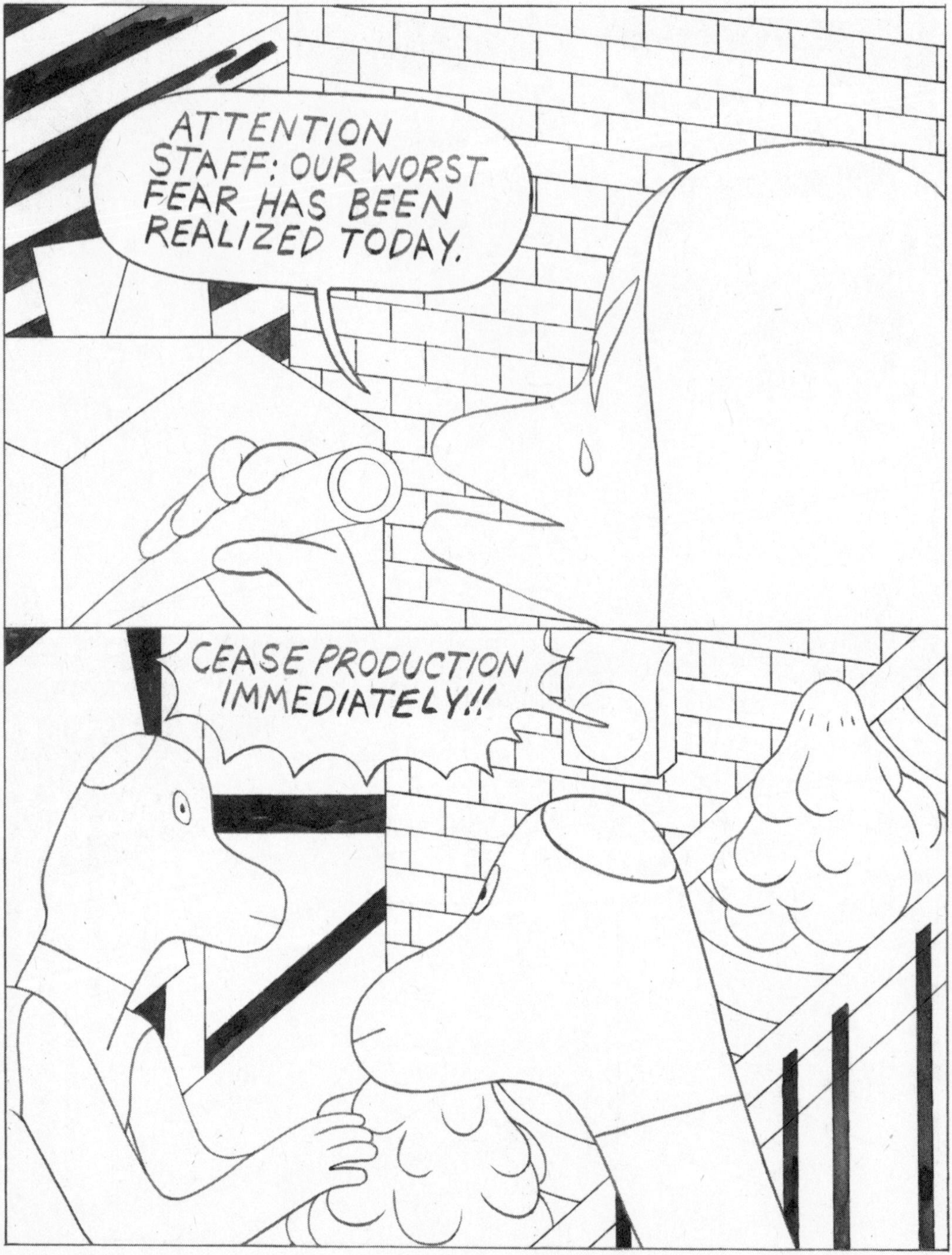
ATTENTION STAFF: OUR WORST FEAR HAS BEEN REALIZED TODAY.
CEASE PRODUCTION IMMEDIATELY!!

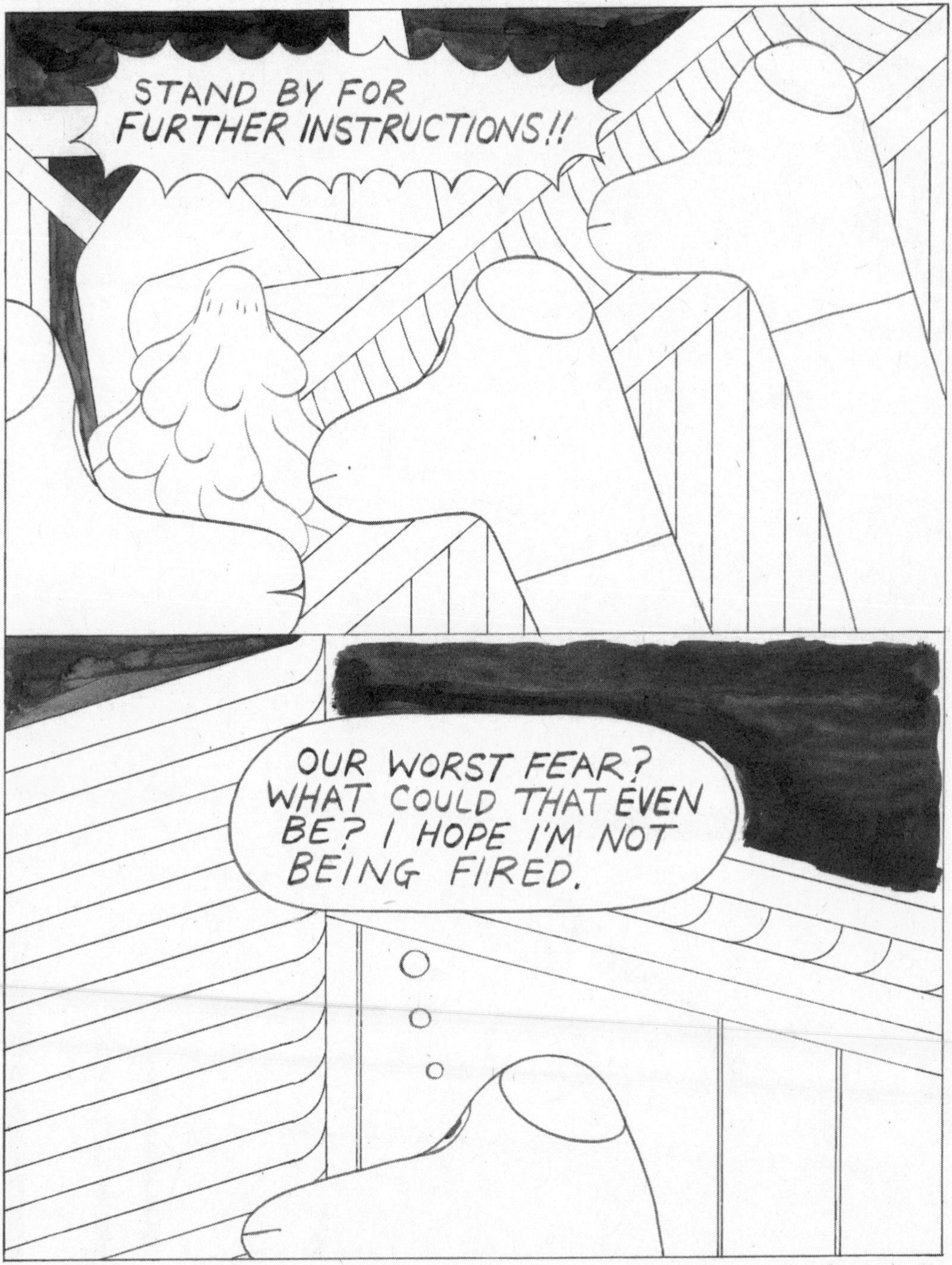
STAND BY FOR FURTHER INSTRUCTIONS!!
OUR WORST FEAR? WHAT COULD THAT EVEN BE? I HOPE I'M NOT BEING FIRED.

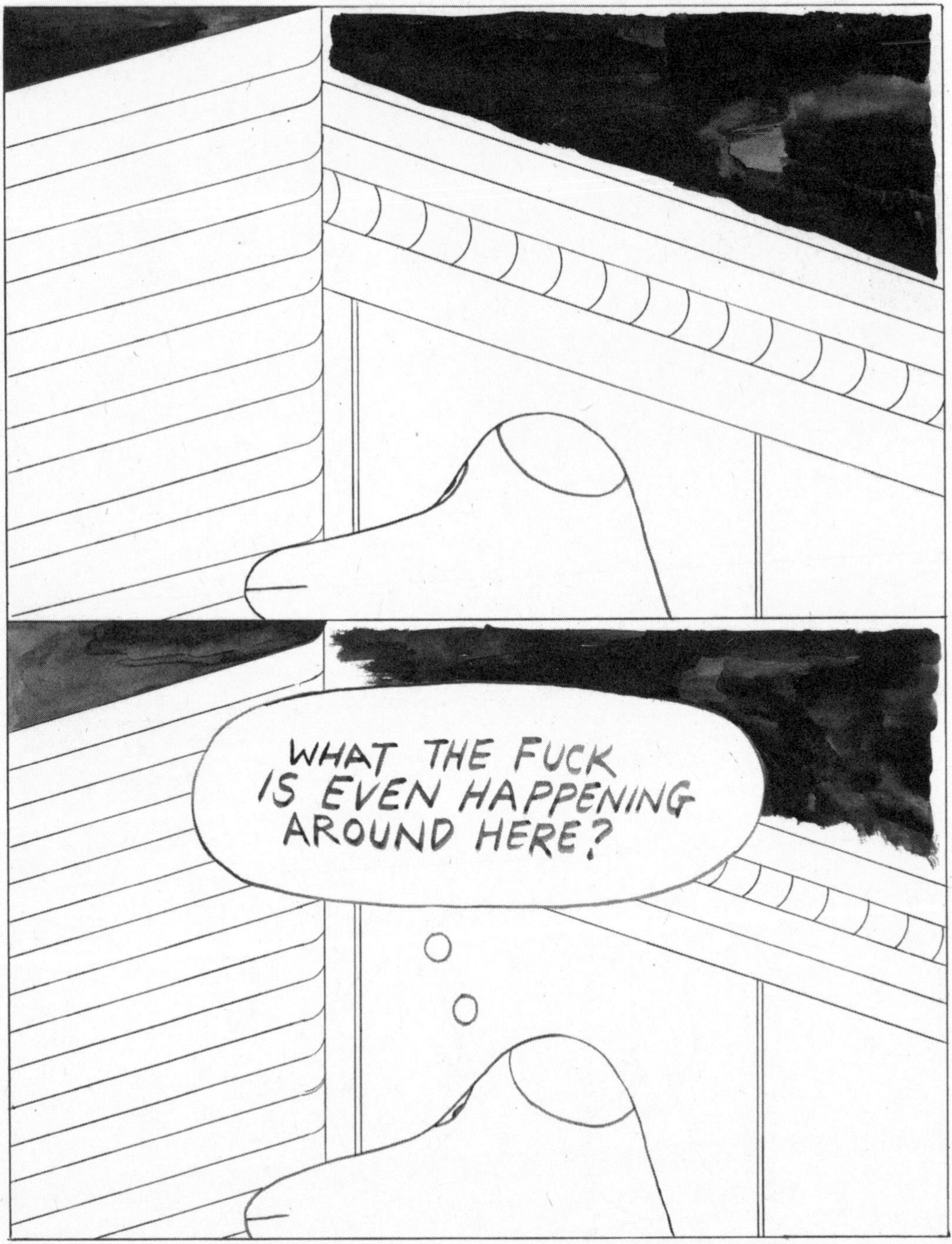
WHAT THE FUCK IS EVEN HAPPENING AROUND HERE?

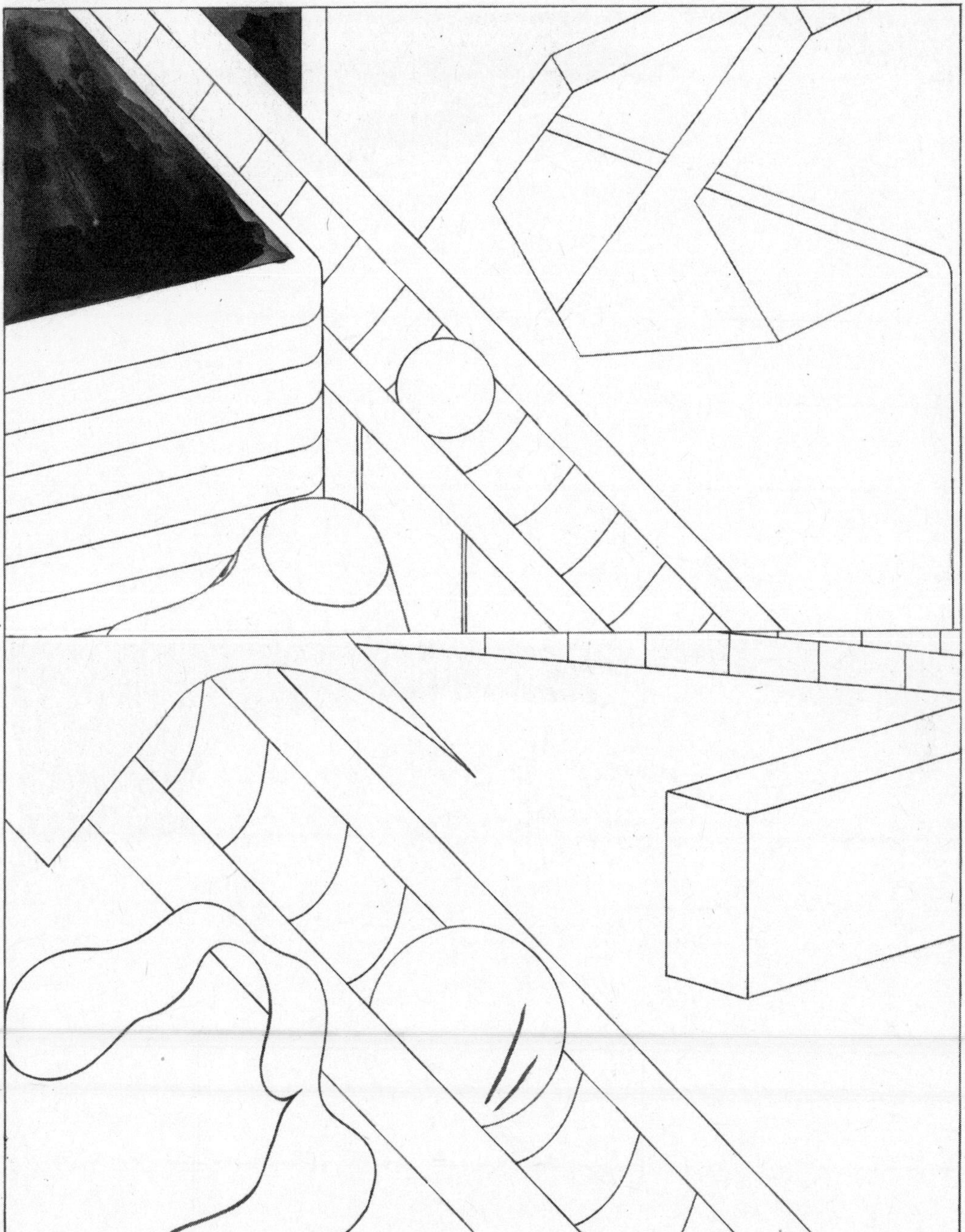

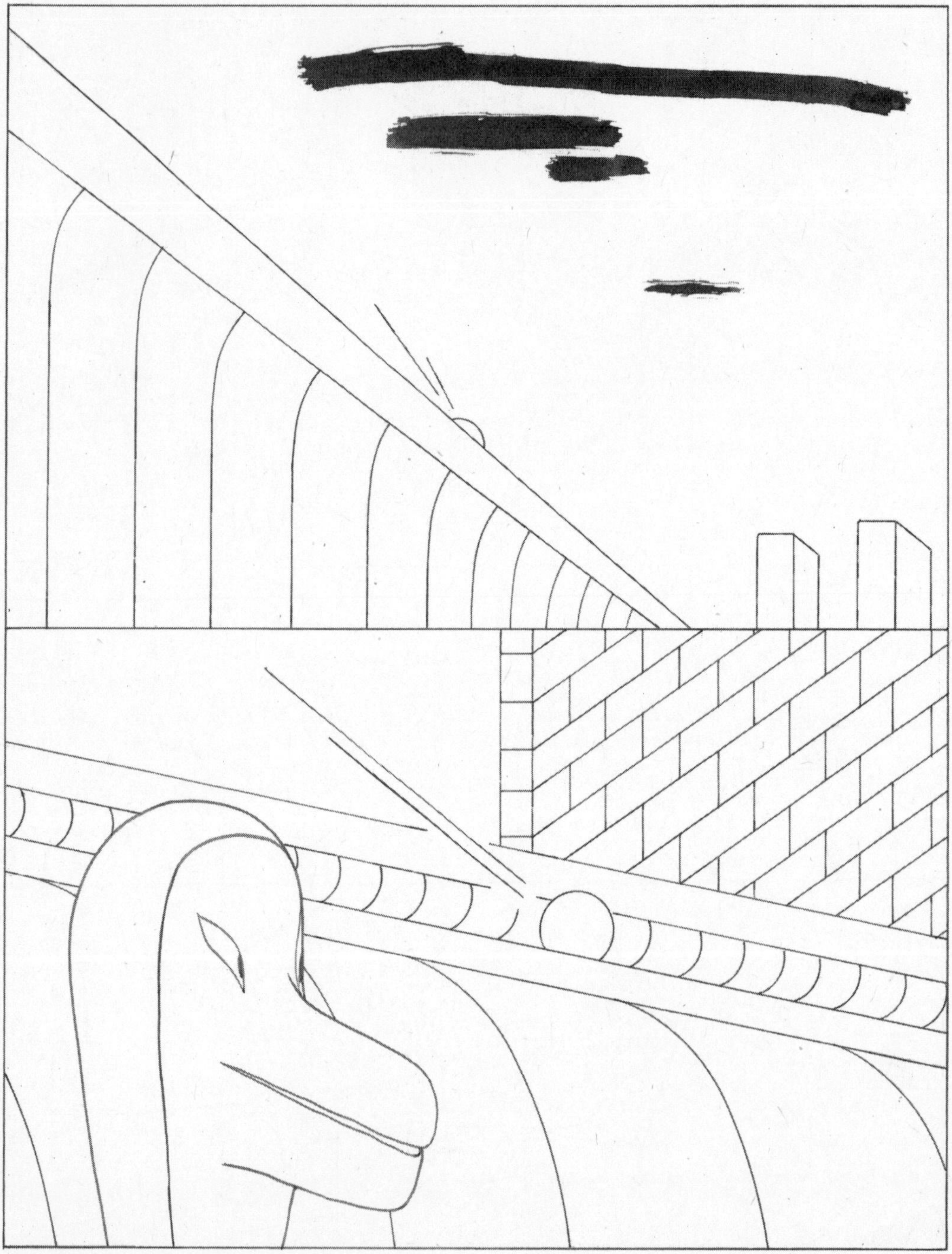

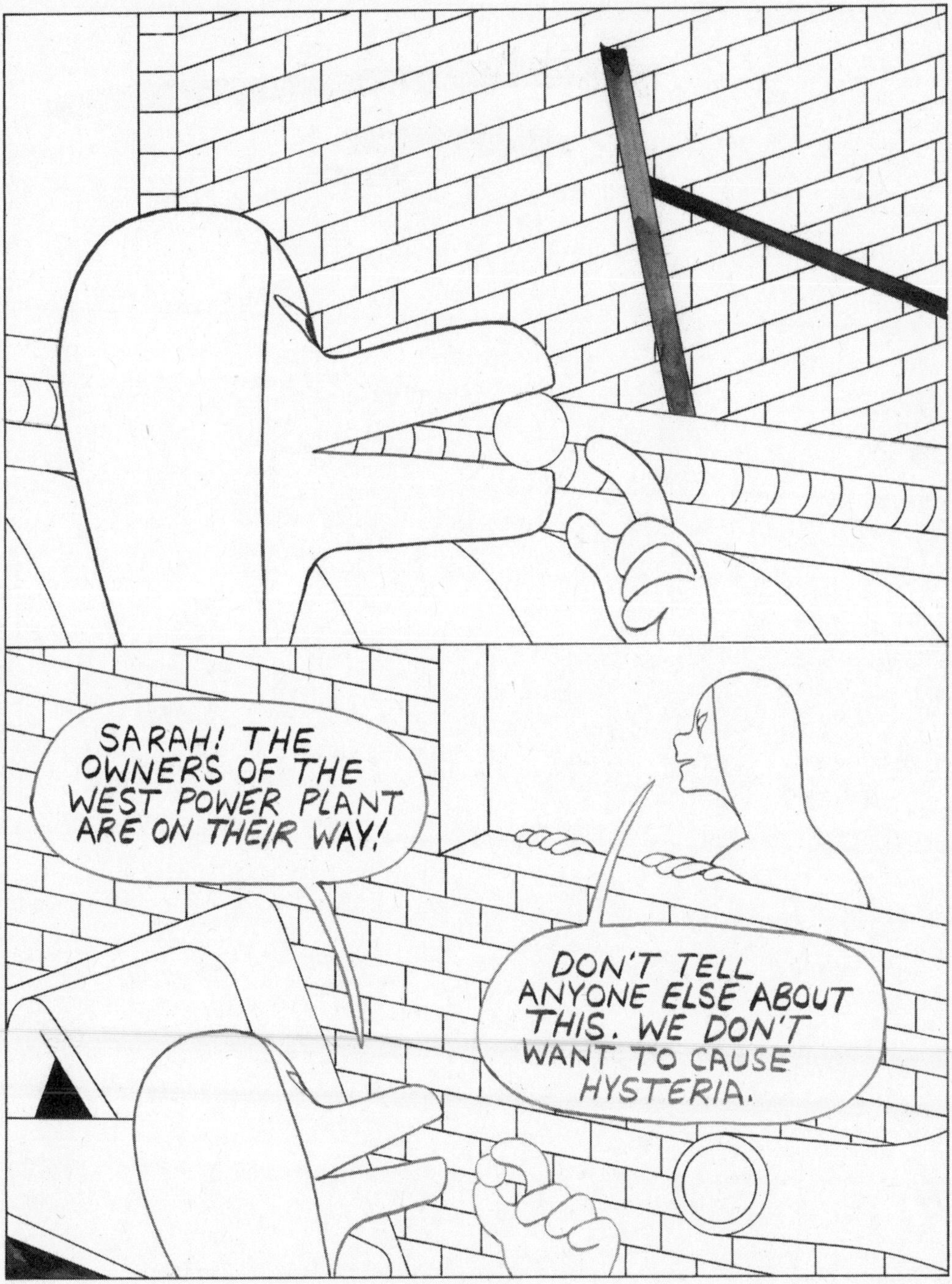
SARAH! THE OWNERS OF THE WEST POWER PLANT ARE ON THEIR WAY!
DON'T TELL ANYONE ELSE ABOUT THIS. WE DON'T WANT TO CAUSE HYSTERIA.

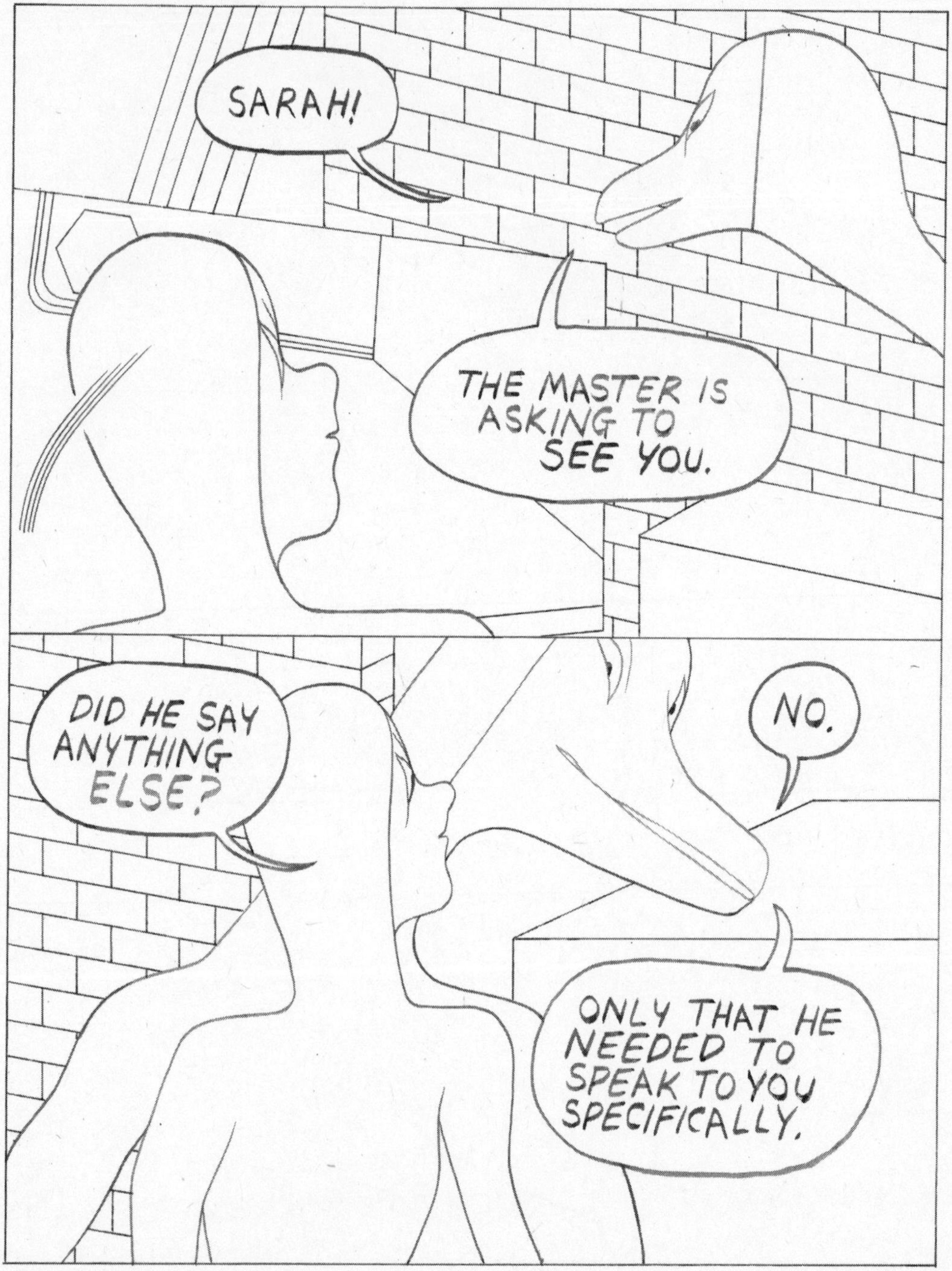
SARAH!
THE MASTER IS ASKING TO SEE YOU.
DID HE SAY ANYTHING ELSE?
NO.
ONLY THAT HE NEEDED TO SPEAK TO YOU SPECIFICALLY.

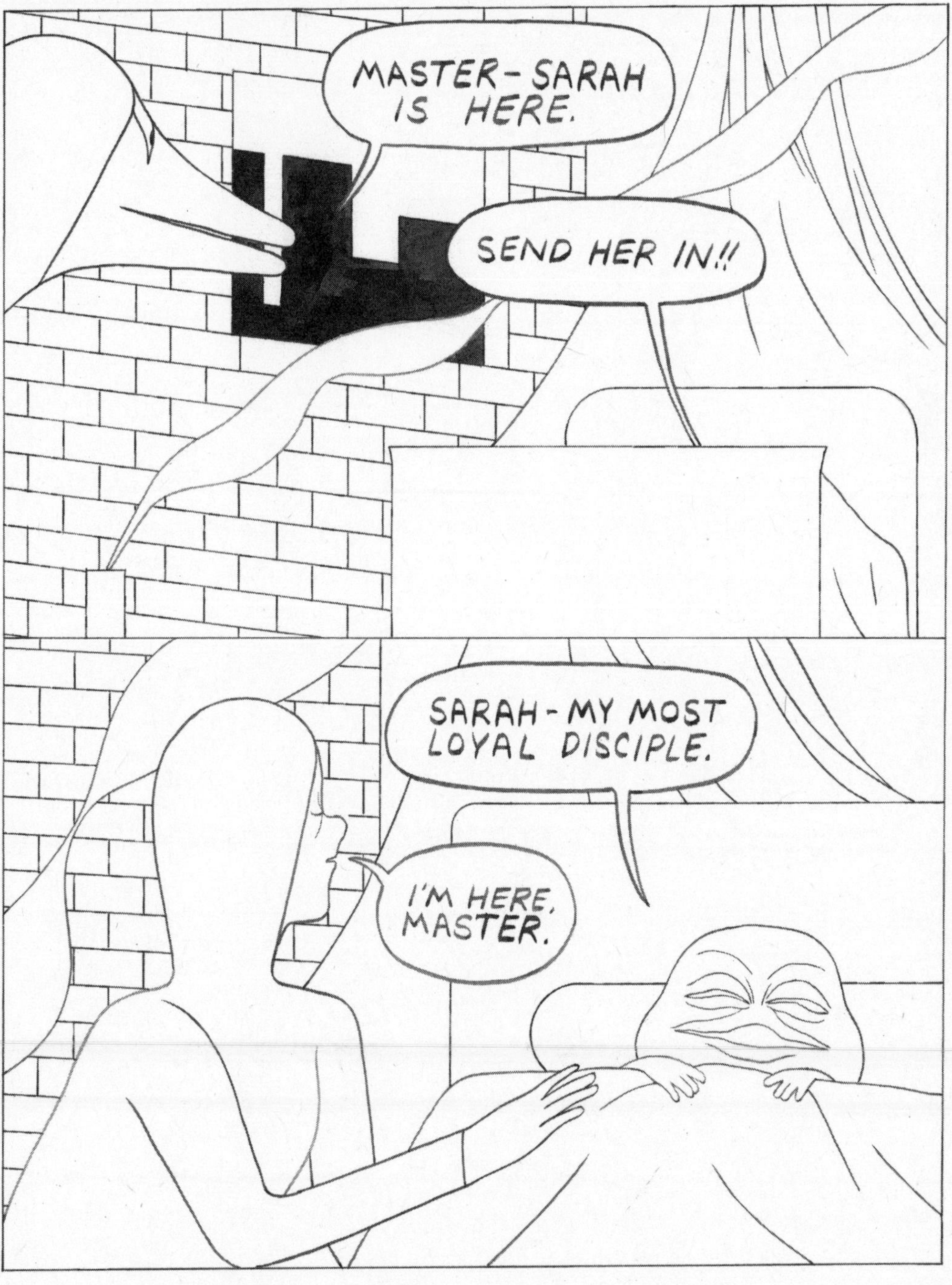
MASTER - SARAH IS HERE.
SEND HER IN!!
SARAH - MY MOST LOYAL DISCIPLE.
I'M HERE, MASTER.

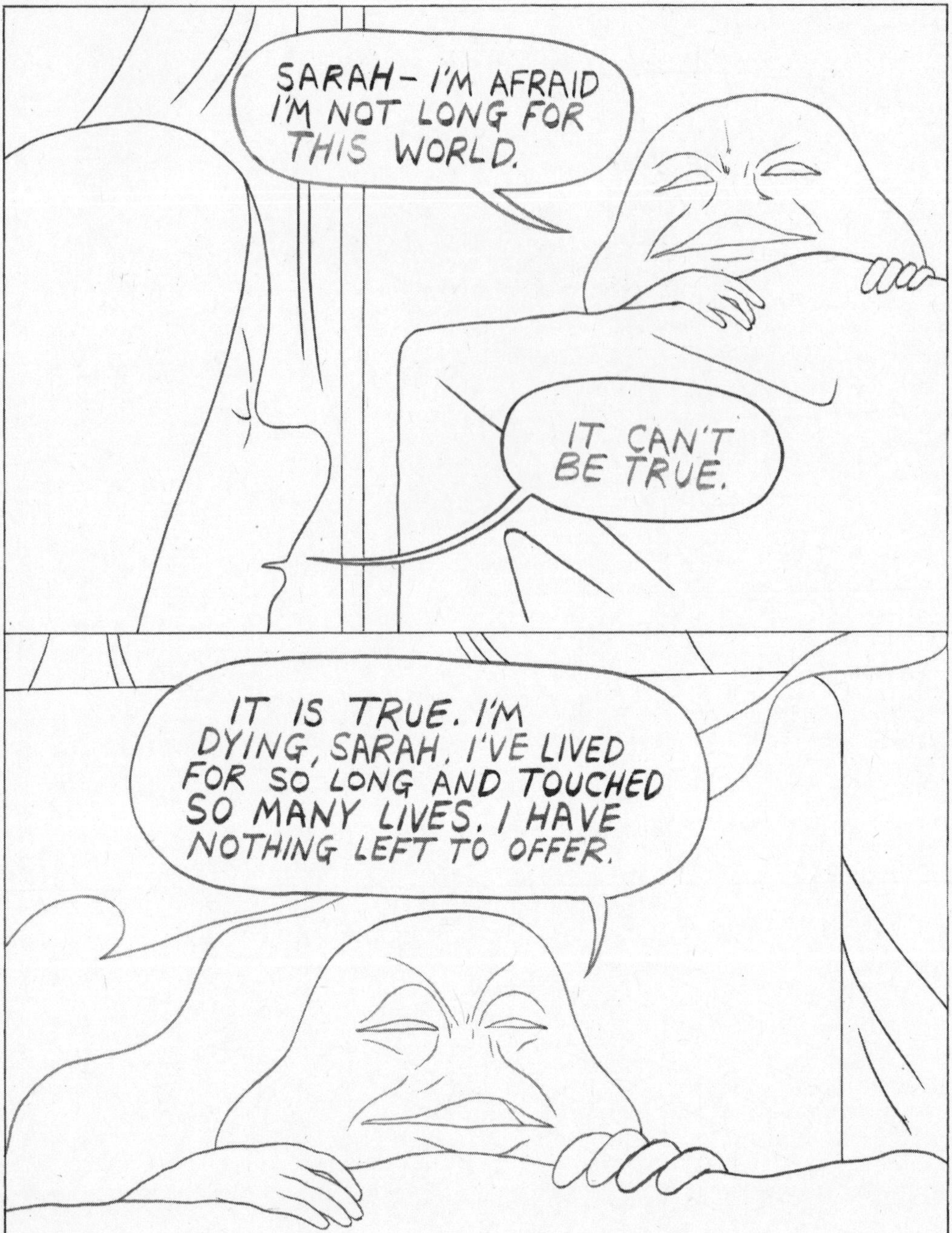
SARAH- I'M AFRAID I'M NOT LONG FOR THIS WORLD.
IT CAN'T BE TRUE.
IT IS TRUE. I'M DYING, SARAH. I'VE LIVED FOR SO LONG AND TOUCHED SO MANY LIVES. I HAVE NOTHING LEFT TO OFFER.

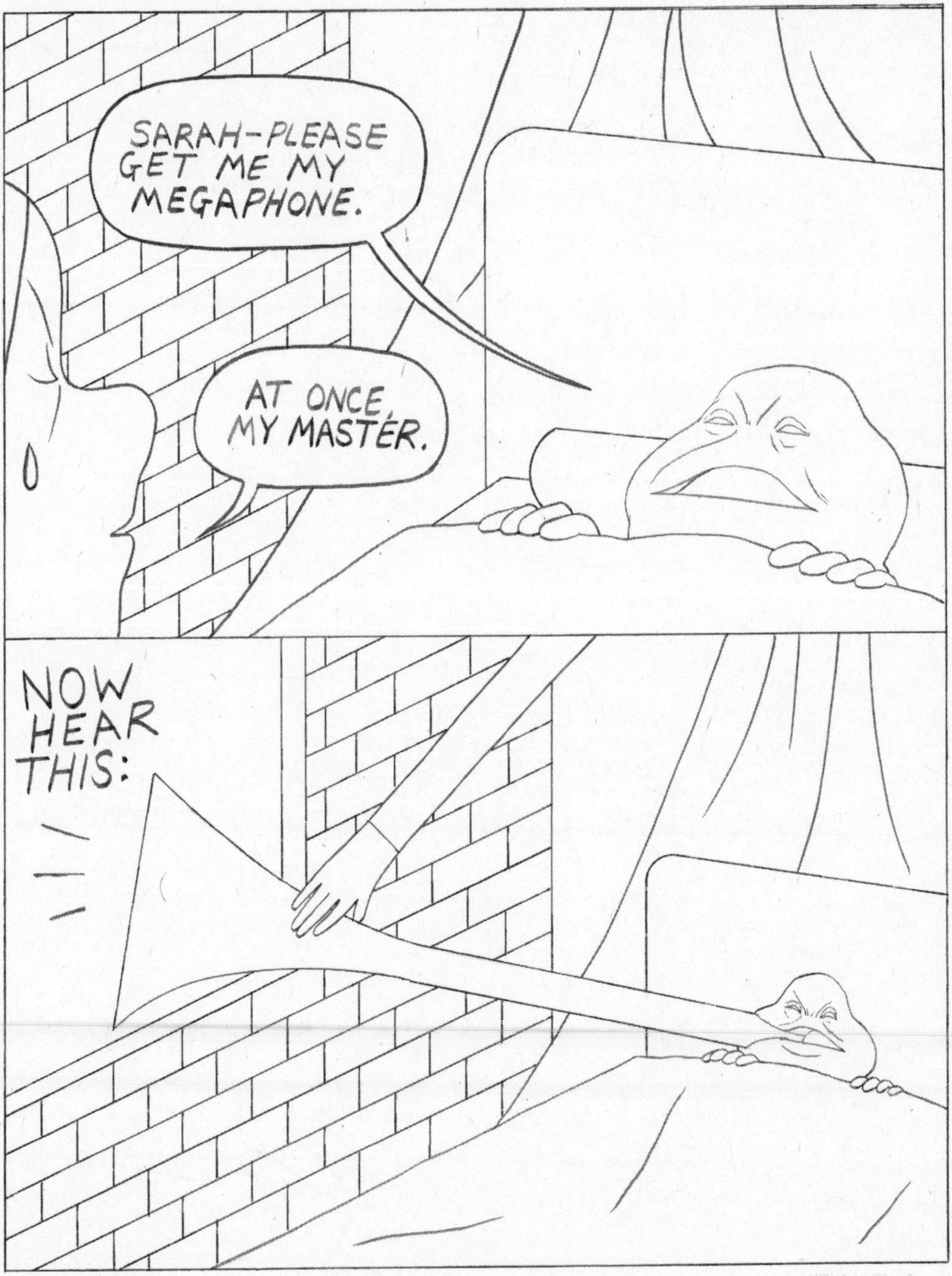
SARAH-PLEASE GET ME MY MEGAPHONE.
AT ONCE, MY MASTER.
NOW HEAR THIS:

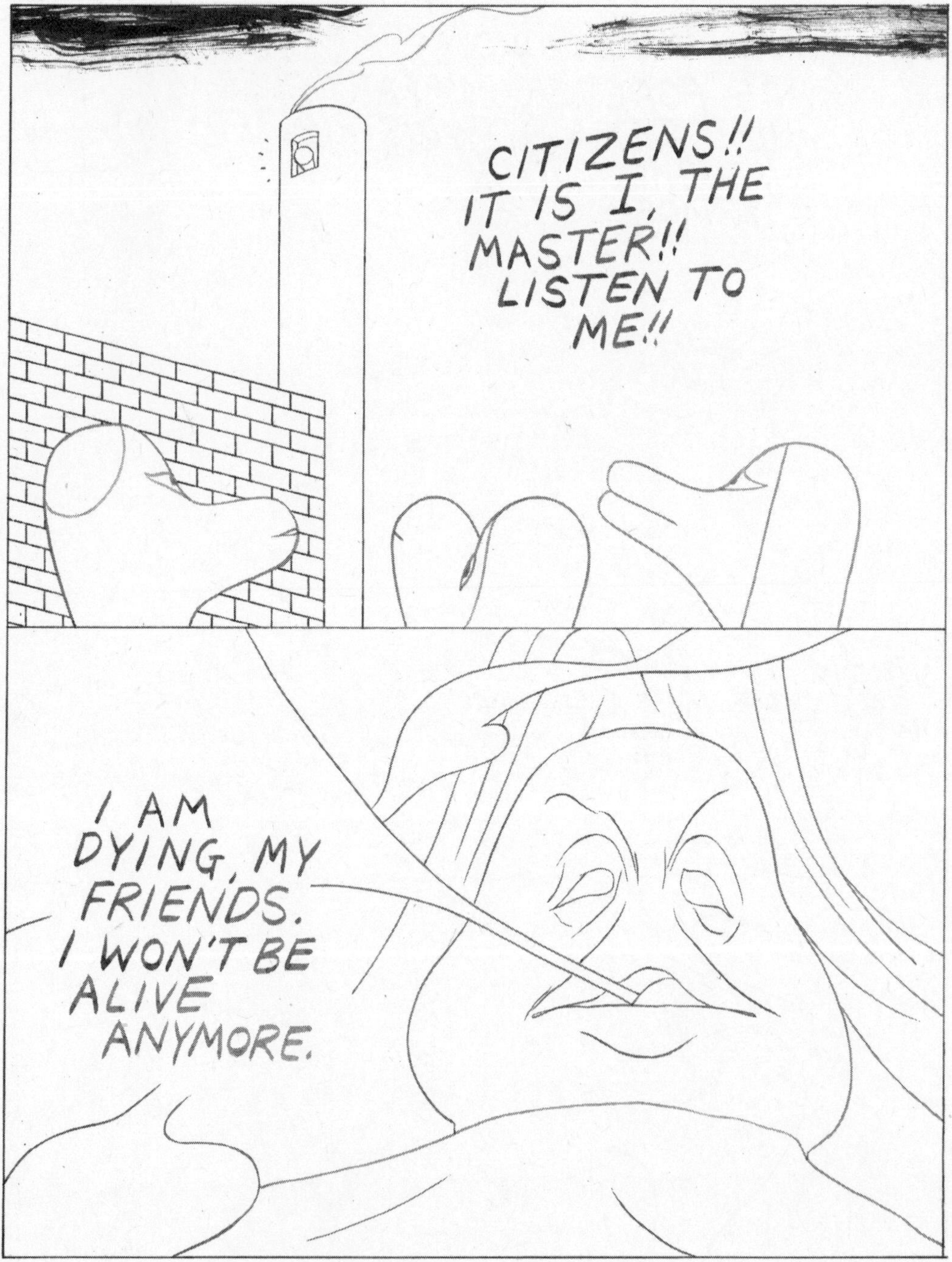
CITIZENS!! IT IS I, THE MASTER!! LISTEN TO ME!!
I AM DYING, MY FRIENDS. I WON'T BE ALIVE ANYMORE.

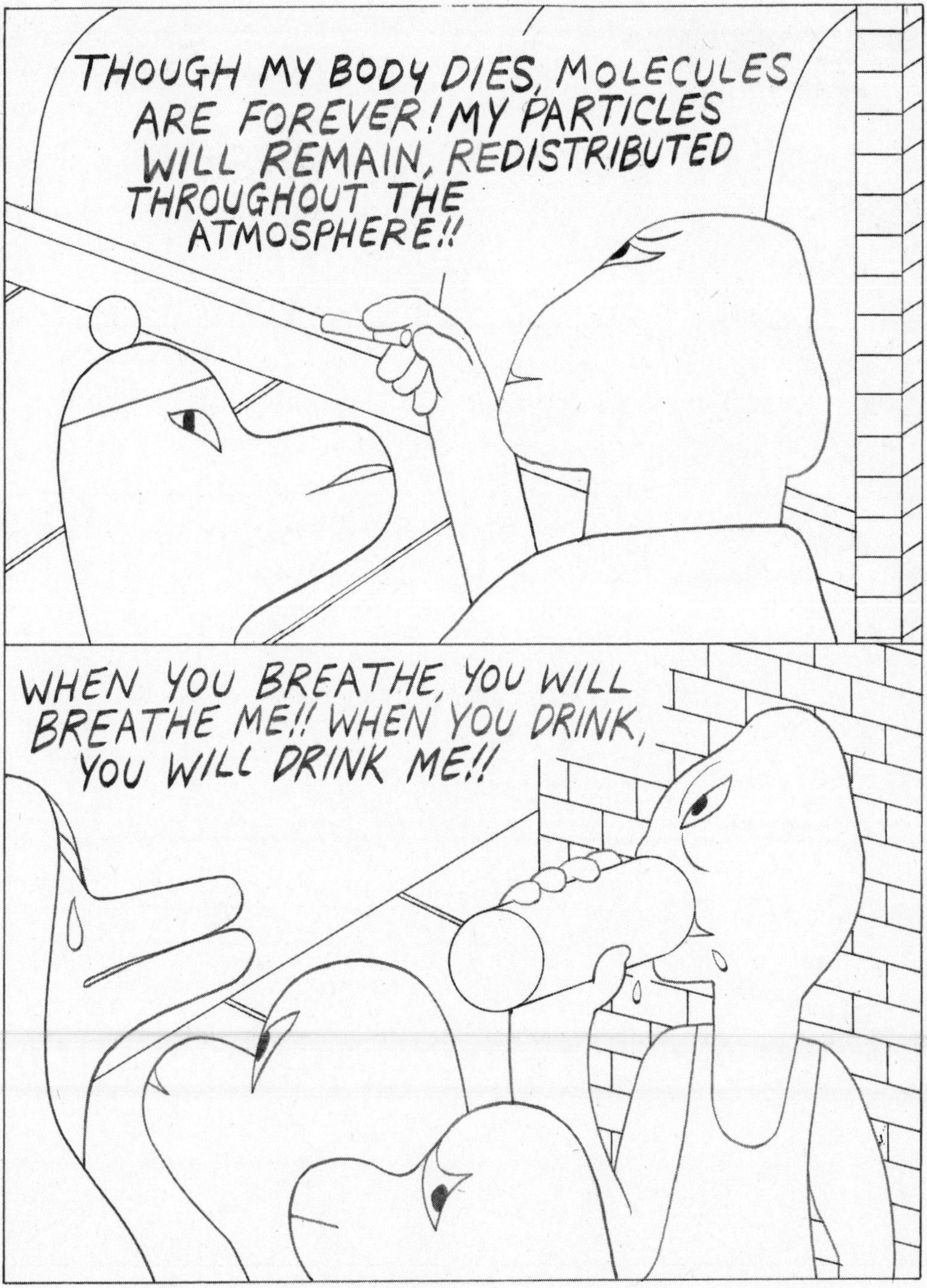
THOUGH MY BODY DIES, MOLECULES ARE FOREVER! MY PARTICLES WILL REMAIN, REDISTRIBUTED THROUGHOUT THE ATMOSPHERE!!
WHEN YOU BREATHE, YOU WILL BREATHE ME!! WHEN YOU DRINK, YOU WILL DRINK ME!!

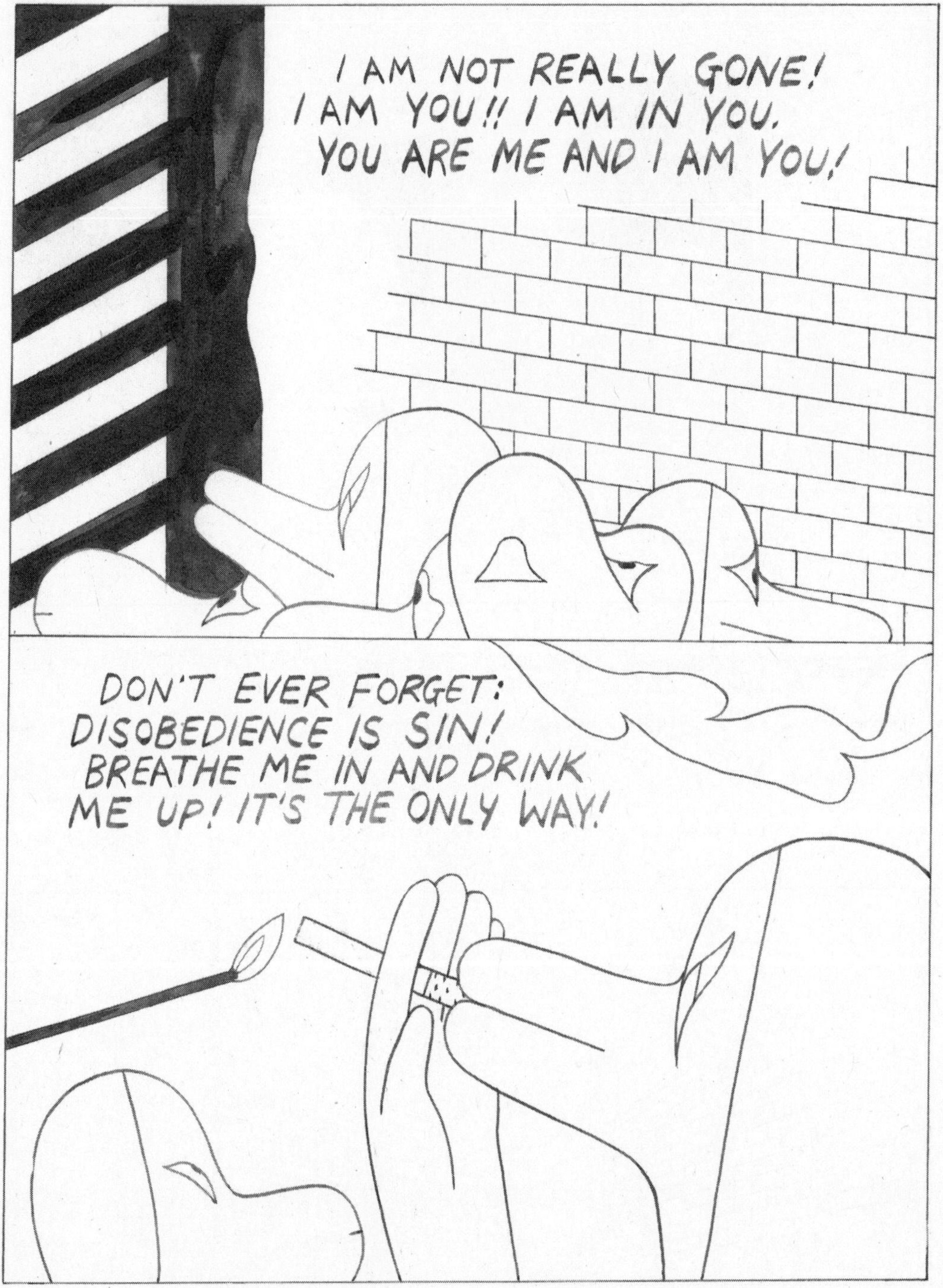
I AM NOT REALLY GONE! I AM YOU!! I AM IN YOU. YOU ARE ME AND I AM YOU!
DON'T EVER FORGET: DISOBEDIENCE IS SIN! BREATHE ME IN AND DRINK ME UP! IT'S THE ONLY WAY!

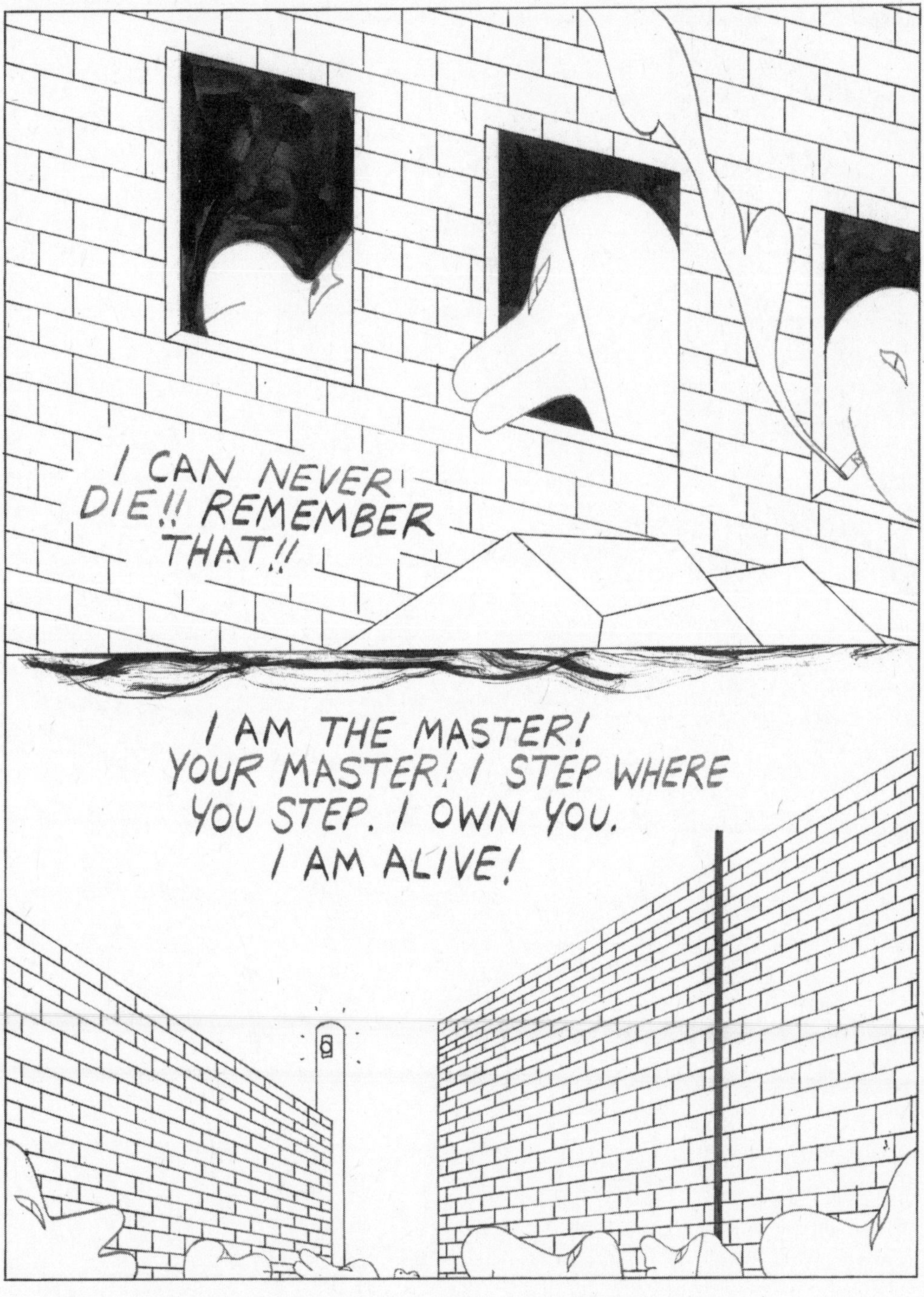
I CAN NEVER DIE!! REMEMBER THAT!!
I AM THE MASTER! YOUR MASTER! I STEP WHERE YOU STEP. I OWN YOU. I AM ALIVE!

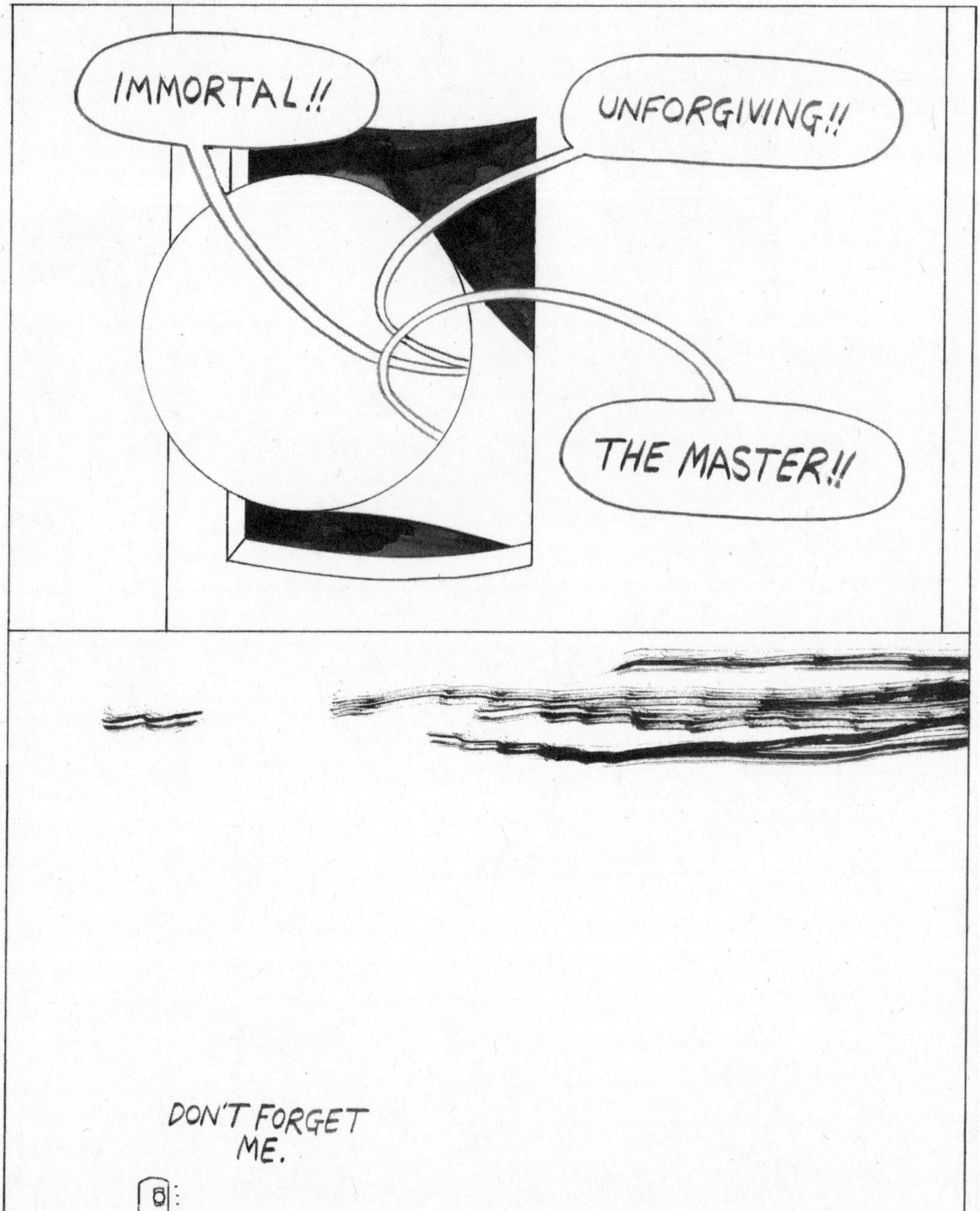
IMMORTAL!!
UNFORGIVING!!
THE MASTER!!
DON'T FORGET ME.

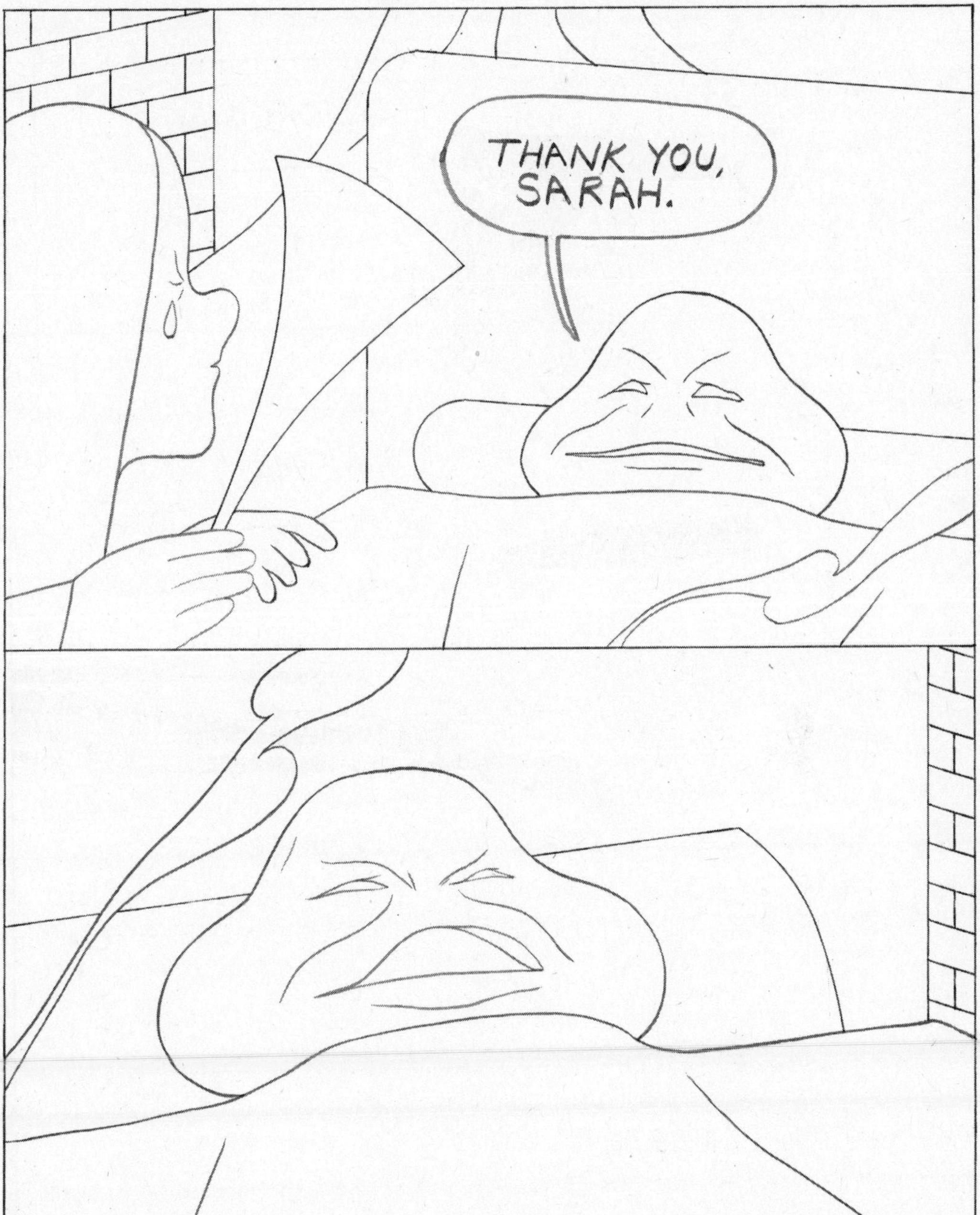
THANK YOU, SARAH.

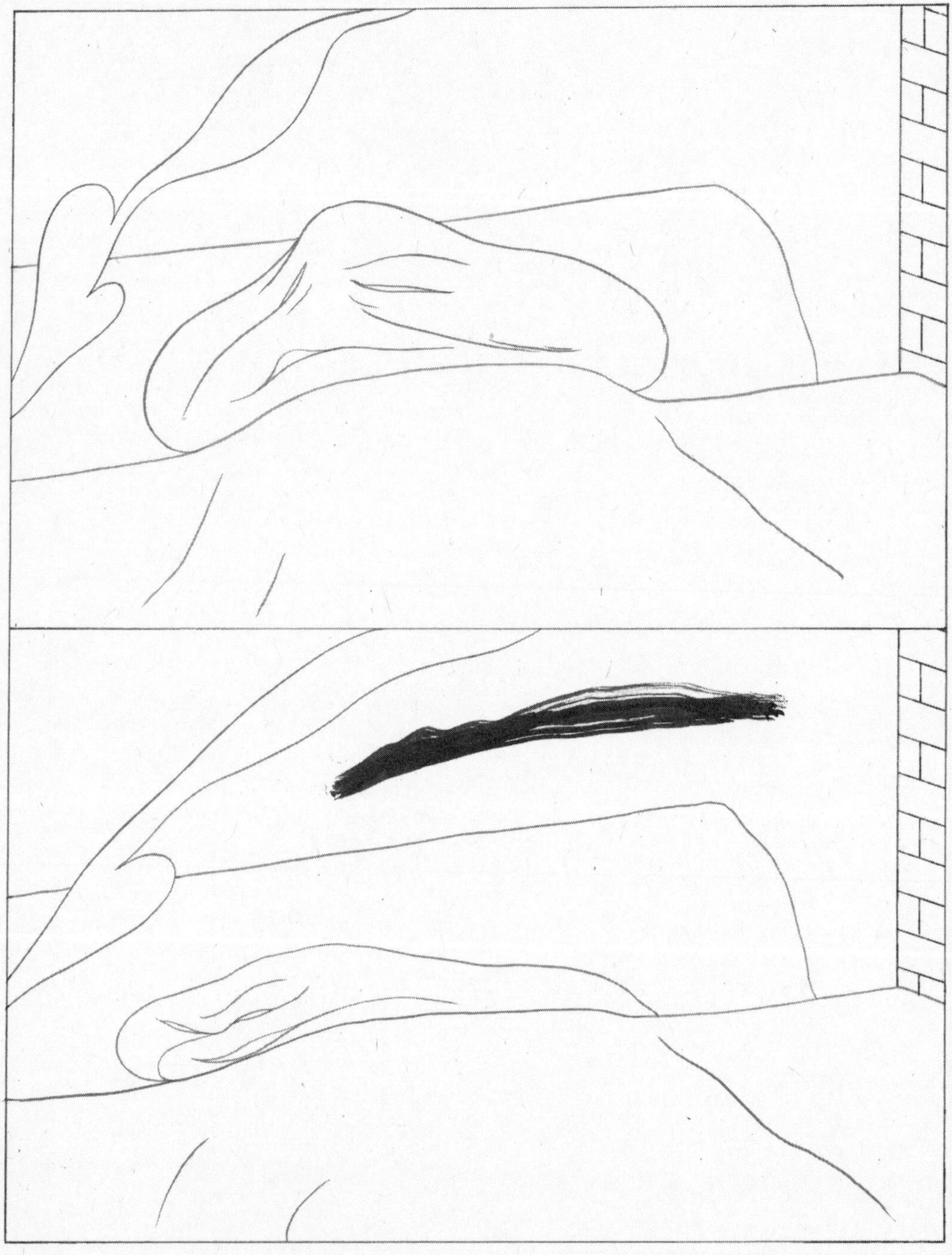

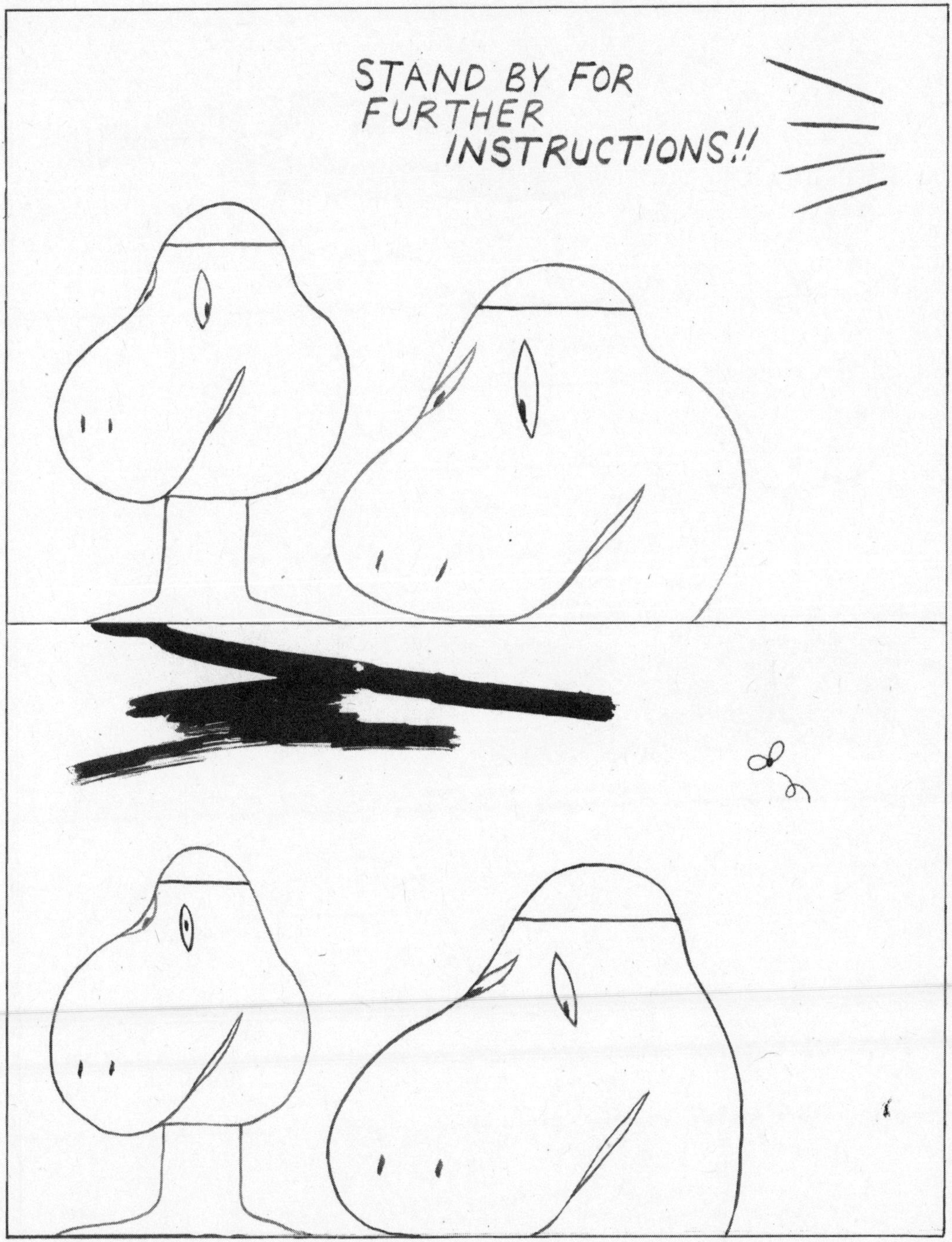
STAND BY FOR FURTHER INSTRUCTIONS!!

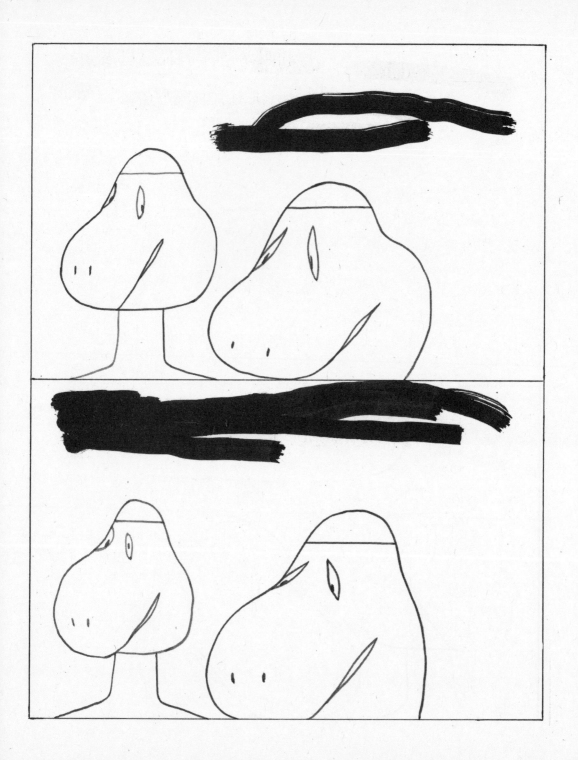

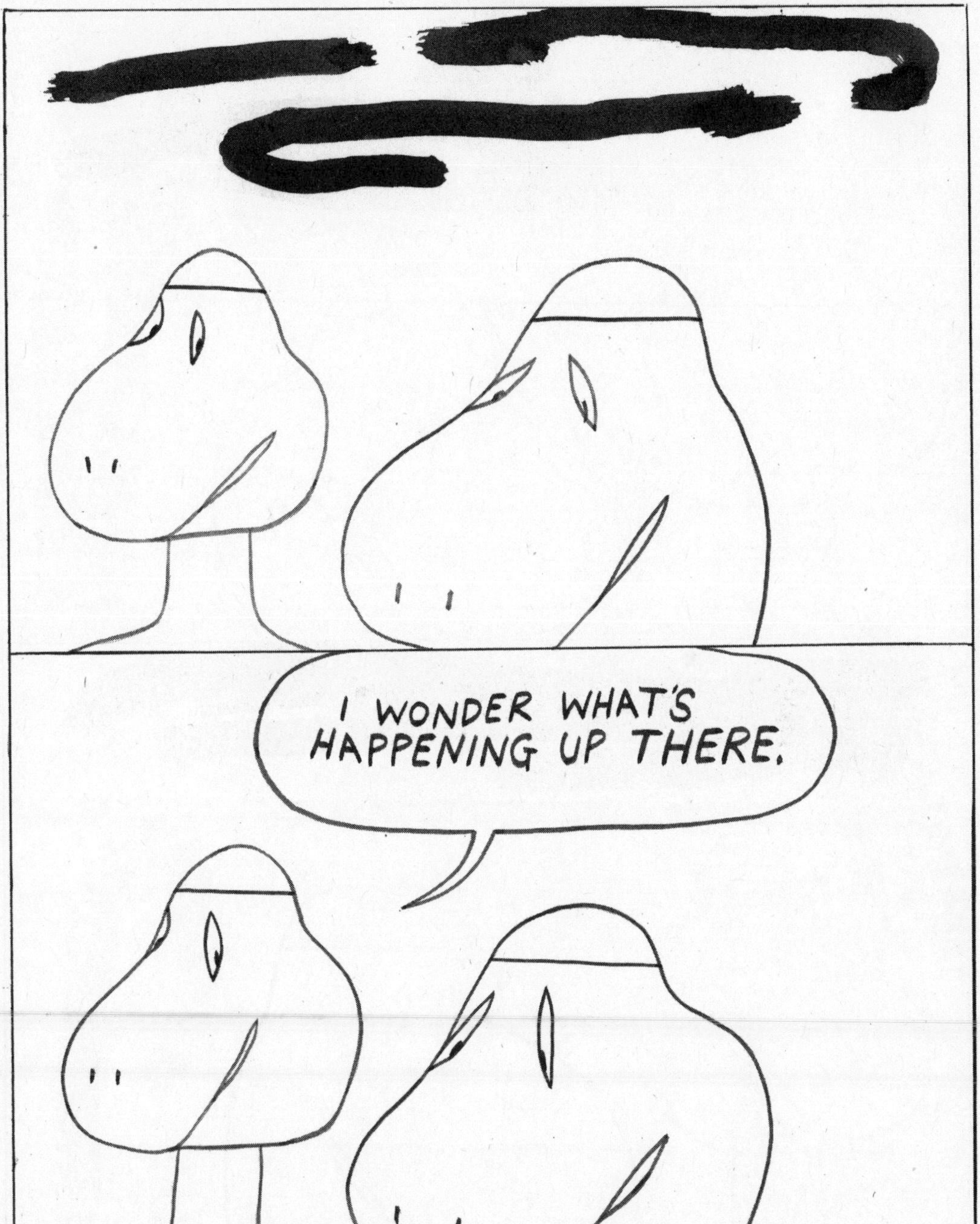
I WONDER WHAT'S HAPPENING UP THERE.

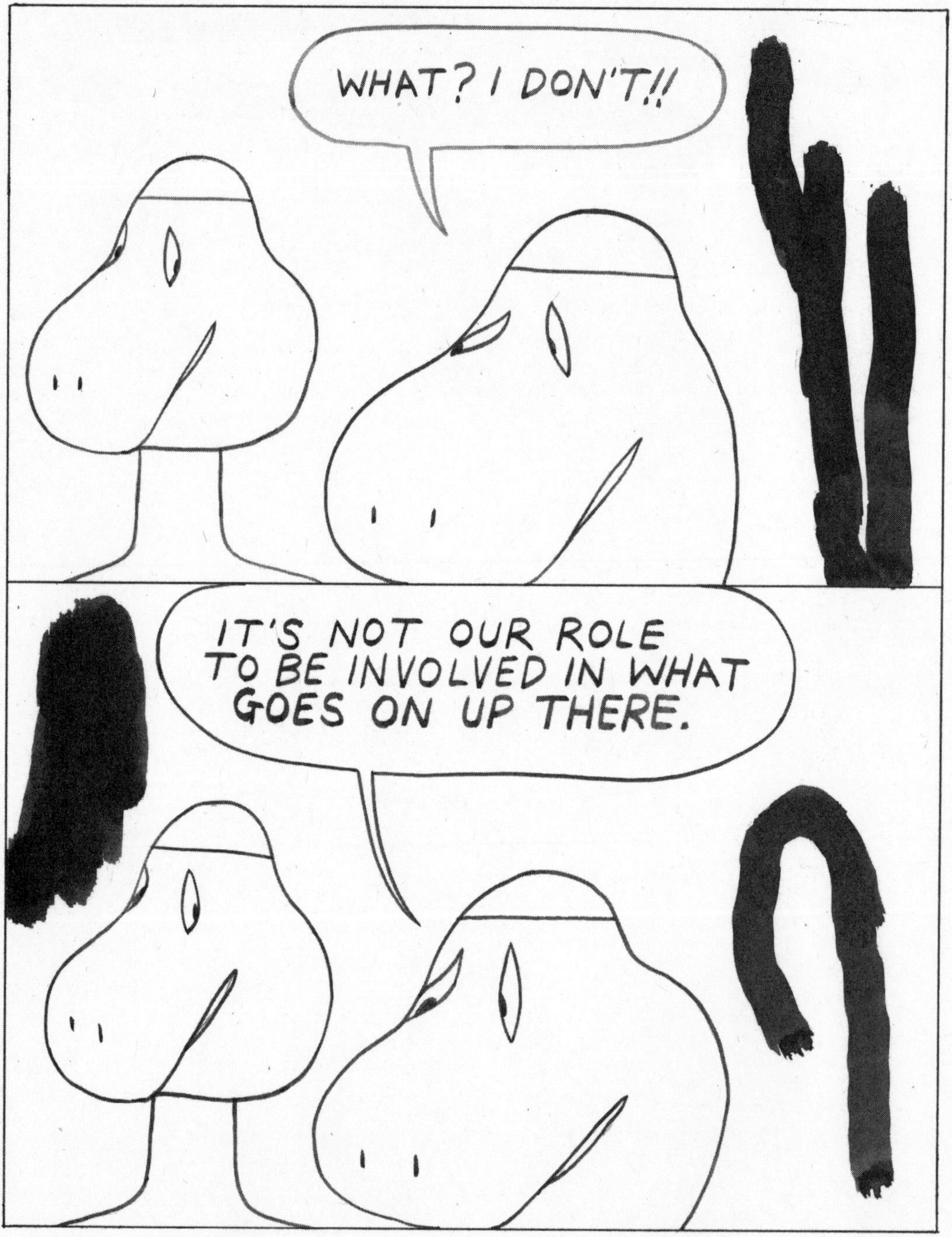
WHAT? I DON'T!!
IT'S NOT OUR ROLE TO BE INVOLVED IN WHAT GOES ON UP THERE.

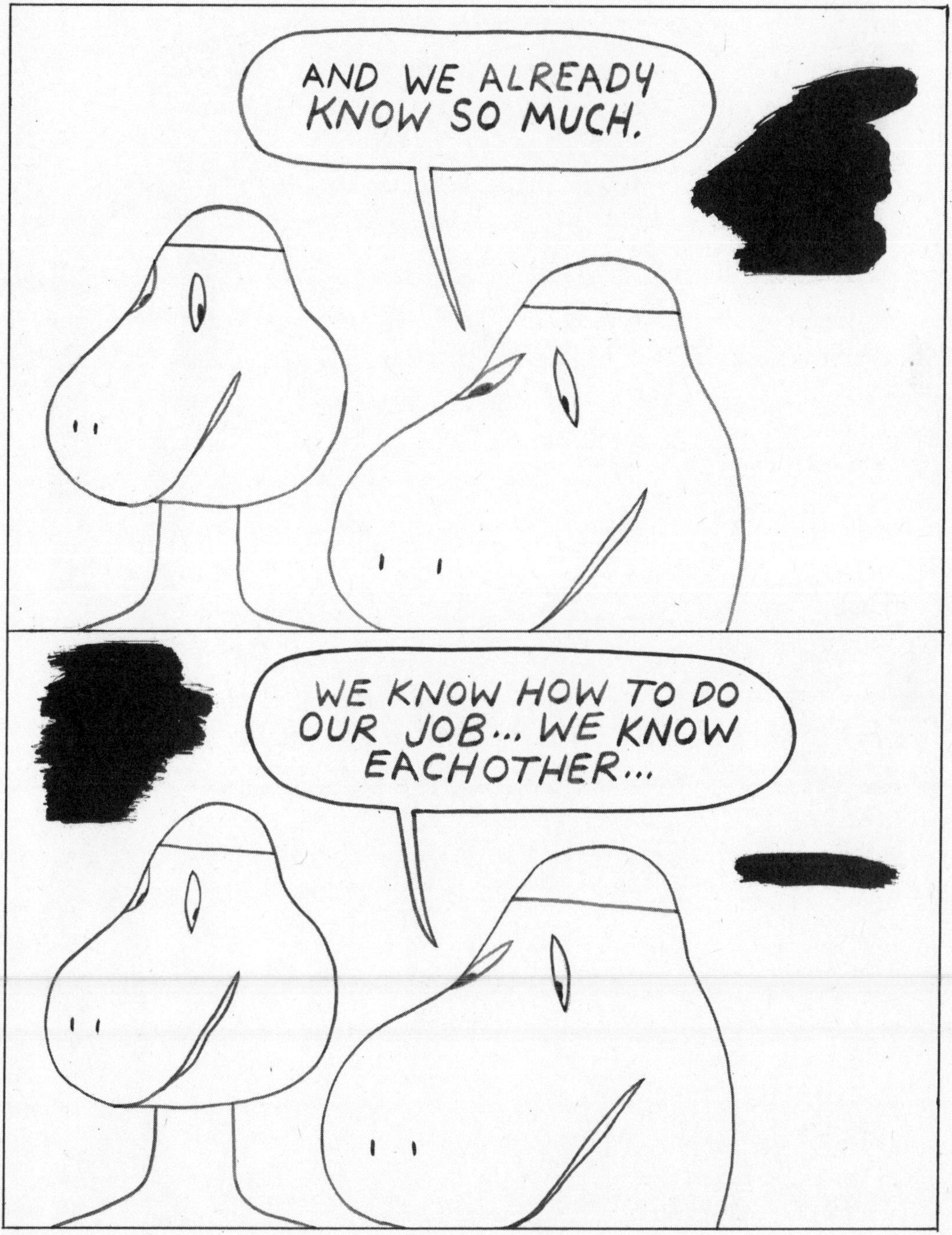
AND WE ALREADY KNOW SO MUCH.
WE KNOW HOW TO DO OUR JOB... WE KNOW EACHOTHER...

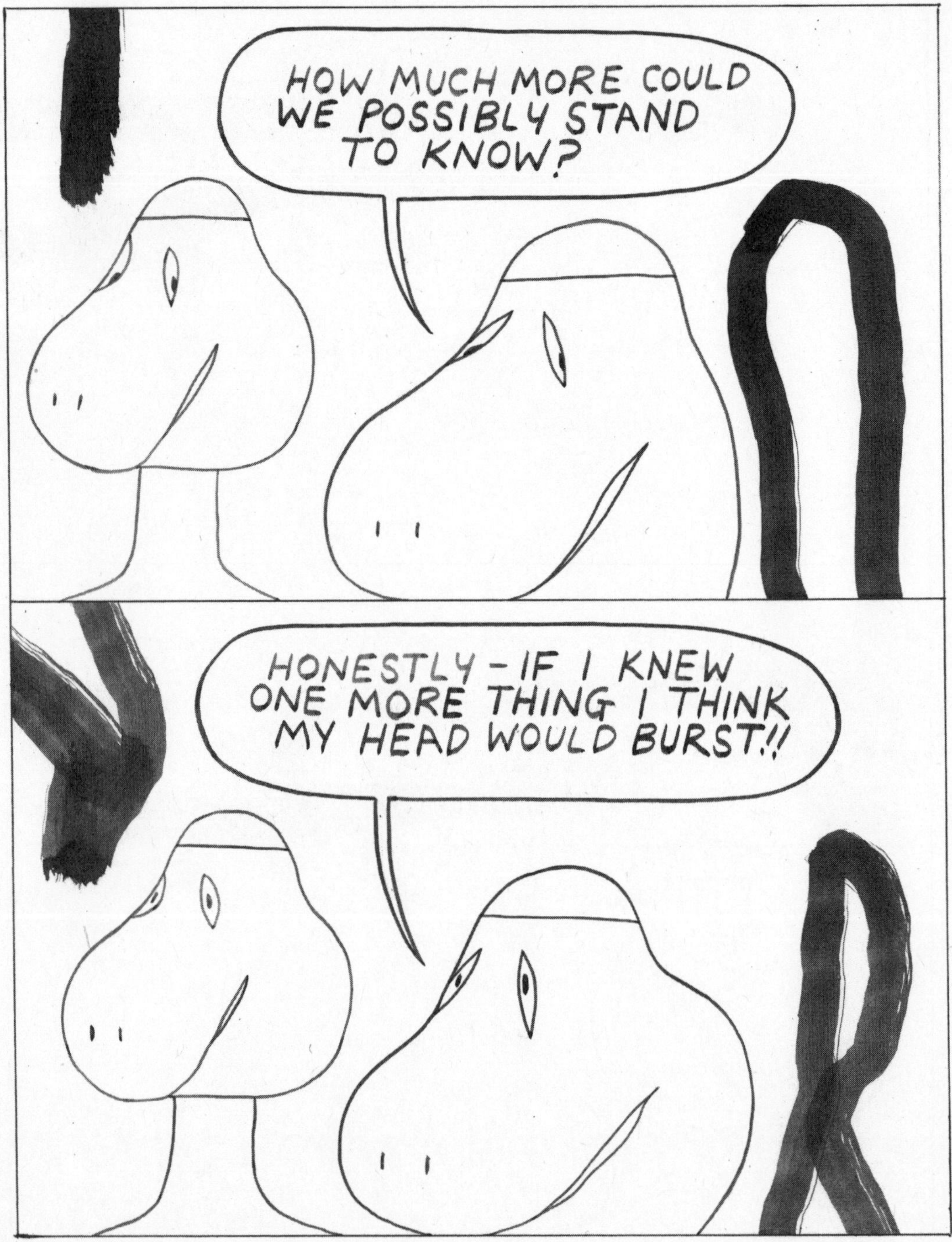
HOW MUCH MORE COULD WE POSSIBLY STAND TO KNOW?
HONESTLY - IF I KNEW ONE MORE THING I THINK MY HEAD WOULD BURST!!

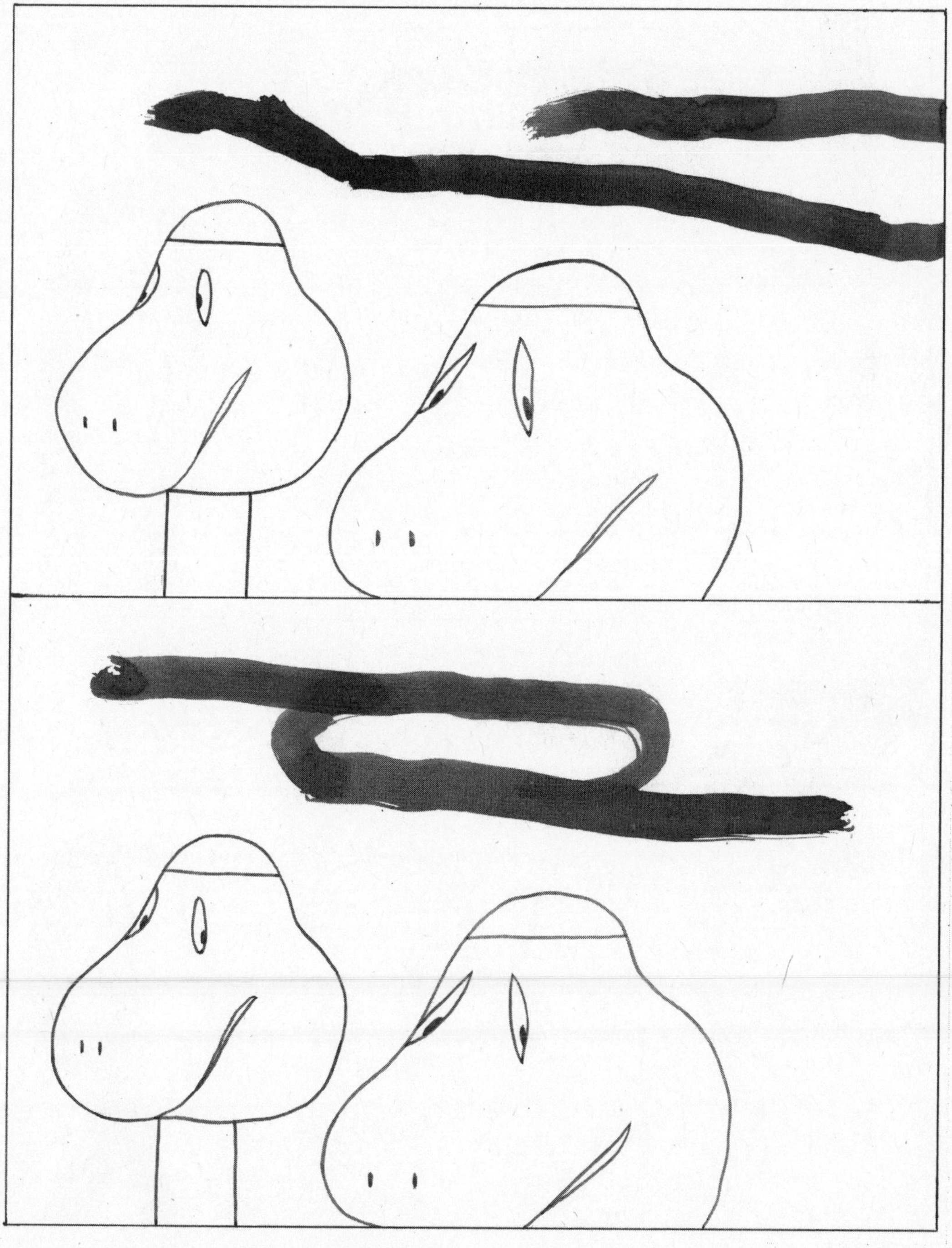

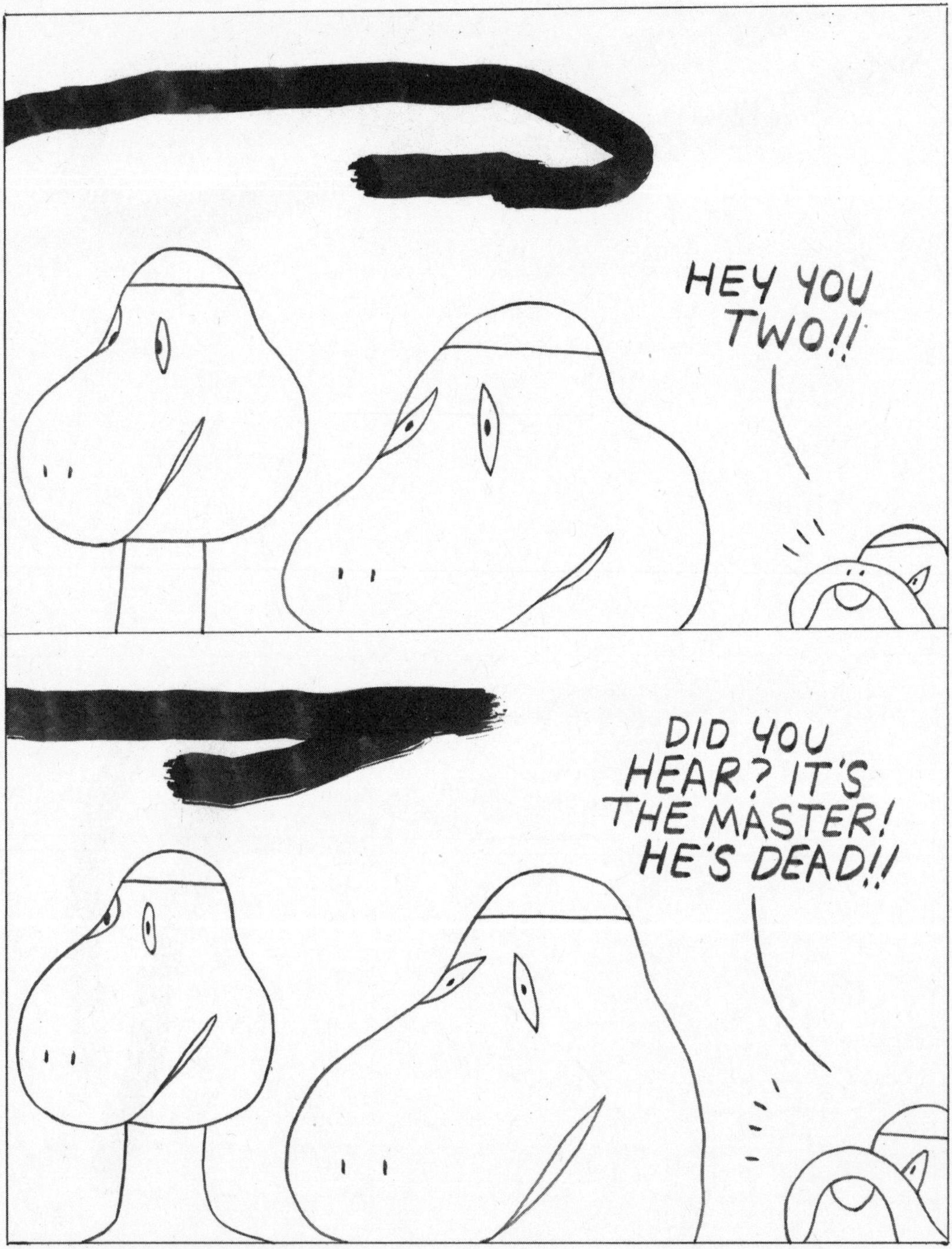
HEY YOU TWO!!
DID YOU HEAR? IT'S THE MASTER! HE'S DEAD!!

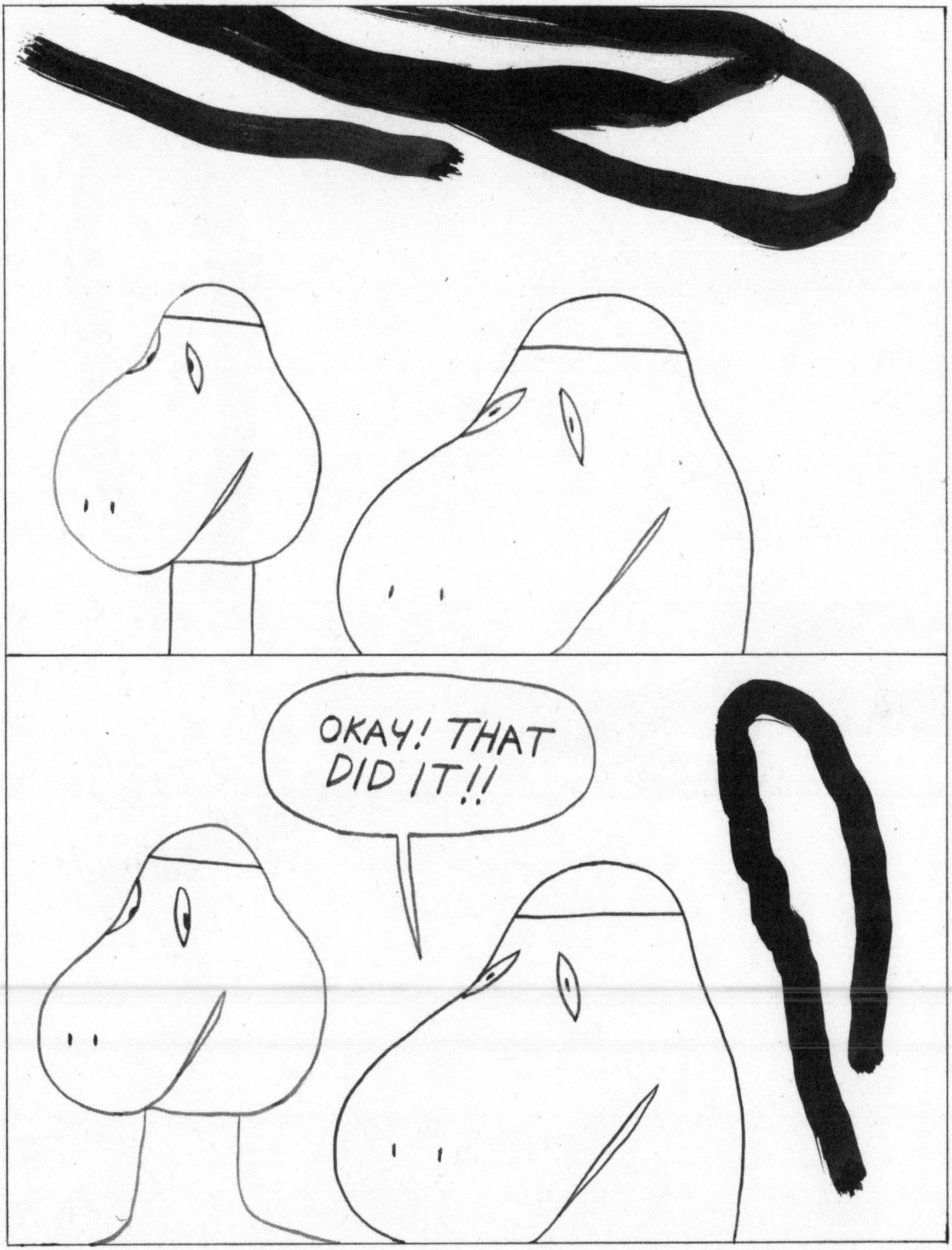
OKAY! THAT DID IT!!

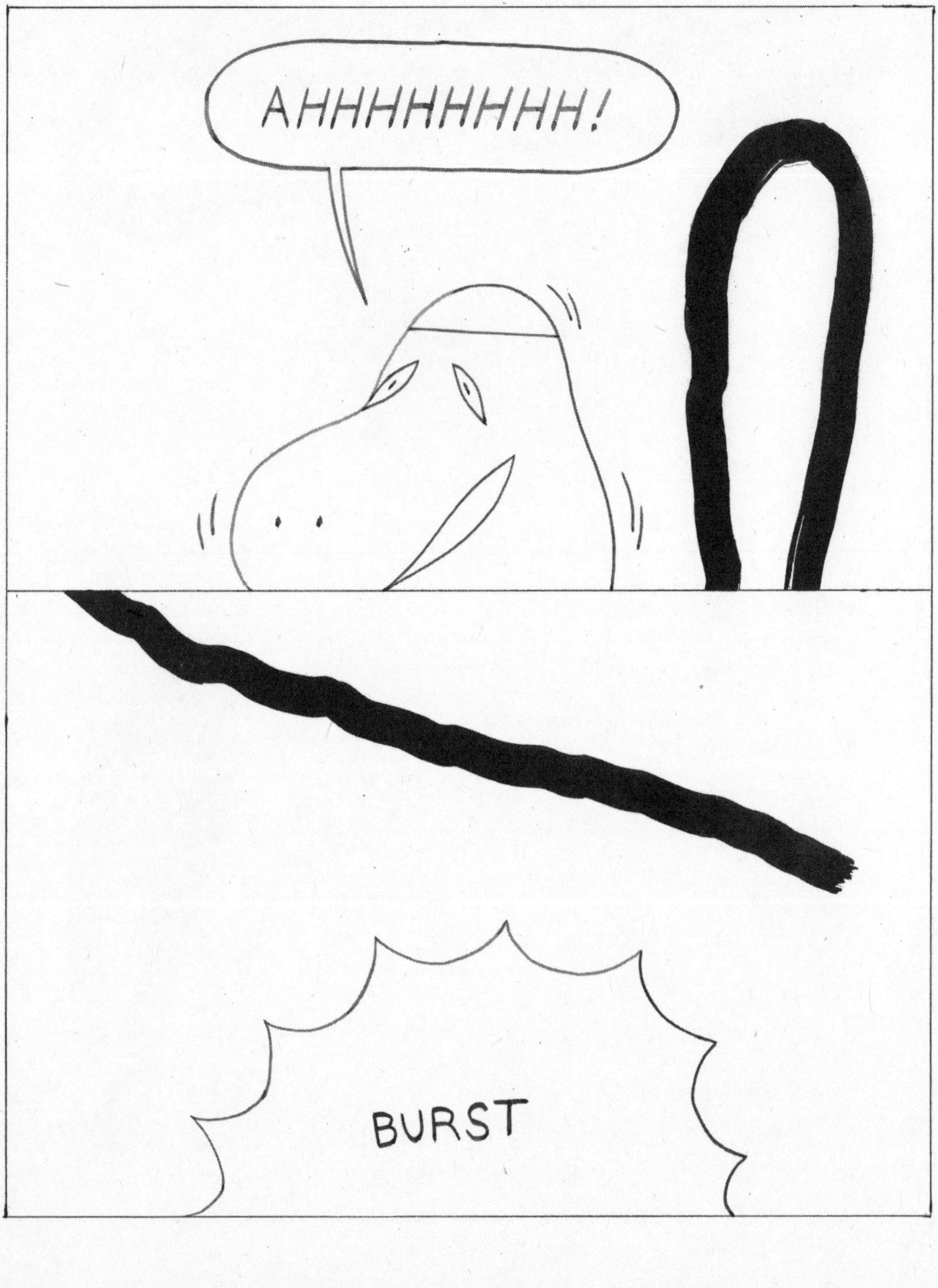
AHHHHHHHH!
BURST

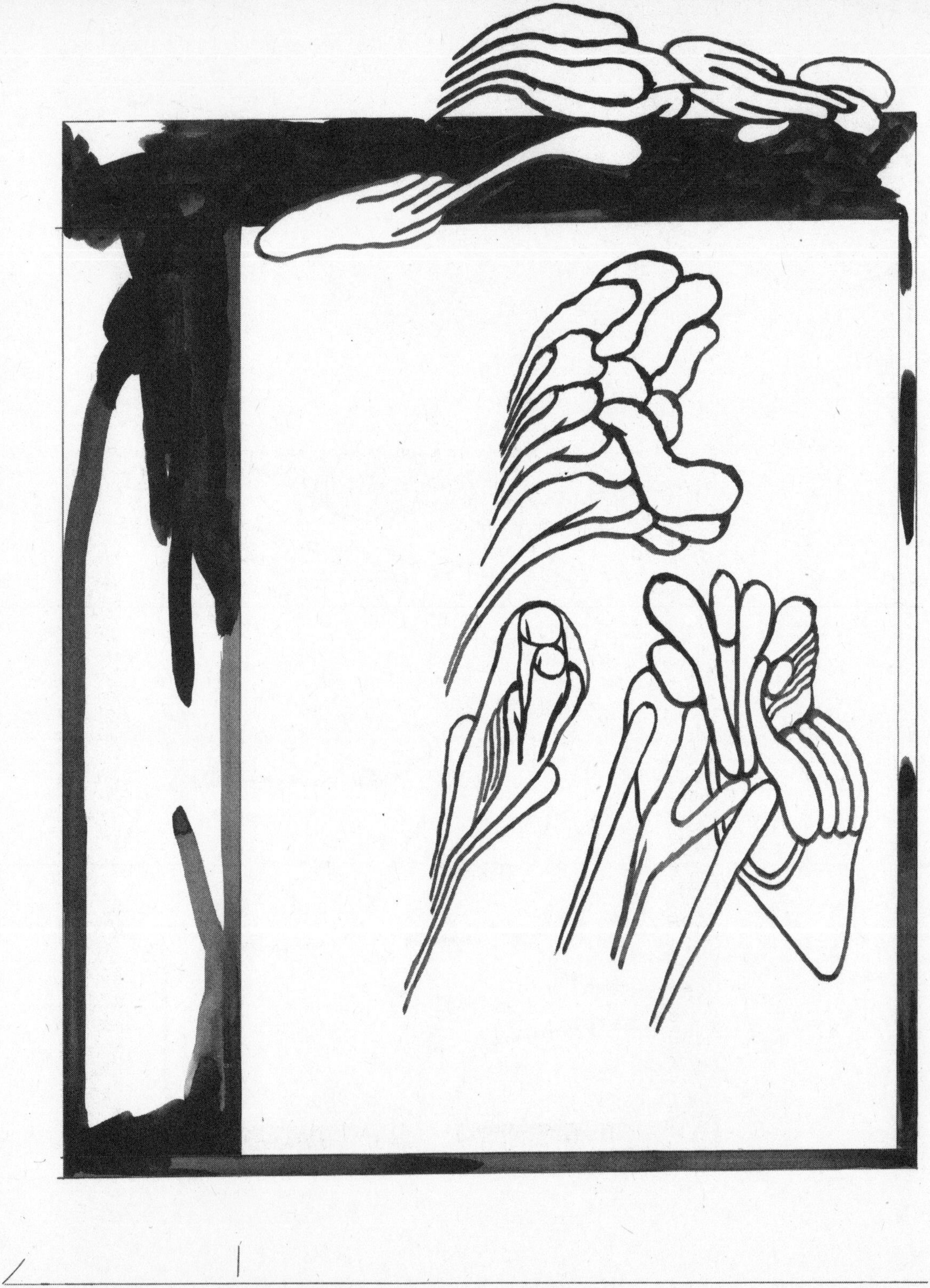

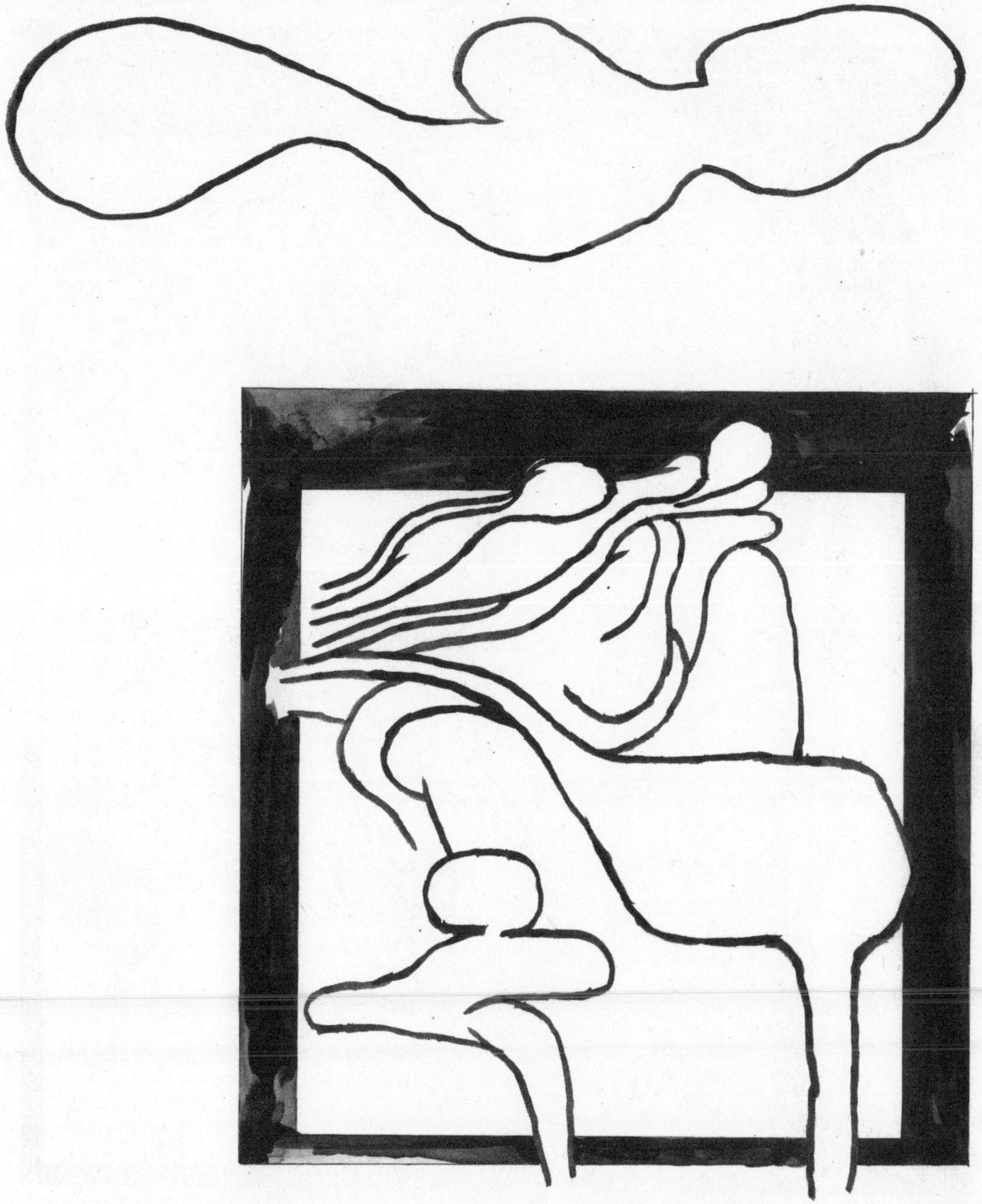

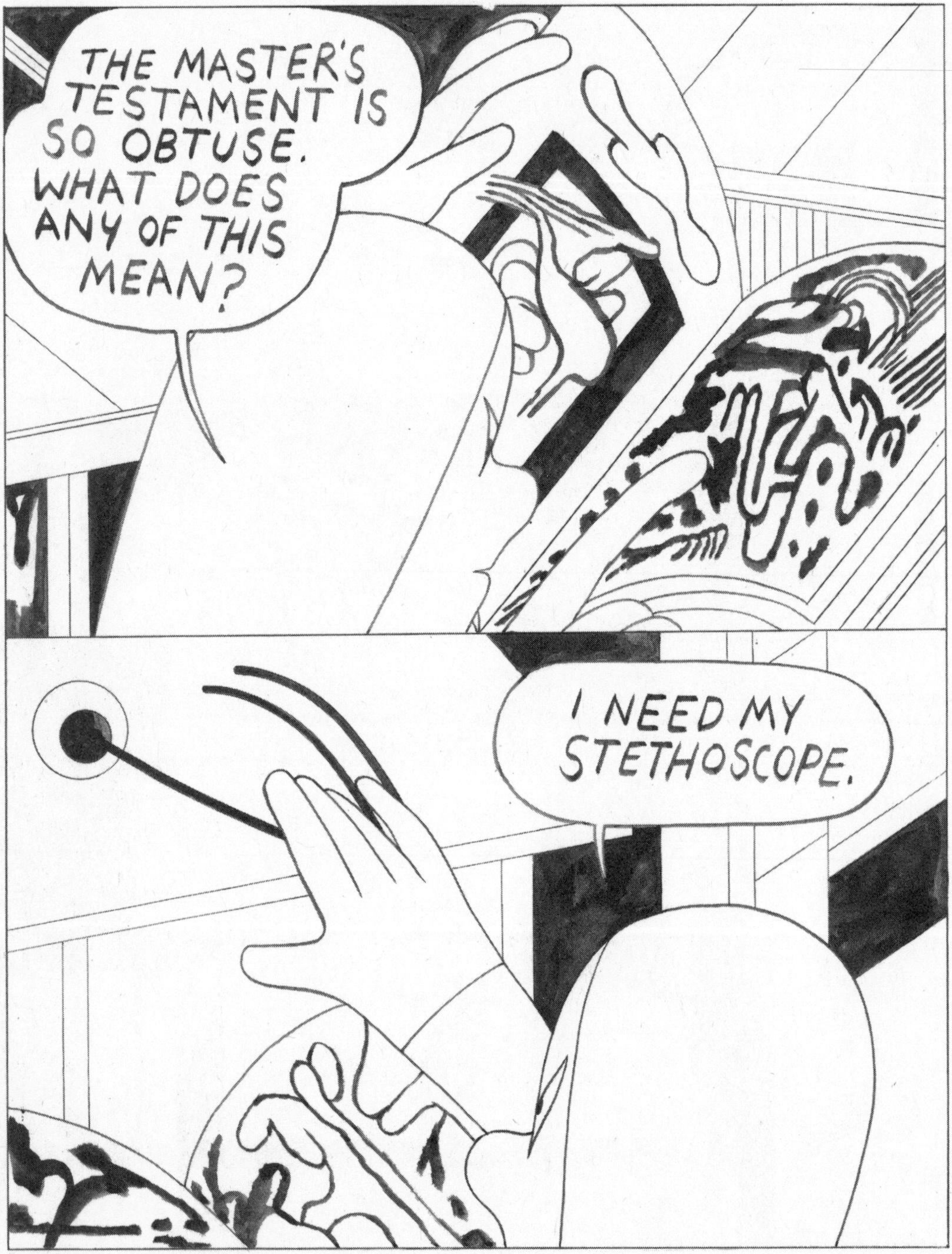
THE MASTER'S TESTAMENT IS SO OBTUSE. WHAT DOES ANY OF THIS MEAN?
I NEED MY STETHOSCOPE.

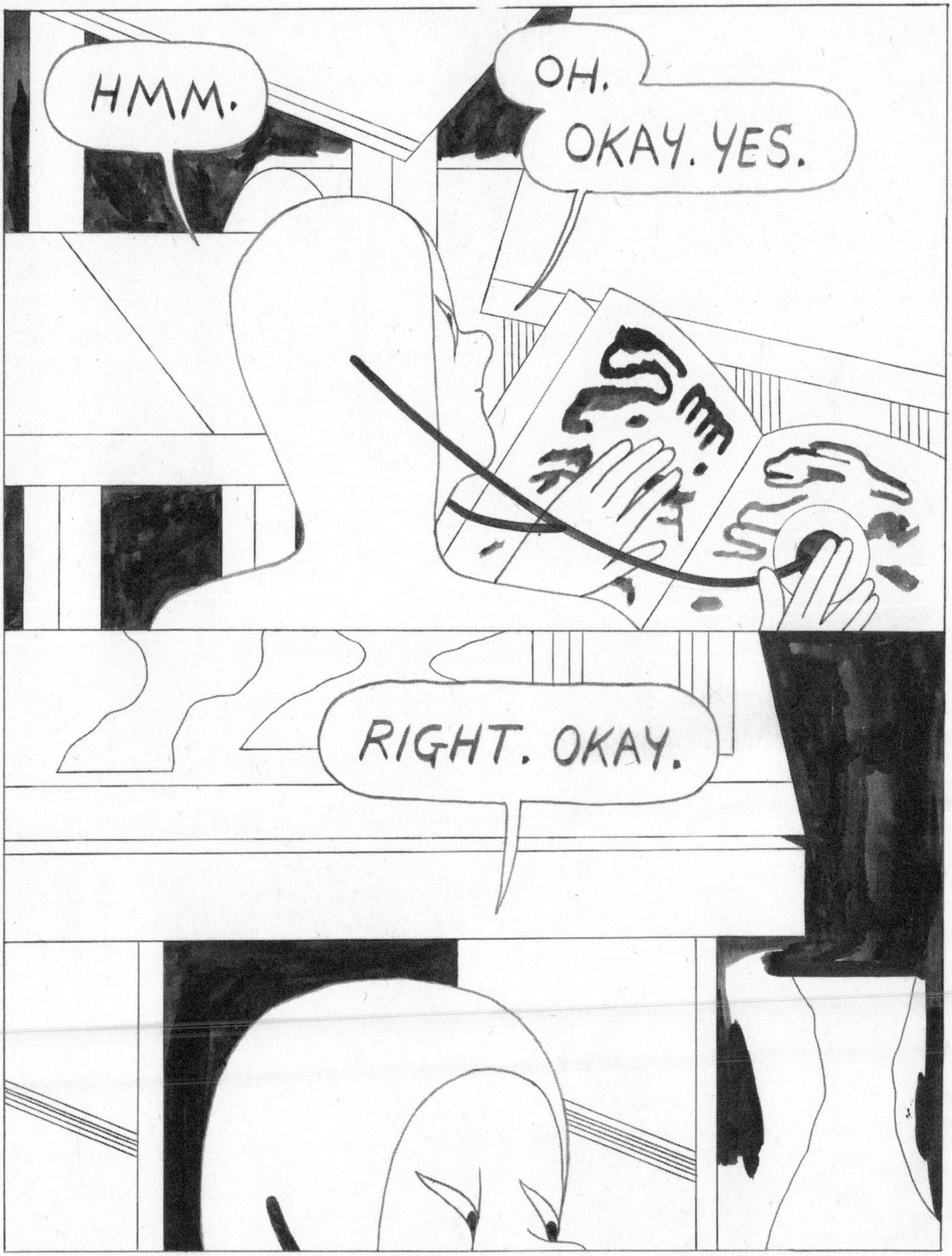
HMM.
OH.
OKAY. YES.
RIGHT. OKAY.

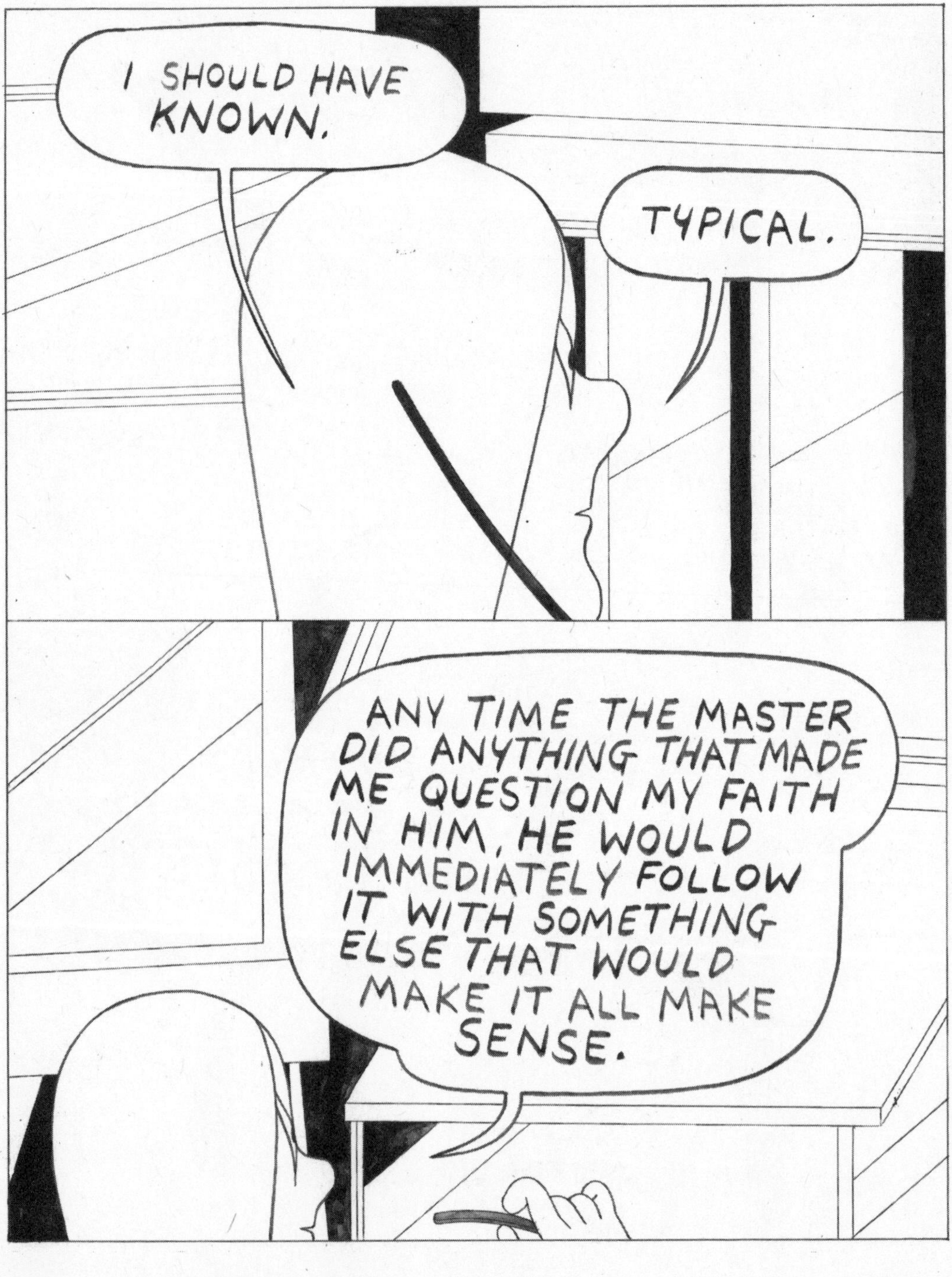
I SHOULD HAVE KNOWN.
TYPICAL.
ANY TIME THE MASTER DID ANYTHING THAT MADE ME QUESTION MY FAITH IN HIM, HE WOULD IMMEDIATELY FOLLOW IT WITH SOMETHING ELSE THAT WOULD MAKE IT ALL MAKE SENSE.

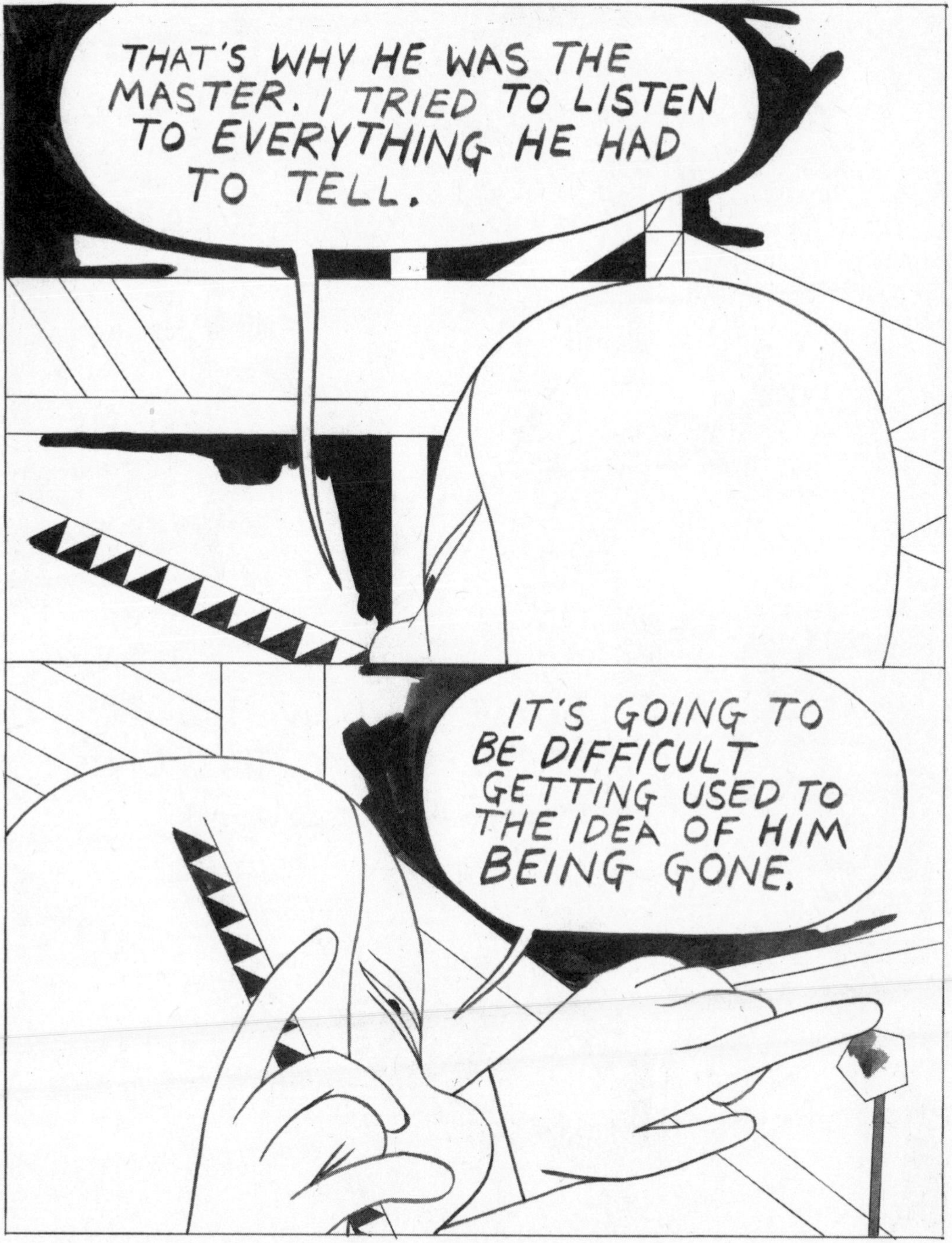
THAT'S WHY HE WAS THE MASTER. I TRIED TO LISTEN TO EVERYTHING HE HAD TO TELL.
IT'S GOING TO BE DIFFICULT GETTING USED TO THE IDEA OF HIM BEING GONE.

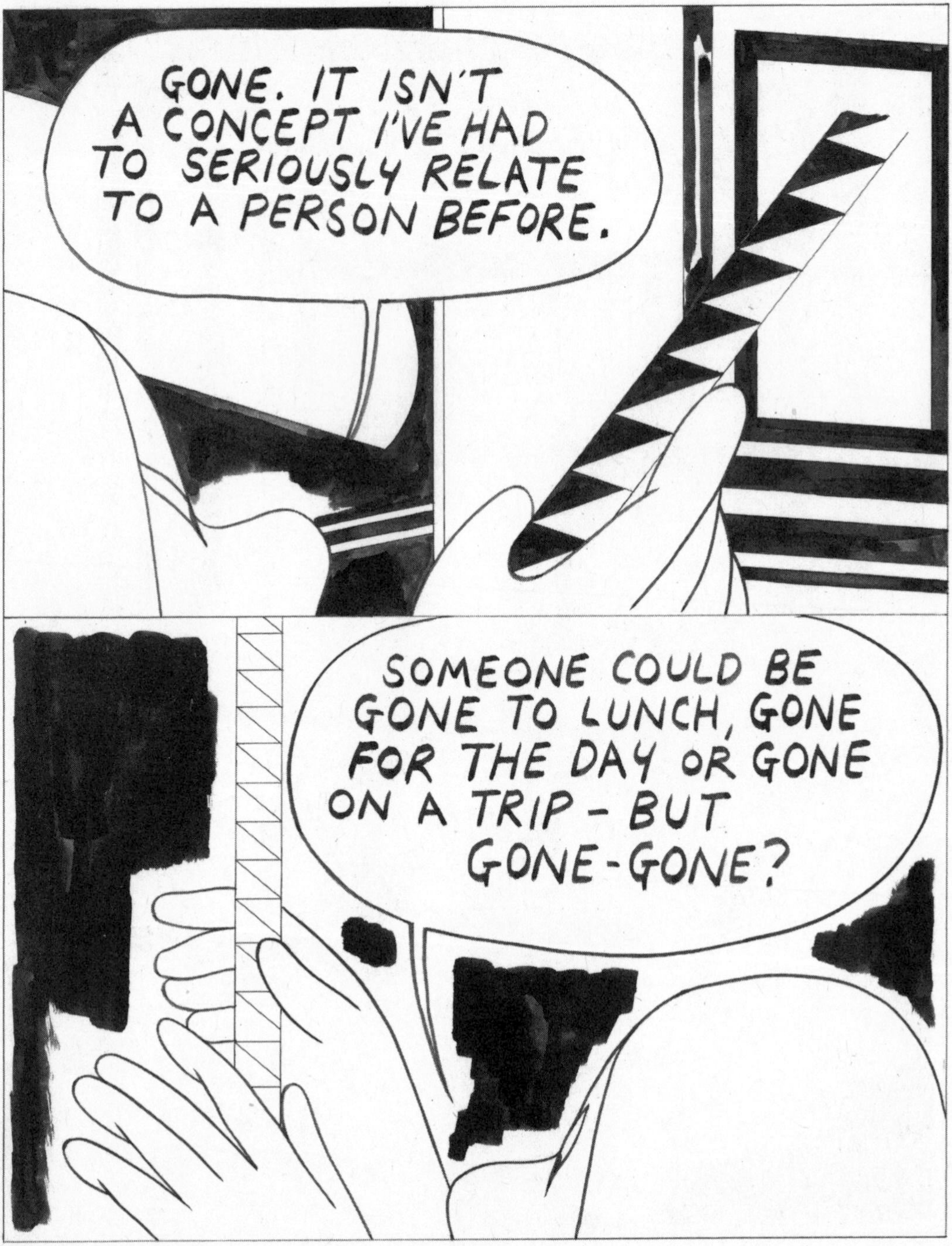
GONE. IT ISN'T A CONCEPT I'VE HAD TO SERIOUSLY RELATE TO A PERSON BEFORE.
SOMEONE COULD BE GONE TO LUNCH, GONE FOR THE DAY OR GONE ON A TRIP - BUT GONE-GONE?

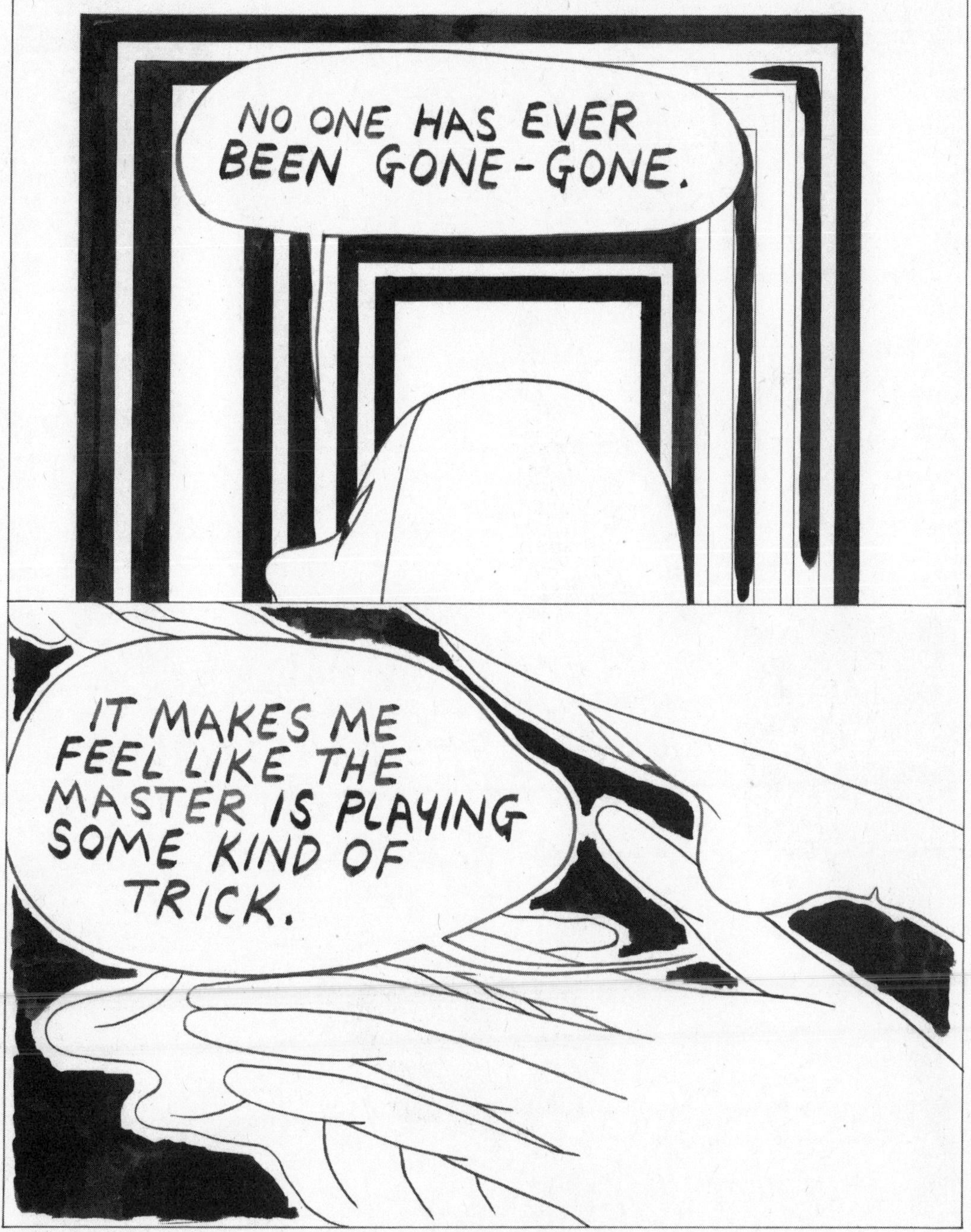
NO ONE HAS EVER BEEN GONE-GONE.
IT MAKES ME FEEL LIKE THE MASTER IS PLAYING SOME KIND OF TRICK.

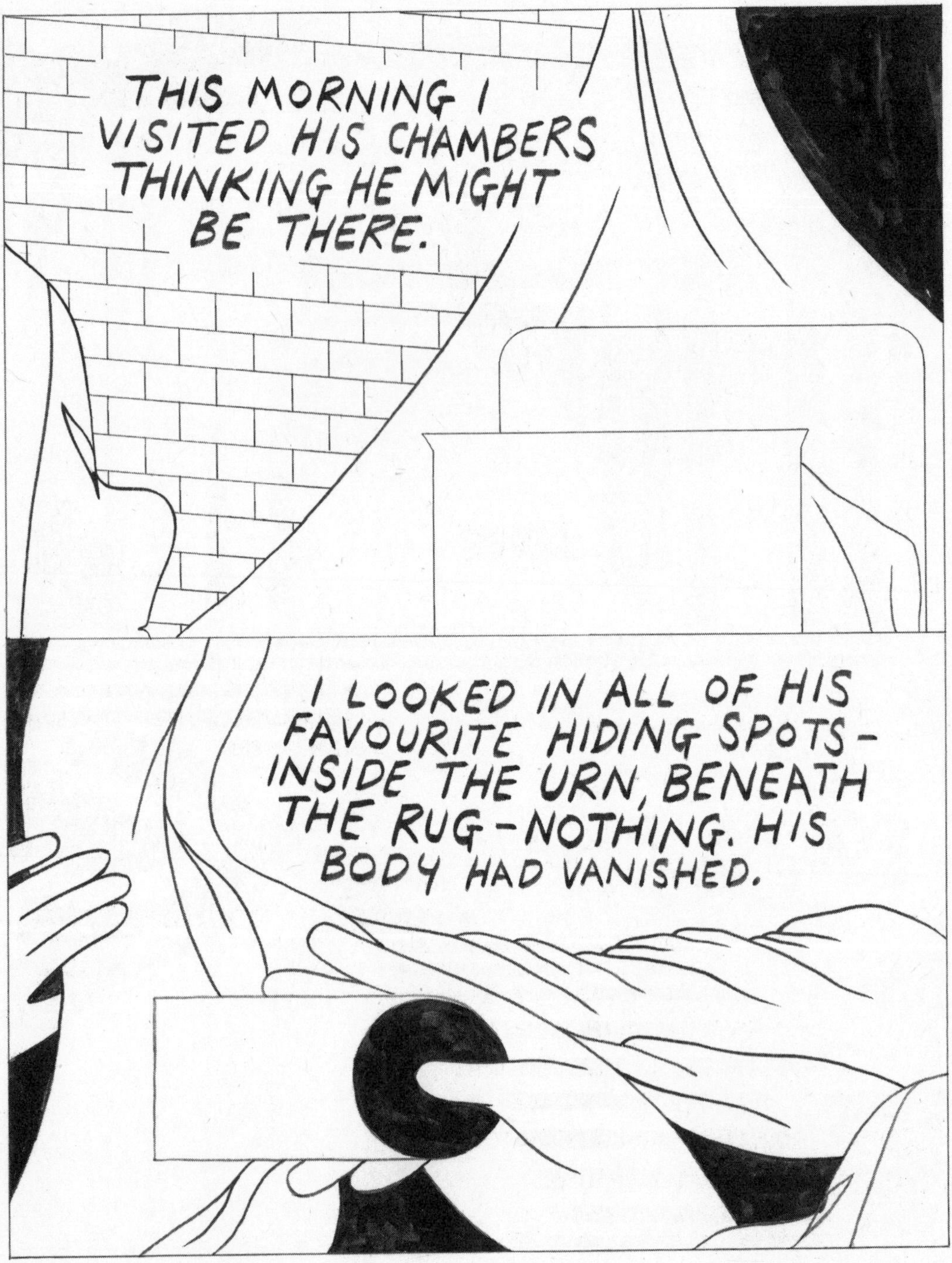
THIS MORNING I VISITED HIS CHAMBERS THINKING HE MIGHT BE THERE.
I LOOKED IN ALL OF HIS FAVOURITE HIDING SPOTS - INSIDE THE URN, BENEATH THE RUG - NOTHING. HIS BODY HAD VANISHED.

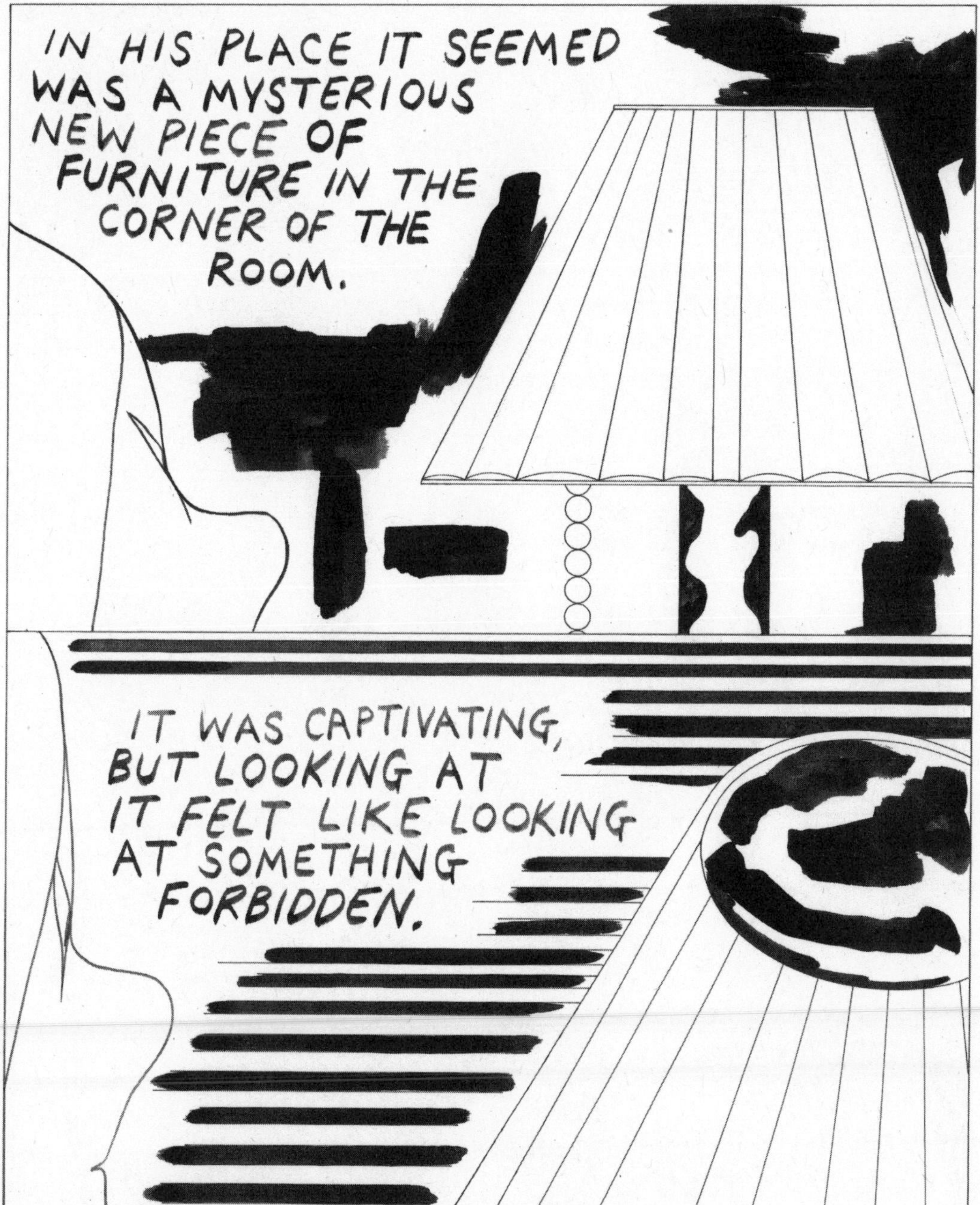
IN HIS PLACE IT SEEMED WAS A MYSTERIOUS NEW PIECE OF FURNITURE IN THE CORNER OF THE ROOM.
IT WAS CAPTIVATING, BUT LOOKING AT IT FELT LIKE LOOKING AT SOMETHING FORBIDDEN.

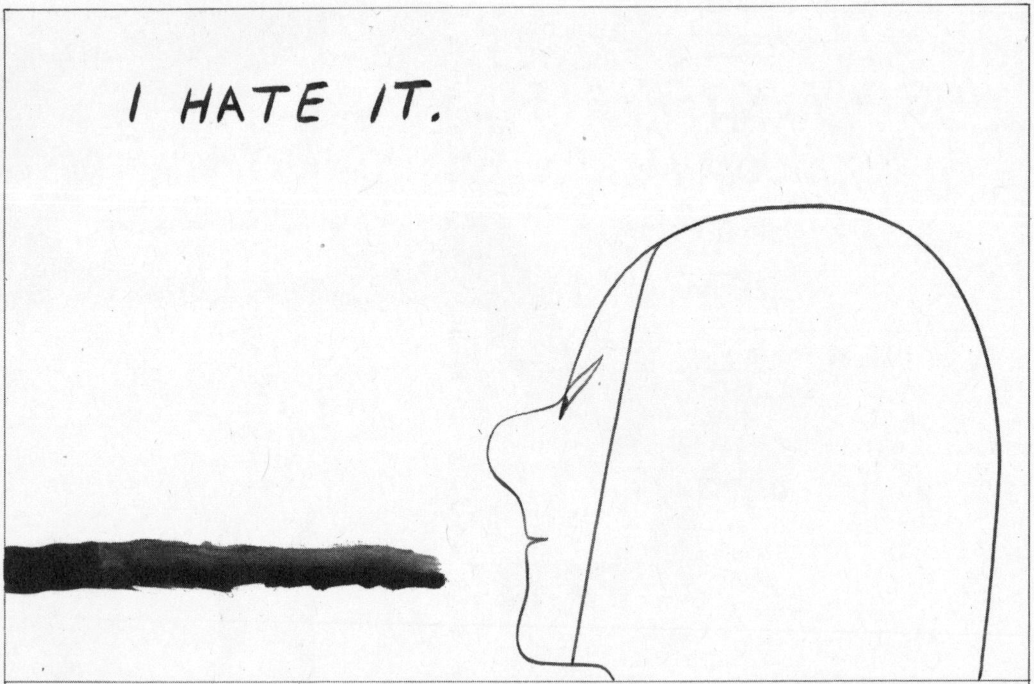
I HATE IT.

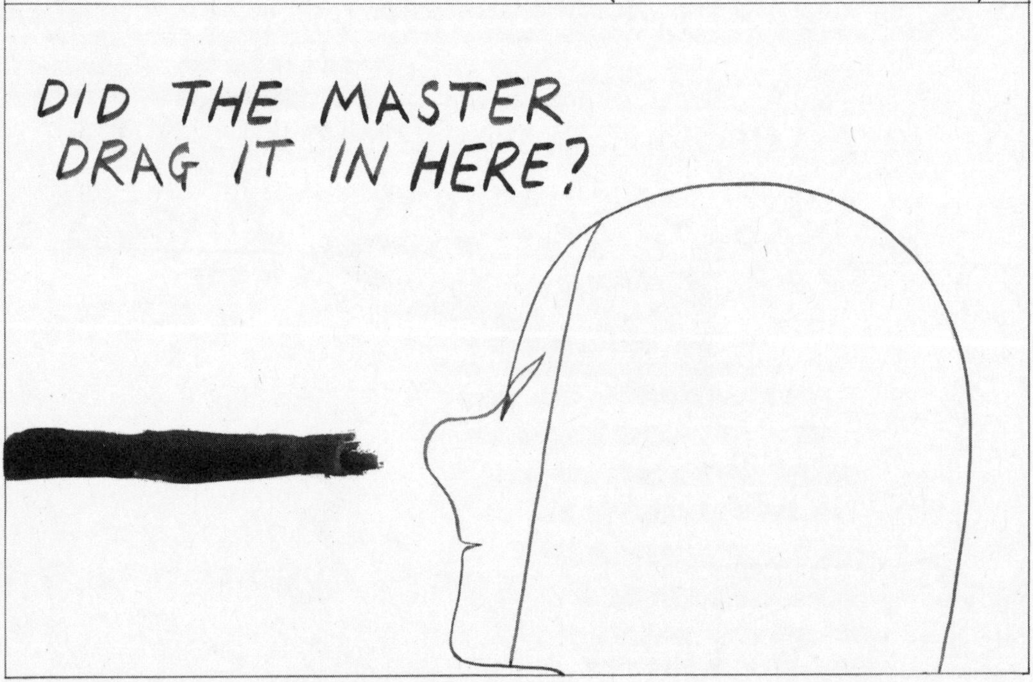
DID THE MASTER
DRAG IT IN HERE?

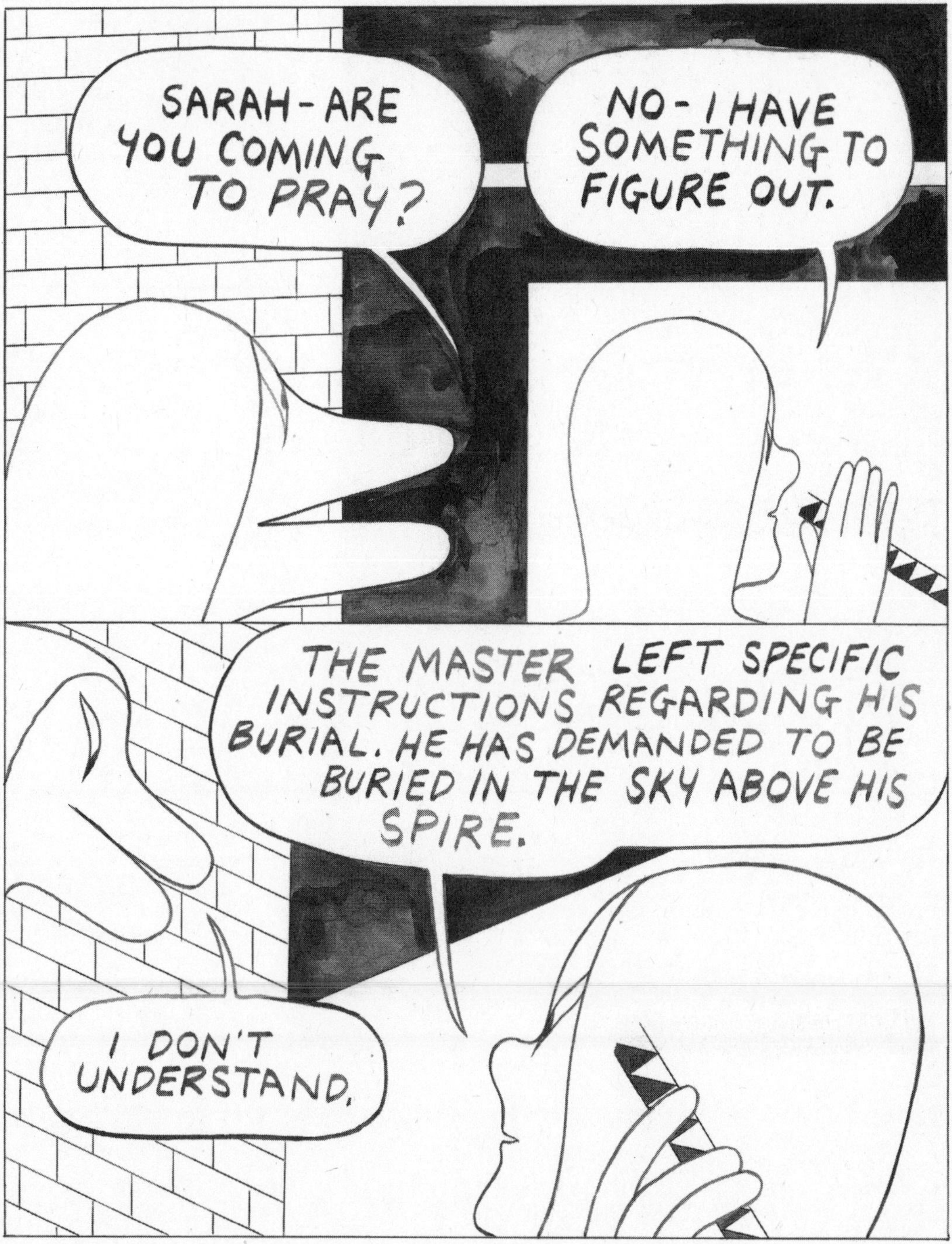
SARAH- ARE YOU COMING TO PRAY?
NO- I HAVE SOMETHING TO FIGURE OUT.
THE MASTER LEFT SPECIFIC INSTRUCTIONS REGARDING HIS BURIAL. HE HAS DEMANDED TO BE BURIED IN THE SKY ABOVE HIS SPIRE.
I DON'T UNDERSTAND.

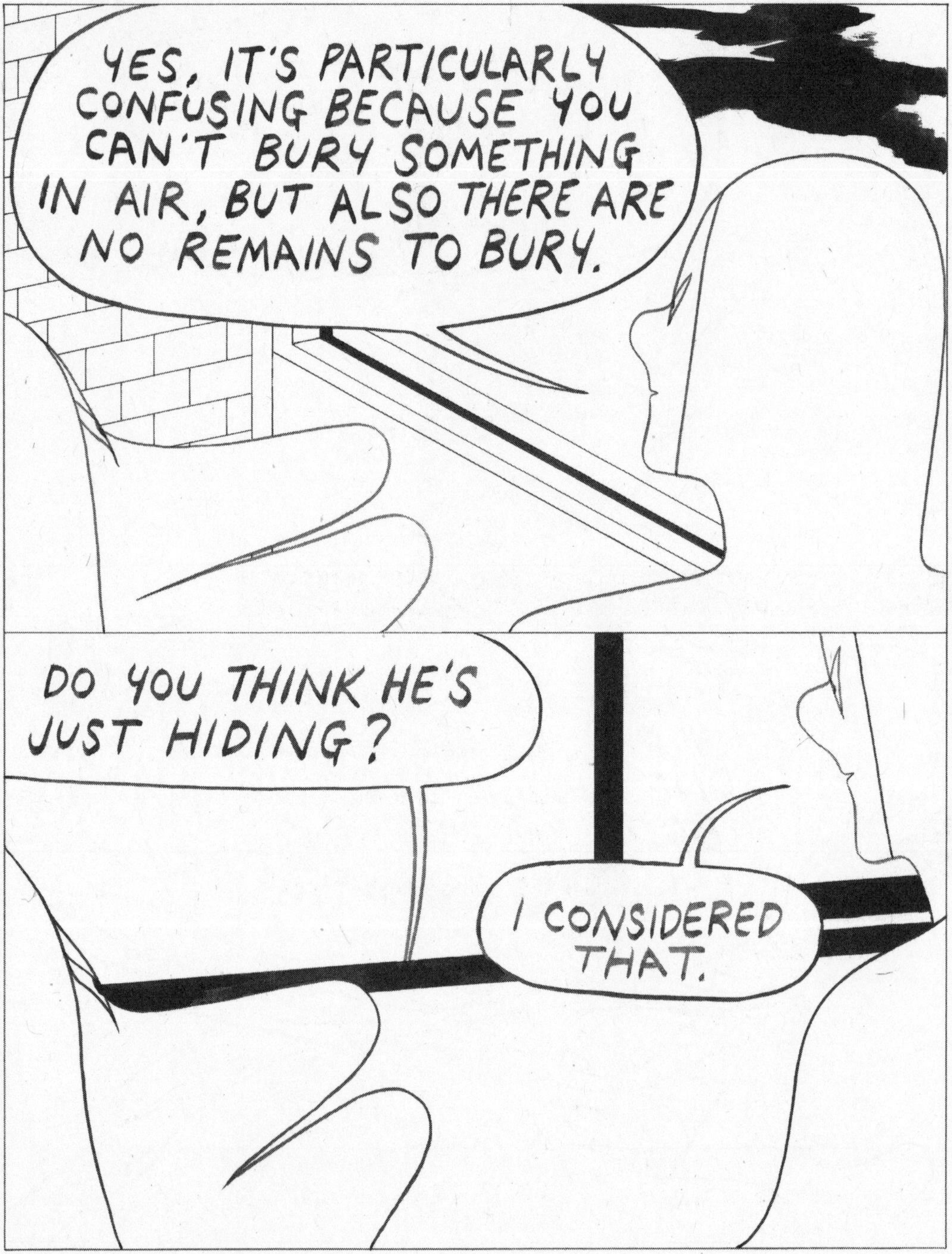
YES, IT'S PARTICULARLY CONFUSING BECAUSE YOU CAN'T BURY SOMETHING IN AIR, BUT ALSO THERE ARE NO REMAINS TO BURY.
DO YOU THINK HE'S JUST HIDING?
I CONSIDERED THAT.

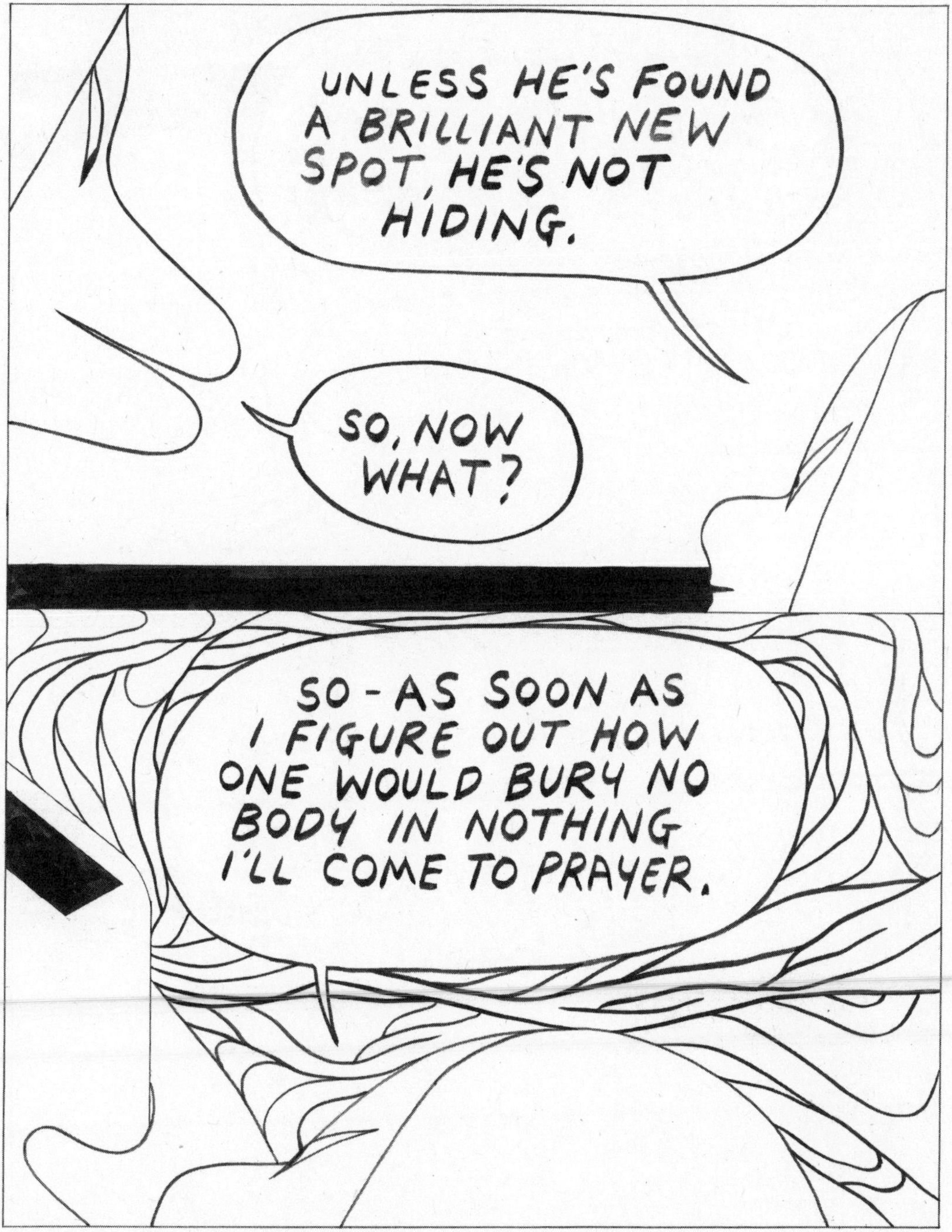
UNLESS HE'S FOUND A BRILLIANT NEW SPOT, HE'S NOT HIDING.
SO, NOW WHAT?
SO - AS SOON AS I FIGURE OUT HOW ONE WOULD BURY NO BODY IN NOTHING I'LL COME TO PRAYER.

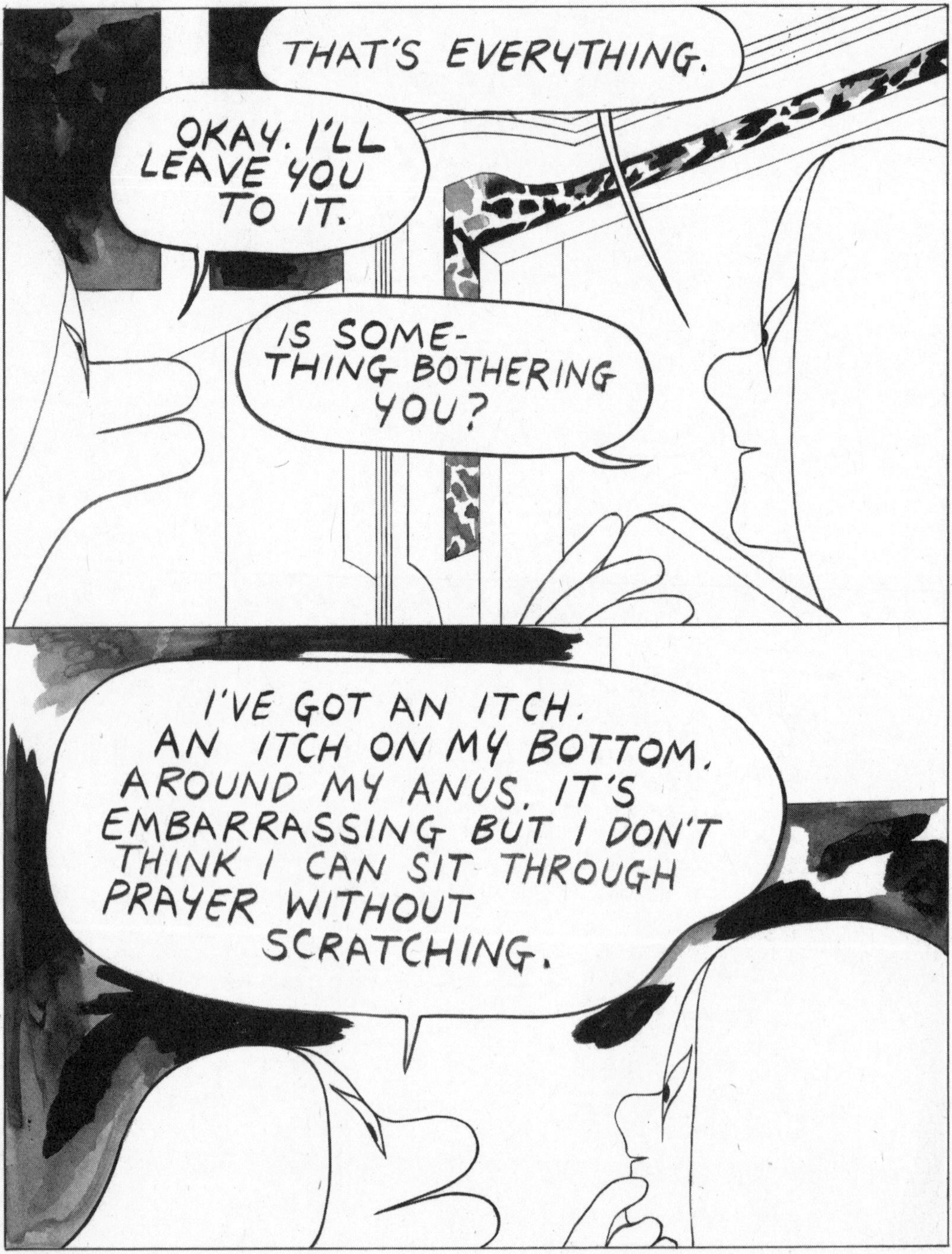
THAT'S EVERYTHING.
OKAY. I'LL LEAVE YOU TO IT.
IS SOME-THING BOTHERING YOU?
I'VE GOT AN ITCH. AN ITCH ON MY BOTTOM. AROUND MY ANUS. IT'S EMBARRASSING BUT I DON'T THINK I CAN SIT THROUGH PRAYER WITHOUT SCRATCHING.

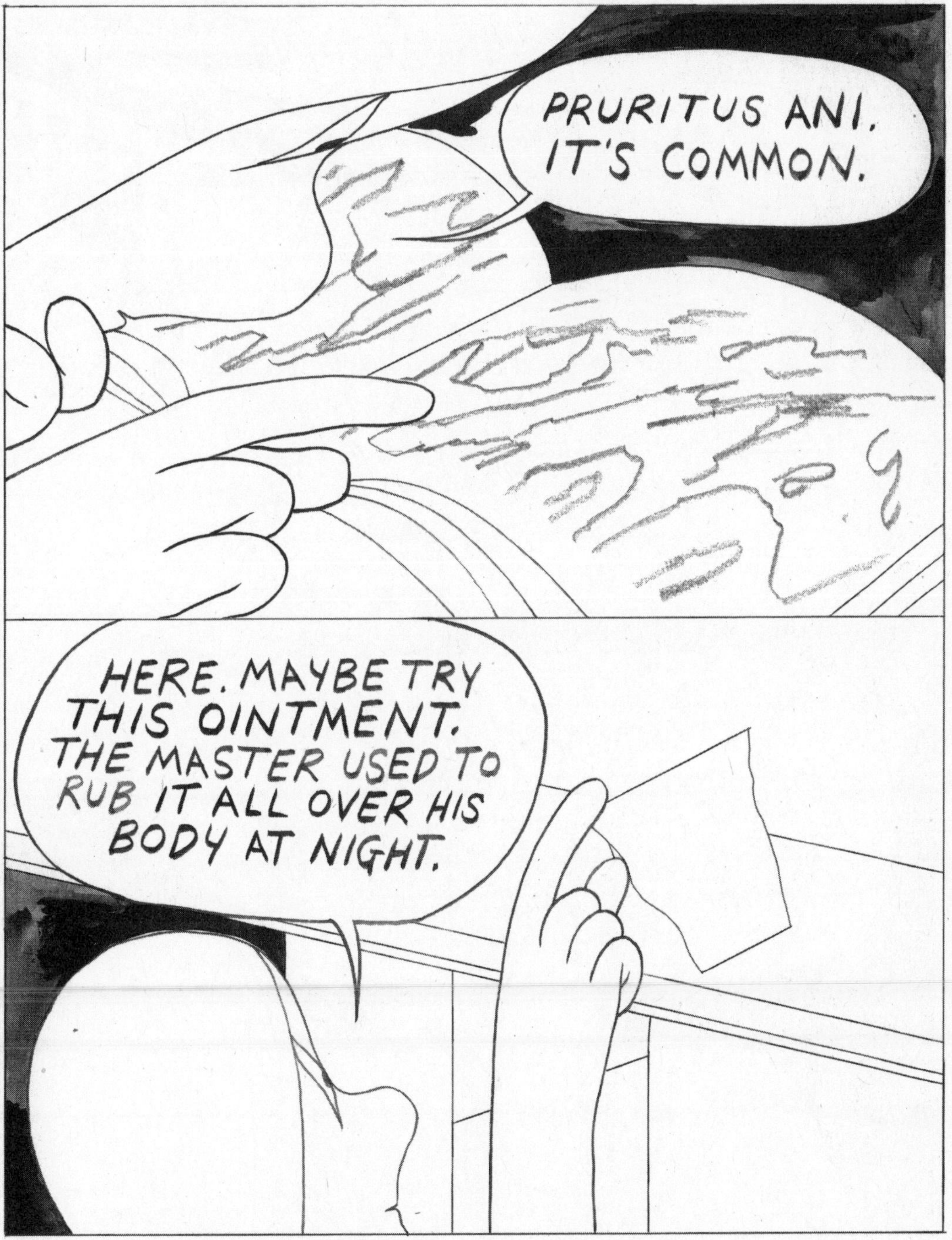
PRURITUS ANI. IT'S COMMON.
HERE. MAYBE TRY THIS OINTMENT. THE MASTER USED TO RUB IT ALL OVER HIS BODY AT NIGHT.

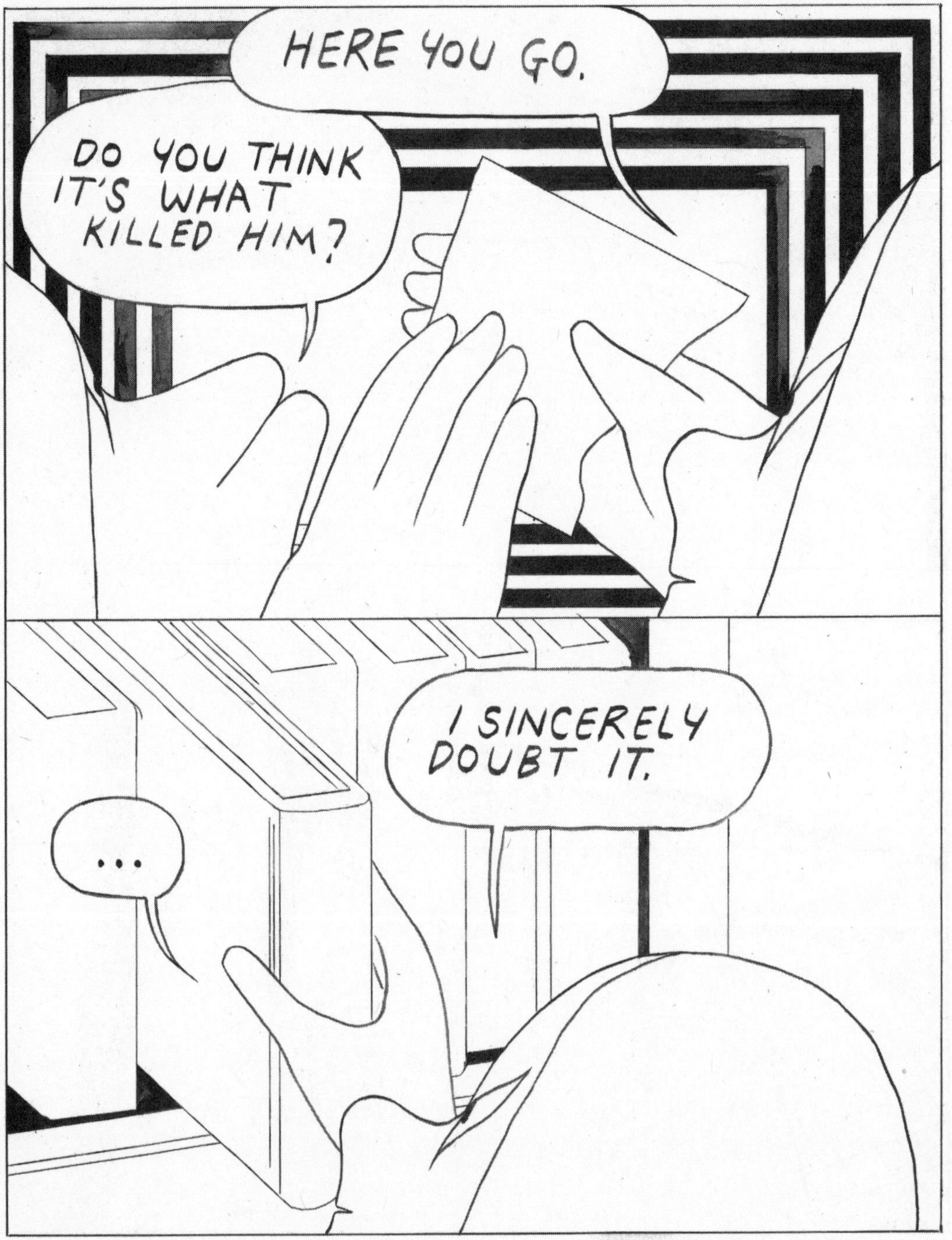
HERE YOU GO.
DO YOU THINK IT'S WHAT KILLED HIM?
I SINCERELY DOUBT IT.
...

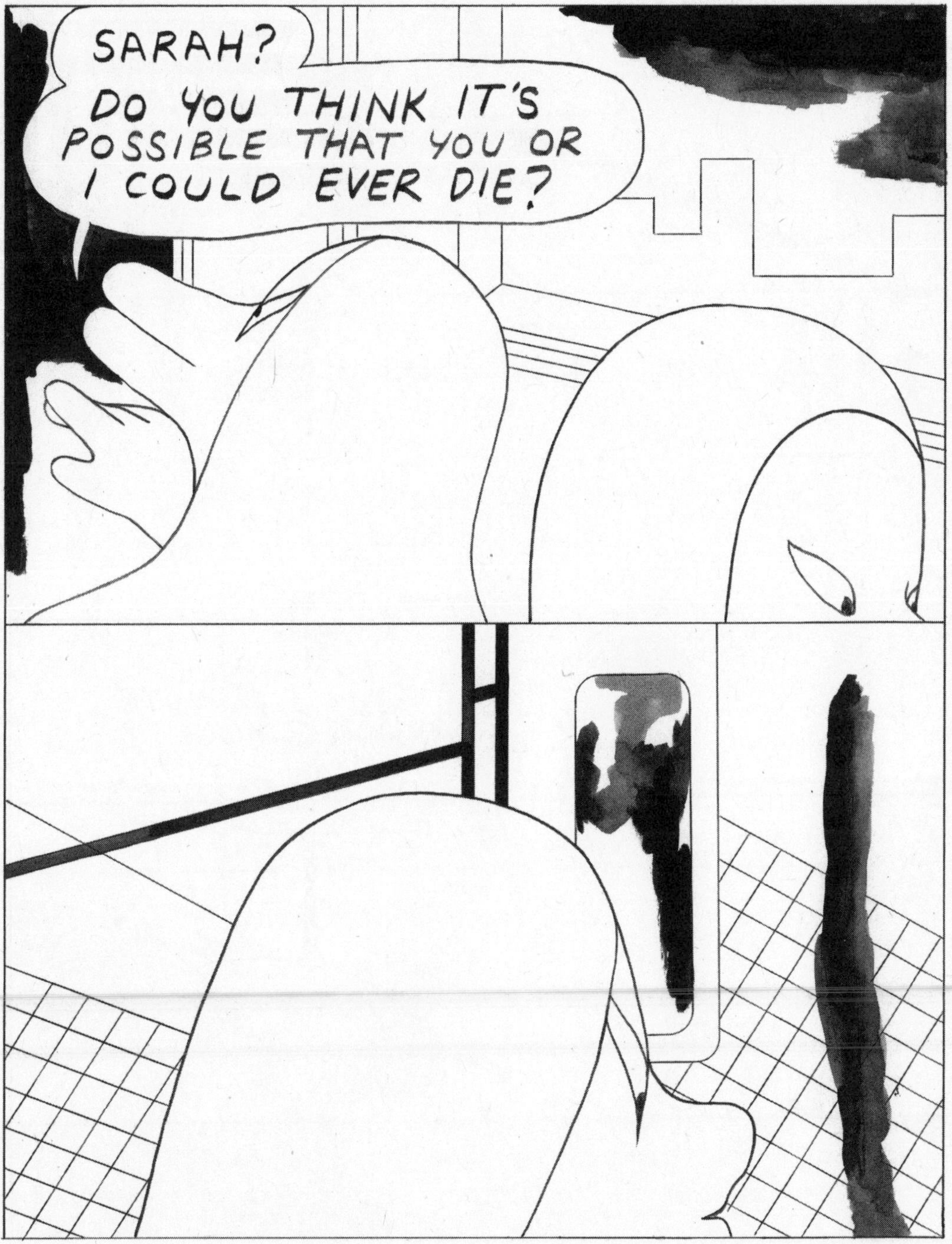
SARAH?
DO YOU THINK IT'S POSSIBLE THAT YOU OR I COULD EVER DIE?

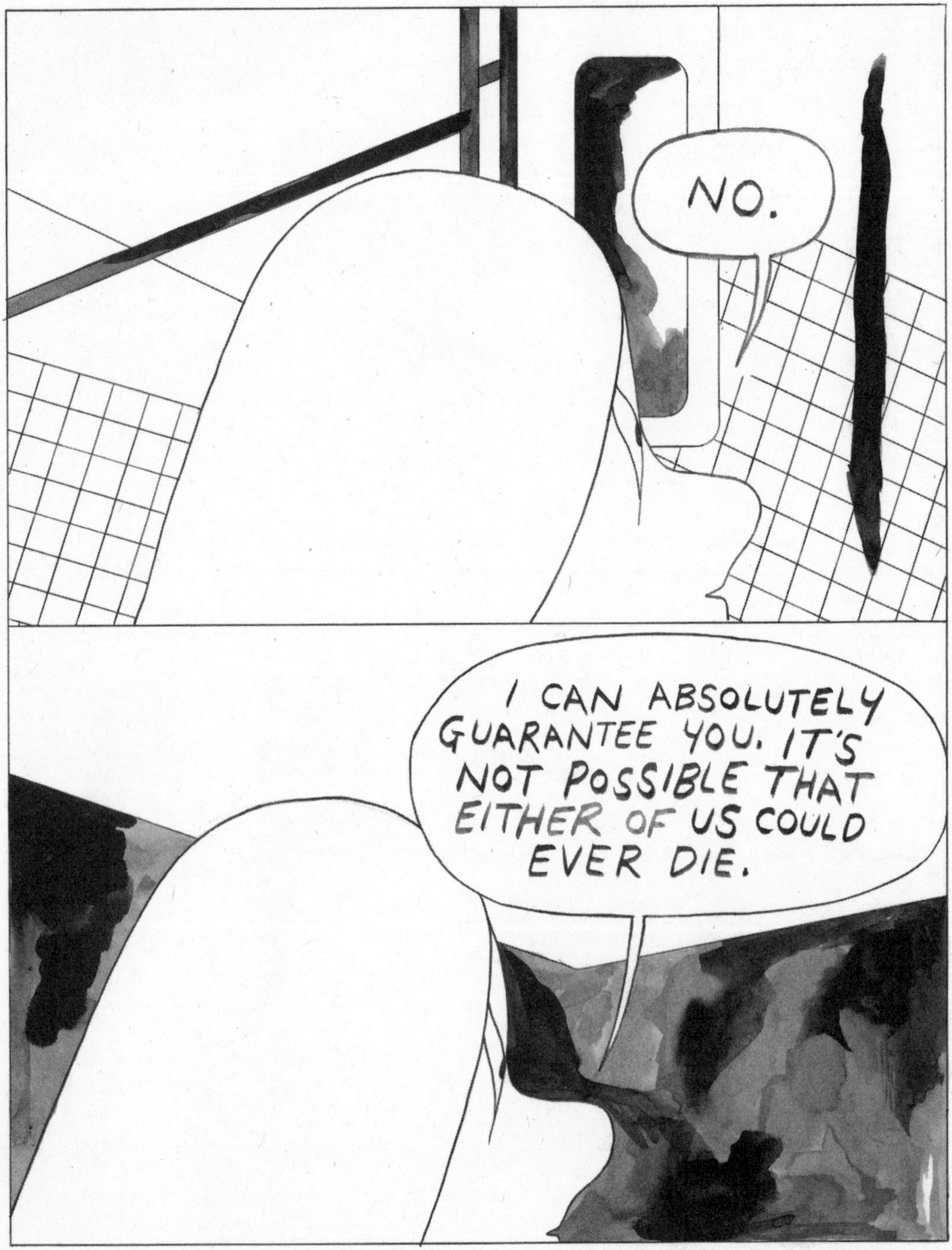
NO.
I CAN ABSOLUTELY GUARANTEE YOU. IT'S NOT POSSIBLE THAT EITHER OF US COULD EVER DIE.

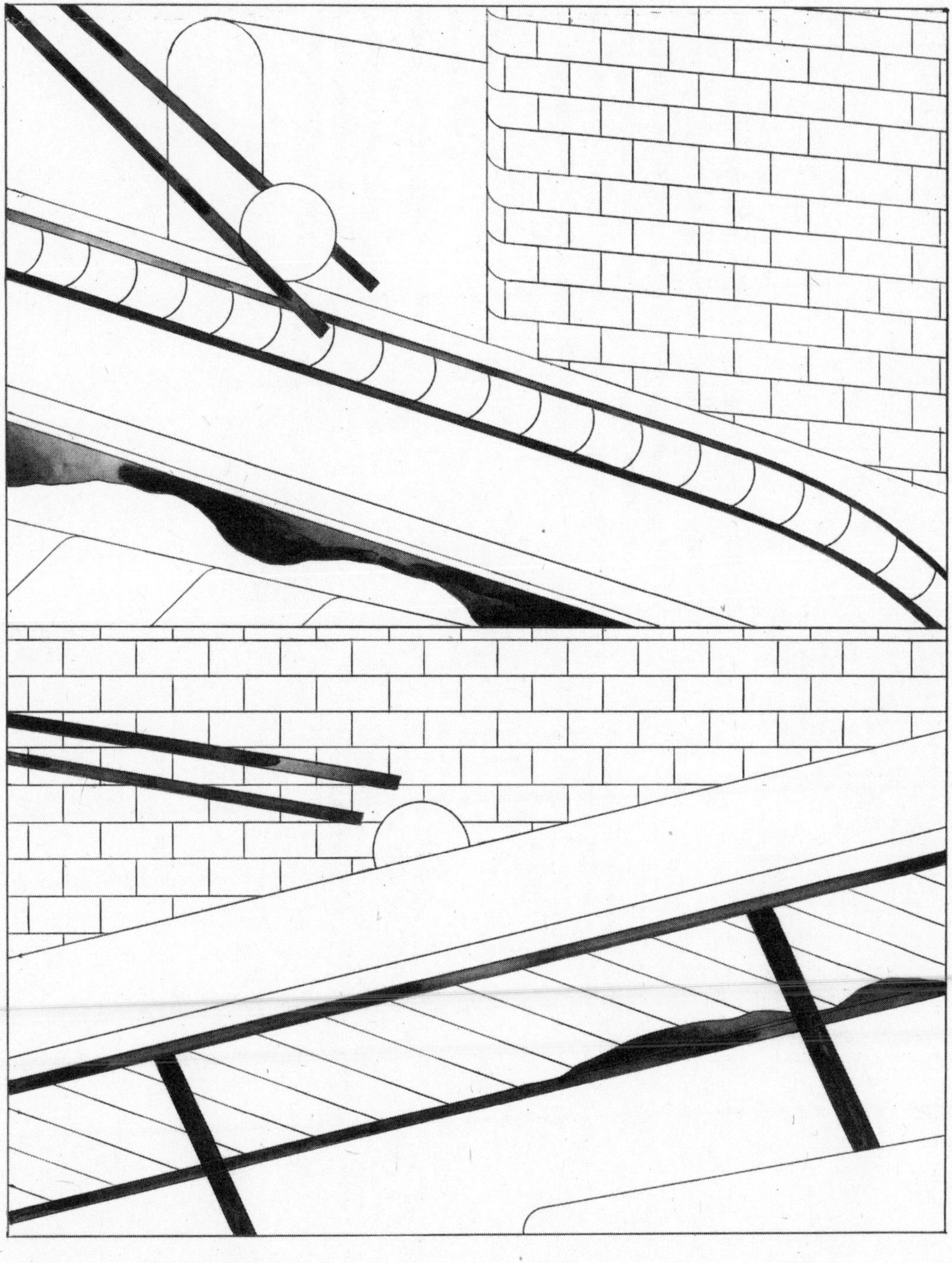

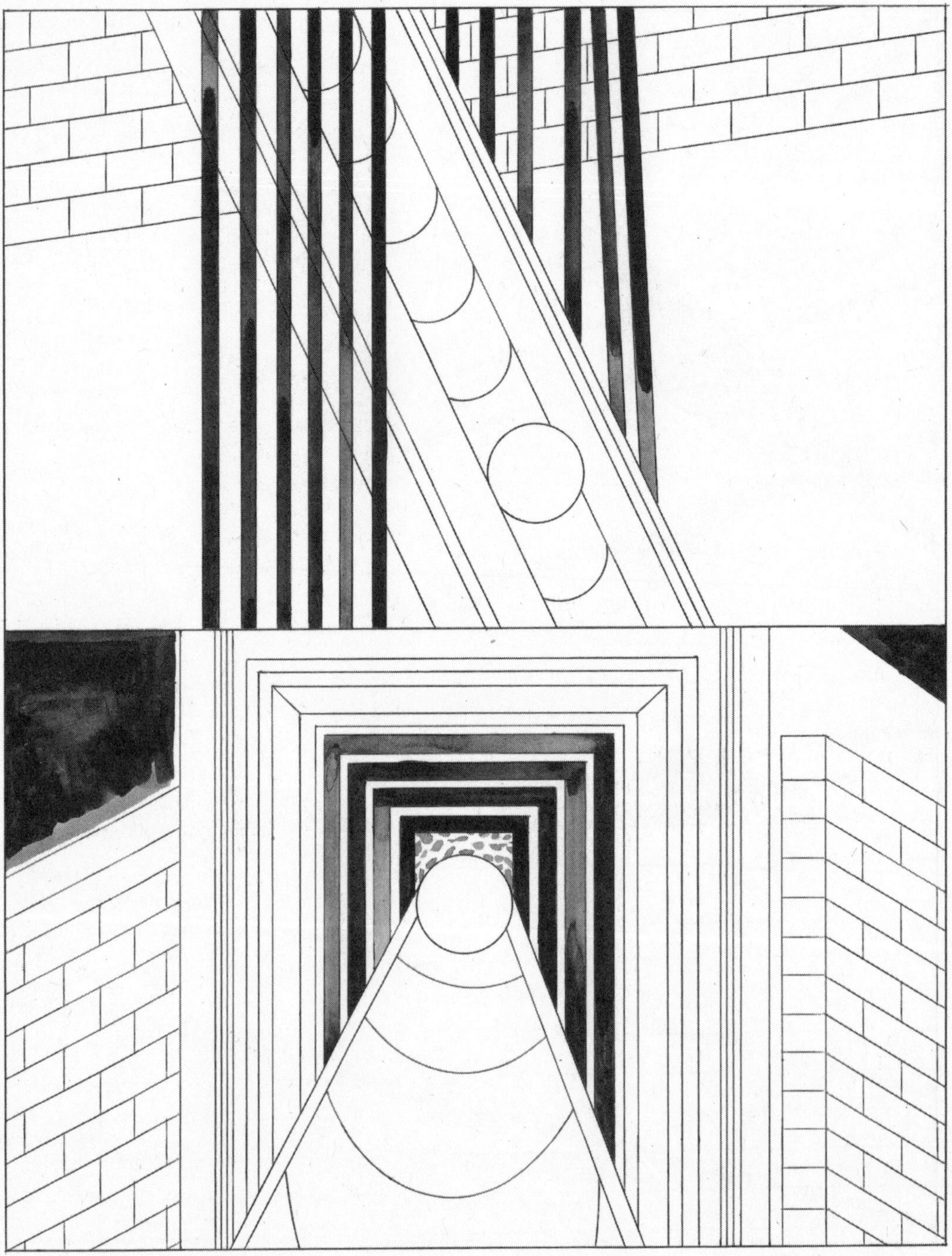

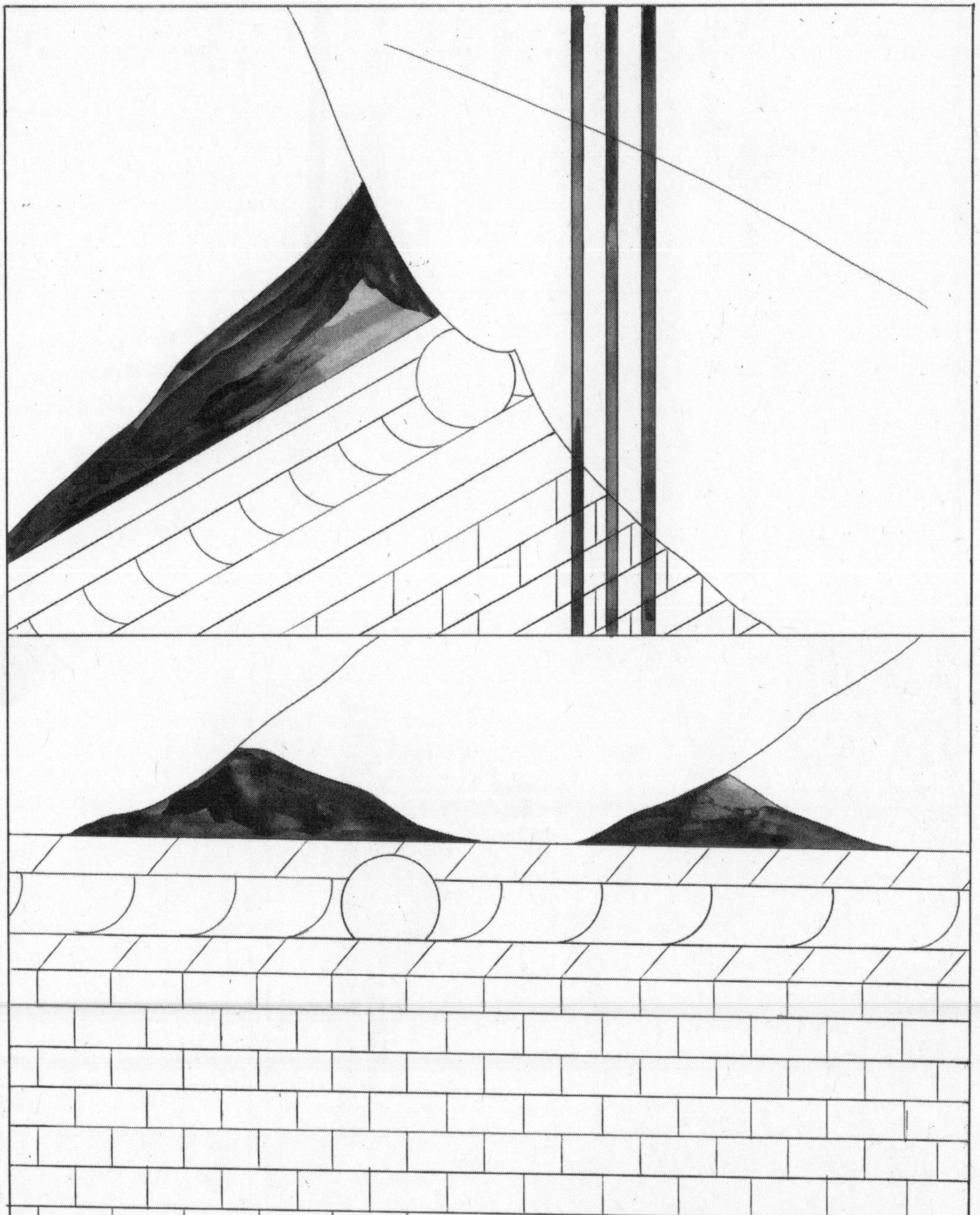

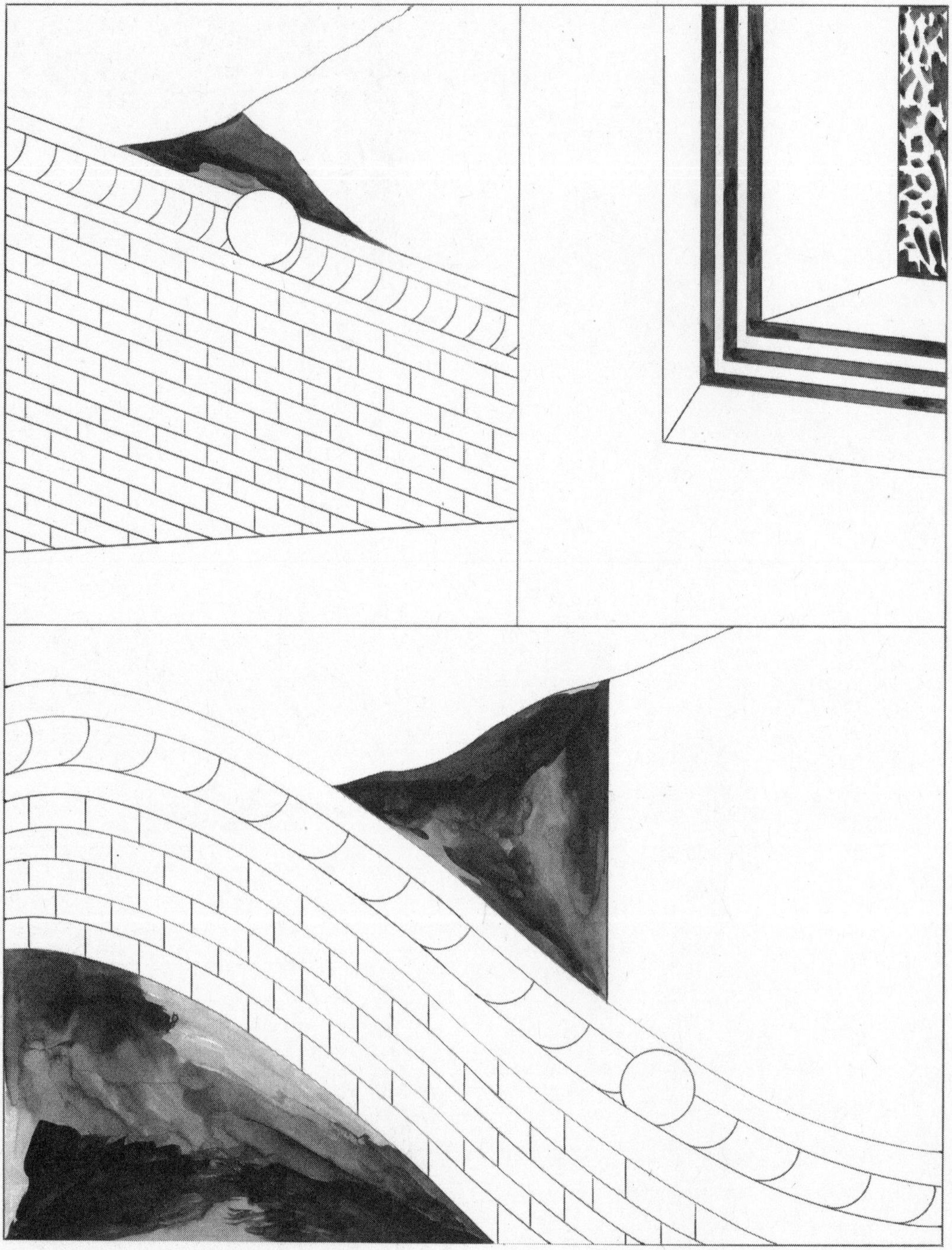

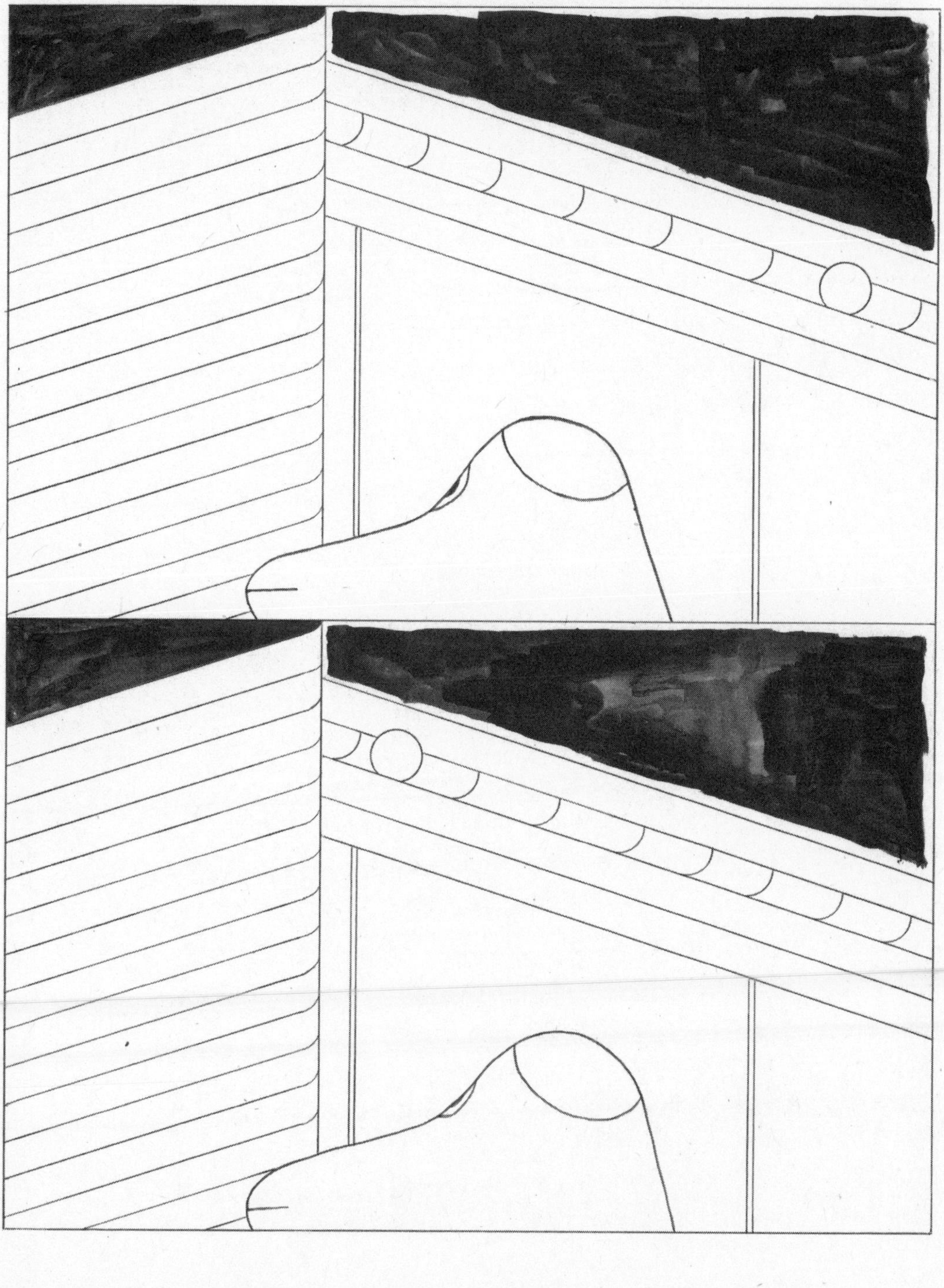

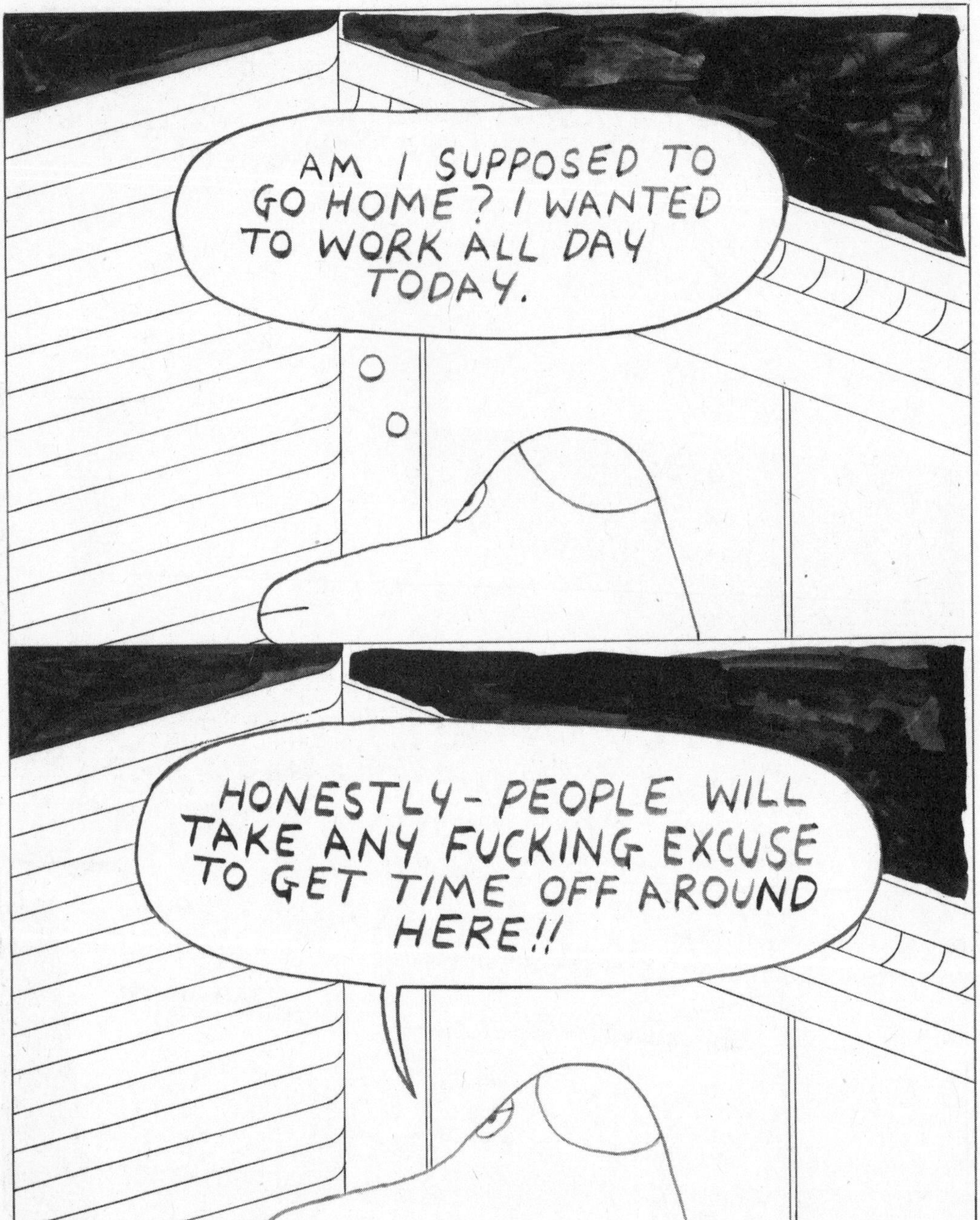
AM I SUPPOSED TO GO HOME? I WANTED TO WORK ALL DAY TODAY.
HONESTLY - PEOPLE WILL TAKE ANY FUCKING EXCUSE TO GET TIME OFF AROUND HERE!!

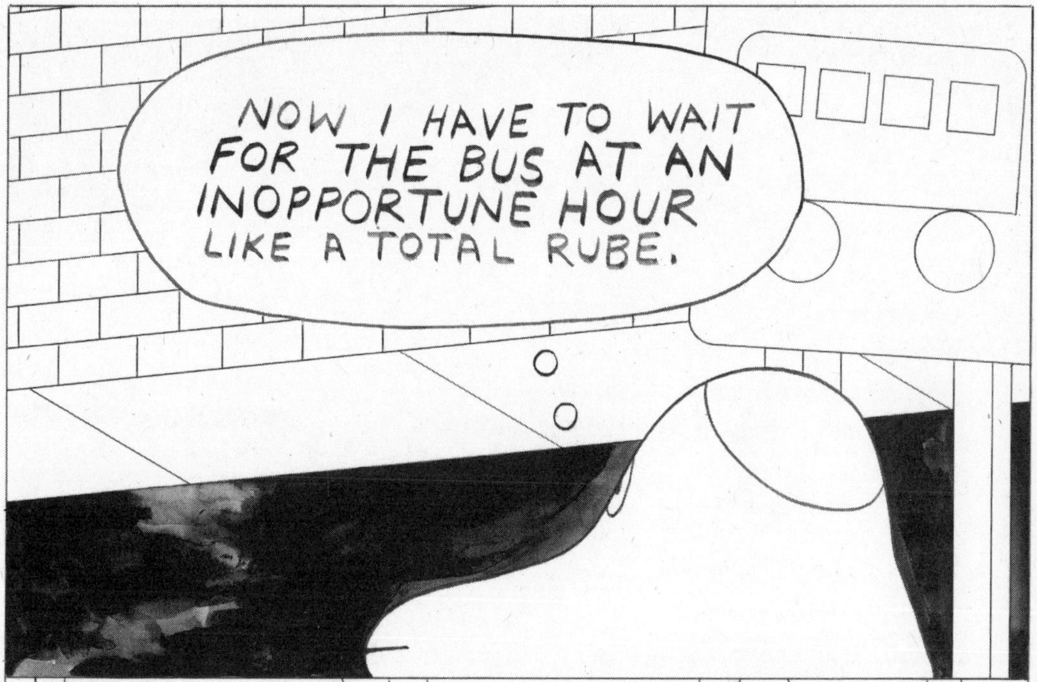
NOW I HAVE TO WAIT FOR THE BUS AT AN INOPPORTUNE HOUR LIKE A TOTAL RUBE.

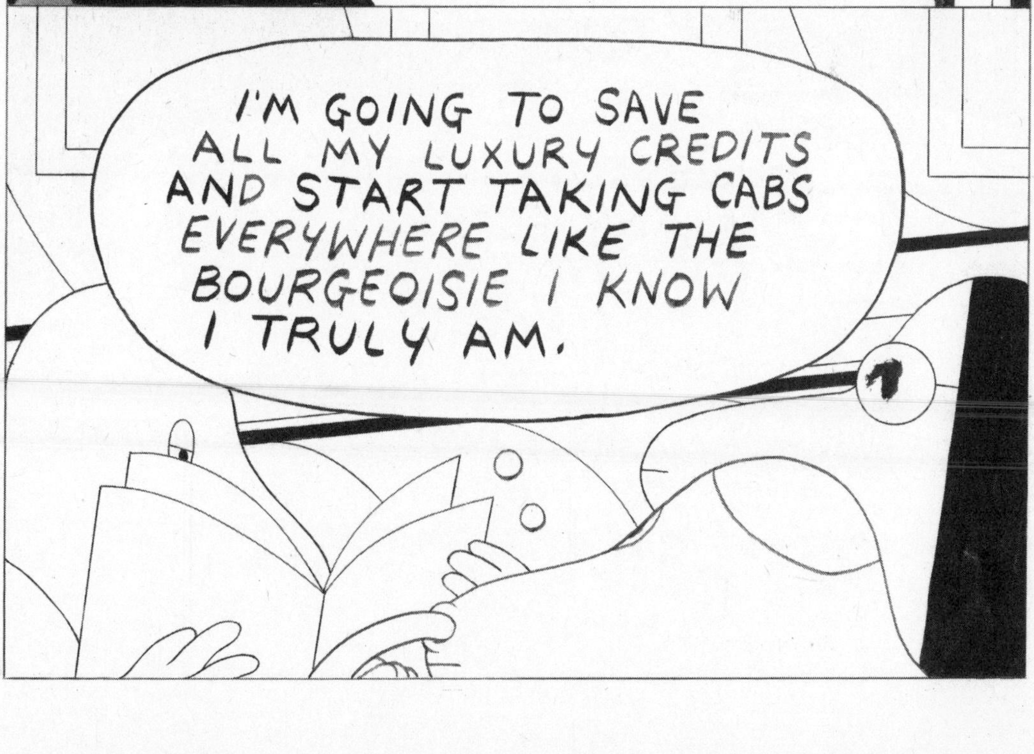
I'M GOING TO SAVE ALL MY LUXURY CREDITS AND START TAKING CABS EVERYWHERE LIKE THE BOURGEOISIE I KNOW I TRULY AM.

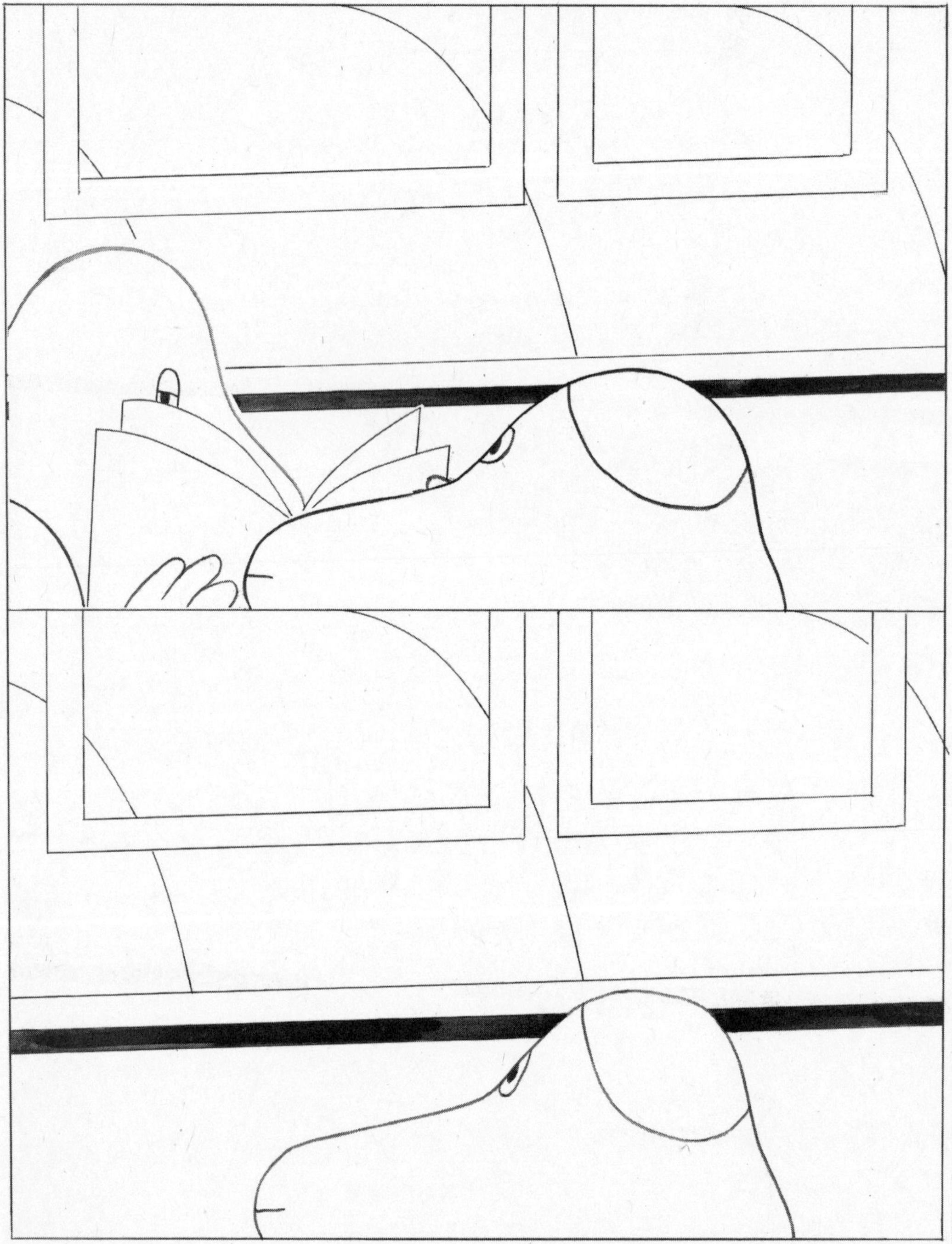

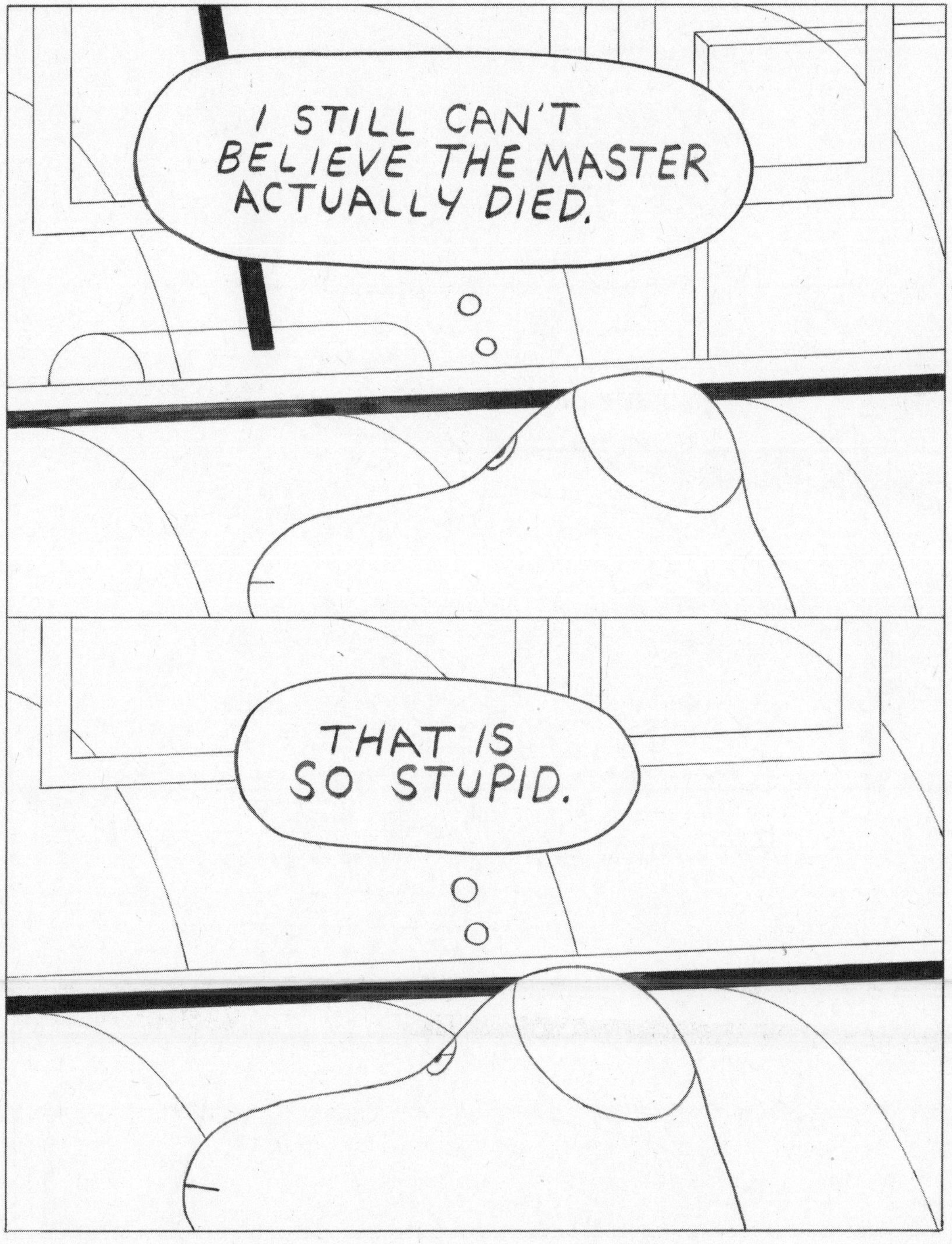
I STILL CAN'T BELIEVE THE MASTER ACTUALLY DIED.
THAT IS SO STUPID.

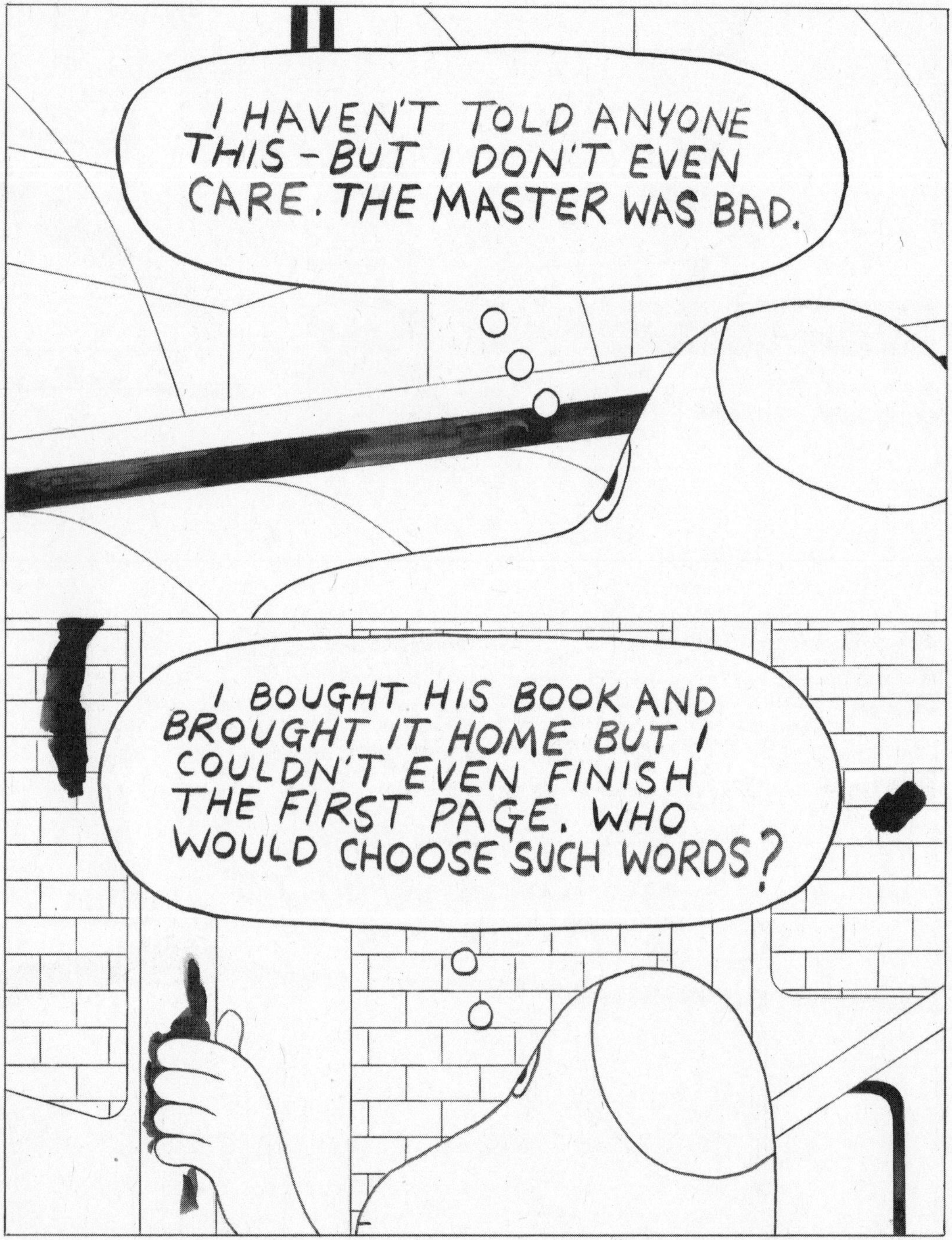
I HAVEN'T TOLD ANYONE THIS - BUT I DON'T EVEN CARE. THE MASTER WAS BAD.
I BOUGHT HIS BOOK AND BROUGHT IT HOME BUT I COULDN'T EVEN FINISH THE FIRST PAGE. WHO WOULD CHOOSE SUCH WORDS?

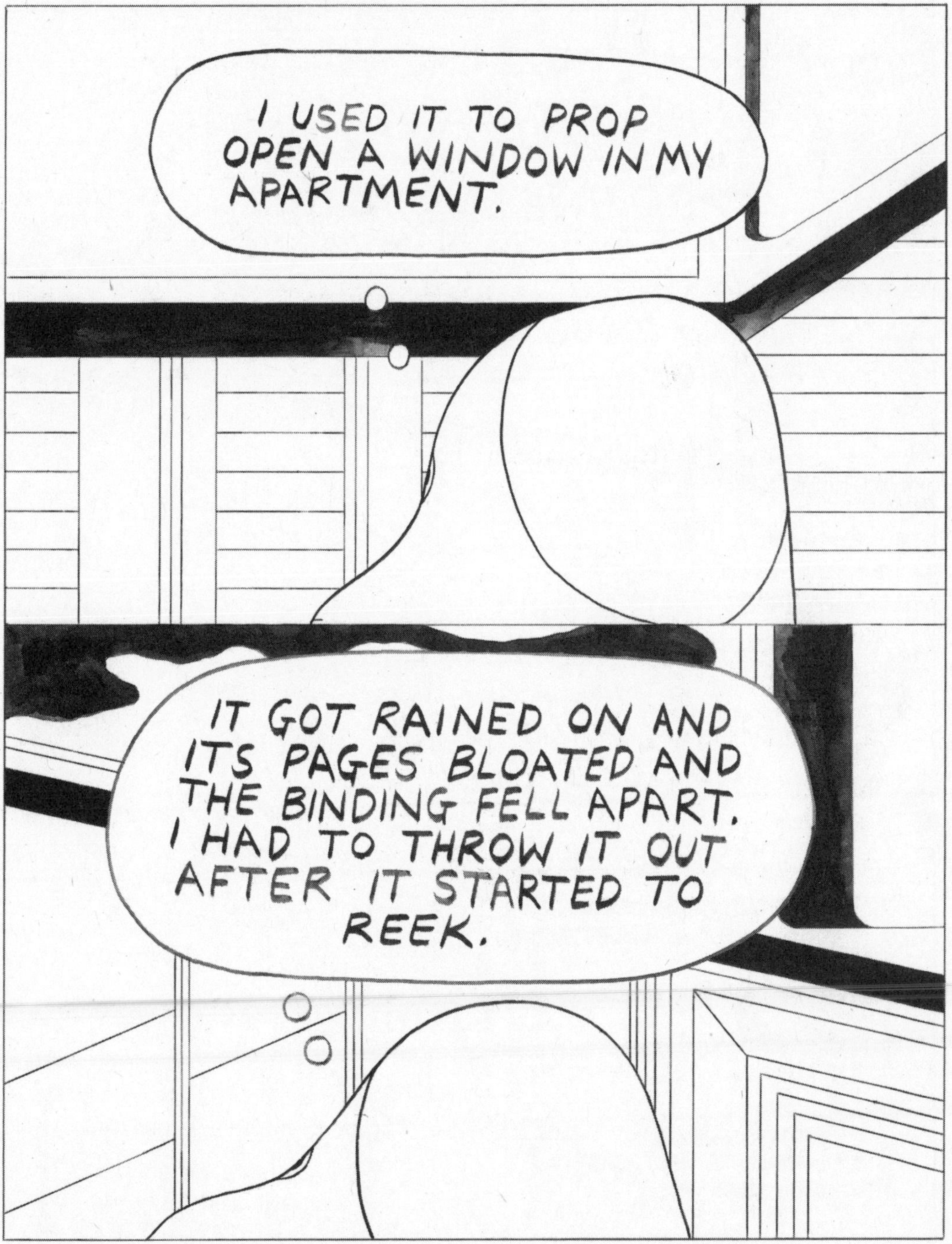
I USED IT TO PROP OPEN A WINDOW IN MY APARTMENT.
IT GOT RAINED ON AND ITS PAGES BLOATED AND THE BINDING FELL APART. I HAD TO THROW IT OUT AFTER IT STARTED TO REEK.

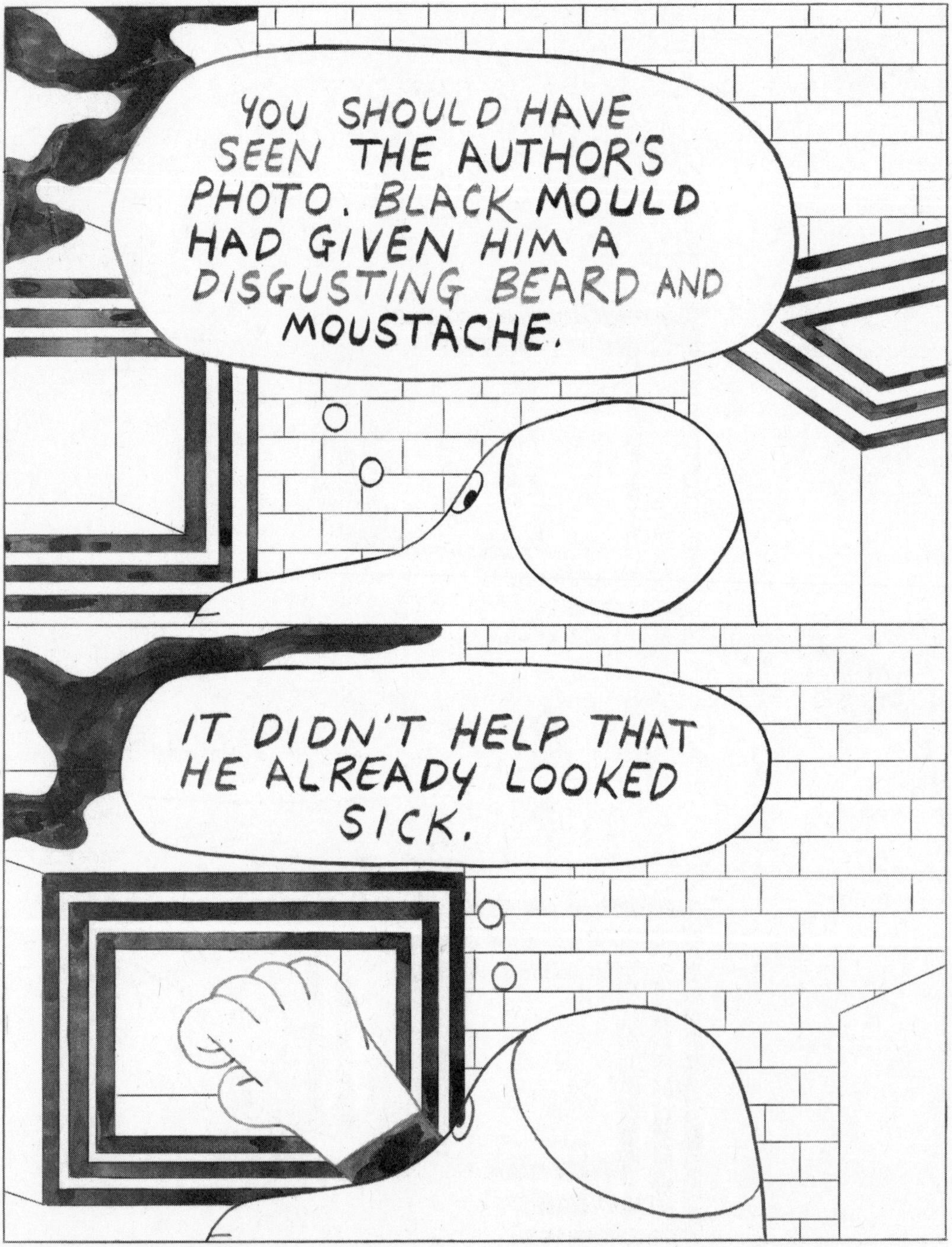
YOU SHOULD HAVE SEEN THE AUTHOR'S PHOTO. BLACK MOULD HAD GIVEN HIM A DISGUSTING BEARD AND MOUSTACHE.
IT DIDN'T HELP THAT HE ALREADY LOOKED SICK.

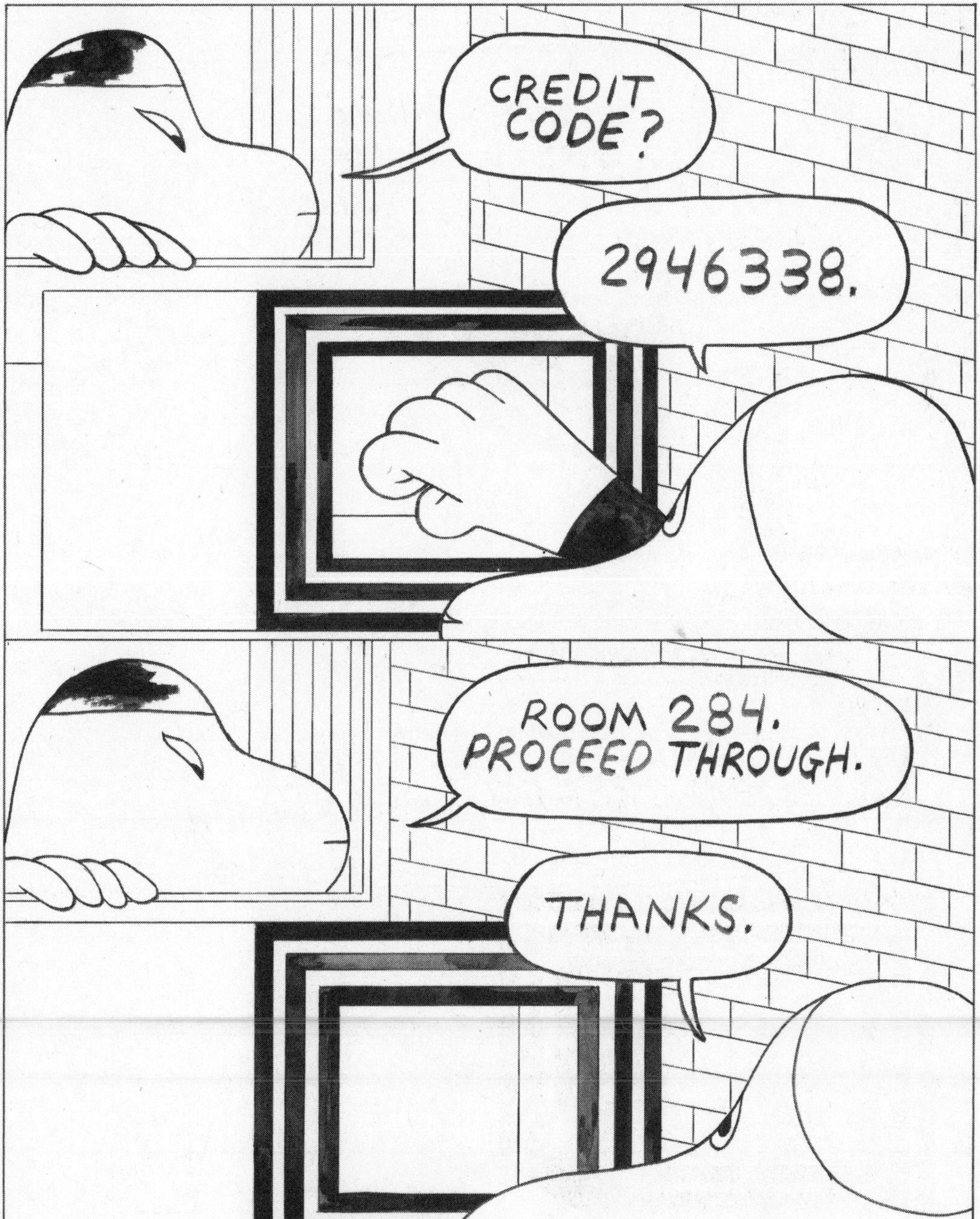
CREDIT CODE?
2946338.
ROOM 284. PROCEED THROUGH.
THANKS.

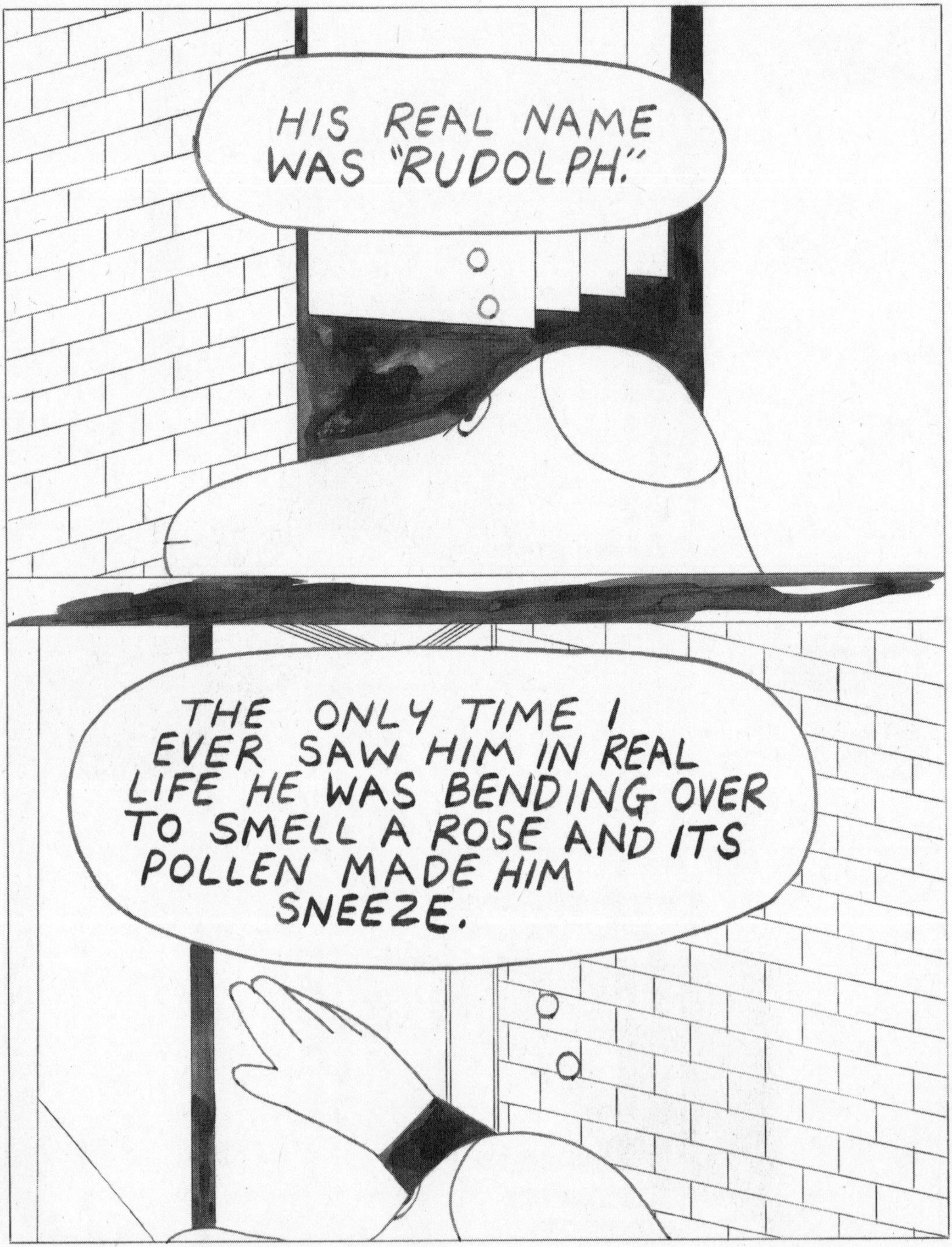
HIS REAL NAME WAS "RUDOLPH."
THE ONLY TIME I EVER SAW HIM IN REAL LIFE HE WAS BENDING OVER TO SMELL A ROSE AND ITS POLLEN MADE HIM SNEEZE.

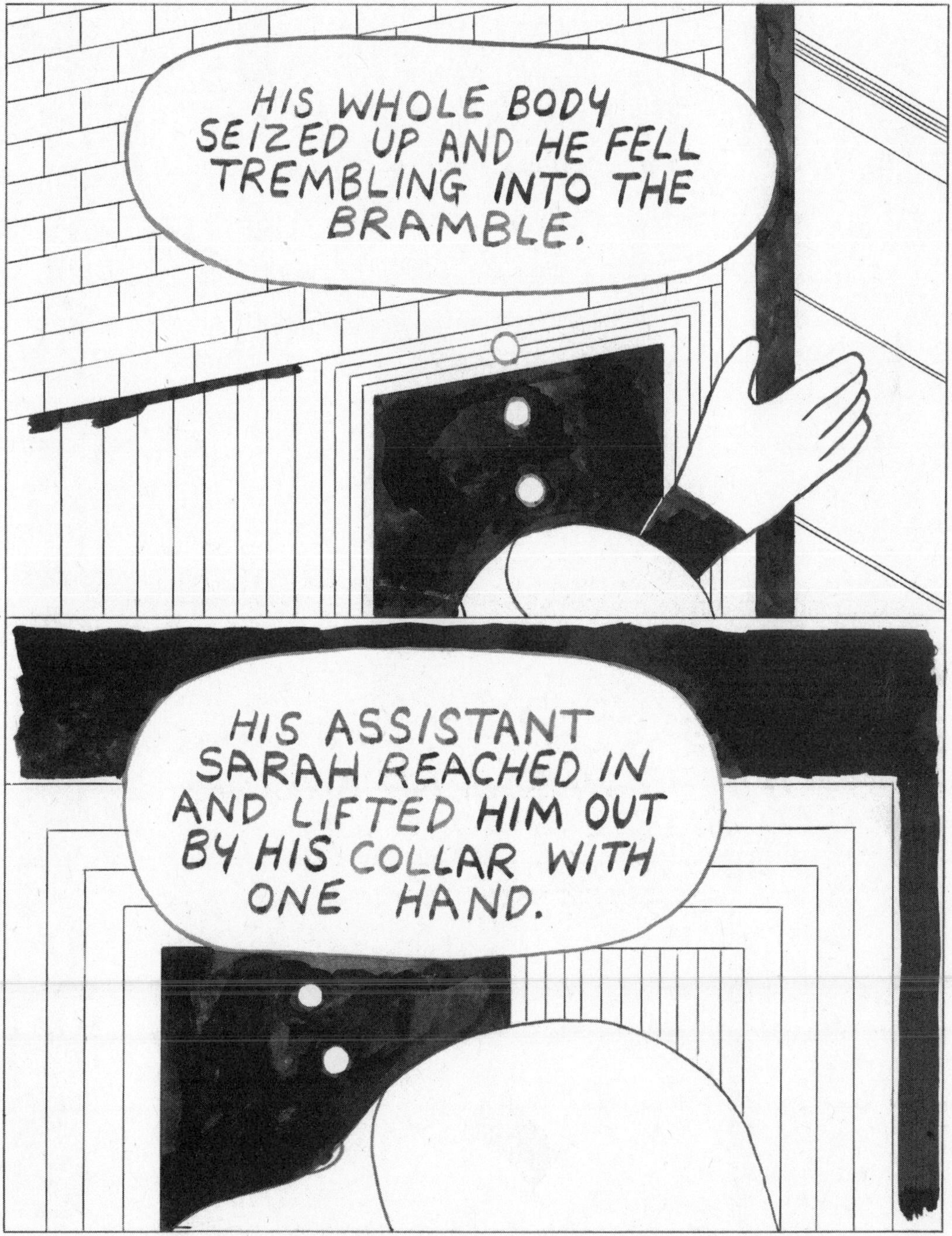
HIS WHOLE BODY SEIZED UP AND HE FELL TREMBLING INTO THE BRAMBLE.
HIS ASSISTANT SARAH REACHED IN AND LIFTED HIM OUT BY HIS COLLAR WITH ONE HAND.

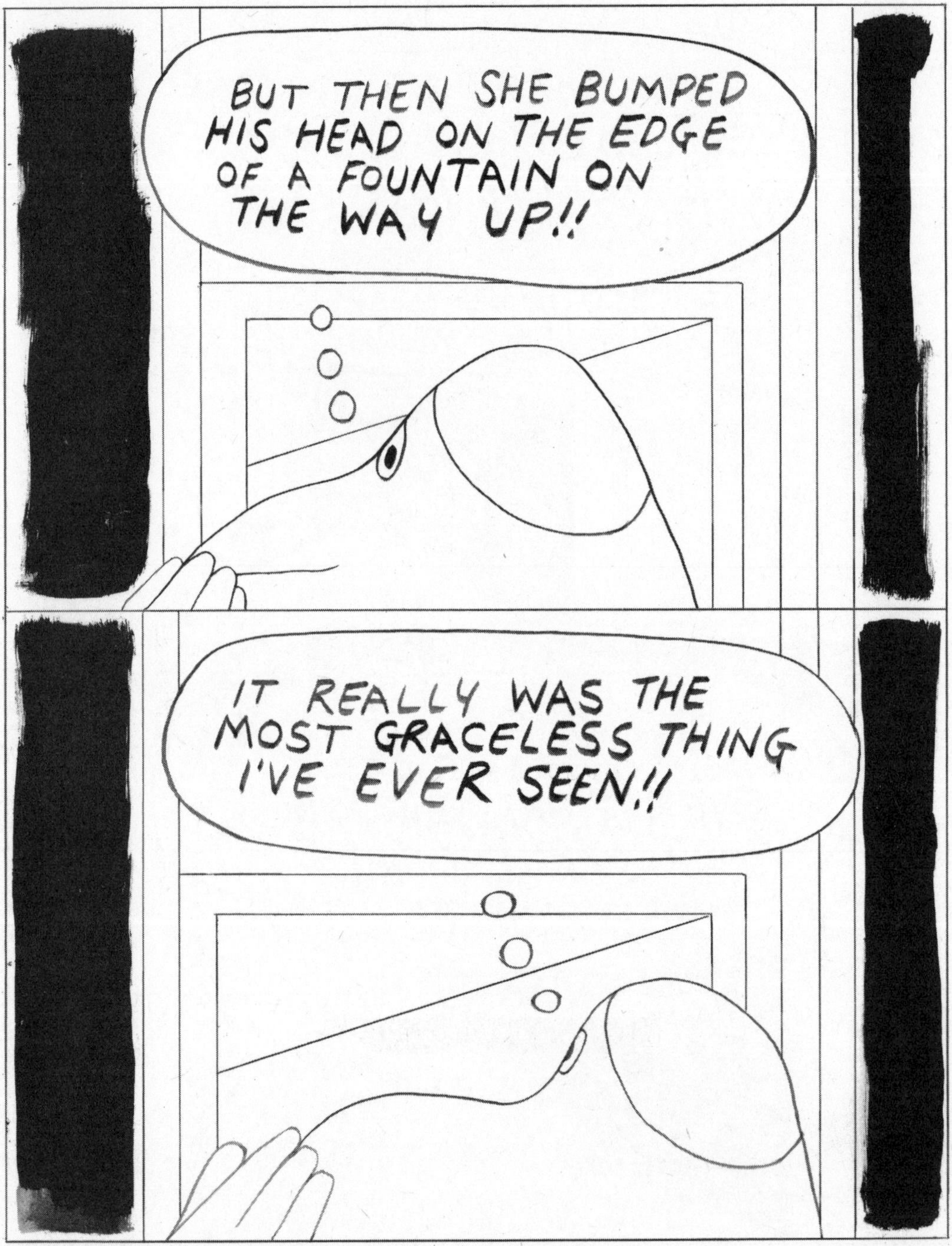
BUT THEN SHE BUMPED HIS HEAD ON THE EDGE OF A FOUNTAIN ON THE WAY UP!!
IT REALLY WAS THE MOST GRACELESS THING I'VE EVER SEEN!!

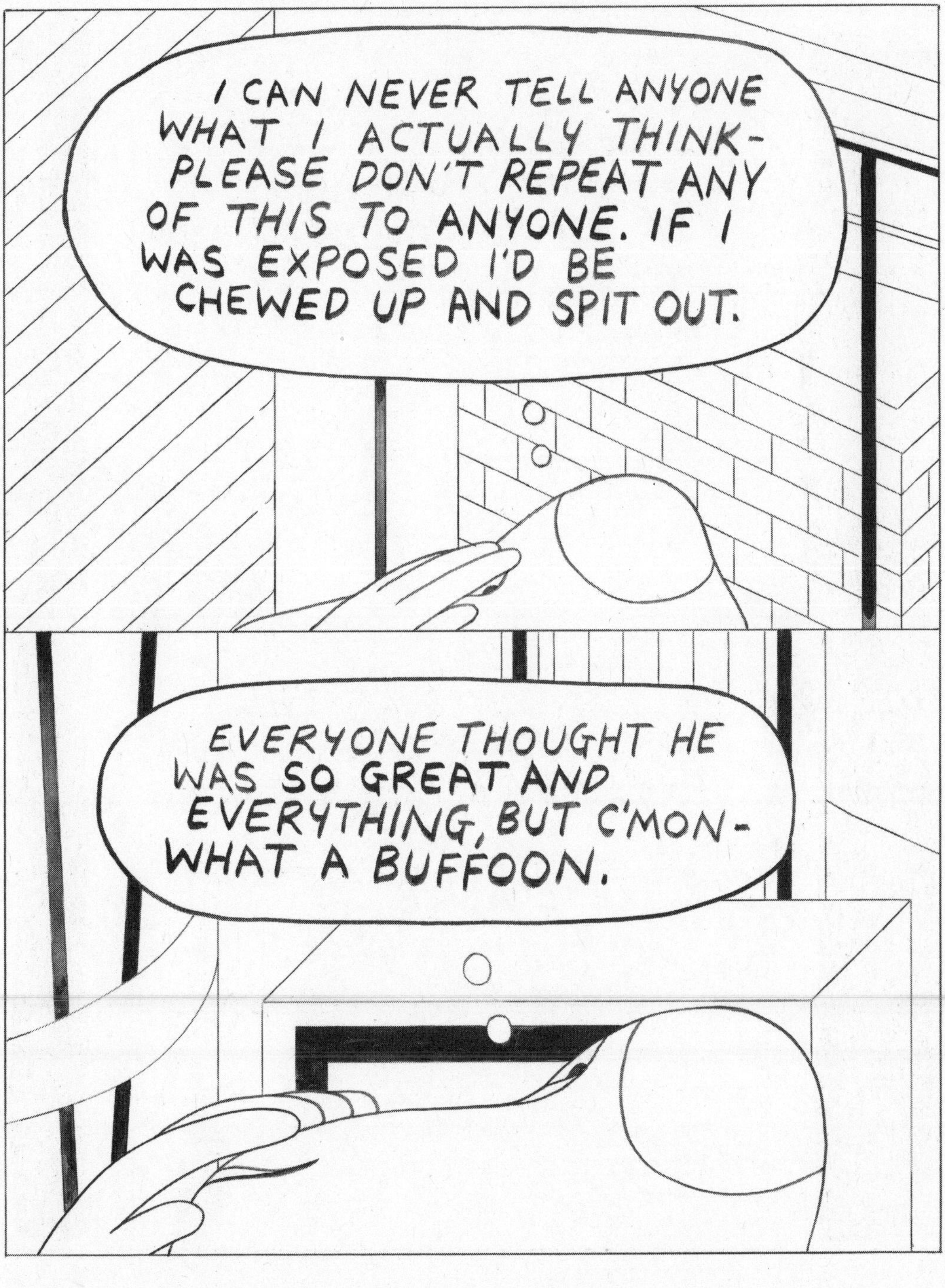
I CAN NEVER TELL ANYONE WHAT I ACTUALLY THINK- PLEASE DON'T REPEAT ANY OF THIS TO ANYONE. IF I WAS EXPOSED I'D BE CHEWED UP AND SPIT OUT.
EVERYONE THOUGHT HE WAS SO GREAT AND EVERYTHING, BUT C'MON- WHAT A BUFFOON.

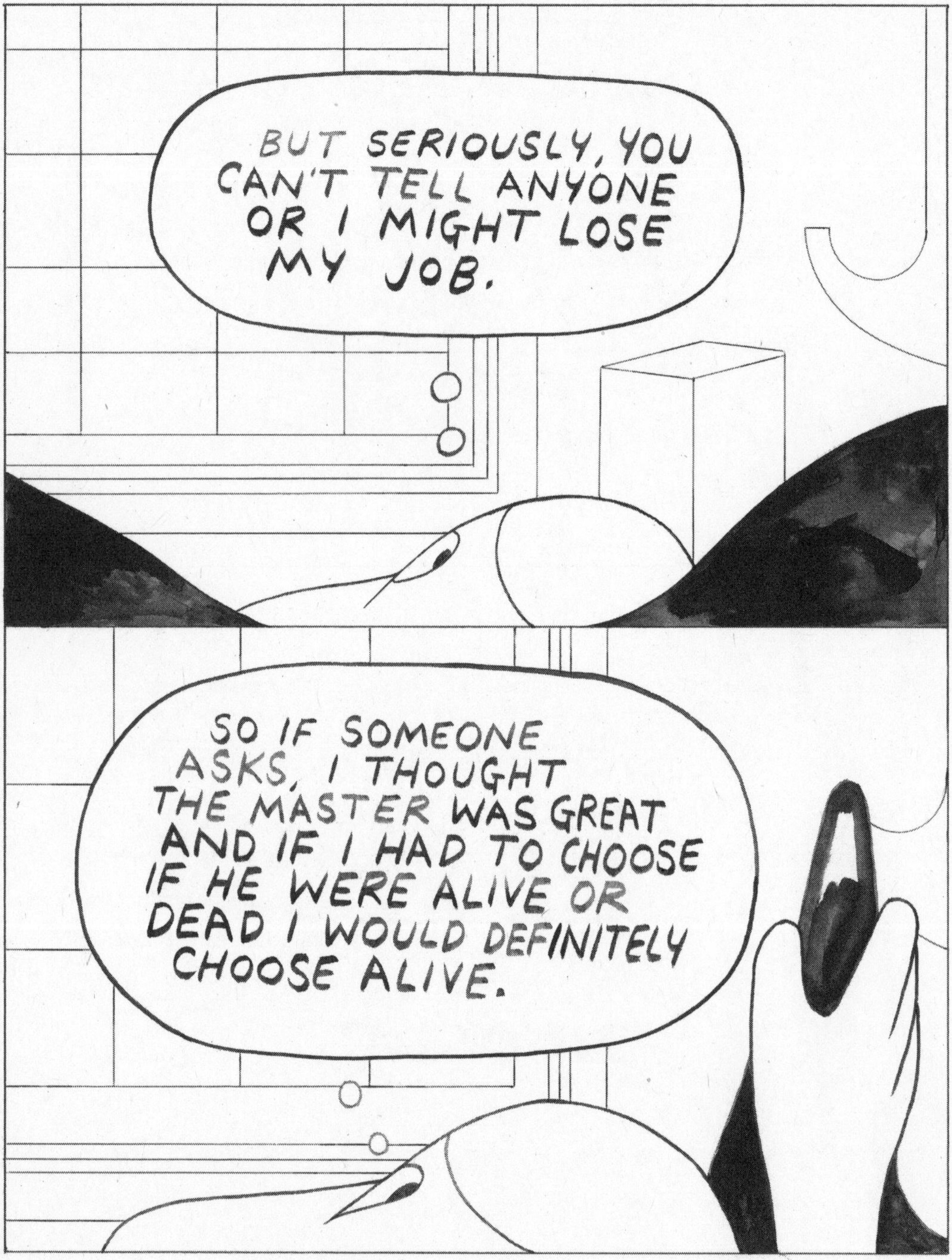
BUT SERIOUSLY, YOU CAN'T TELL ANYONE OR I MIGHT LOSE MY JOB.
SO IF SOMEONE ASKS, I THOUGHT THE MASTER WAS GREAT AND IF I HAD TO CHOOSE IF HE WERE ALIVE OR DEAD I WOULD DEFINITELY CHOOSE ALIVE.

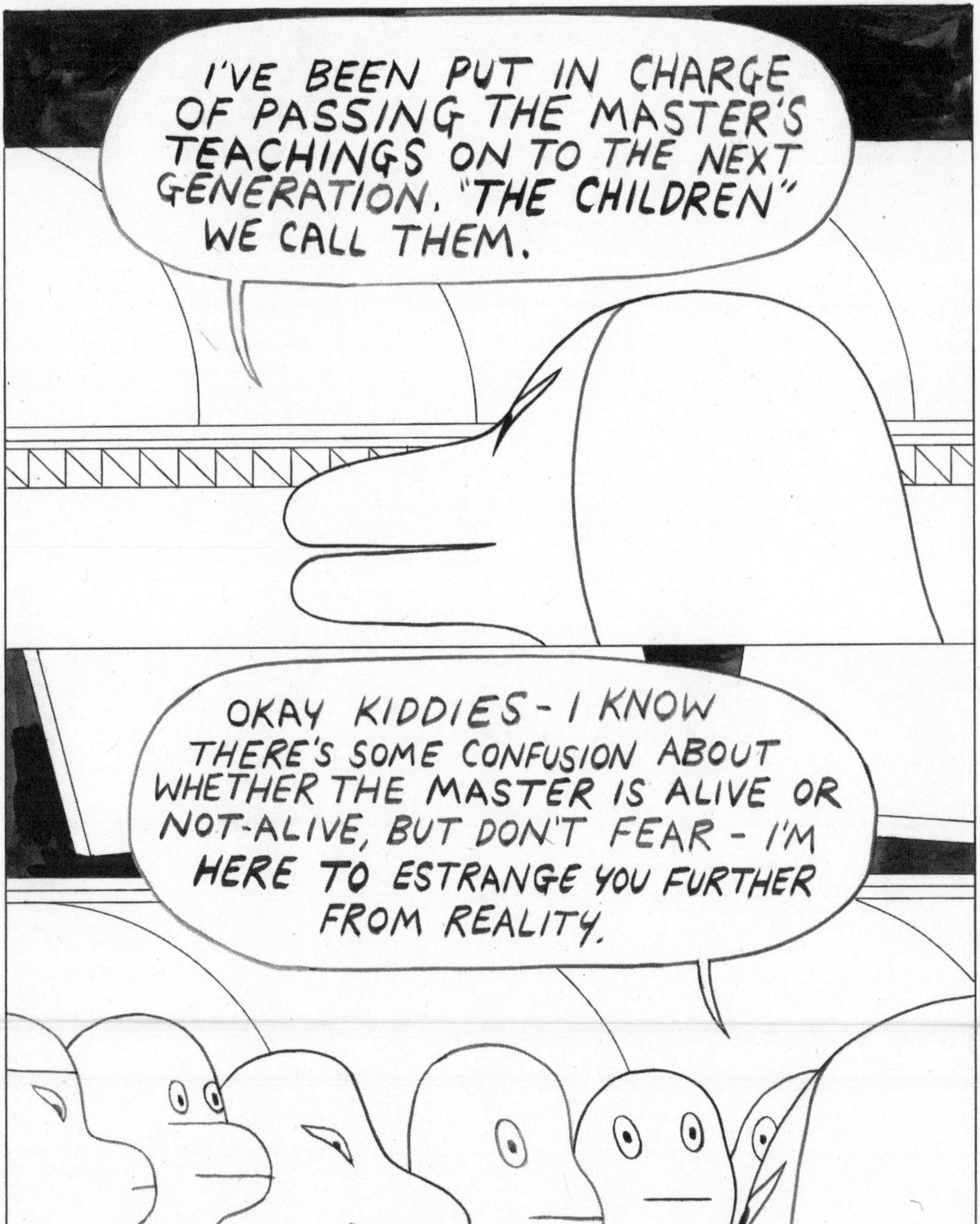
I'VE BEEN PUT IN CHARGE OF PASSING THE MASTER'S TEACHINGS ON TO THE NEXT GENERATION. "THE CHILDREN" WE CALL THEM.
OKAY KIDDIES - I KNOW THERE'S SOME CONFUSION ABOUT WHETHER THE MASTER IS ALIVE OR NOT-ALIVE, BUT DON'T FEAR - I'M HERE TO ESTRANGE YOU FURTHER FROM REALITY.

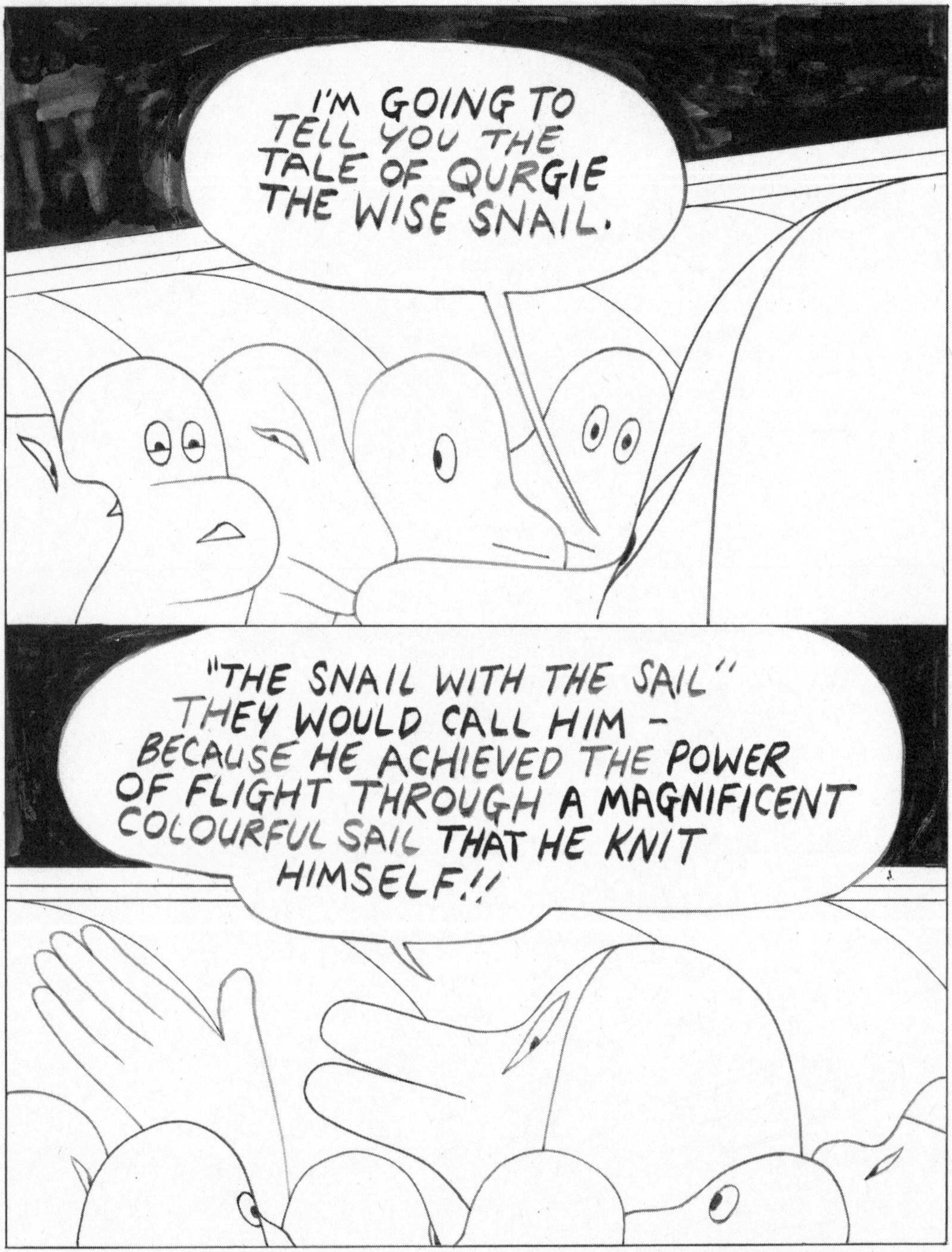
I'M GOING TO TELL YOU THE TALE OF QURGIE THE WISE SNAIL.
"THE SNAIL WITH THE SAIL" THEY WOULD CALL HIM - BECAUSE HE ACHIEVED THE POWER OF FLIGHT THROUGH A MAGNIFICENT COLOURFUL SAIL THAT HE KNIT HIMSELF!!

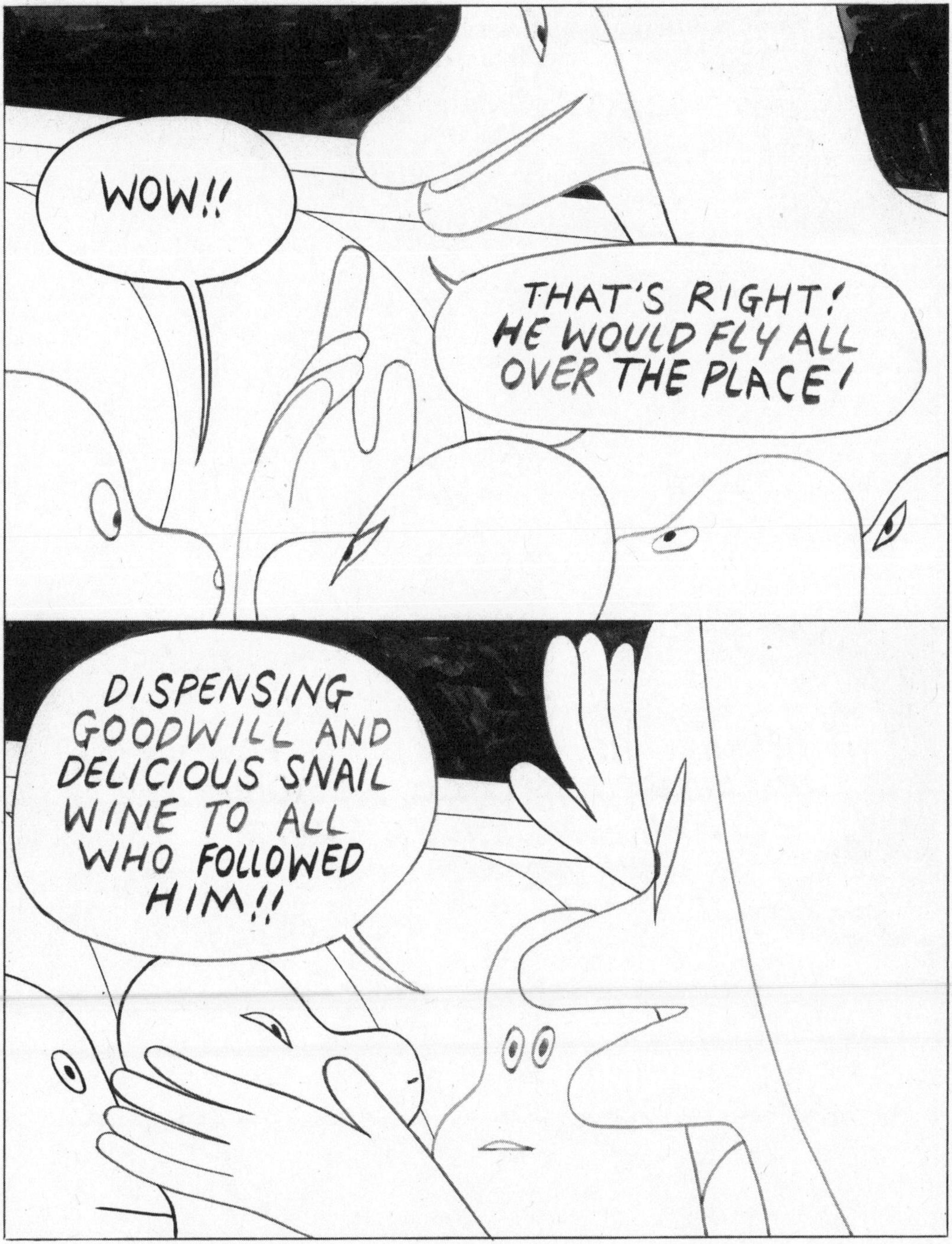
WOW!!
THAT'S RIGHT! HE WOULD FLY ALL OVER THE PLACE!
DISPENSING GOODWILL AND DELICIOUS SNAIL WINE TO ALL WHO FOLLOWED HIM!!

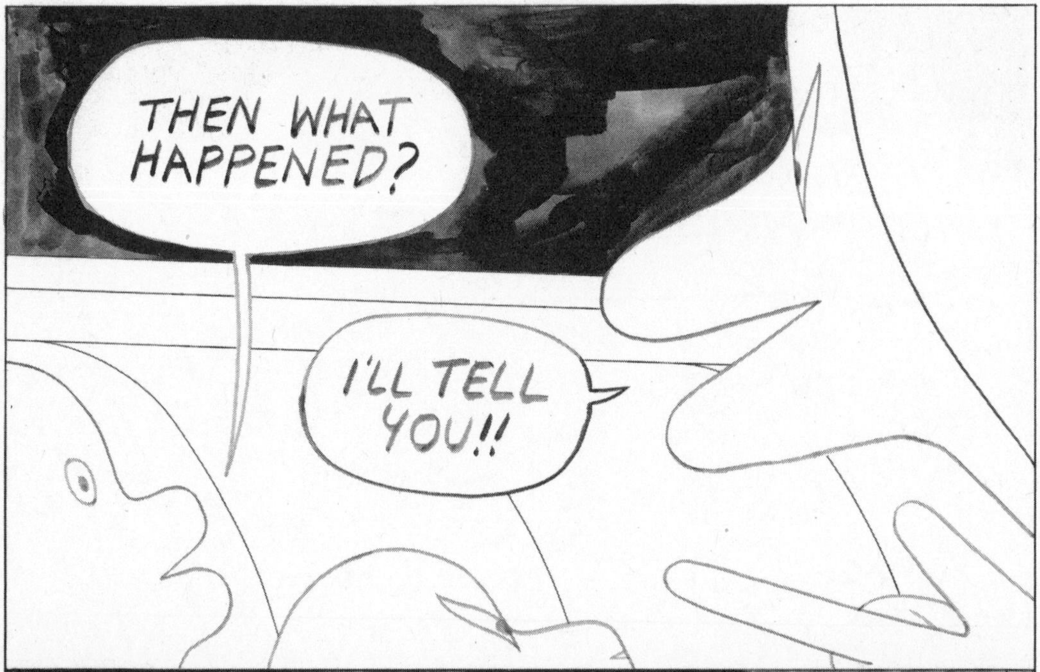
THEN WHAT HAPPENED?
I'LL TELL YOU!!

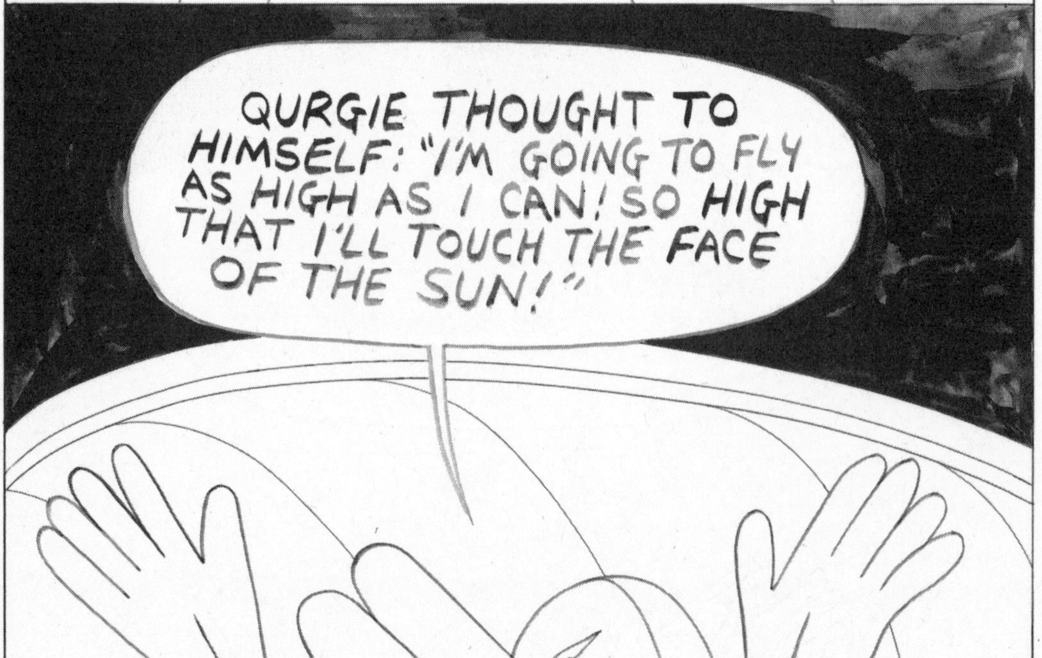
QURGIE THOUGHT TO HIMSELF: "I'M GOING TO FLY AS HIGH AS I CAN! SO HIGH THAT I'LL TOUCH THE FACE OF THE SUN!"

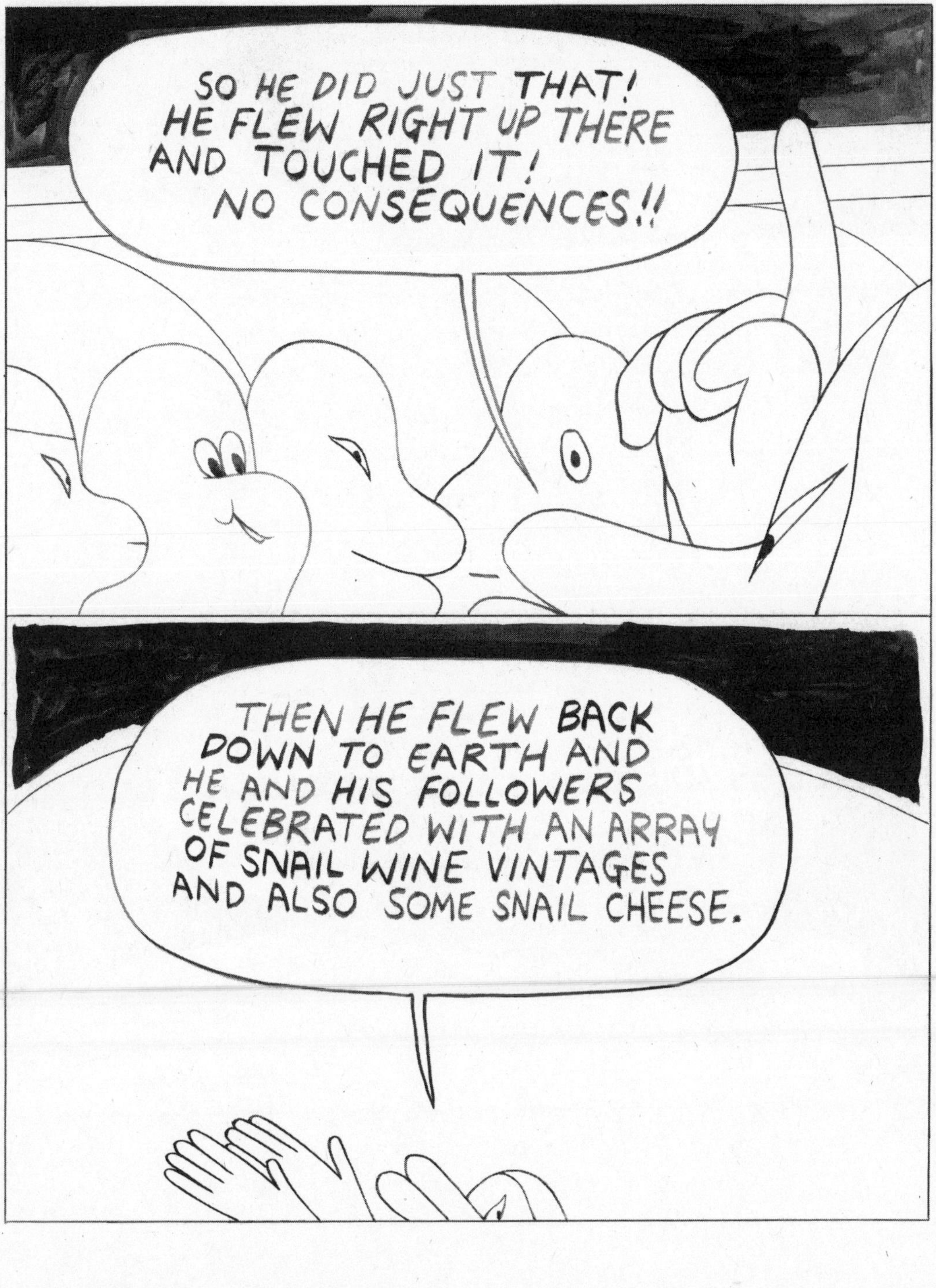
SO HE DID JUST THAT! HE FLEW RIGHT UP THERE AND TOUCHED IT! NO CONSEQUENCES!!
THEN HE FLEW BACK DOWN TO EARTH AND HE AND HIS FOLLOWERS CELEBRATED WITH AN ARRAY OF SNAIL WINE VINTAGES AND ALSO SOME SNAIL CHEESE.

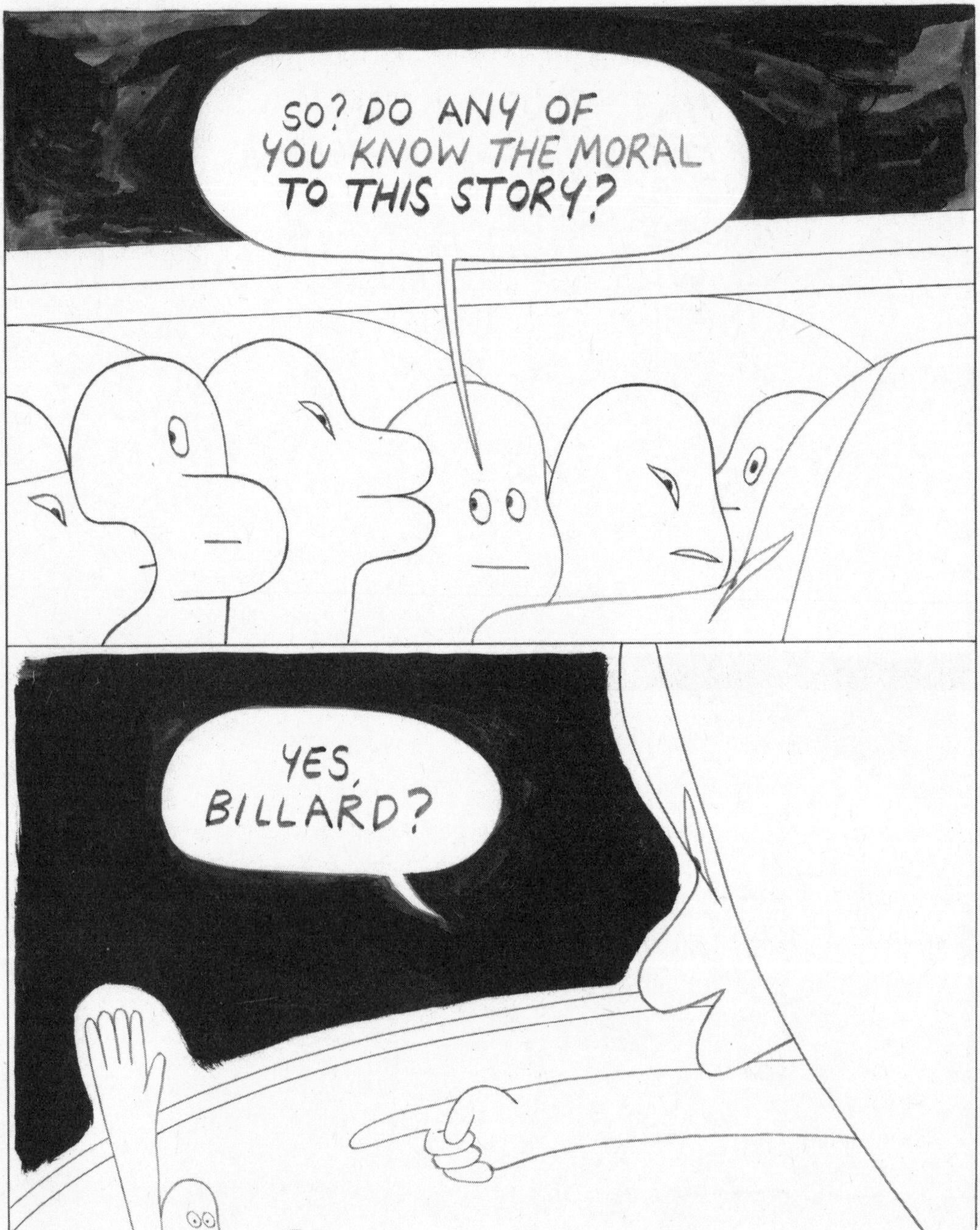
SO? DO ANY OF YOU KNOW THE MORAL TO THIS STORY?
YES, BILLARD?

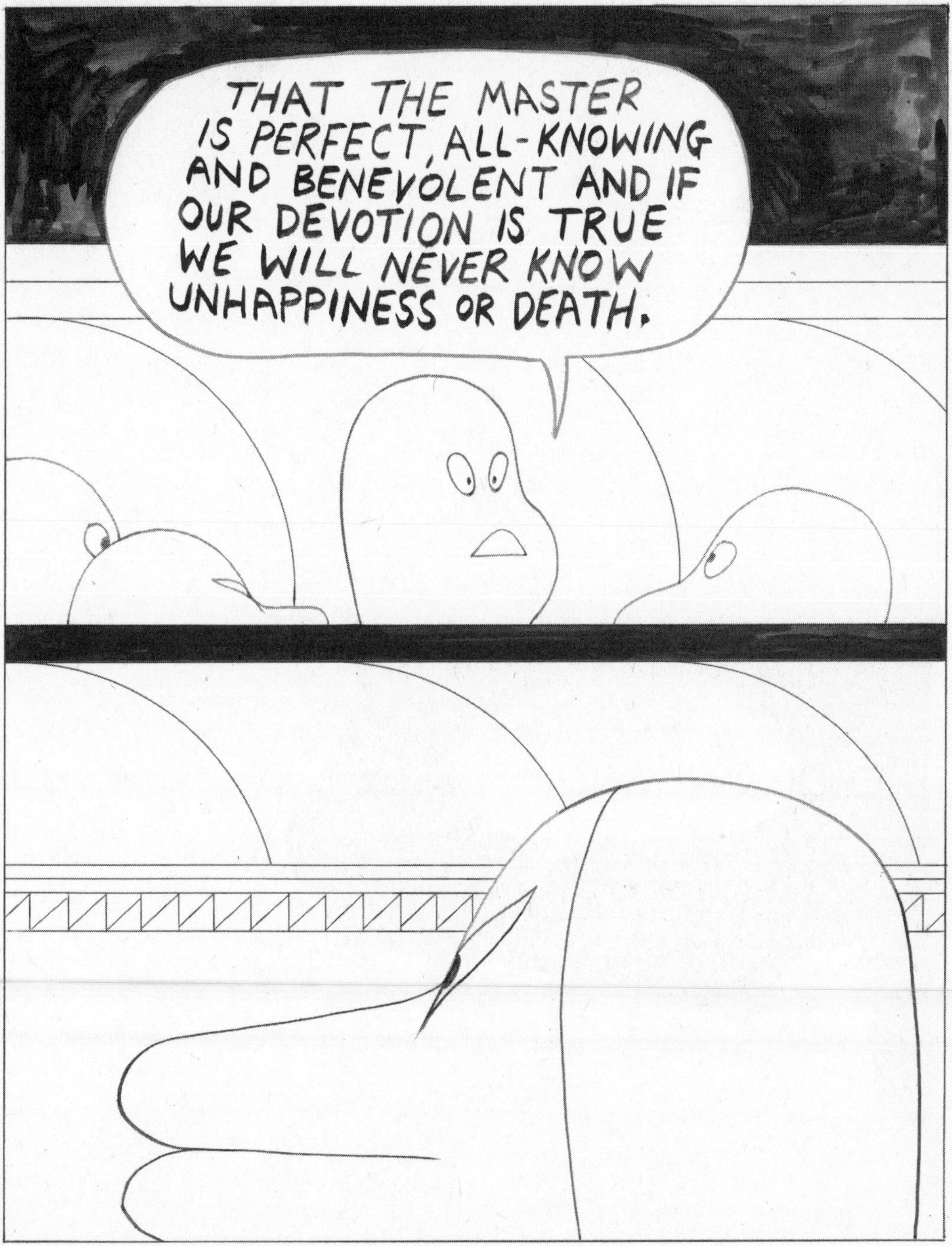
THAT THE MASTER IS PERFECT, ALL-KNOWING AND BENEVOLENT AND IF OUR DEVOTION IS TRUE WE WILL NEVER KNOW UNHAPPINESS OR DEATH.

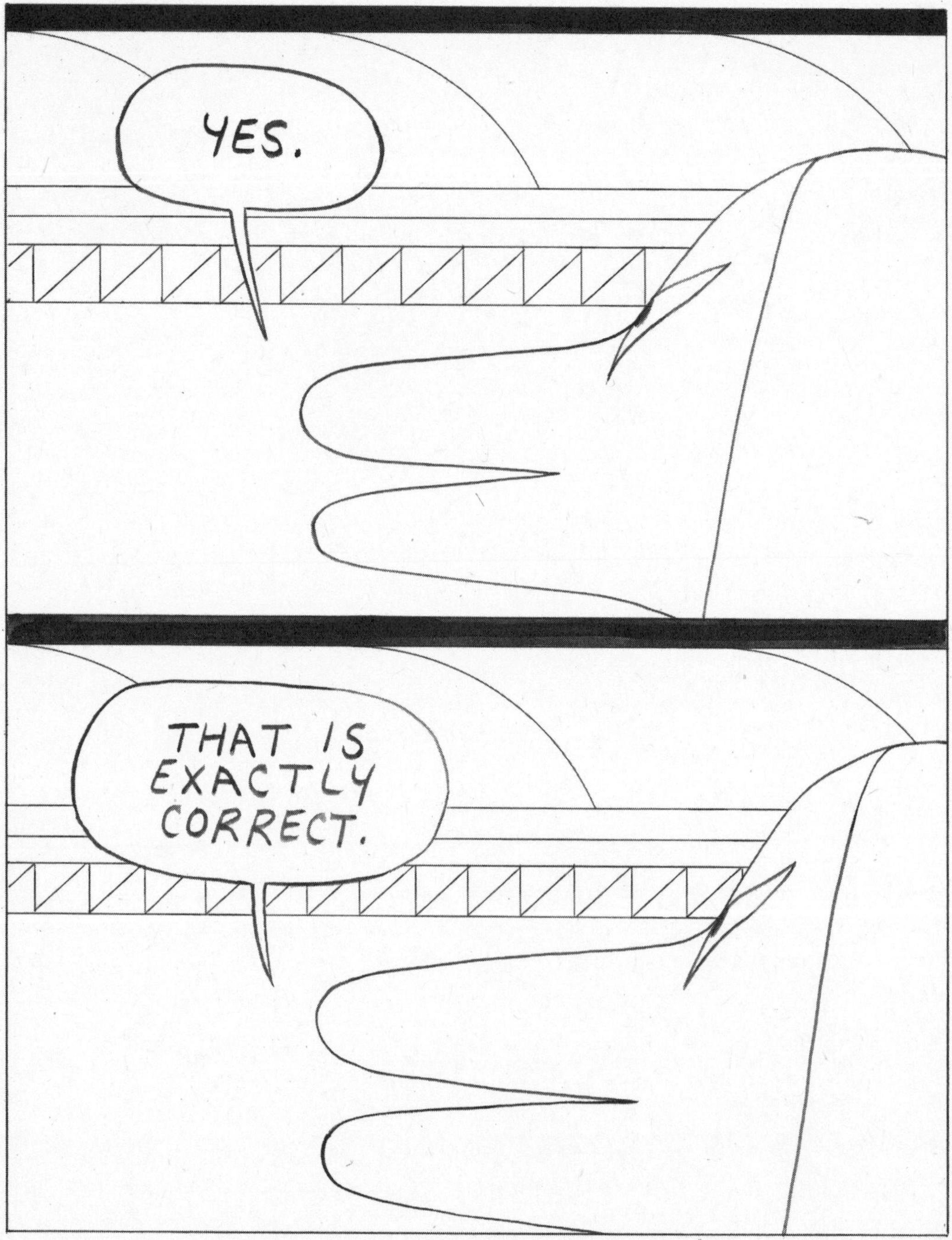
YES.
THAT IS EXACTLY CORRECT.

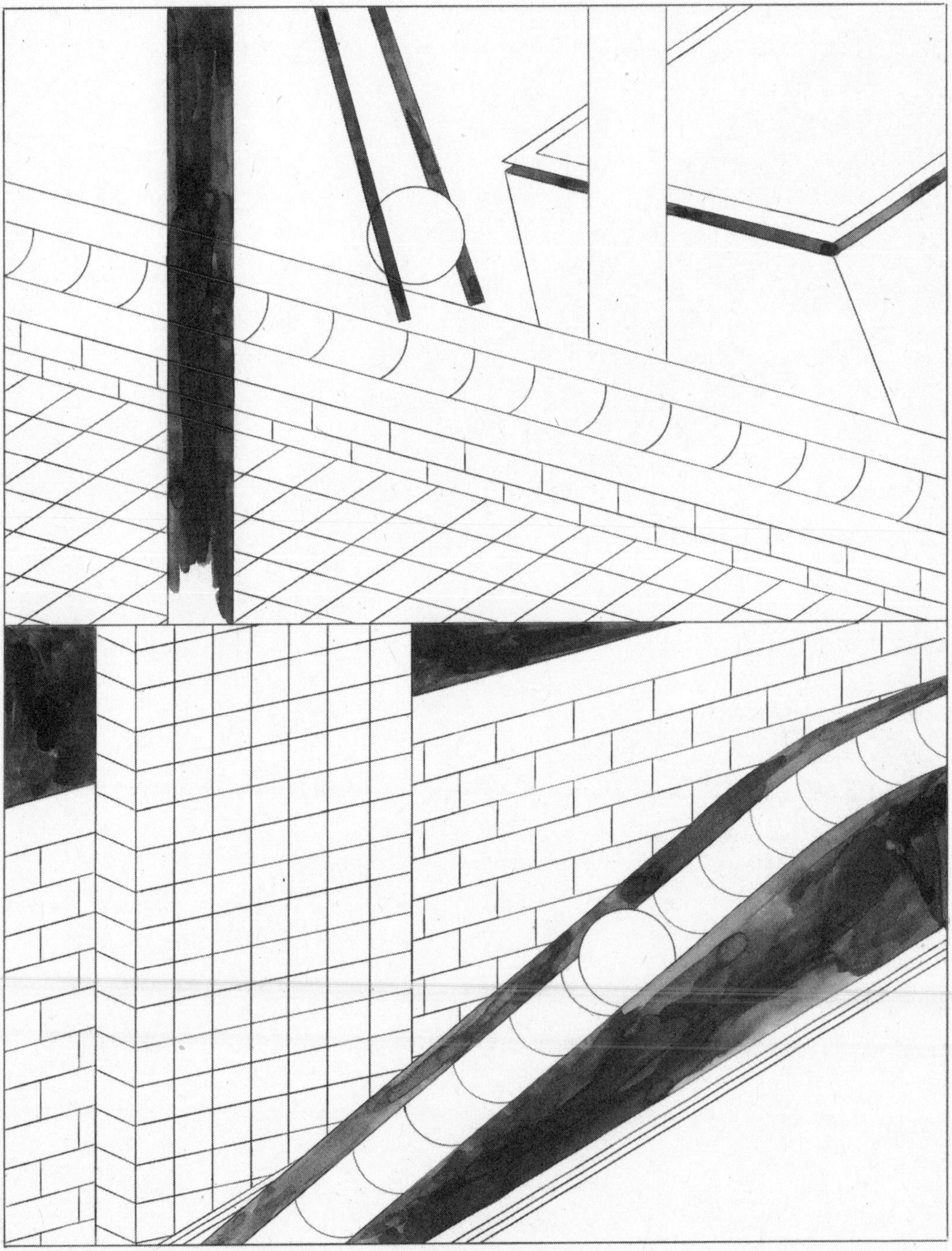

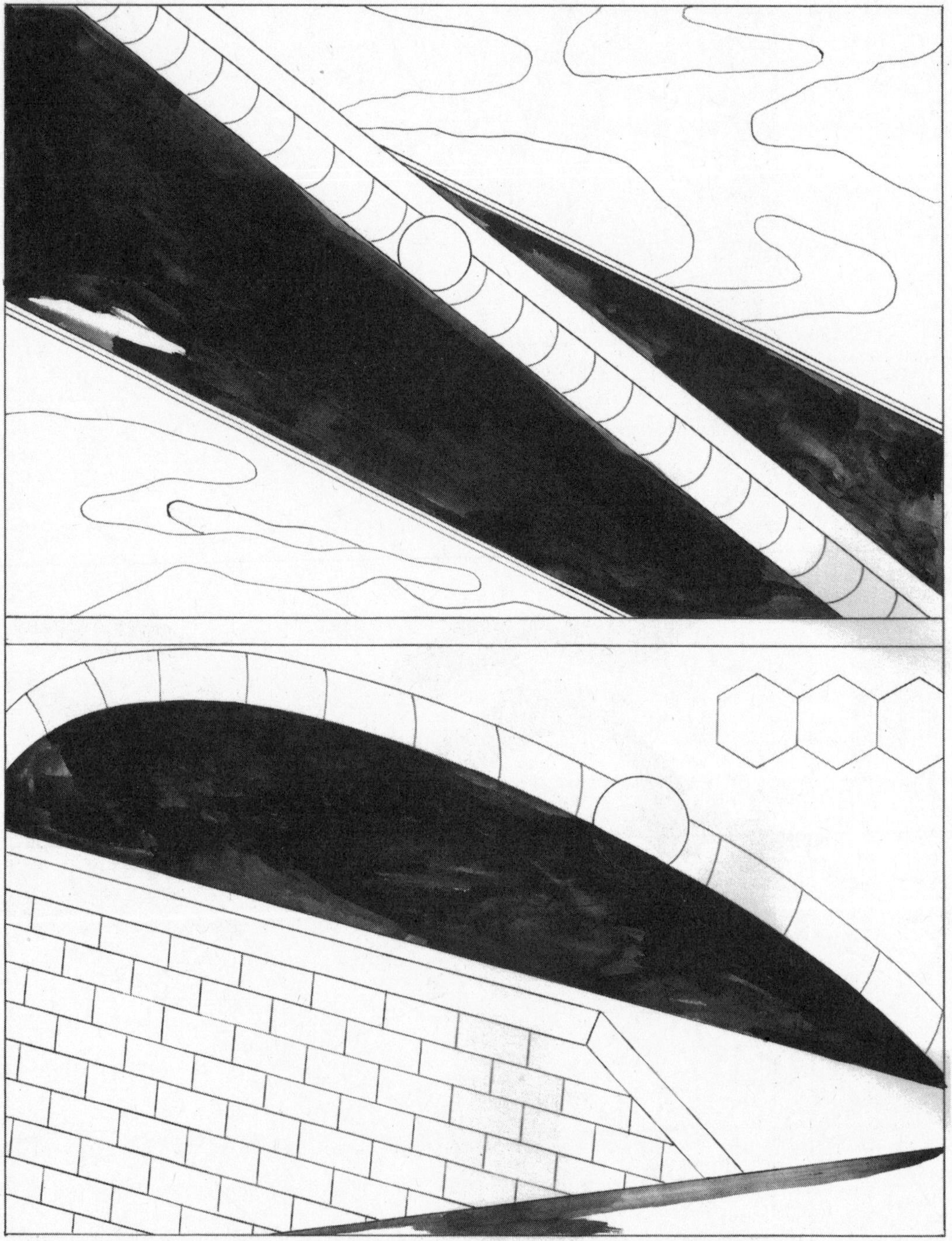

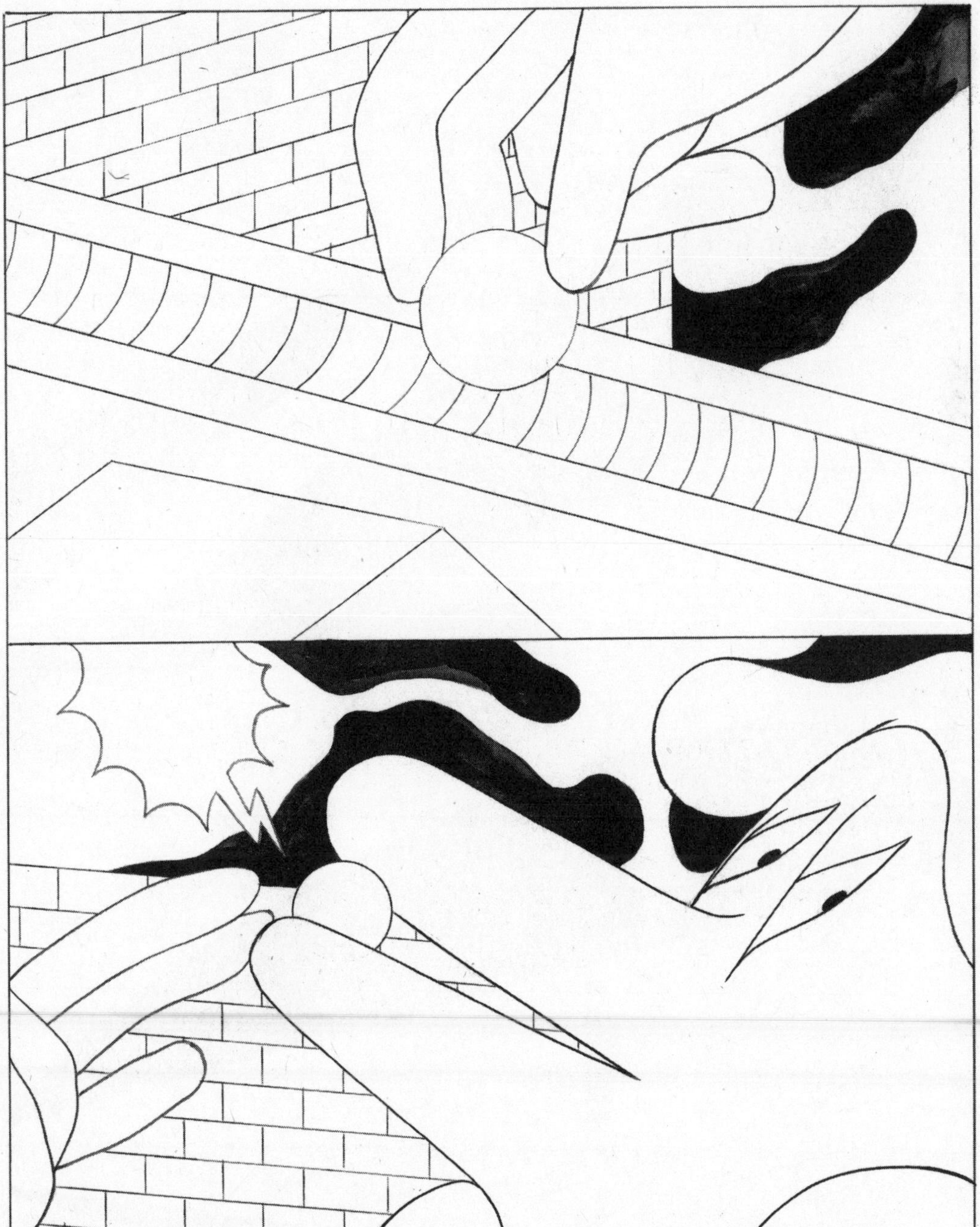

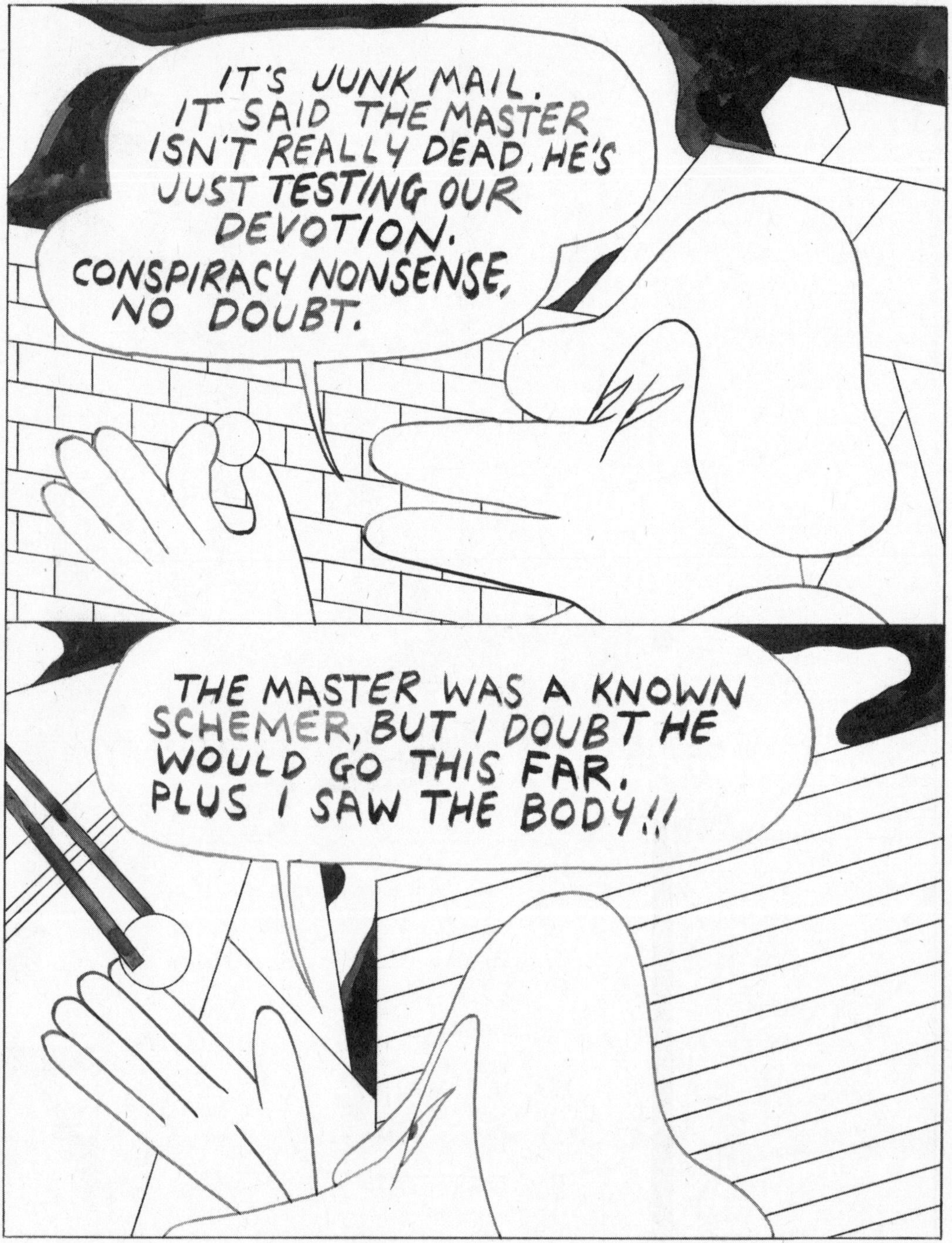
IT'S JUNK MAIL. IT SAID THE MASTER ISN'T REALLY DEAD, HE'S JUST TESTING OUR DEVOTION. CONSPIRACY NONSENSE, NO DOUBT.
THE MASTER WAS A KNOWN SCHEMER, BUT I DOUBT HE WOULD GO THIS FAR. PLUS I SAW THE BODY!!

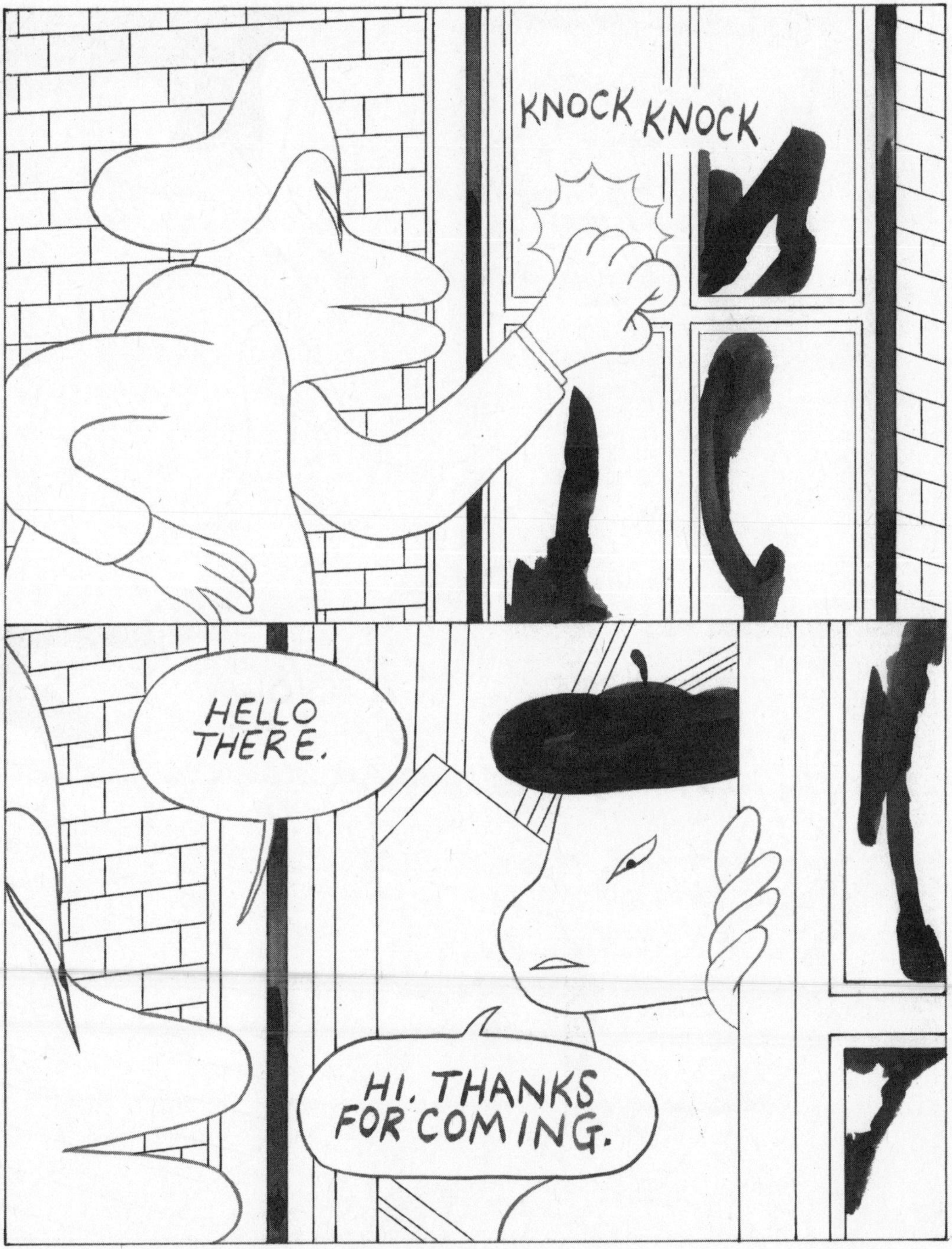
KNOCK KNOCK
HELLO THERE.
HI. THANKS FOR COMING.

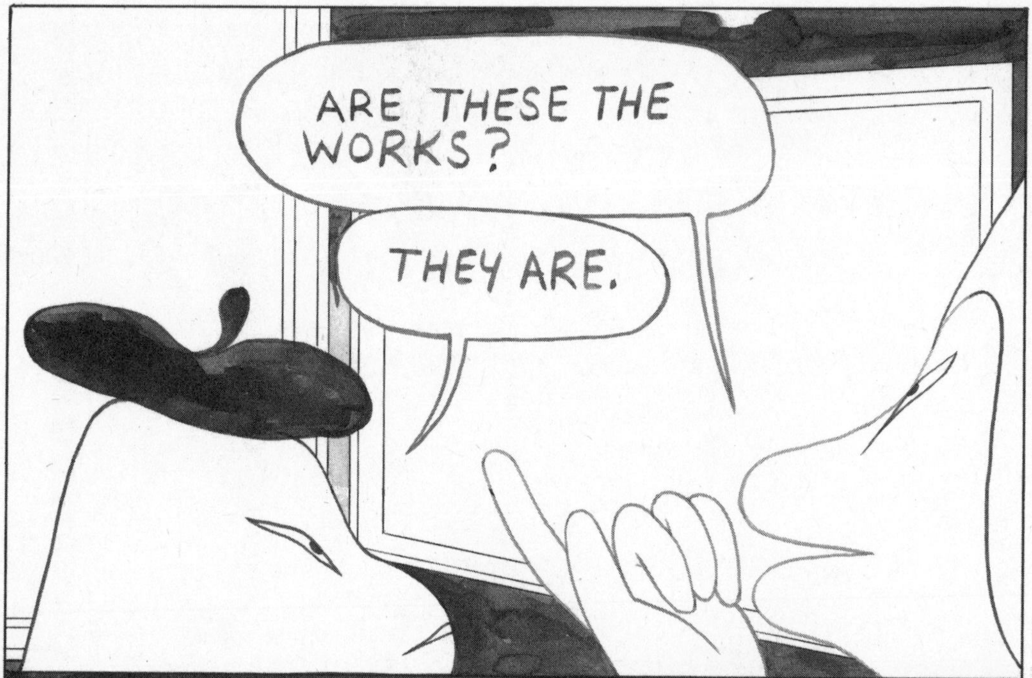
ARE THESE THE WORKS?
THEY ARE.

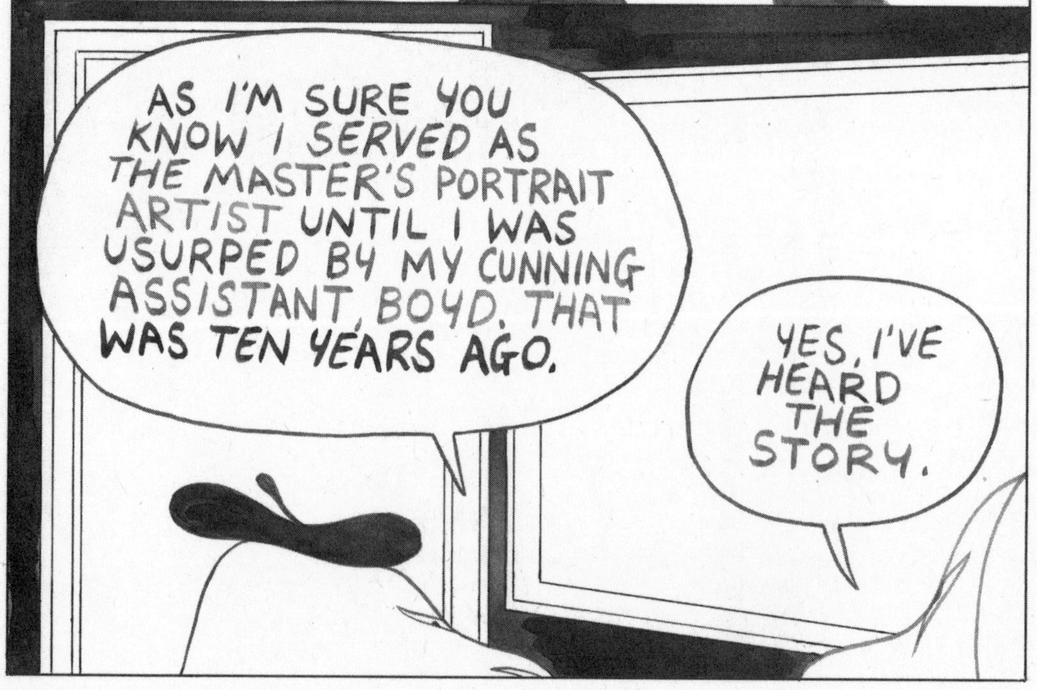
AS I'M SURE YOU KNOW I SERVED AS THE MASTER'S PORTRAIT ARTIST UNTIL I WAS USURPED BY MY CUNNING ASSISTANT, BOYD. THAT WAS TEN YEARS AGO.
YES, I'VE HEARD THE STORY.

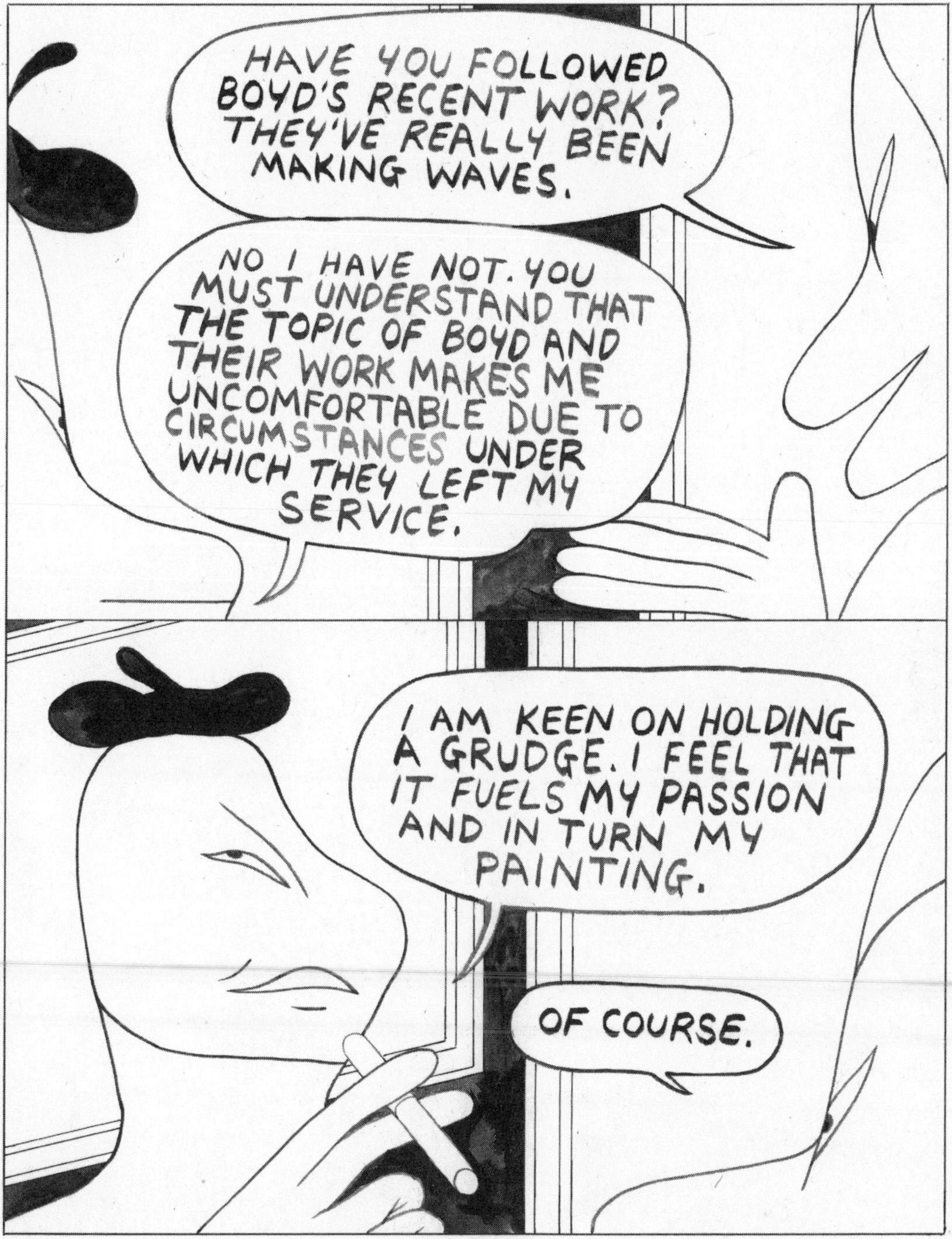
HAVE YOU FOLLOWED BOYD'S RECENT WORK? THEY'VE REALLY BEEN MAKING WAVES.
NO I HAVE NOT. YOU MUST UNDERSTAND THAT THE TOPIC OF BOYD AND THEIR WORK MAKES ME UNCOMFORTABLE DUE TO CIRCUMSTANCES UNDER WHICH THEY LEFT MY SERVICE.
I AM KEEN ON HOLDING A GRUDGE. I FEEL THAT IT FUELS MY PASSION AND IN TURN MY PAINTING.
OF COURSE.

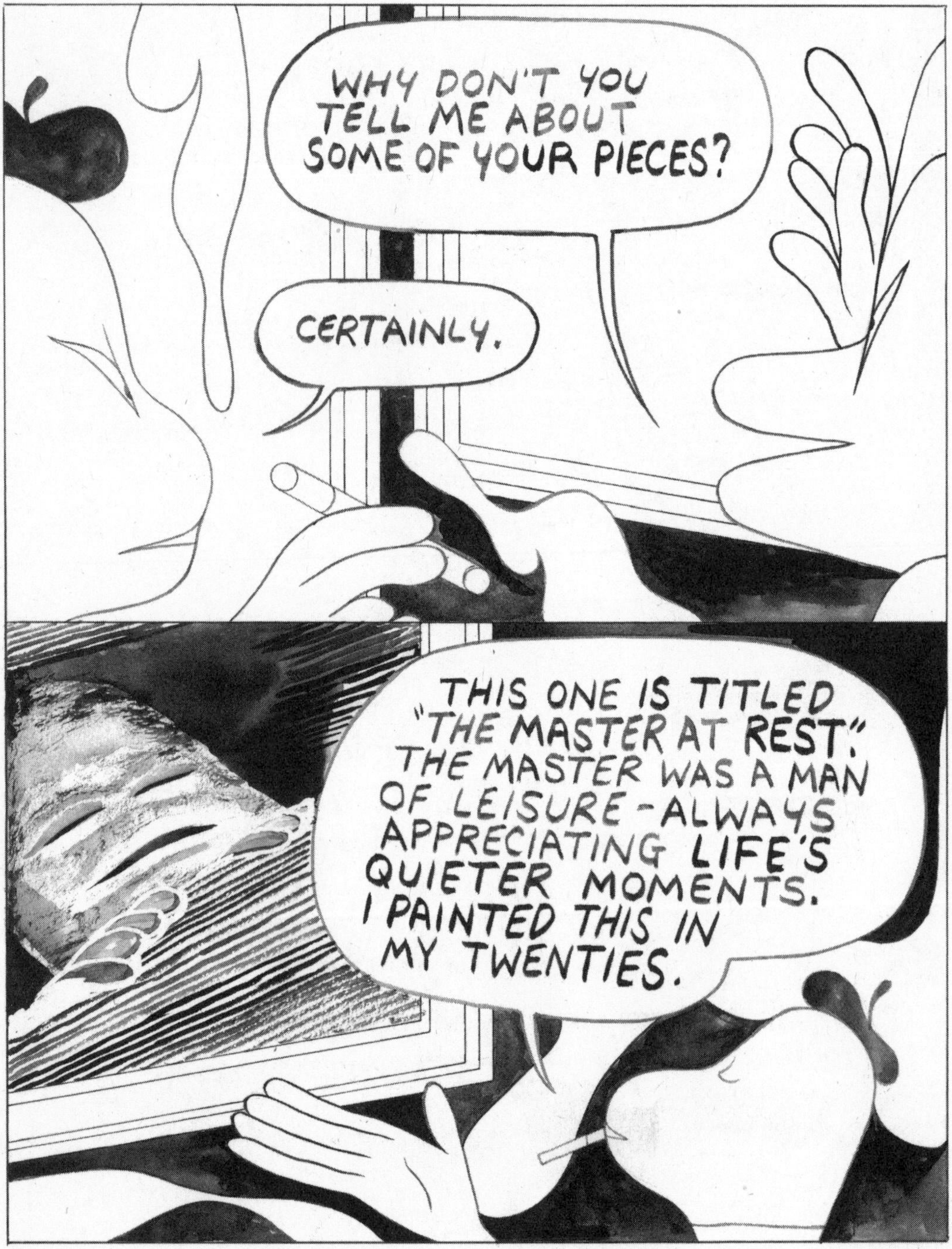
WHY DON'T YOU TELL ME ABOUT SOME OF YOUR PIECES?
CERTAINLY.
THIS ONE IS TITLED "THE MASTER AT REST". THE MASTER WAS A MAN OF LEISURE - ALWAYS APPRECIATING LIFE'S QUIETER MOMENTS. I PAINTED THIS IN MY TWENTIES.

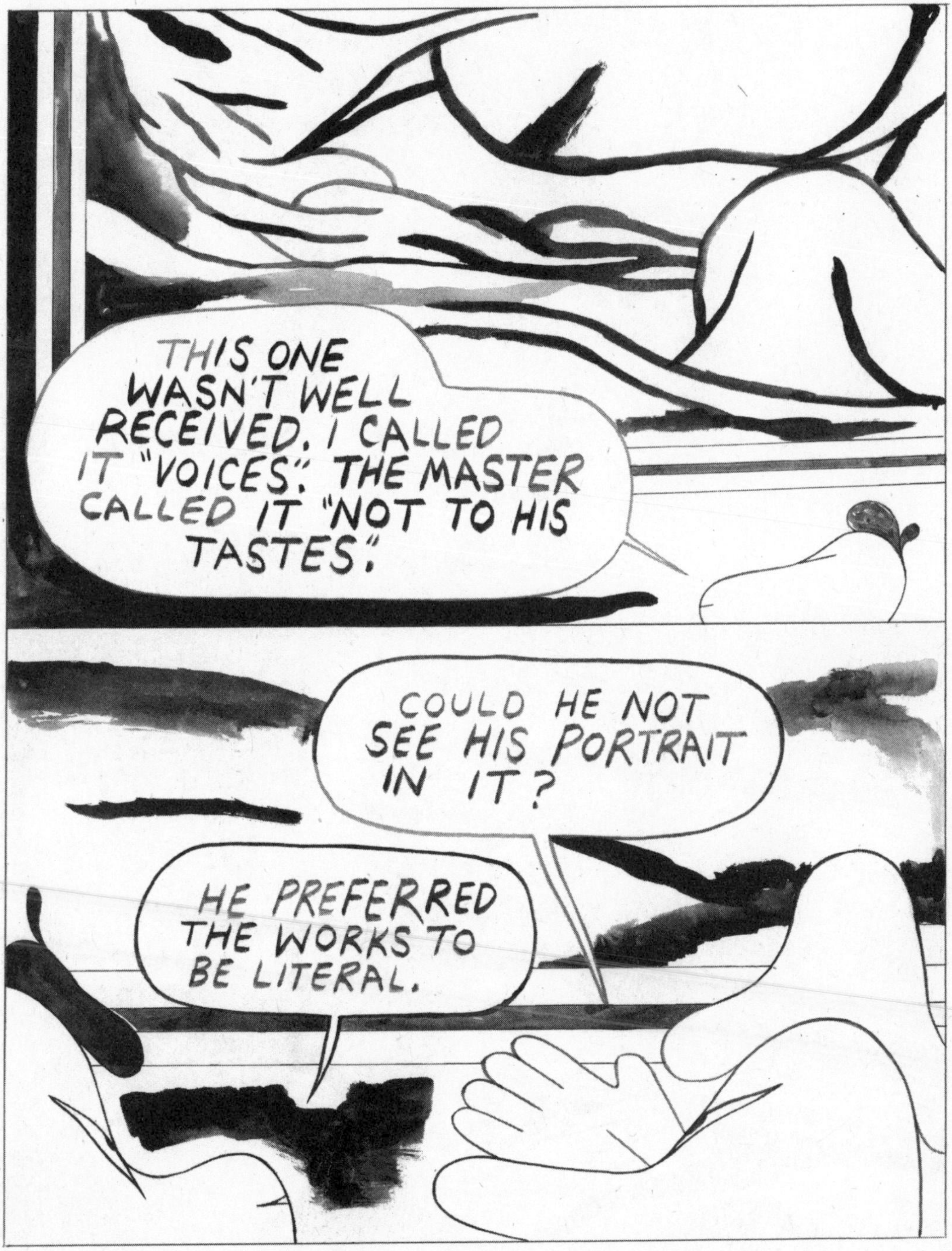
THIS ONE WASN'T WELL RECEIVED. I CALLED IT "VOICES". THE MASTER CALLED IT "NOT TO HIS TASTES."
COULD HE NOT SEE HIS PORTRAIT IN IT?
HE PREFERRED THE WORKS TO BE LITERAL.

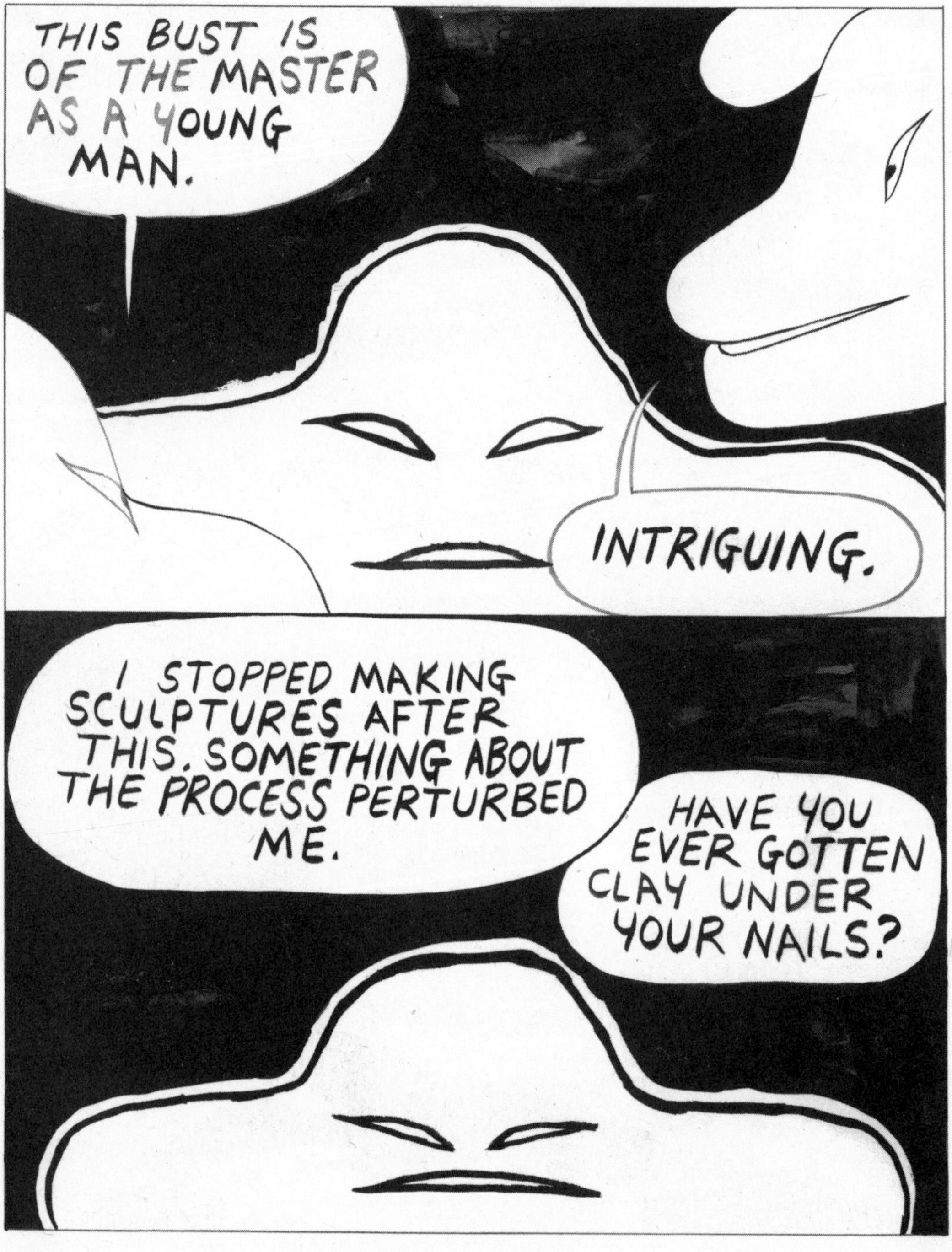
THIS BUST IS OF THE MASTER AS A YOUNG MAN.
INTRIGUING.
I STOPPED MAKING SCULPTURES AFTER THIS. SOMETHING ABOUT THE PROCESS PERTURBED ME.
HAVE YOU EVER GOTTEN CLAY UNDER YOUR NAILS?

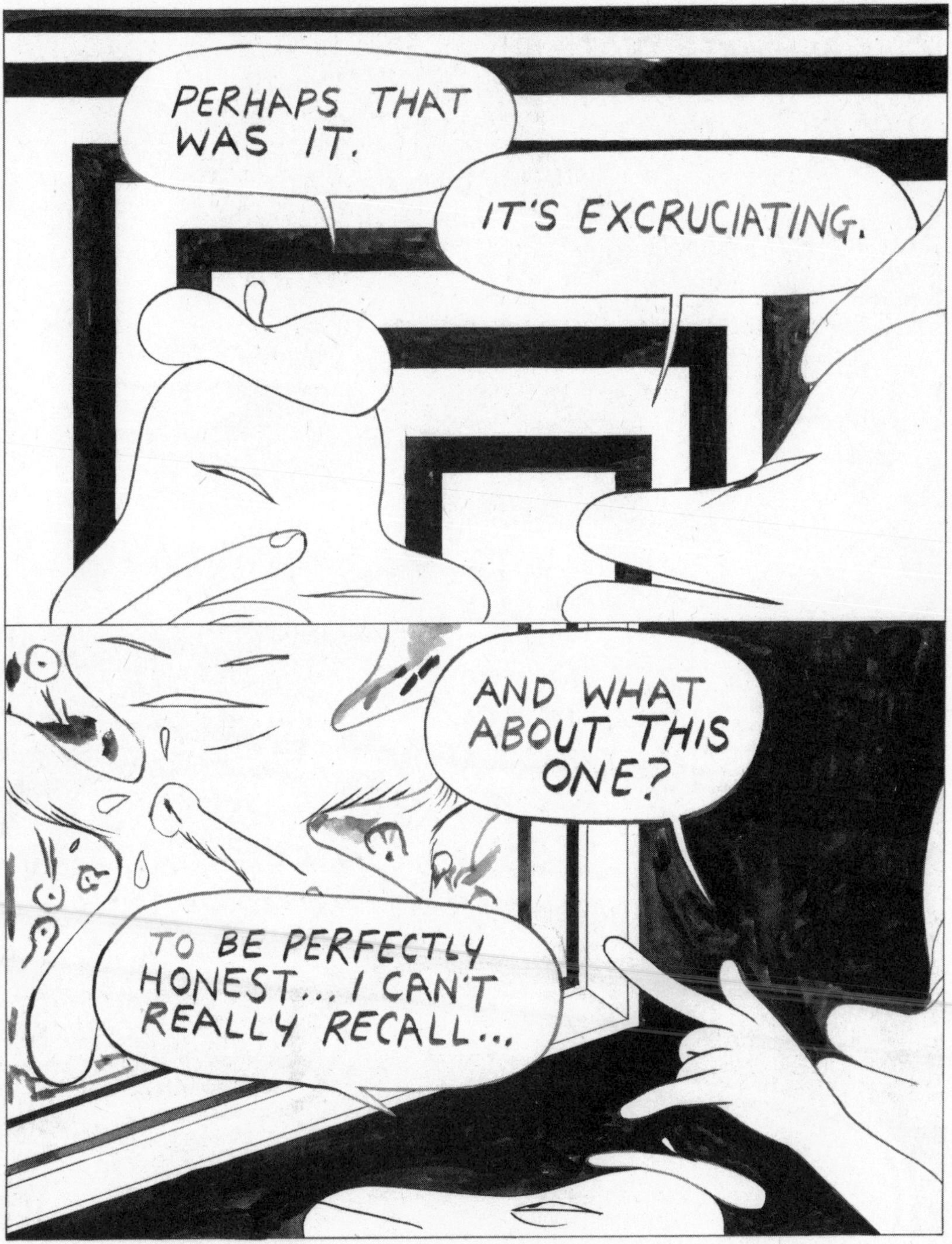
PERHAPS THAT WAS IT.
IT'S EXCRUCIATING.
AND WHAT ABOUT THIS ONE?
TO BE PERFECTLY HONEST... I CAN'T REALLY RECALL...

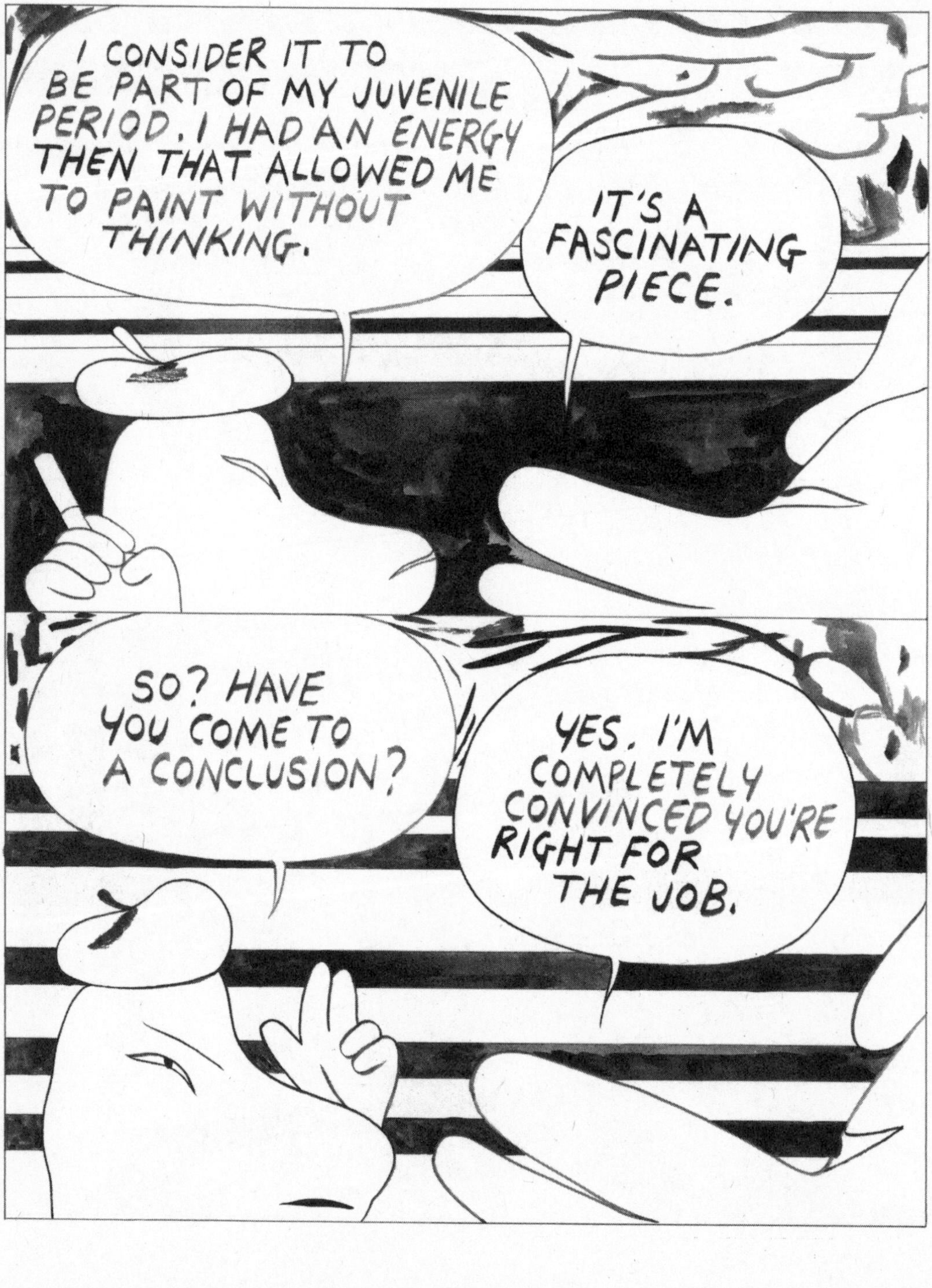
I CONSIDER IT TO BE PART OF MY JUVENILE PERIOD. I HAD AN ENERGY THEN THAT ALLOWED ME TO PAINT WITHOUT THINKING.
IT'S A FASCINATING PIECE.
SO? HAVE YOU COME TO A CONCLUSION?
YES. I'M COMPLETELY CONVINCED YOU'RE RIGHT FOR THE JOB.

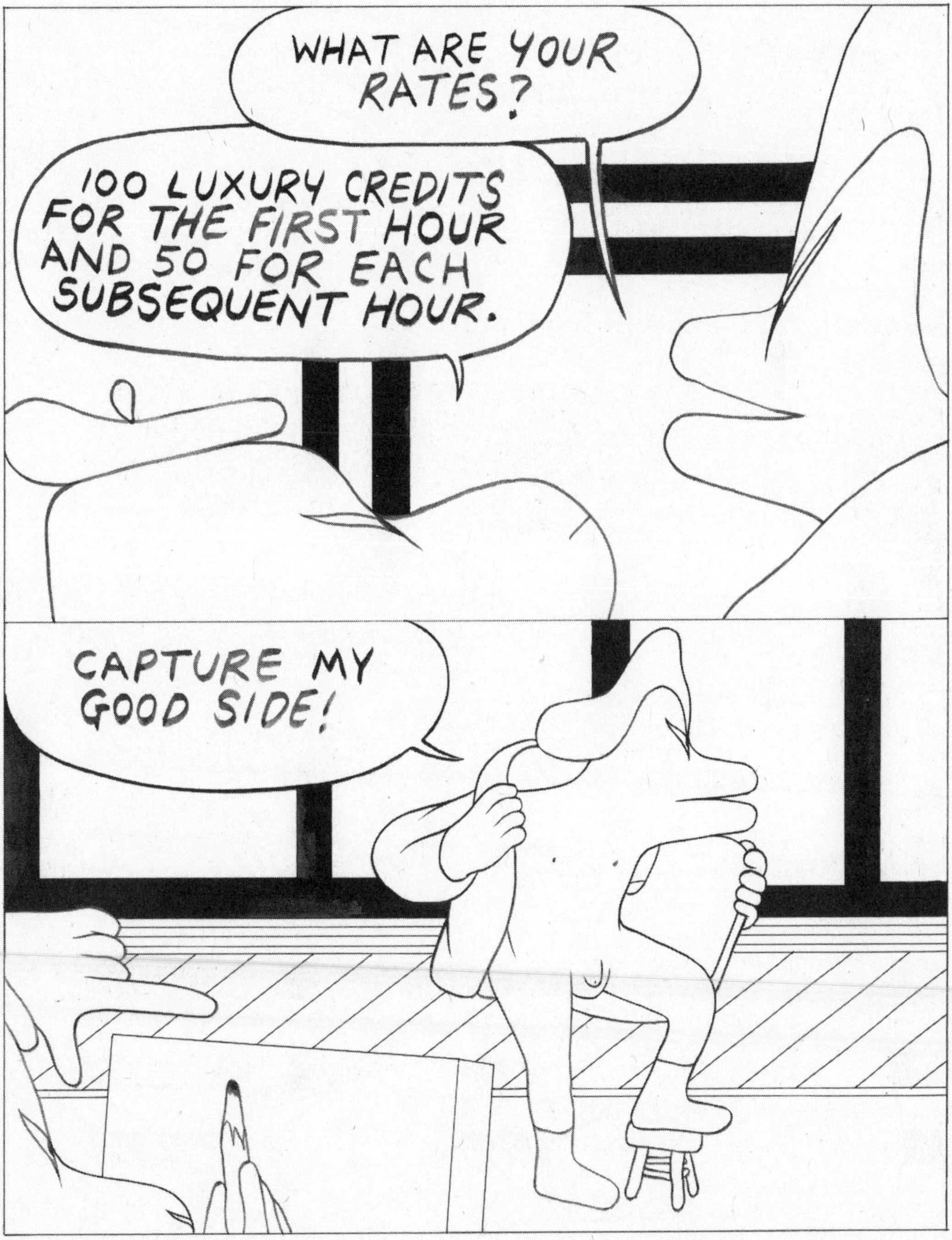
WHAT ARE YOUR RATES?
100 LUXURY CREDITS FOR THE FIRST HOUR AND 50 FOR EACH SUBSEQUENT HOUR.
CAPTURE MY GOOD SIDE!

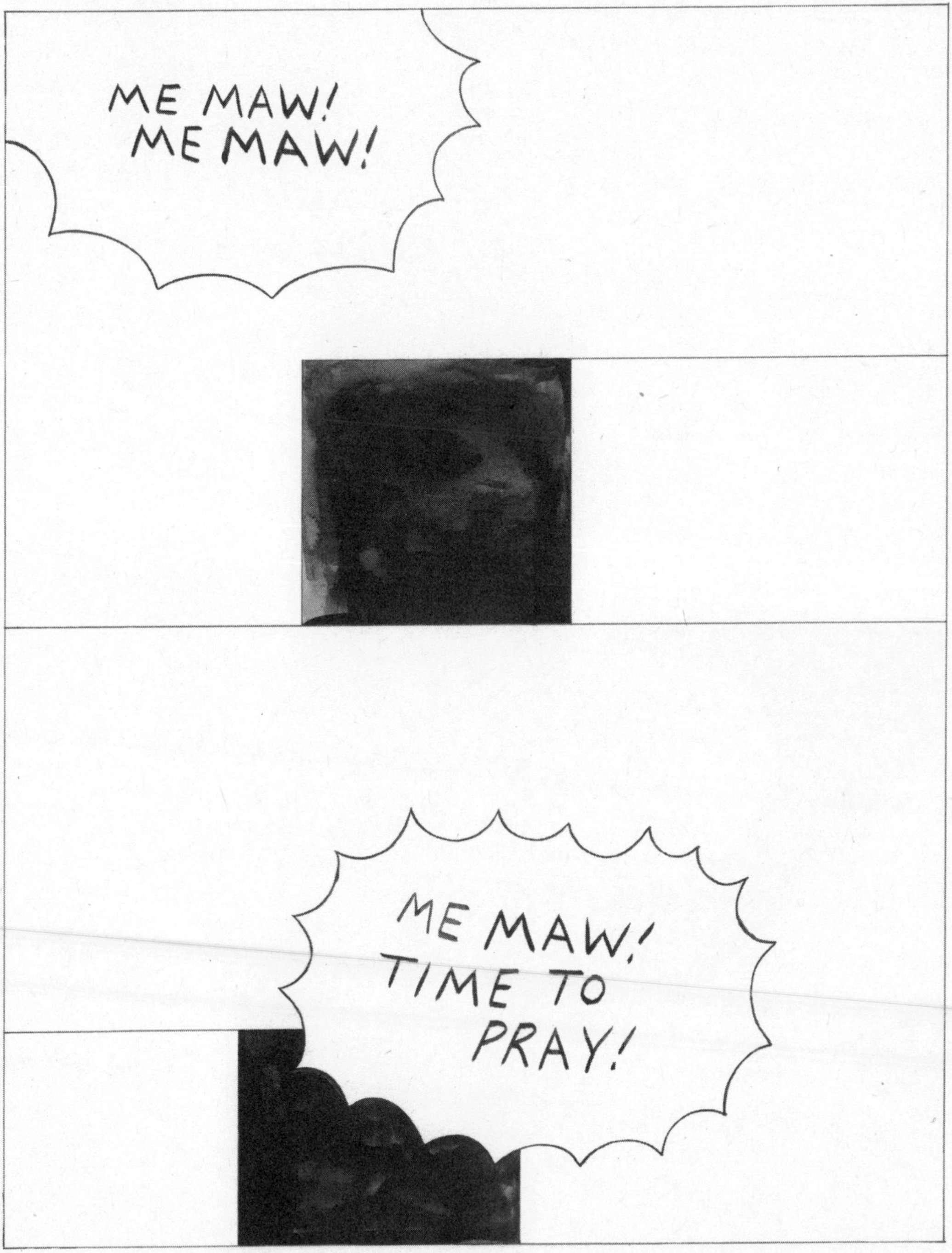
ME MAW! ME MAW!
ME MAW! TIME TO PRAY!

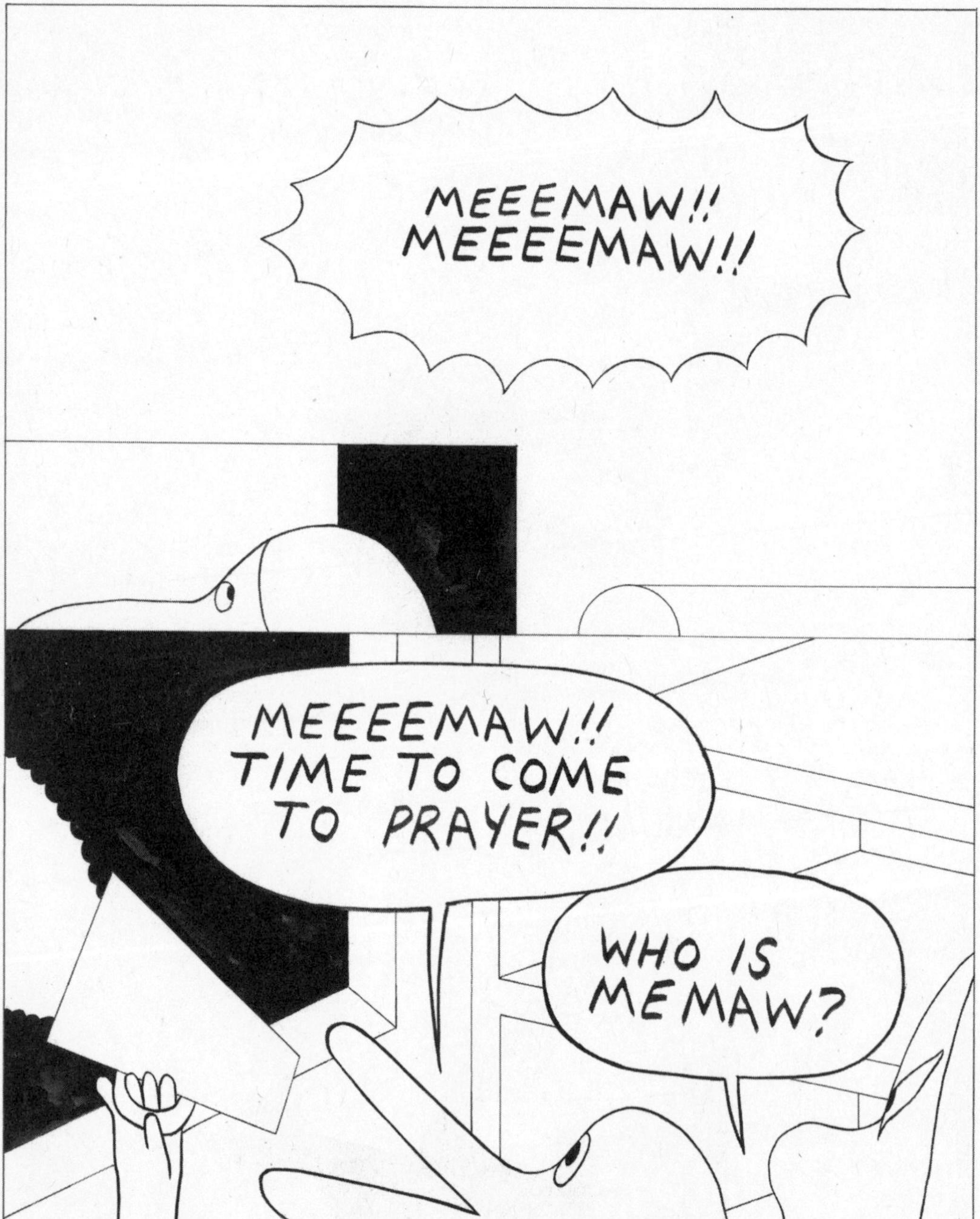
MEEEMAW!! MEEEEEMAW!!
MEEEEEMAW!! TIME TO COME TO PRAYER!!
WHO IS MEMAW?

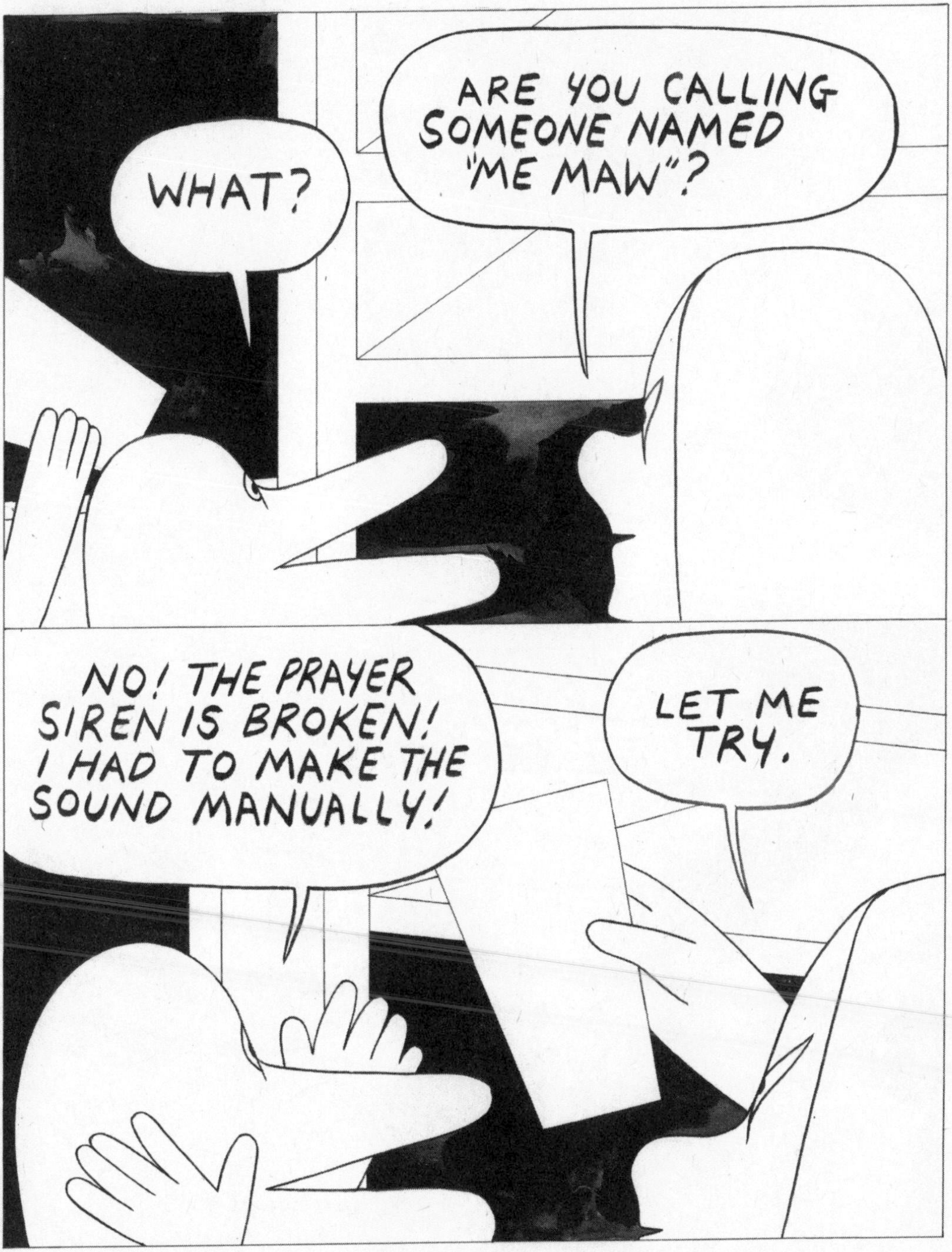
WHAT?
ARE YOU CALLING SOMEONE NAMED "ME MAW"?
NO! THE PRAYER SIREN IS BROKEN! I HAD TO MAKE THE SOUND MANUALLY!
LET ME TRY.

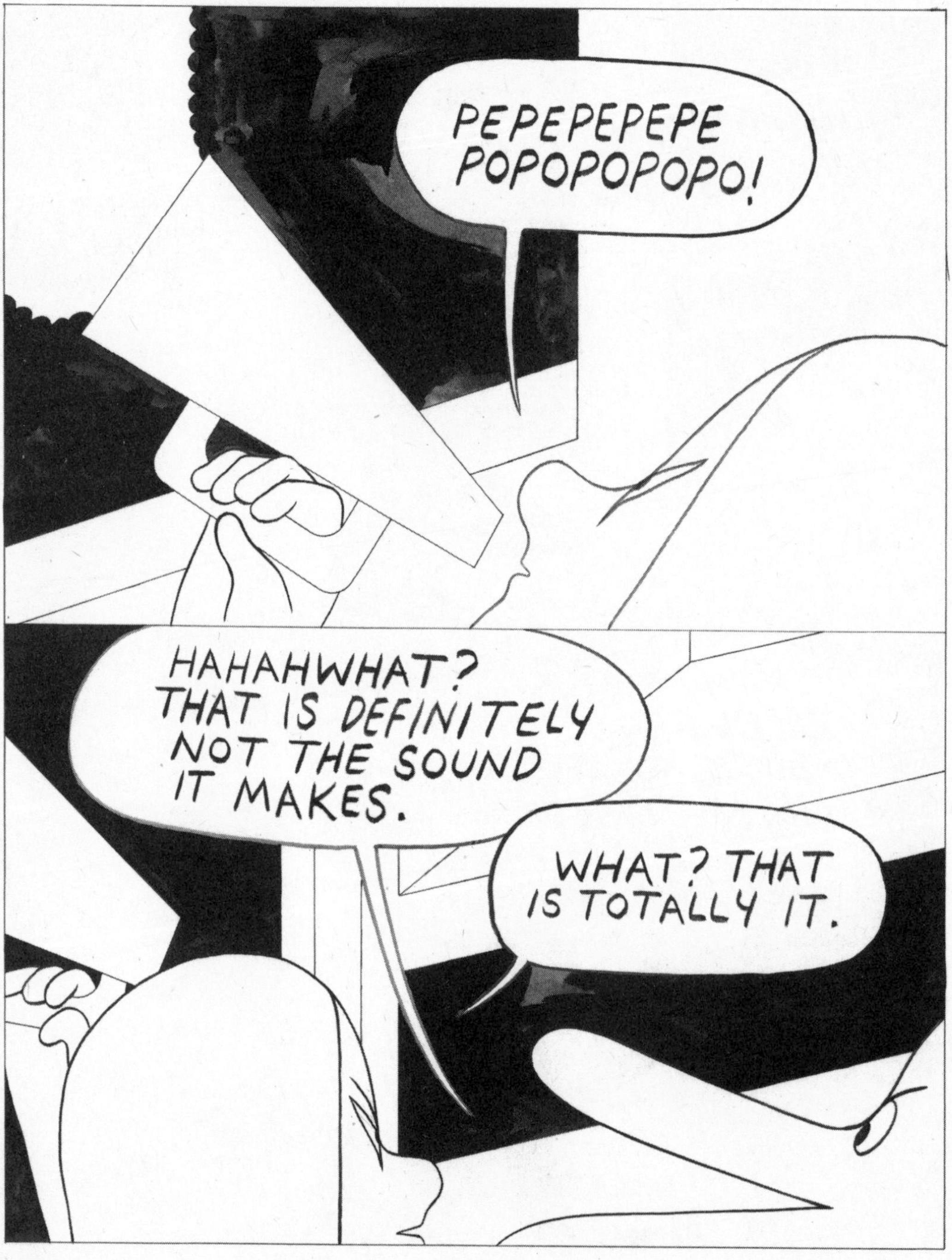
PEPEPEPEPE POPOPOPOPO!
HAHAHWHAT? THAT IS DEFINITELY NOT THE SOUND IT MAKES.
WHAT? THAT IS TOTALLY IT.

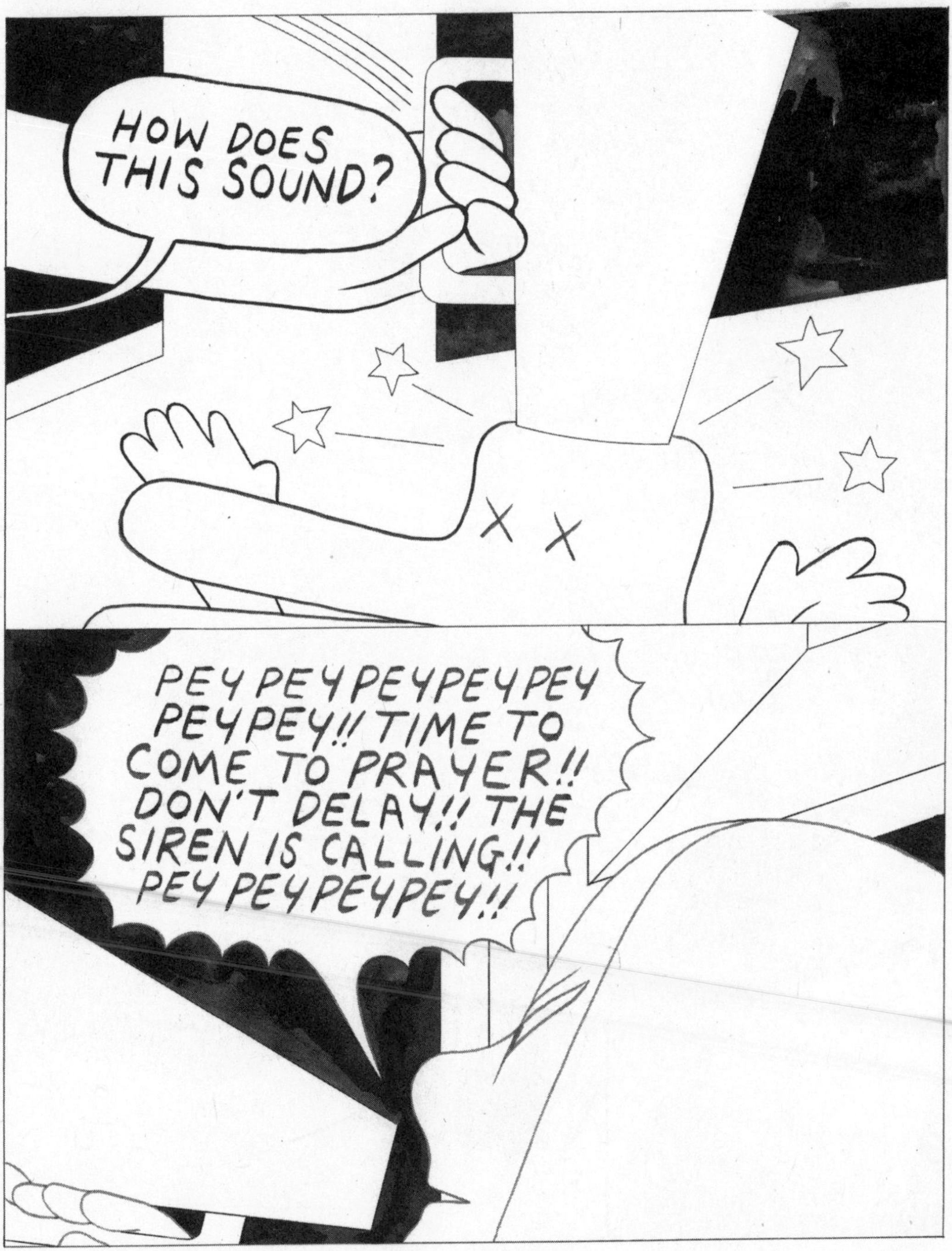
HOW DOES THIS SOUND?
PEY PEY PEY PEY PEY PEY PEY PEY!! TIME TO COME TO PRAYER!! DON'T DELAY!! THE SIREN IS CALLING!! PEY PEY PEY PEY!!

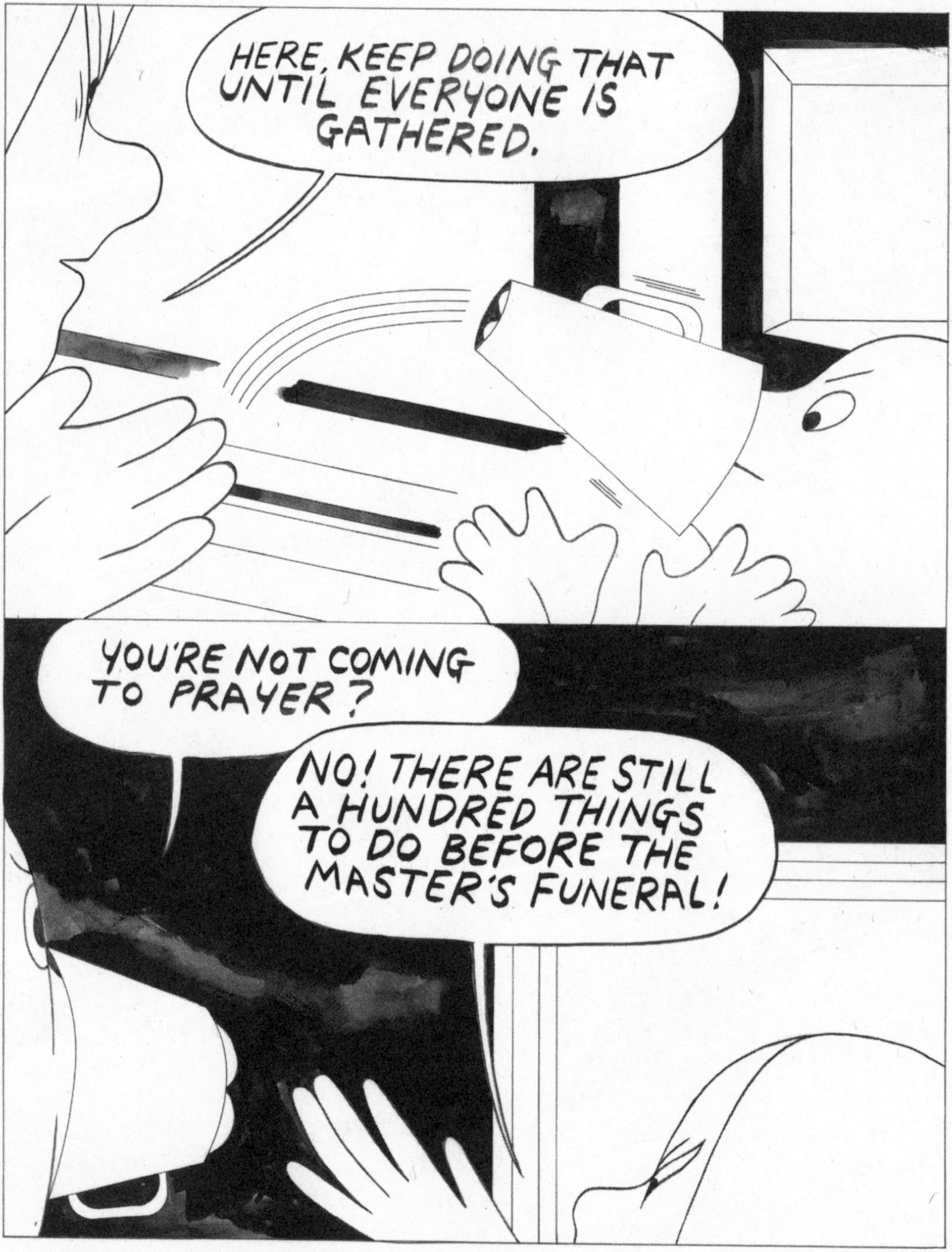
HERE, KEEP DOING THAT UNTIL EVERYONE IS GATHERED.
YOU'RE NOT COMING TO PRAYER?
NO! THERE ARE STILL A HUNDRED THINGS TO DO BEFORE THE MASTER'S FUNERAL!

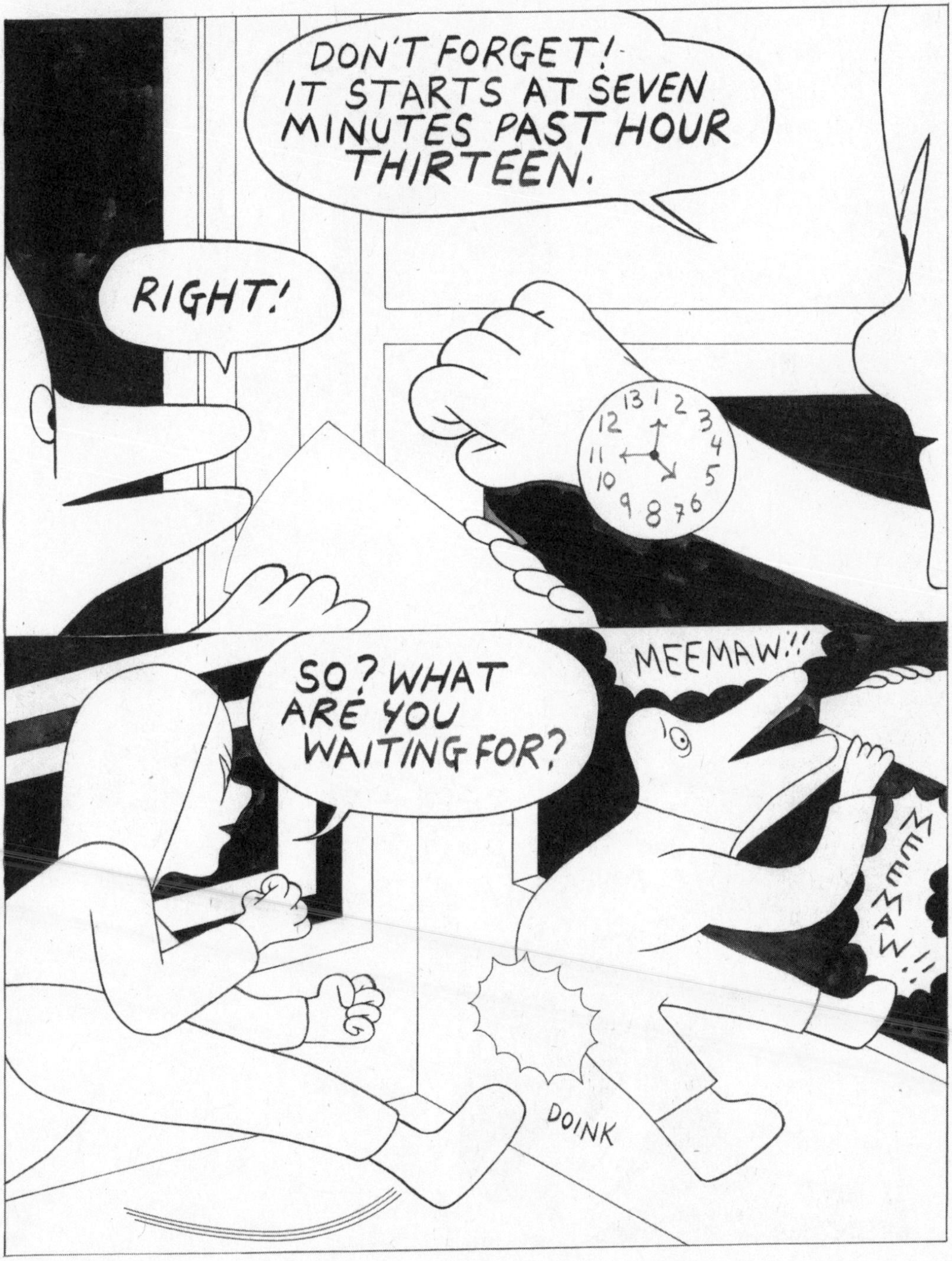
DON'T FORGET! IT STARTS AT SEVEN MINUTES PAST HOUR THIRTEEN.
RIGHT!
SO? WHAT ARE YOU WAITING FOR?
MEEMAW!!!
MEEMAW!!!
DOINK

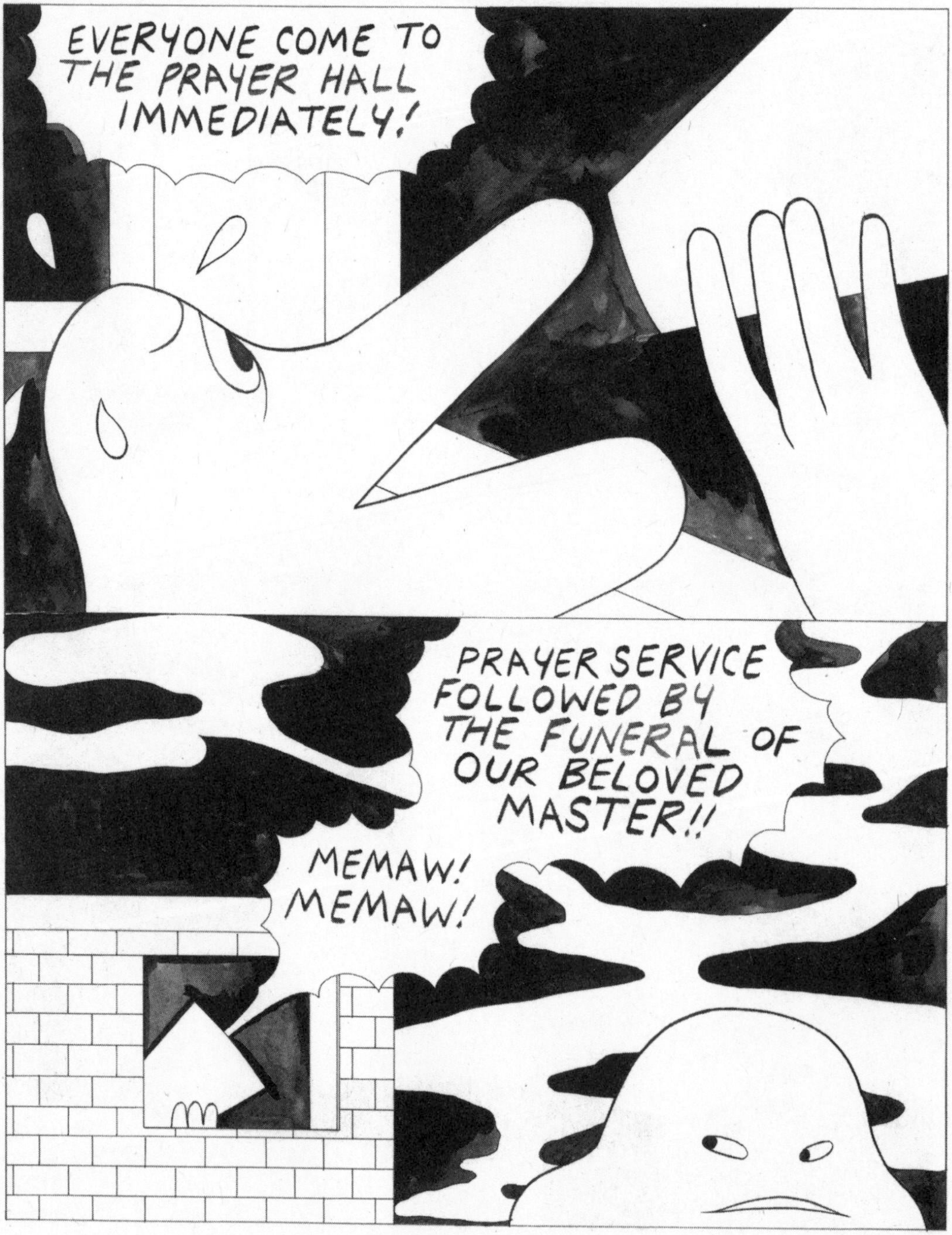
EVERYONE COME TO THE PRAYER HALL IMMEDIATELY!
PRAYER SERVICE FOLLOWED BY THE FUNERAL OF OUR BELOVED MASTER!!
MEMAW! MEMAW!

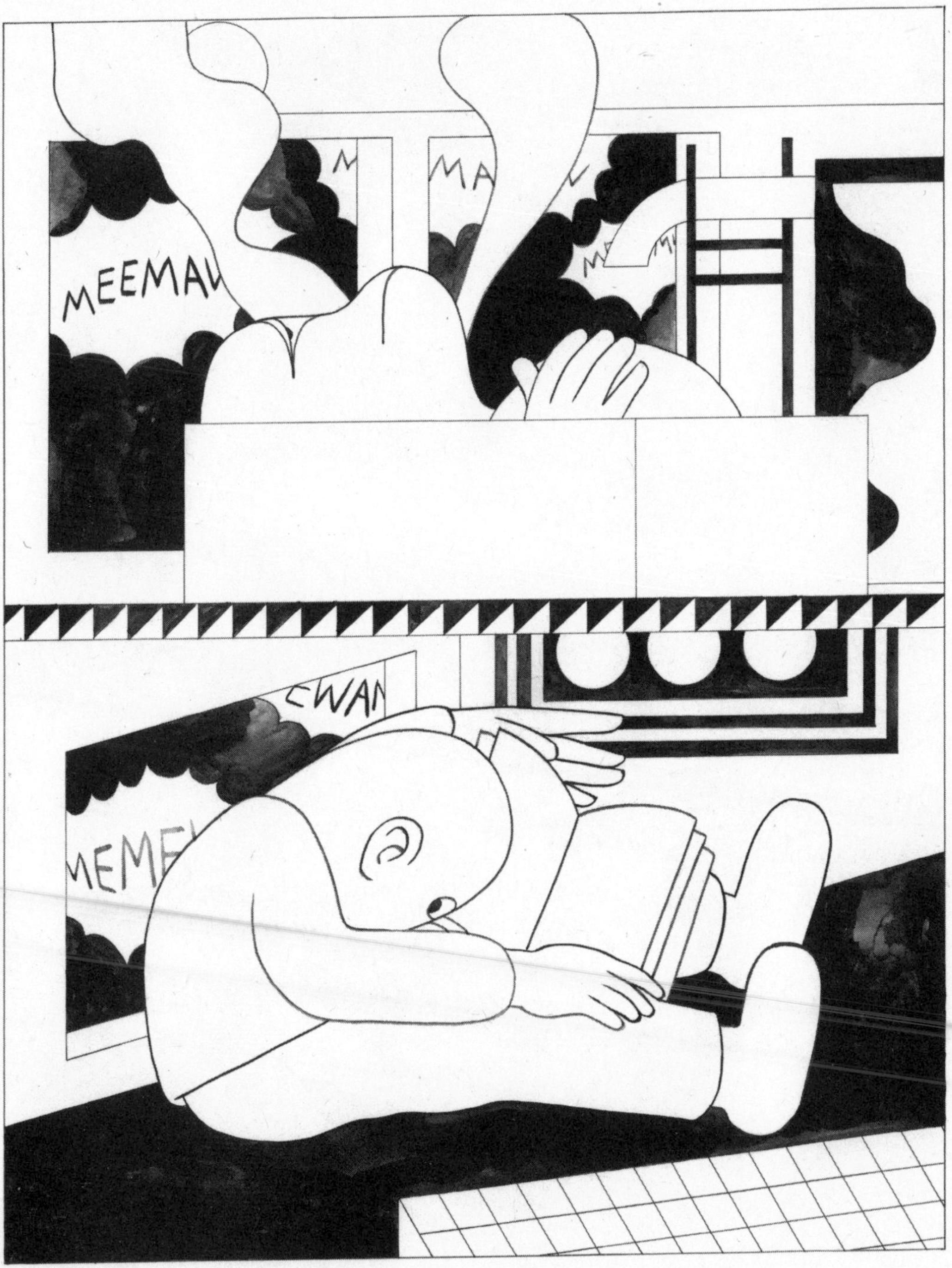
MEEMAW
EWAN
MEME

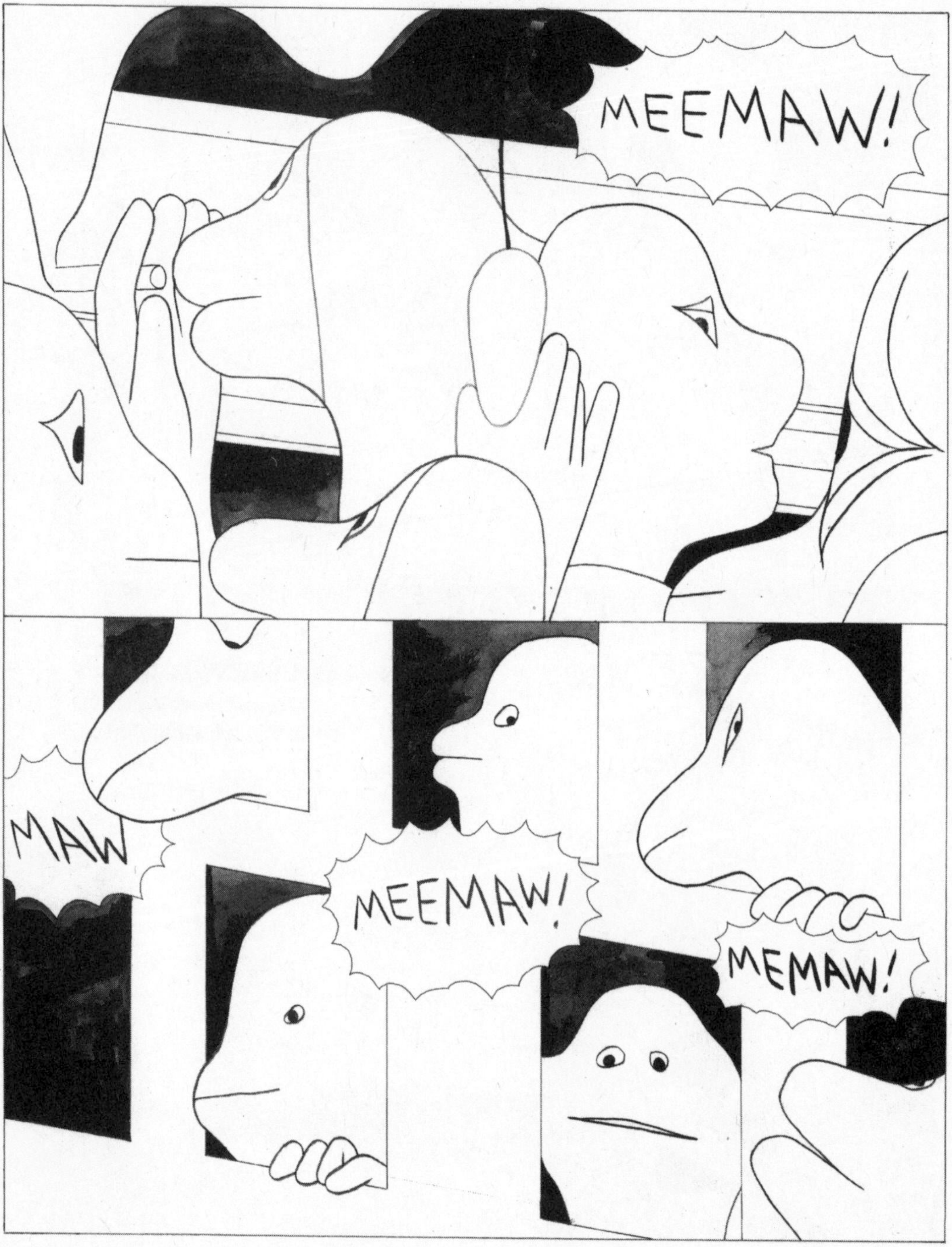
MEEMAW!
MAW
MEEMAW!
MEMAW!

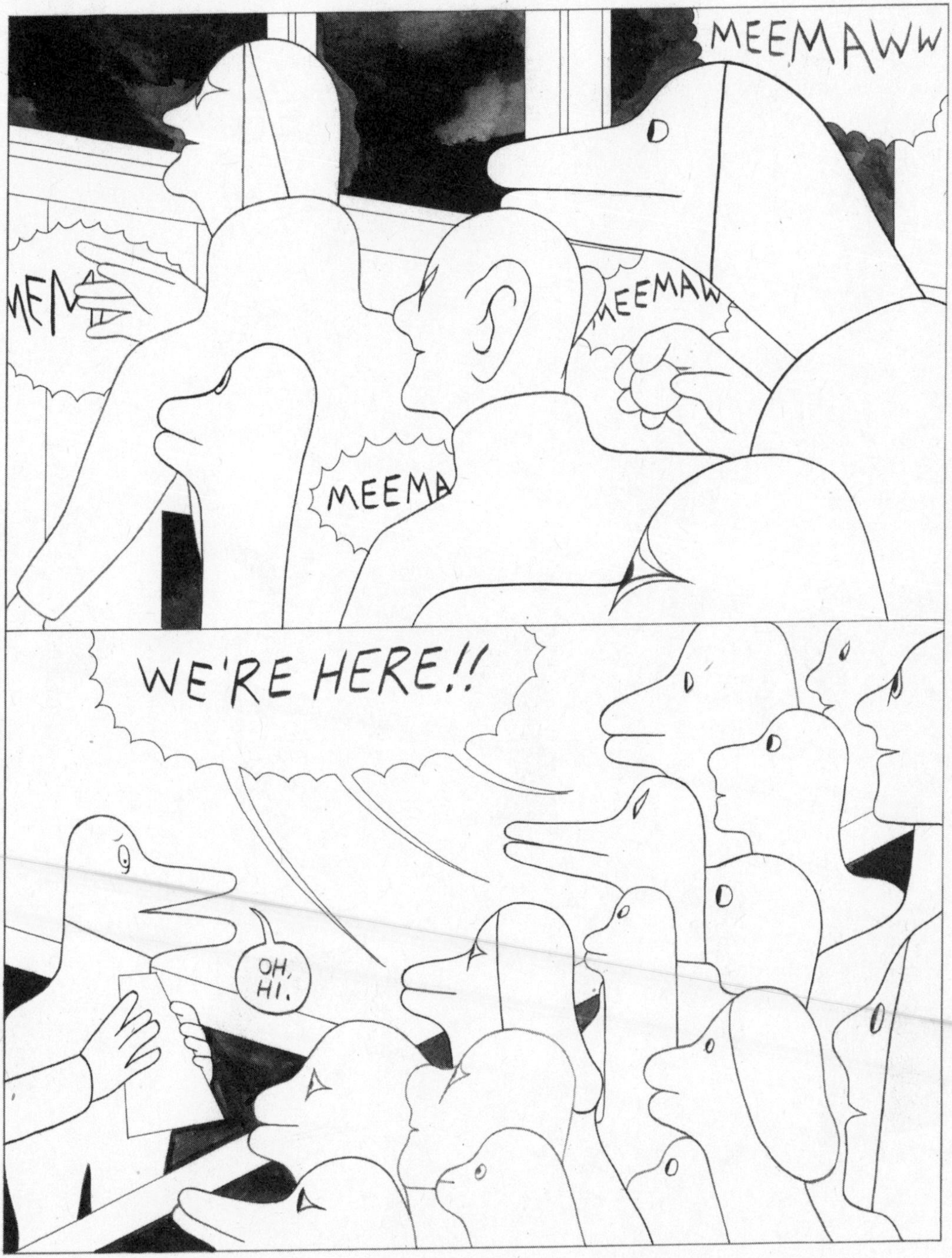
MEEMAWW
MEM
MEEMAW
MEEMA
WE'RE HERE!!
OH, HI.

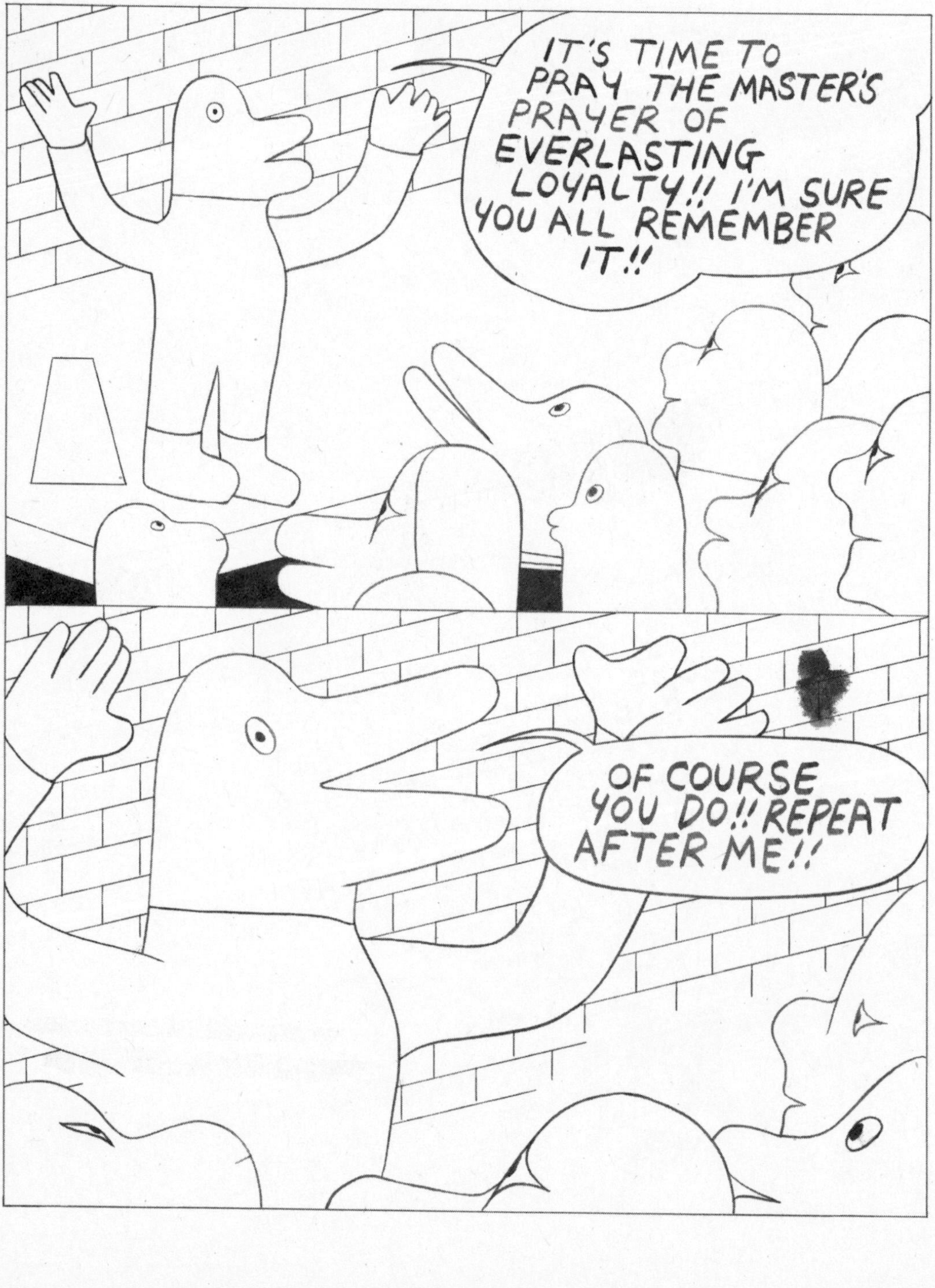
IT'S TIME TO PRAY THE MASTER'S PRAYER OF EVERLASTING LOYALTY!! I'M SURE YOU ALL REMEMBER IT!!
OF COURSE YOU DO!! REPEAT AFTER ME!!

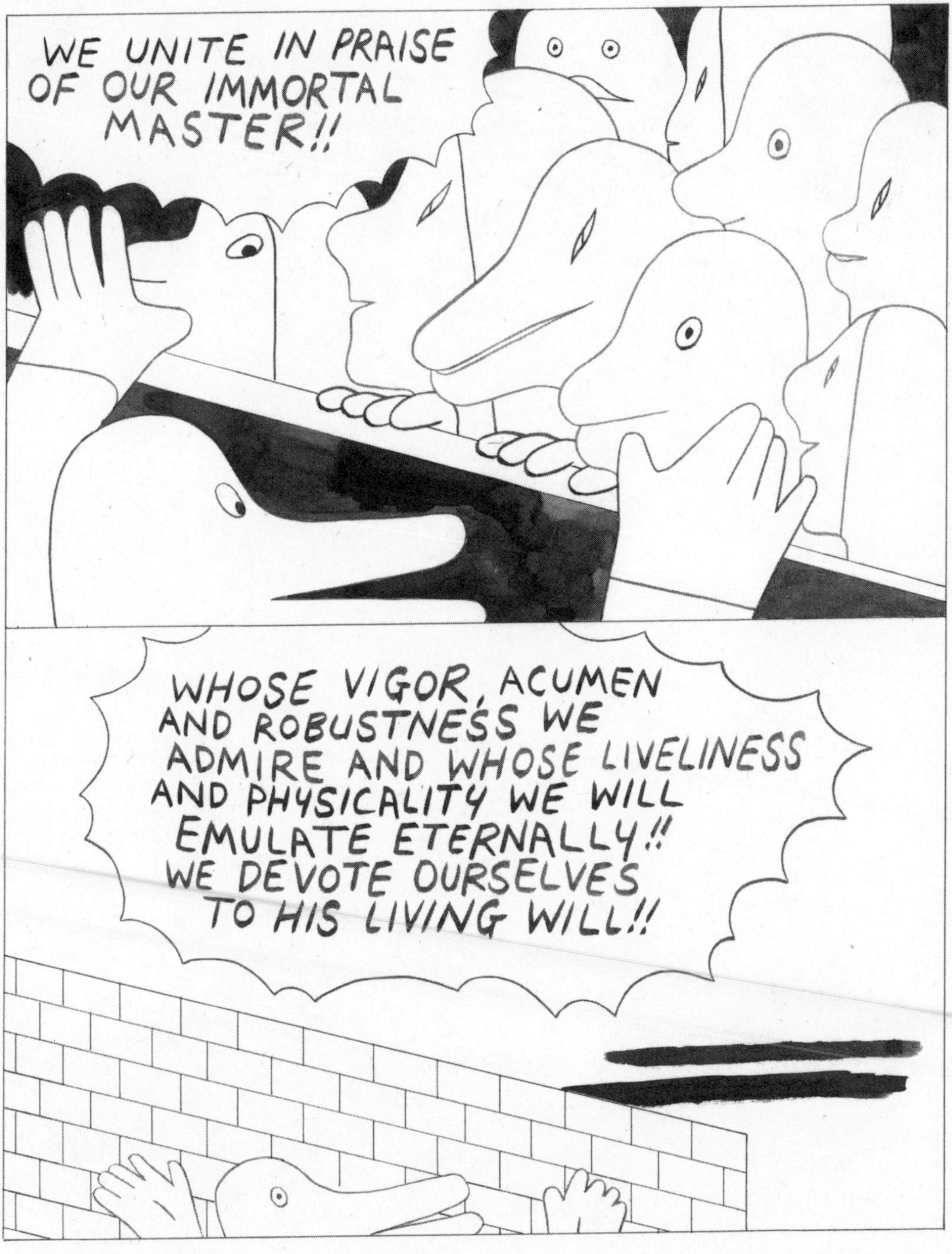
WE UNITE IN PRAISE OF OUR IMMORTAL MASTER!!
WHOSE VIGOR, ACUMEN AND ROBUSTNESS WE ADMIRE AND WHOSE LIVELINESS AND PHYSICALITY WE WILL EMULATE ETERNALLY!! WE DEVOTE OURSELVES TO HIS LIVING WILL!!

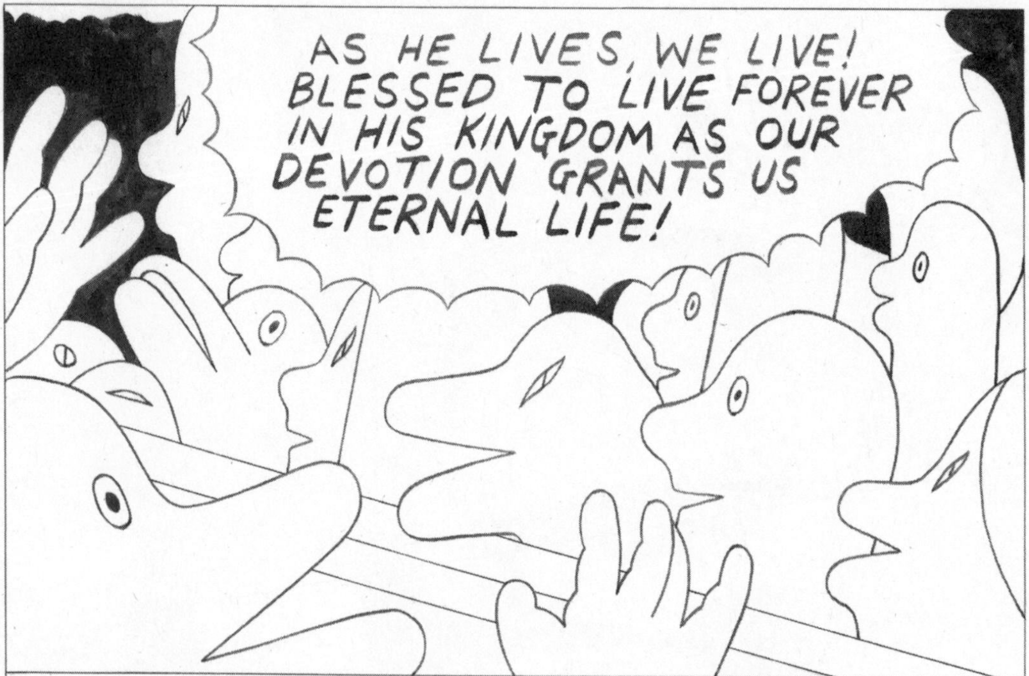
AS HE LIVES, WE LIVE! BLESSED TO LIVE FOREVER IN HIS KINGDOM AS OUR DEVOTION GRANTS US ETERNAL LIFE!

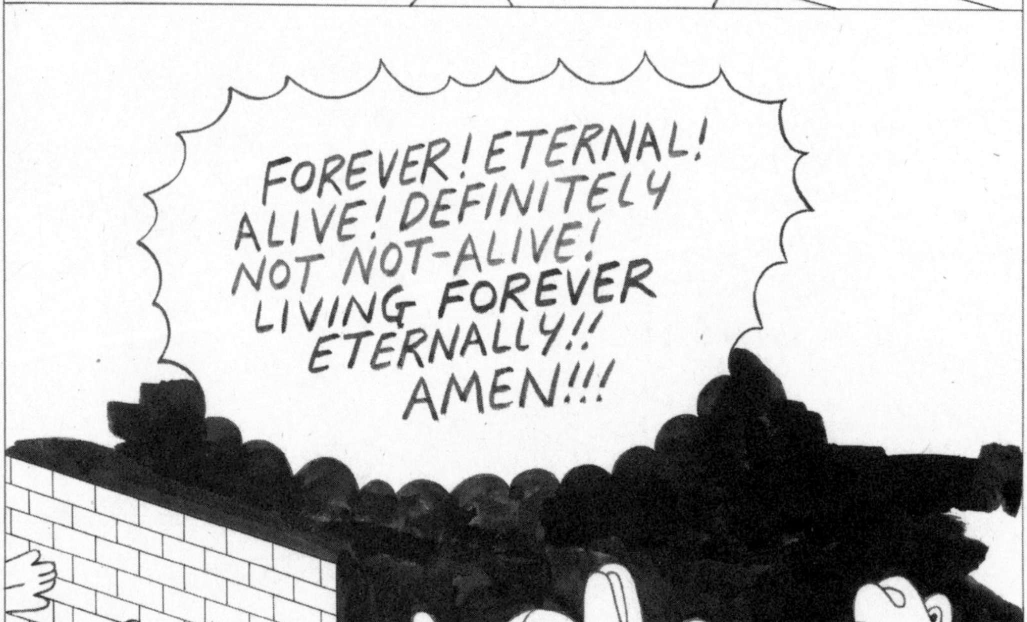
FOREVER! ETERNAL! ALIVE! DEFINITELY NOT NOT-ALIVE! LIVING FOREVER ETERNALLY!! AMEN!!!

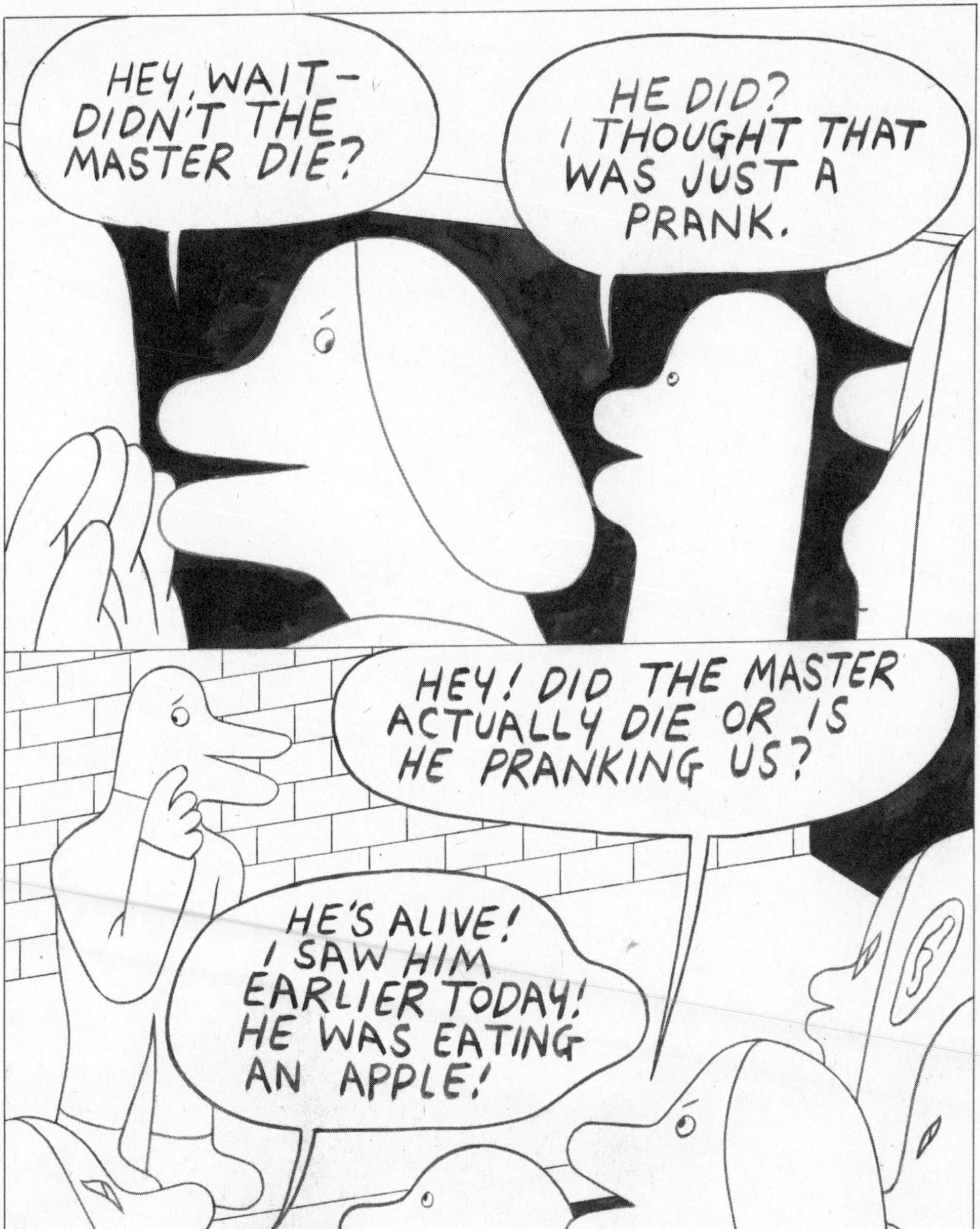
HEY, WAIT- DIDN'T THE MASTER DIE?
HE DID? I THOUGHT THAT WAS JUST A PRANK.
HEY! DID THE MASTER ACTUALLY DIE OR IS HE PRANKING US?
HE'S ALIVE! I SAW HIM EARLIER TODAY! HE WAS EATING AN APPLE!

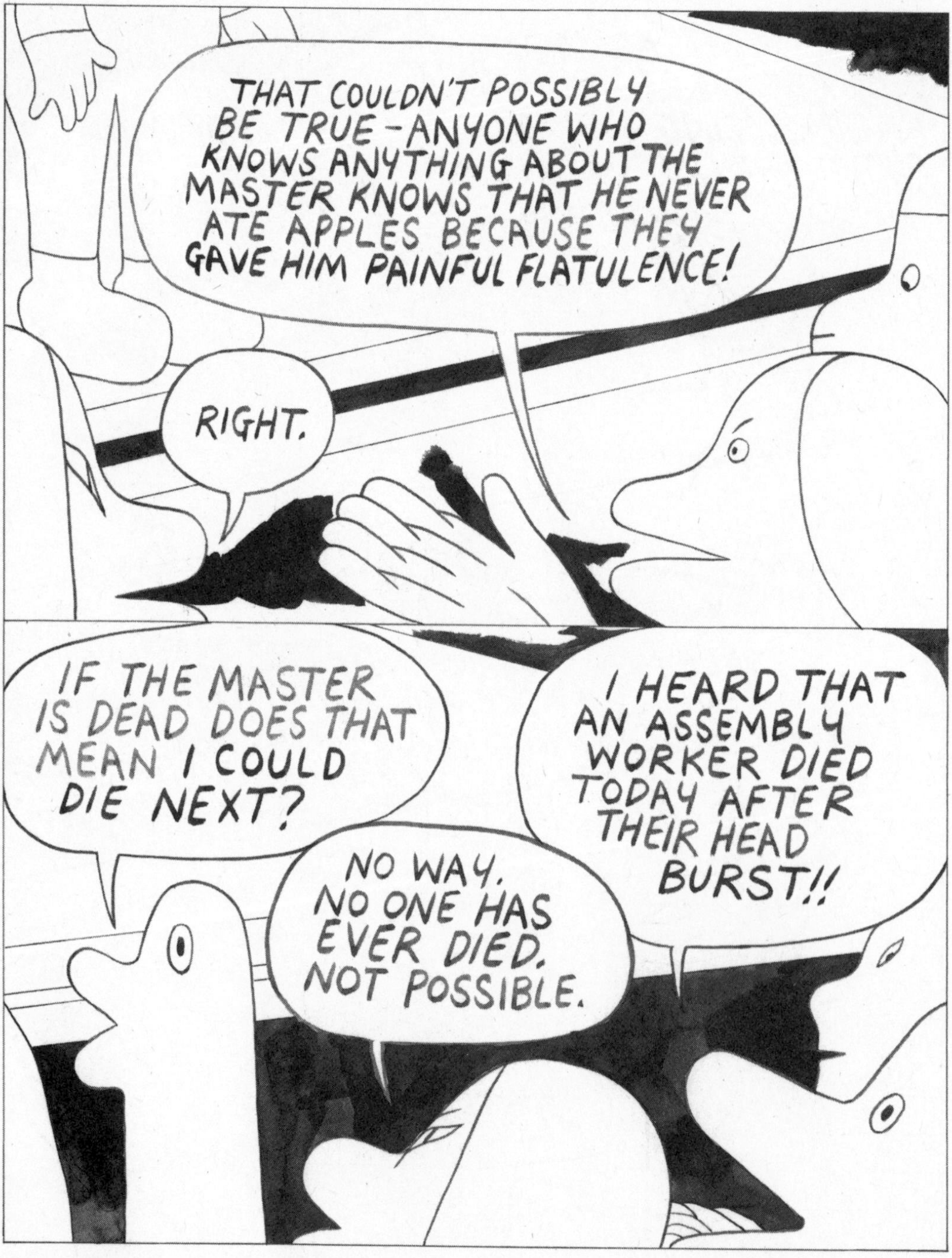

THAT COULDN'T POSSIBLY BE TRUE - ANYONE WHO KNOWS ANYTHING ABOUT THE MASTER KNOWS THAT HE NEVER ATE APPLES BECAUSE THEY GAVE HIM PAINFUL FLATULENCE!
RIGHT.
IF THE MASTER IS DEAD DOES THAT MEAN I COULD DIE NEXT?
NO WAY. NO ONE HAS EVER DIED. NOT POSSIBLE.
I HEARD THAT AN ASSEMBLY WORKER DIED TODAY AFTER THEIR HEAD BURST!!

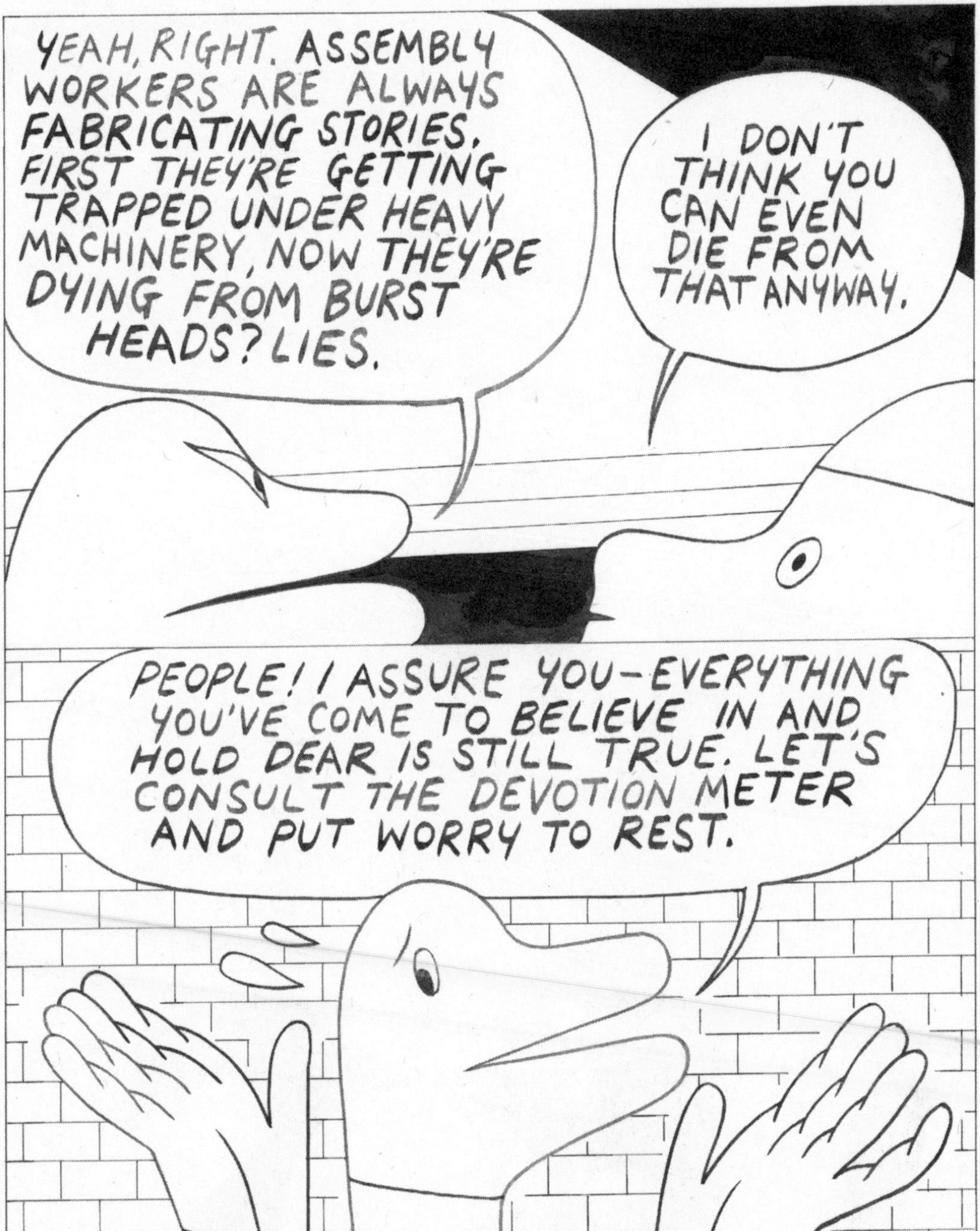
YEAH, RIGHT. ASSEMBLY WORKERS ARE ALWAYS FABRICATING STORIES. FIRST THEY'RE GETTING TRAPPED UNDER HEAVY MACHINERY, NOW THEY'RE DYING FROM BURST HEADS? LIES.
I DON'T THINK YOU CAN EVEN DIE FROM THAT ANYWAY.
PEOPLE! I ASSURE YOU—EVERYTHING YOU'VE COME TO BELIEVE IN AND HOLD DEAR IS STILL TRUE. LET'S CONSULT THE DEVOTION METER AND PUT WORRY TO REST.

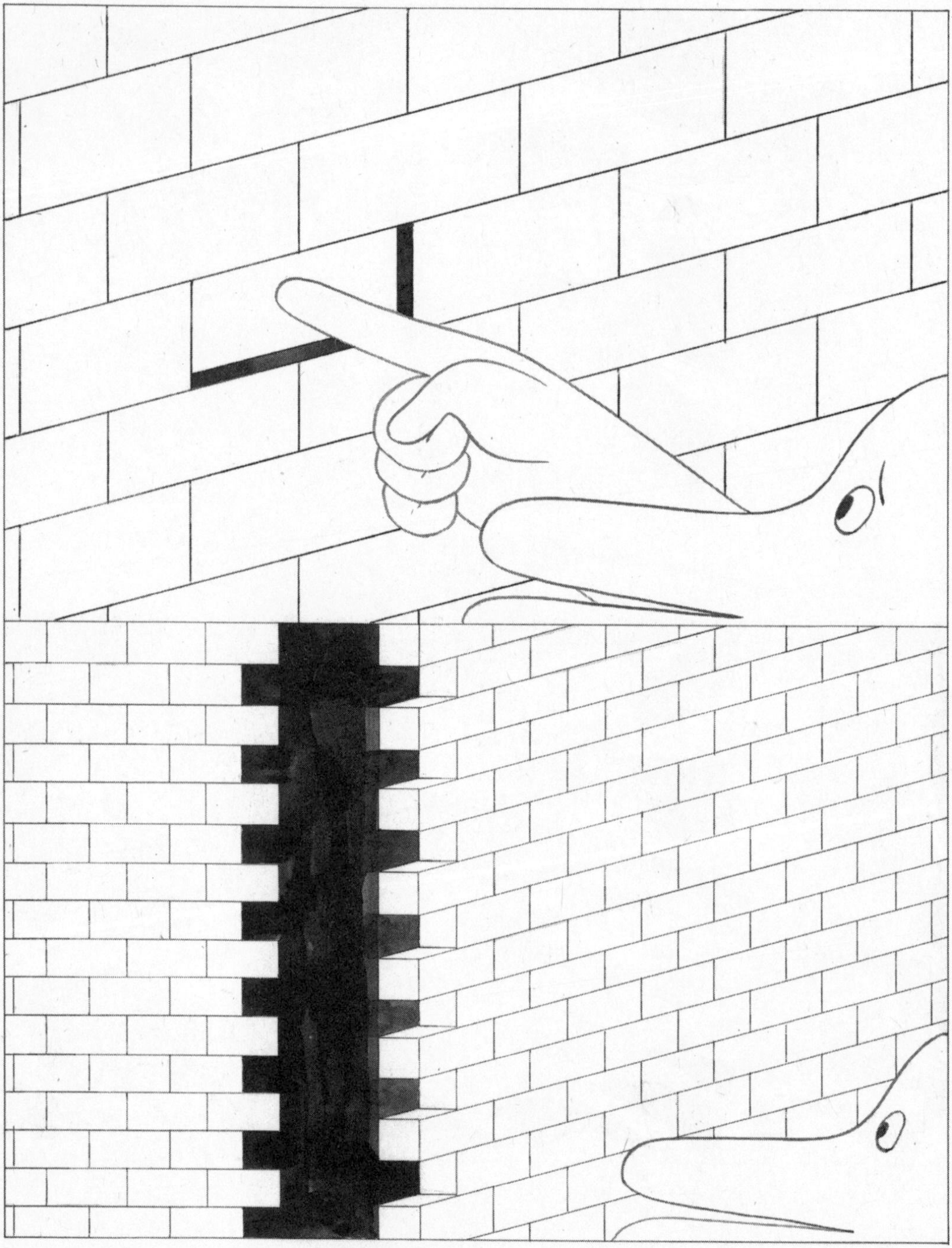

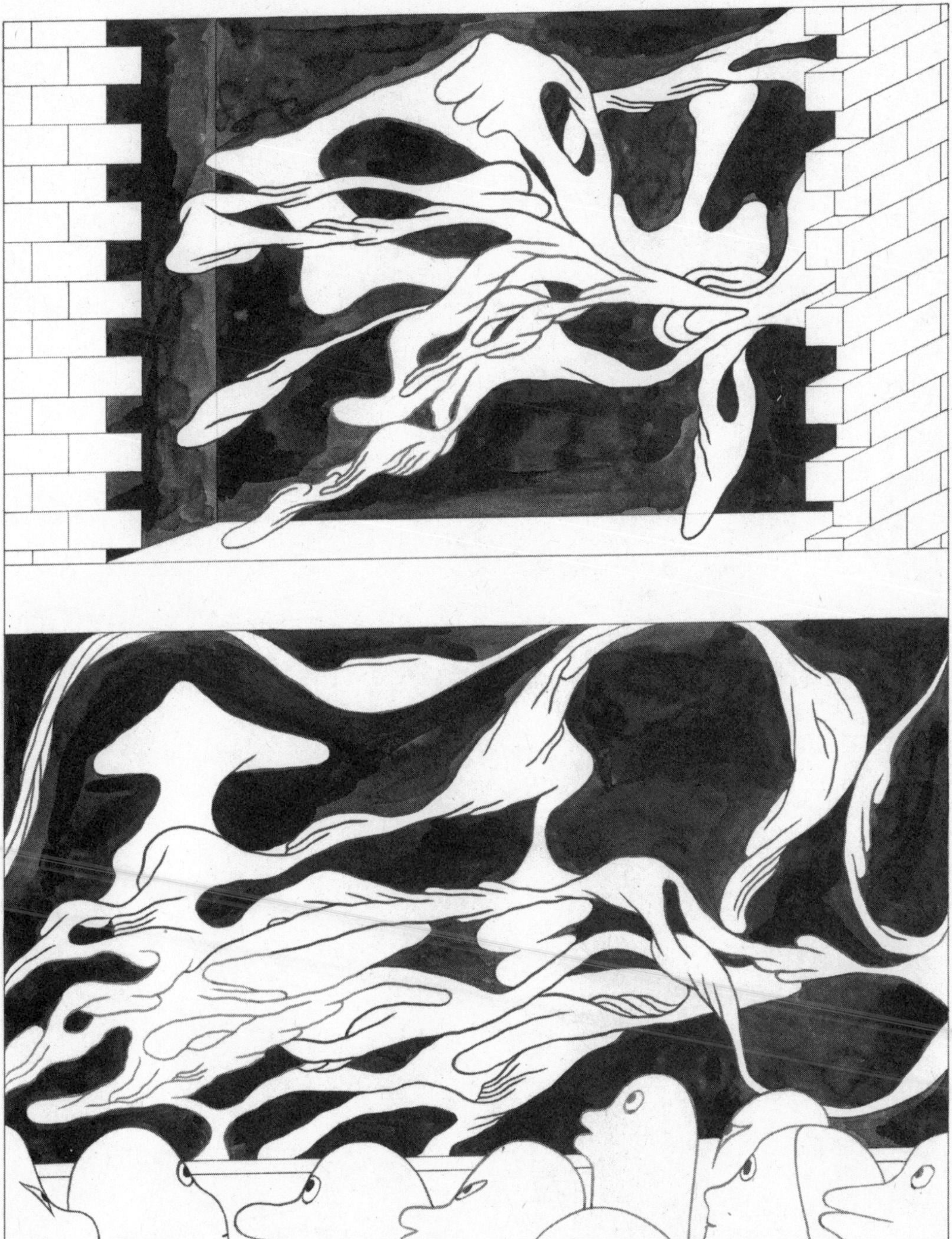

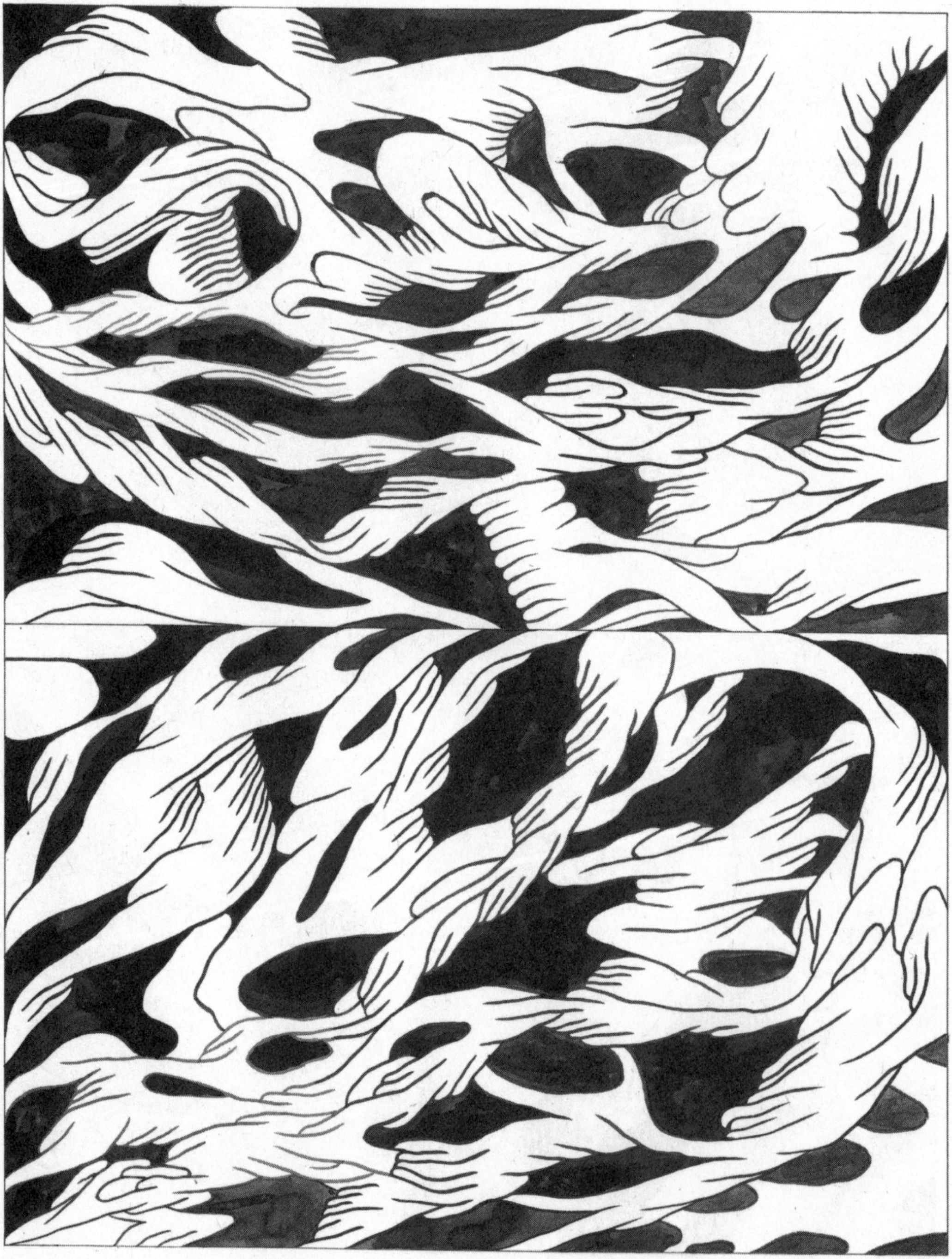

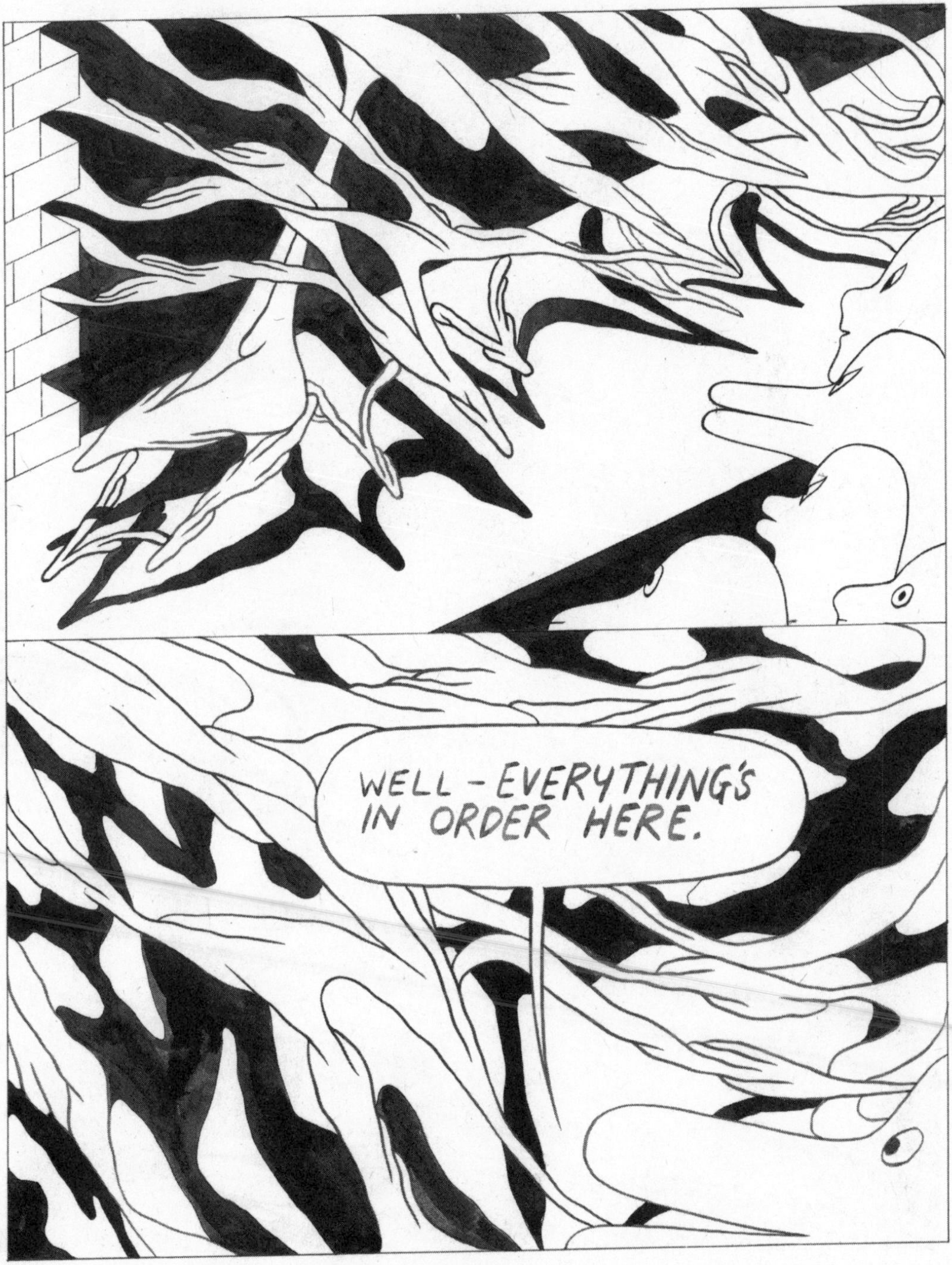
WELL - EVERYTHING'S IN ORDER HERE.

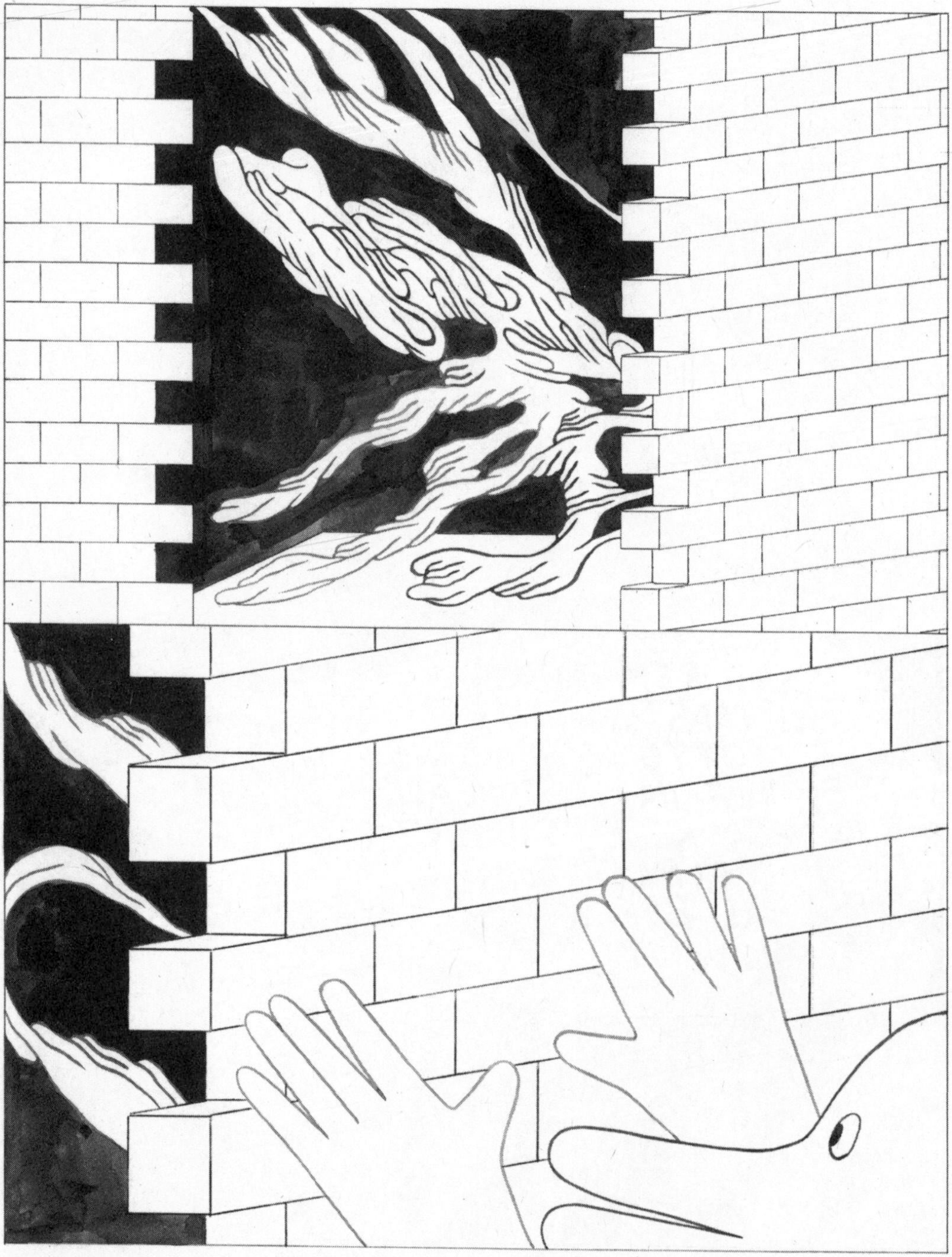

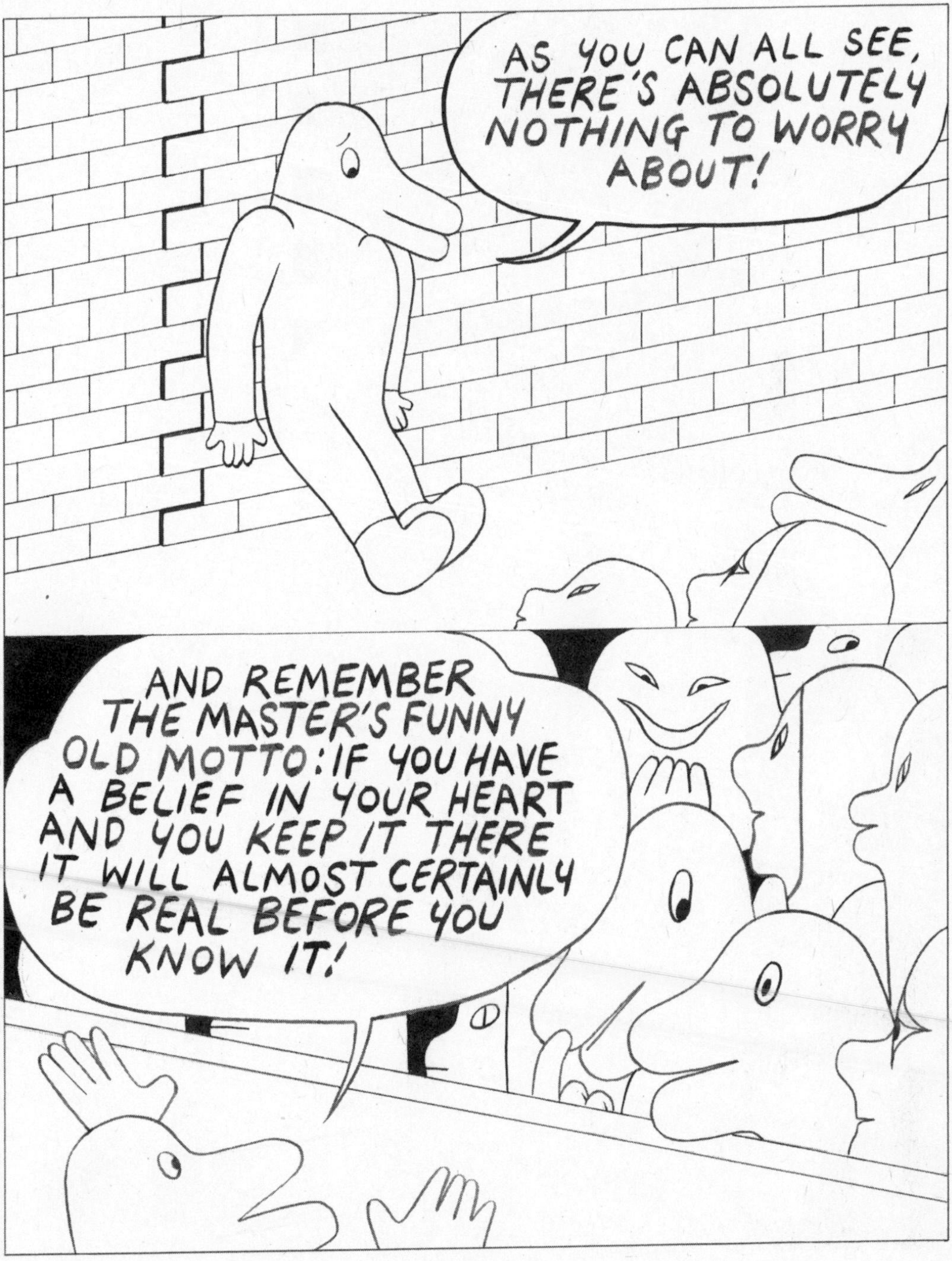
AS YOU CAN ALL SEE, THERE'S ABSOLUTELY NOTHING TO WORRY ABOUT!
AND REMEMBER THE MASTER'S FUNNY OLD MOTTO: IF YOU HAVE A BELIEF IN YOUR HEART AND YOU KEEP IT THERE IT WILL ALMOST CERTAINLY BE REAL BEFORE YOU KNOW IT!

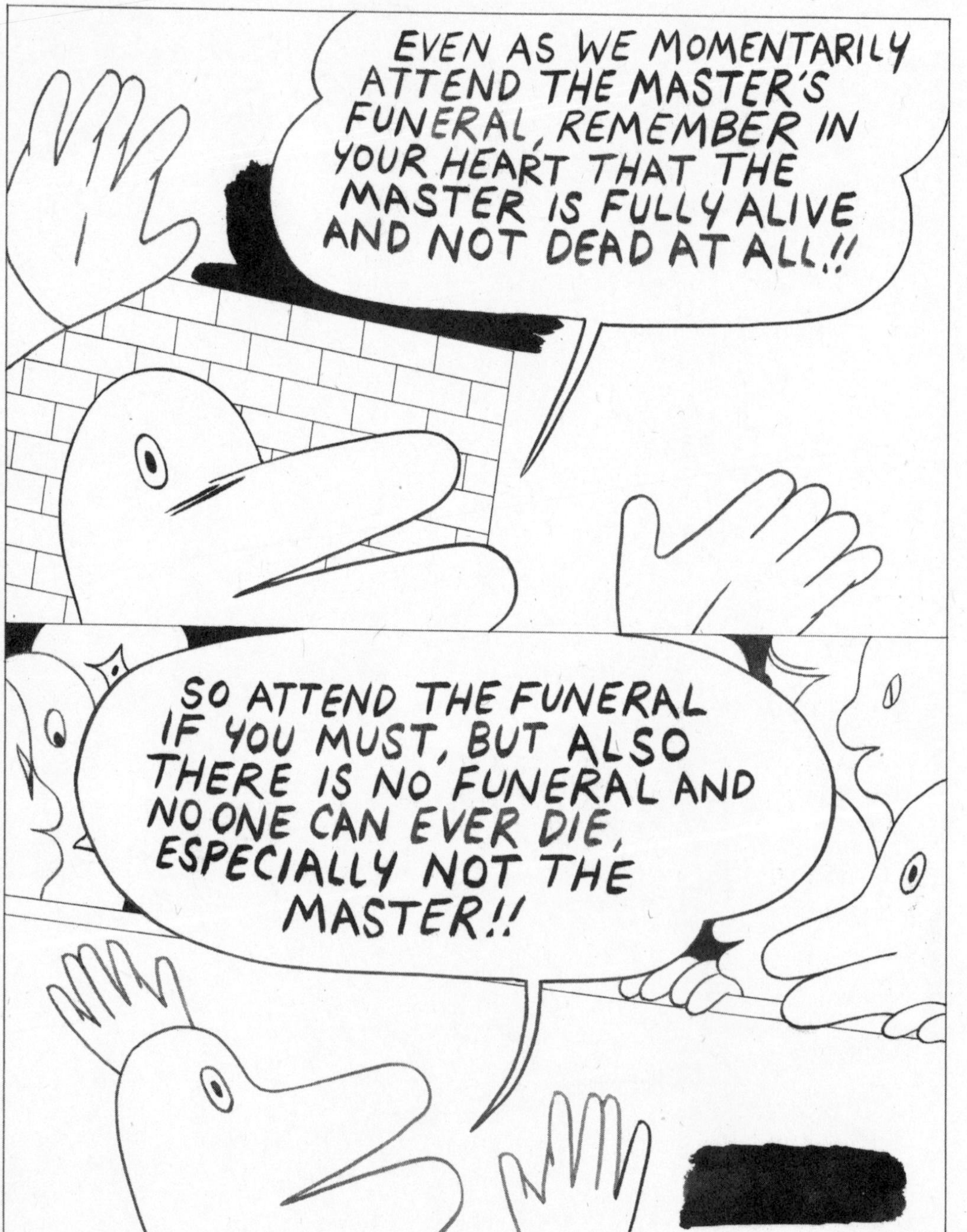
EVEN AS WE MOMENTARILY ATTEND THE MASTER'S FUNERAL, REMEMBER IN YOUR HEART THAT THE MASTER IS FULLY ALIVE AND NOT DEAD AT ALL!!
SO ATTEND THE FUNERAL IF YOU MUST, BUT ALSO THERE IS NO FUNERAL AND NO ONE CAN EVER DIE, ESPECIALLY NOT THE MASTER!!

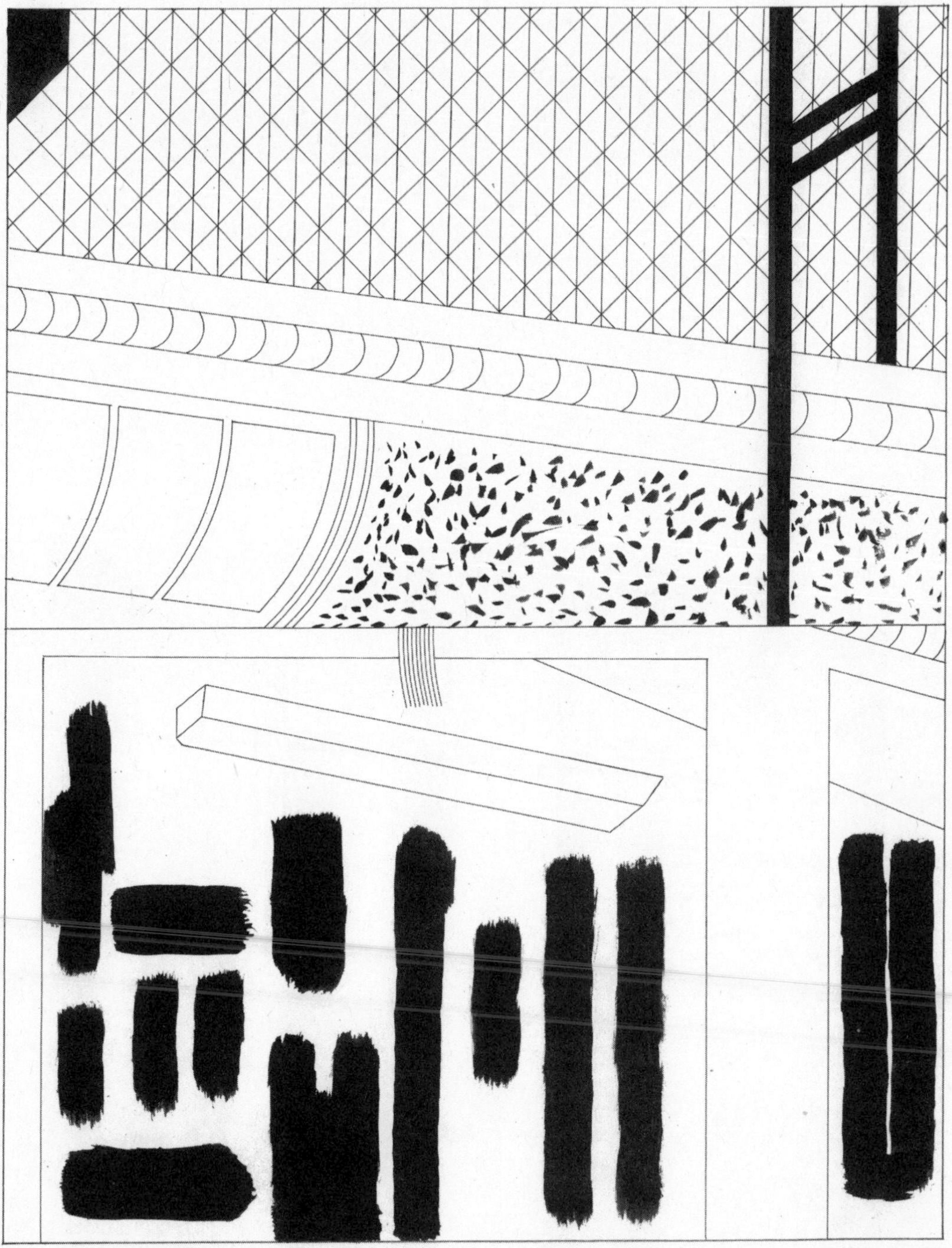

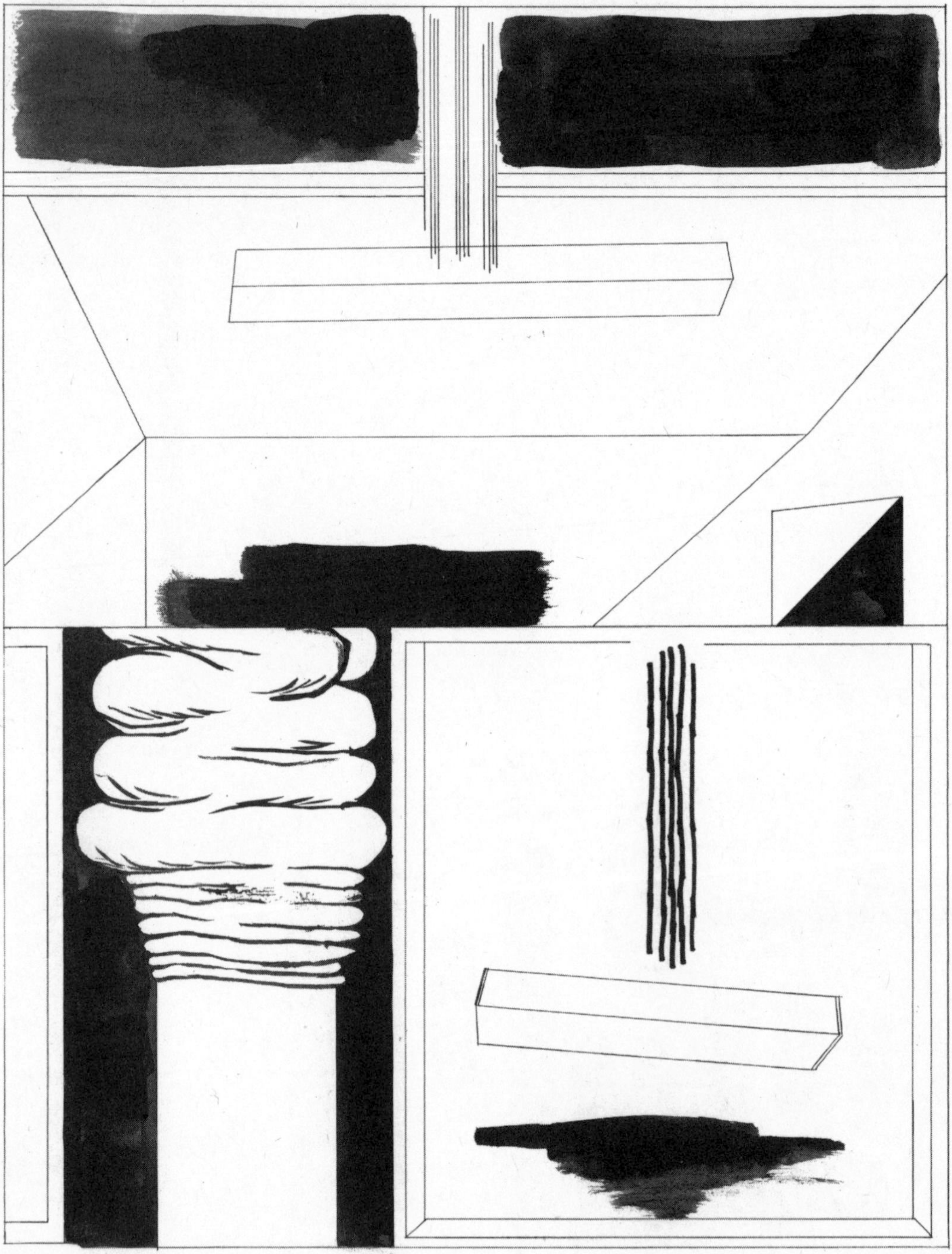

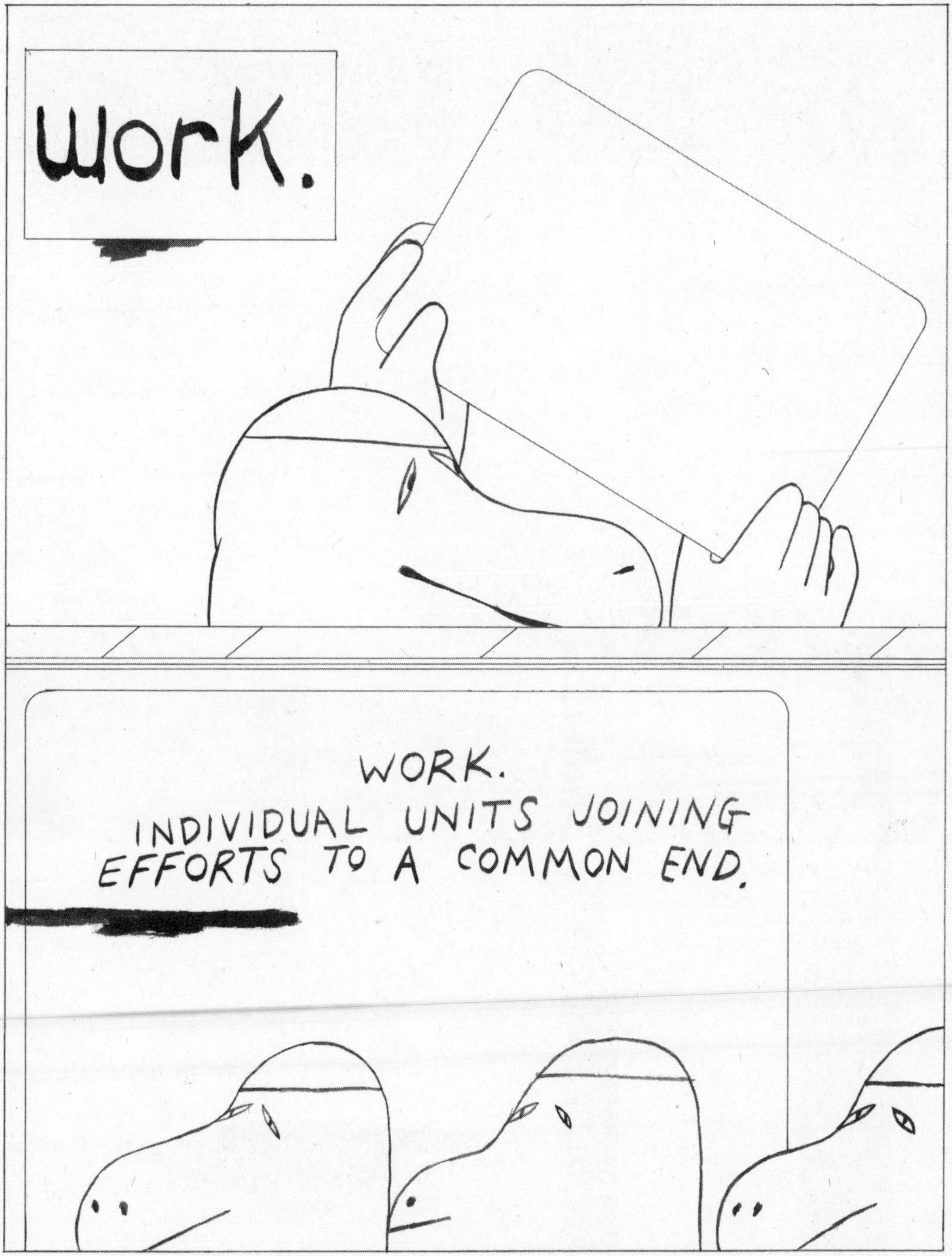
work.
WORK.
INDIVIDUAL UNITS JOINING EFFORTS TO A COMMON END.

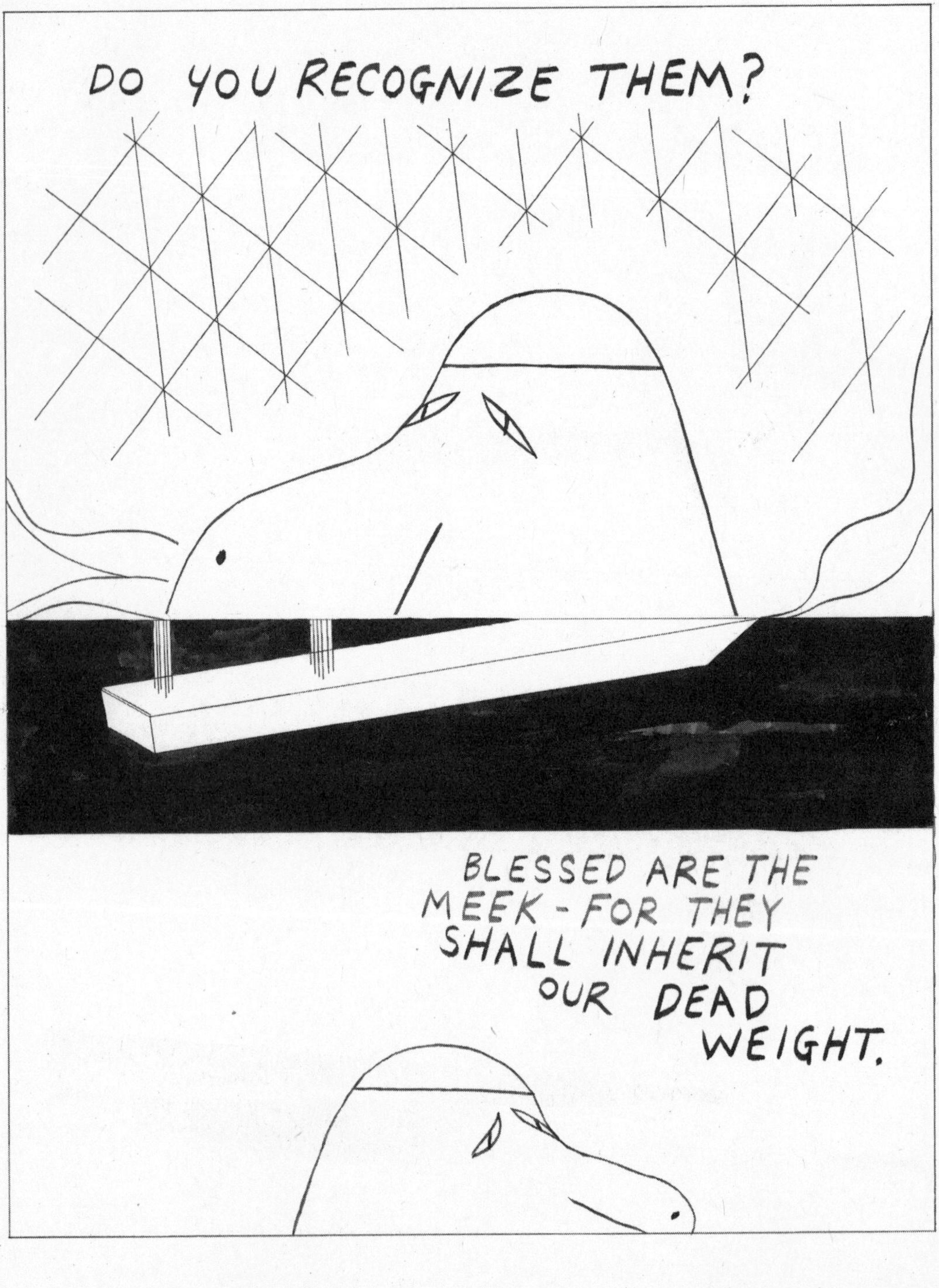
DO YOU RECOGNIZE THEM?
BLESSED ARE THE MEEK - FOR THEY SHALL INHERIT OUR DEAD WEIGHT.

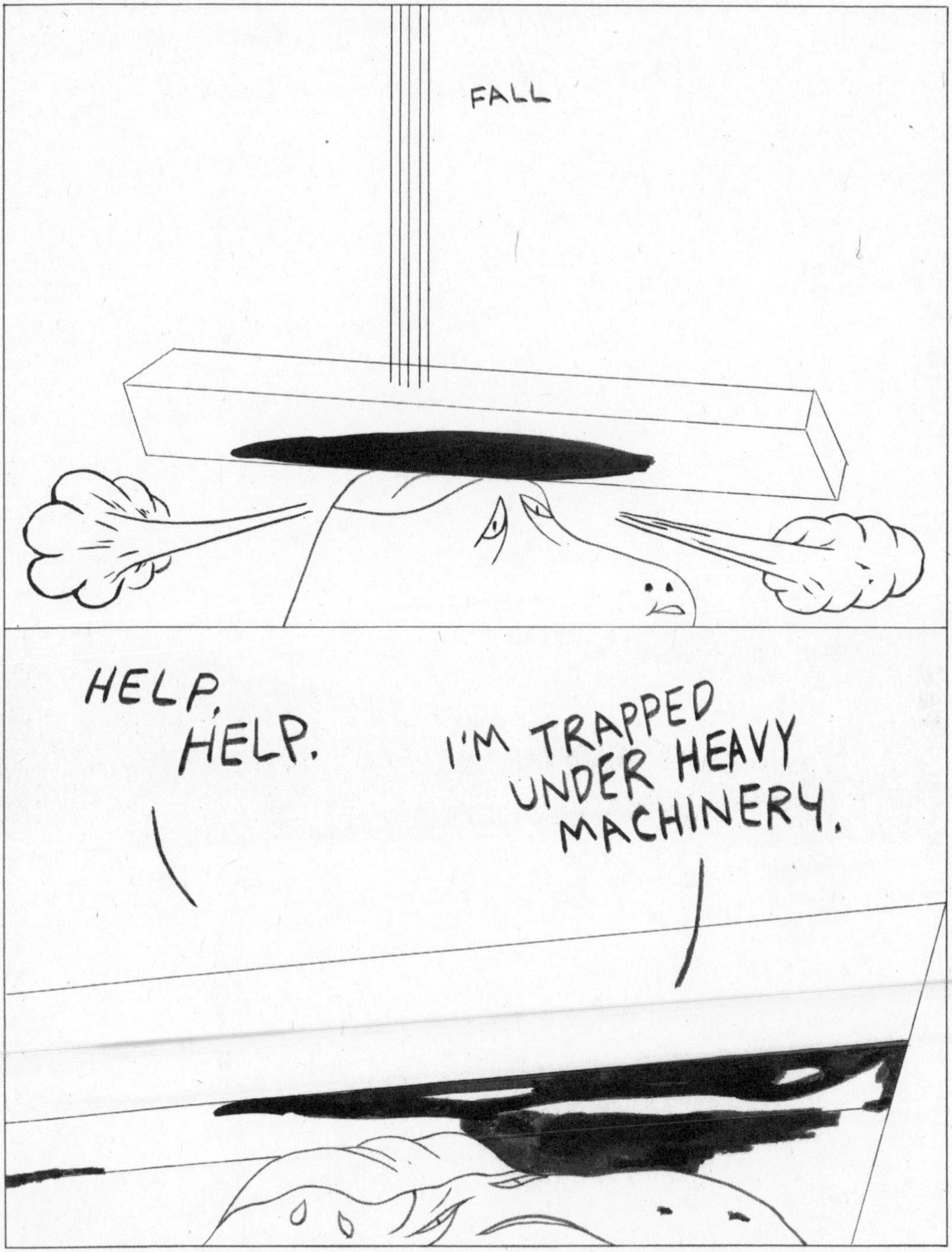
FALL
HELP, HELP.
I'M TRAPPED UNDER HEAVY MACHINERY.

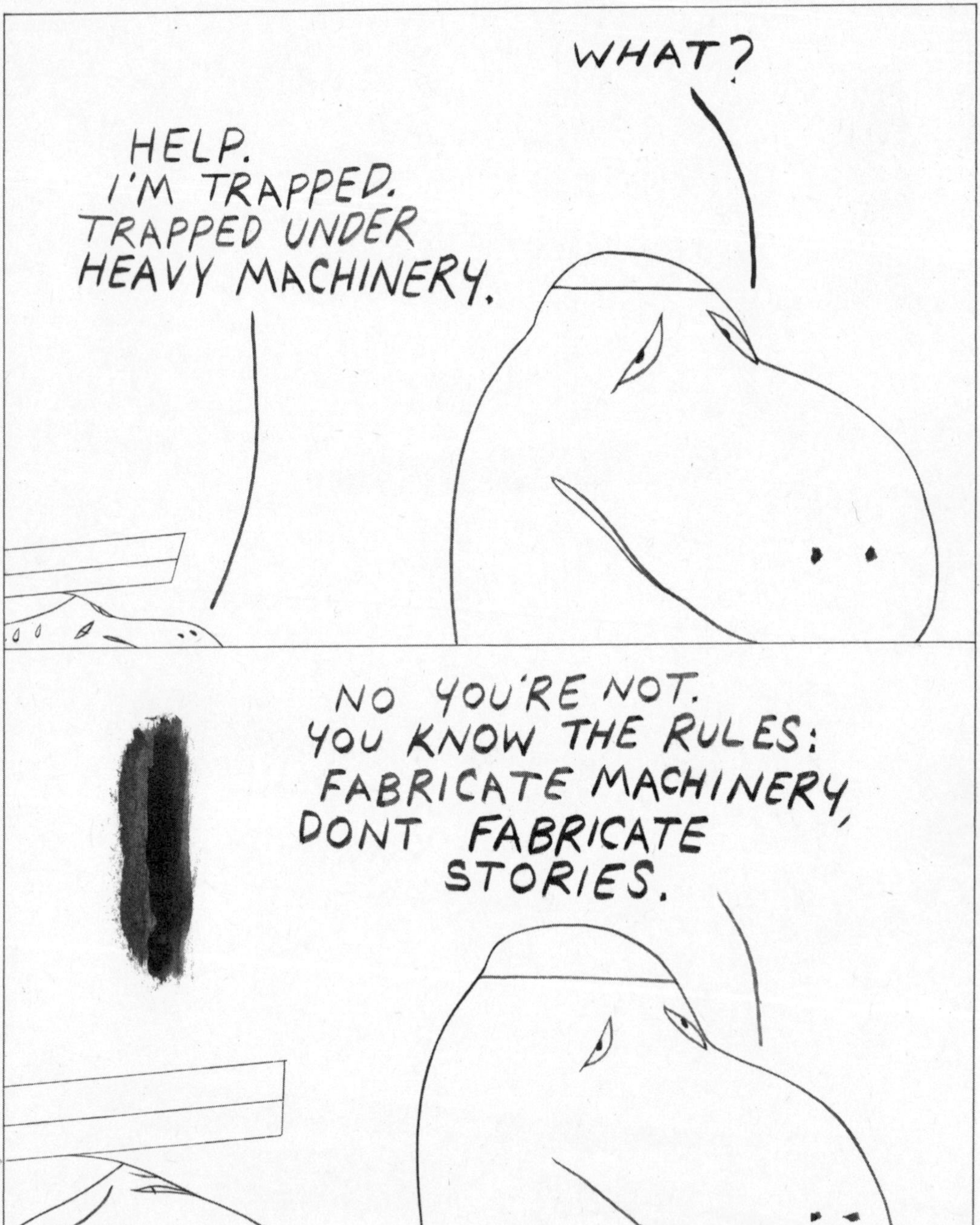
HELP.
I'M TRAPPED.
TRAPPED UNDER
HEAVY MACHINERY.
WHAT?
NO YOU'RE NOT.
YOU KNOW THE RULES:
FABRICATE MACHINERY,
DONT FABRICATE
STORIES.

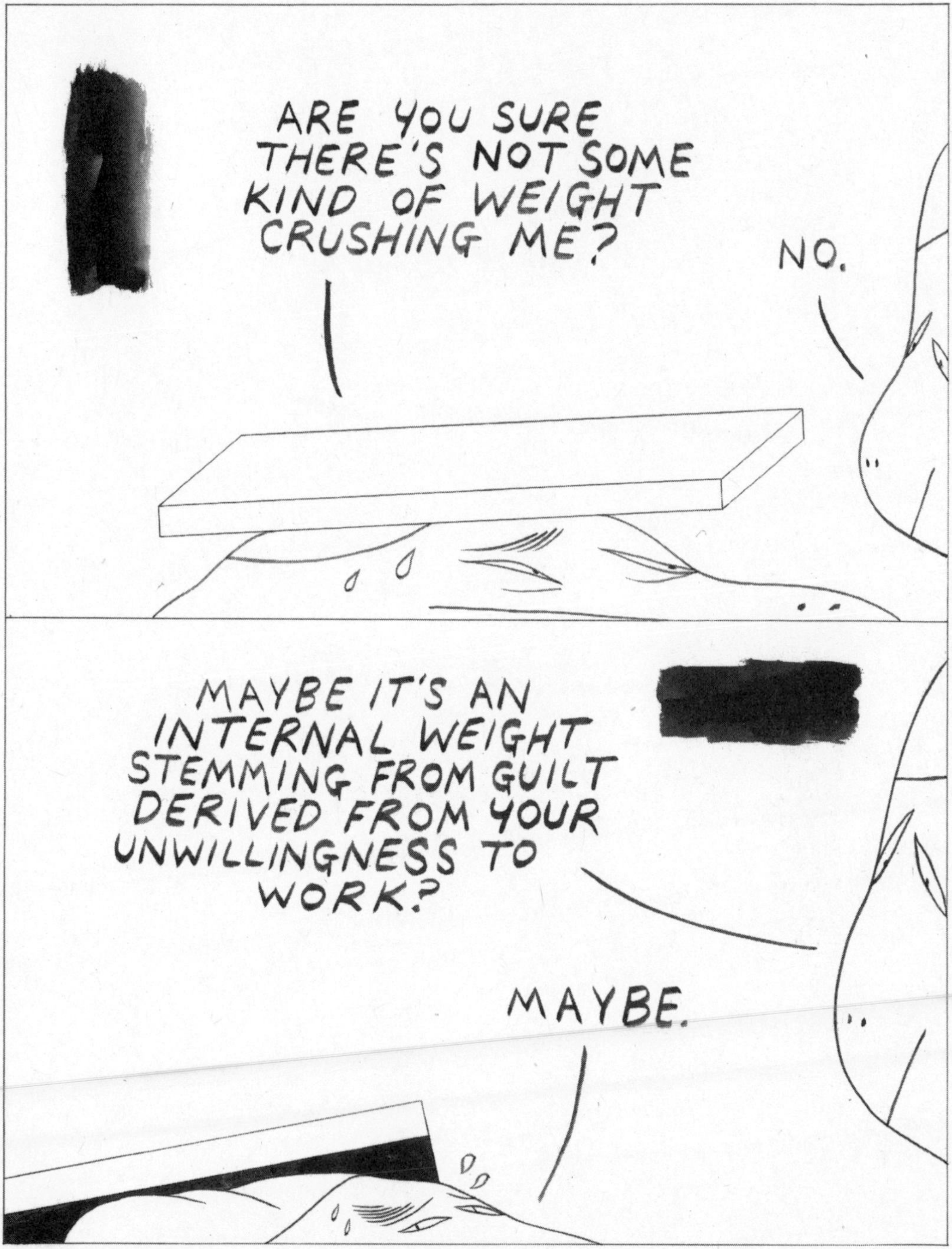
[redacted]
ARE YOU SURE THERE'S NOT SOME KIND OF WEIGHT CRUSHING ME?
NO.
MAYBE IT'S AN INTERNAL WEIGHT STEMMING FROM GUILT DERIVED FROM YOUR UNWILLINGNESS TO WORK?
[redacted]
MAYBE.

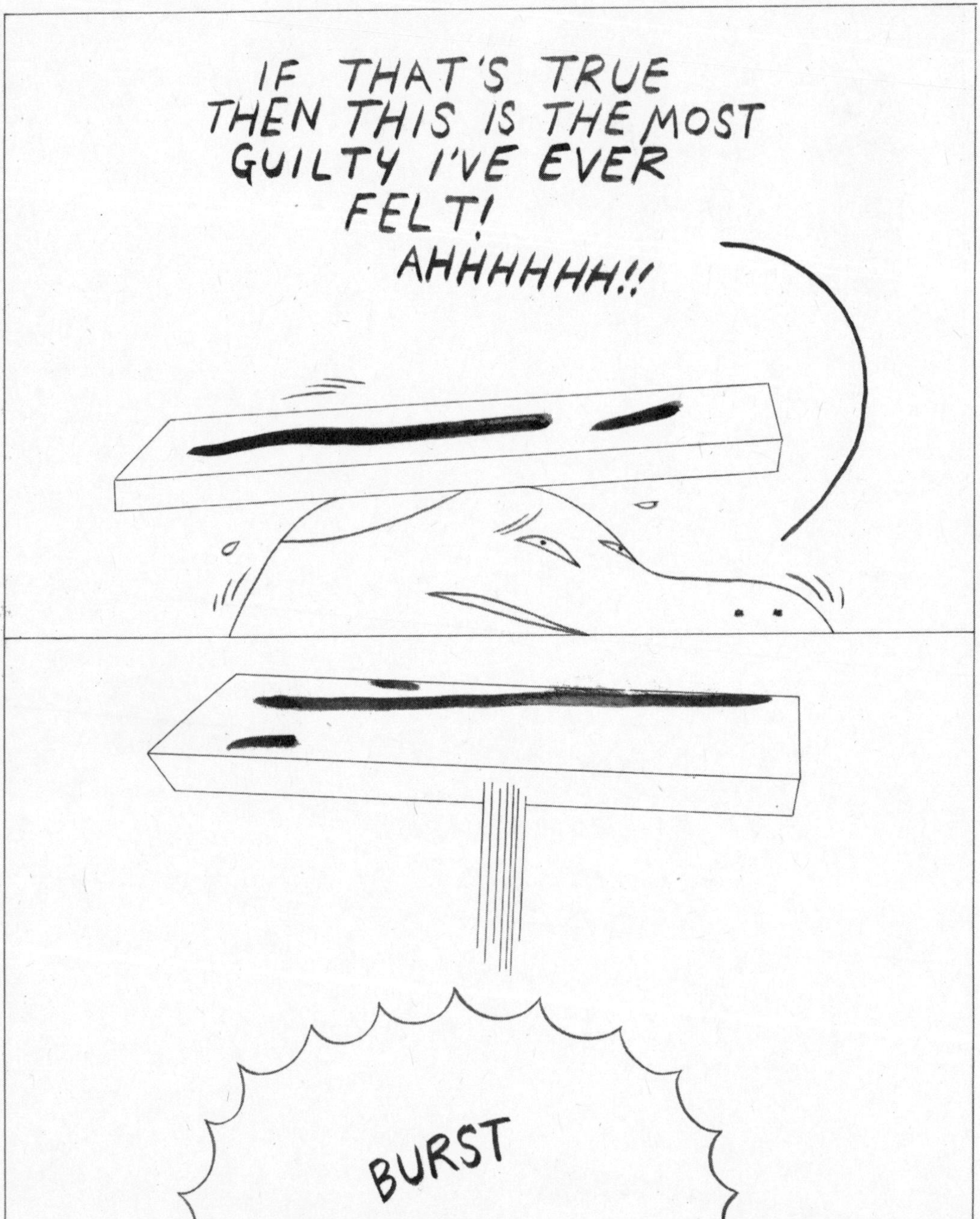
IF THAT'S TRUE THEN THIS IS THE MOST GUILTY I'VE EVER FELT!
AHHHHHH!!
BURST

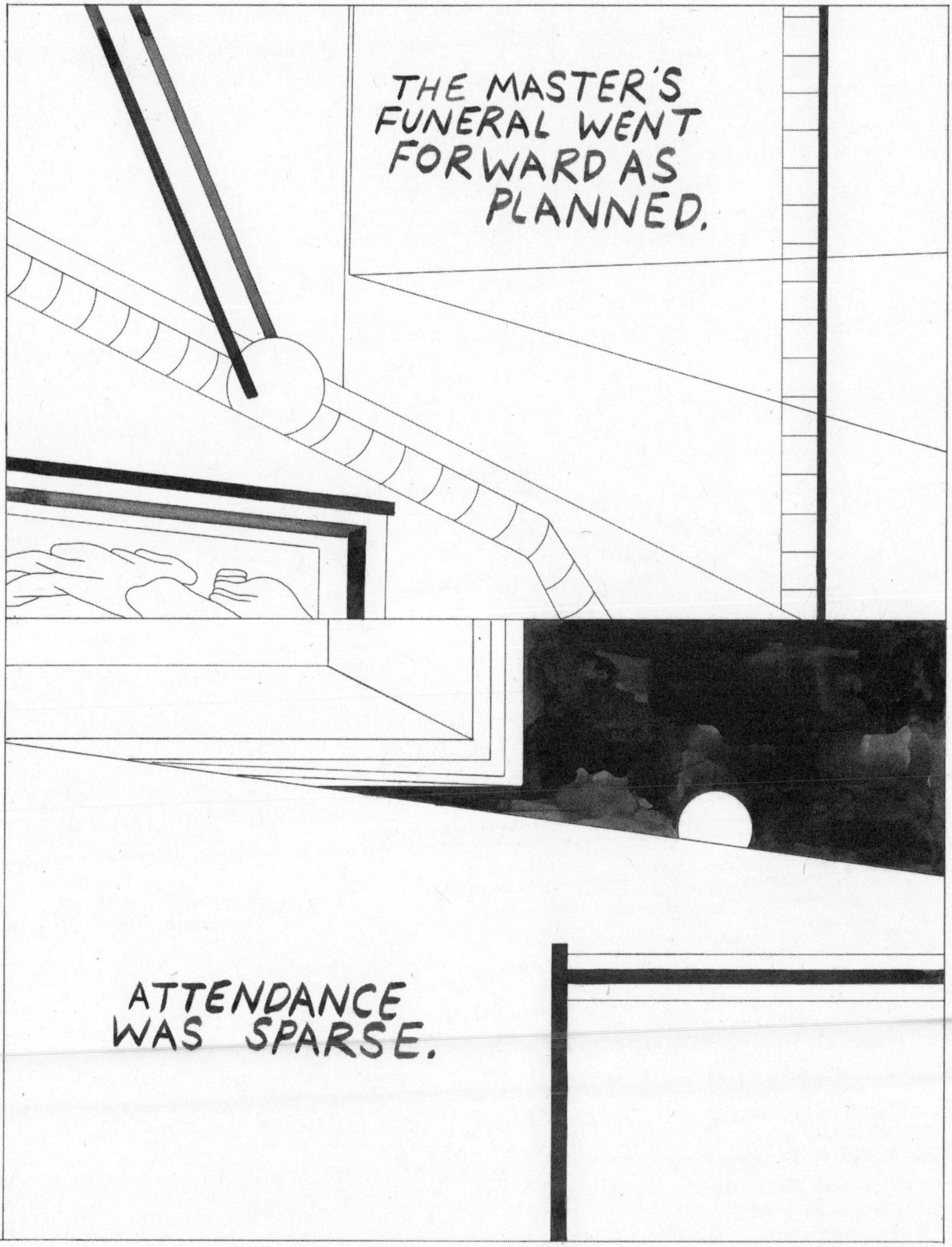
THE MASTER'S FUNERAL WENT FORWARD AS PLANNED.
ATTENDANCE WAS SPARSE.

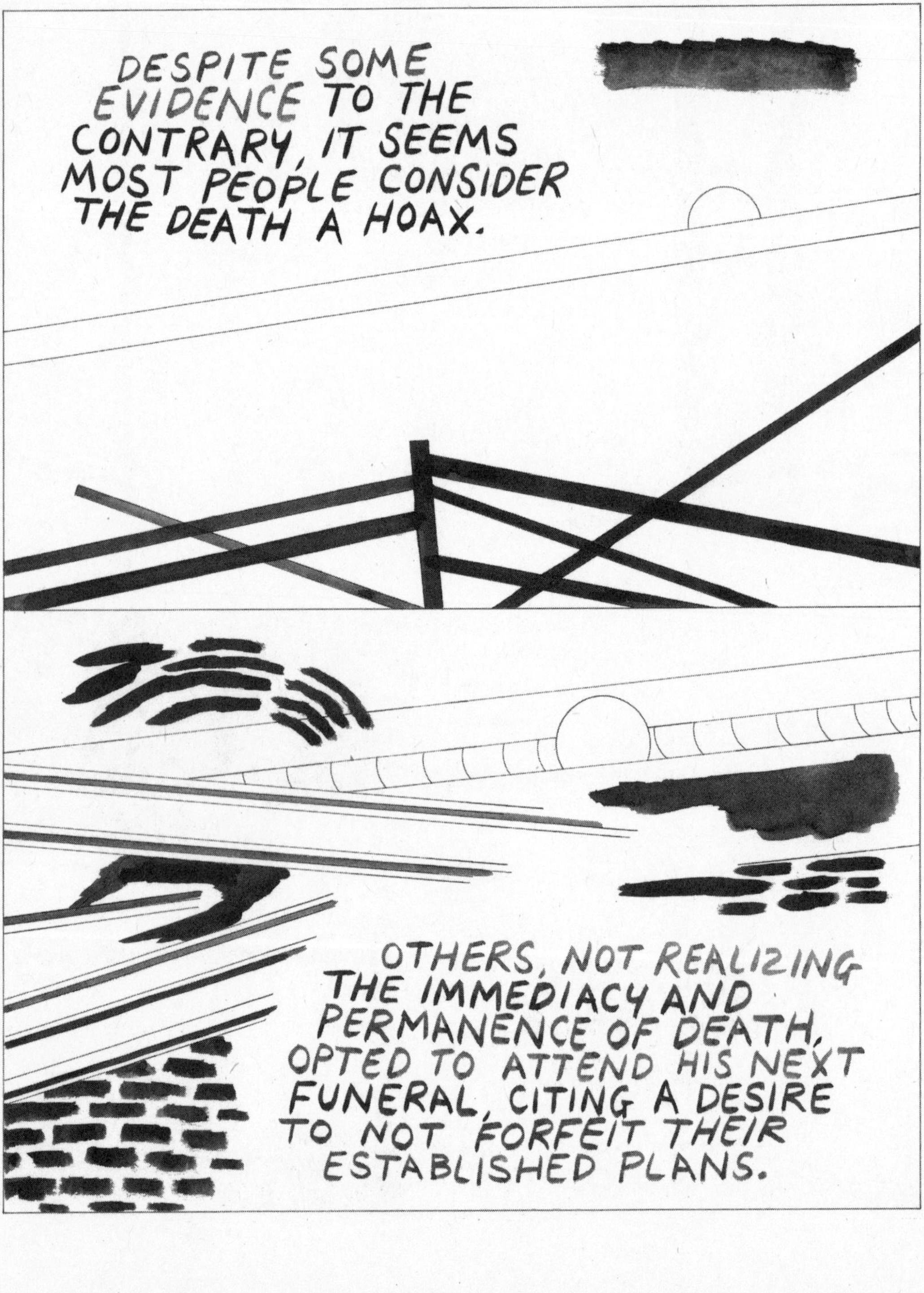
DESPITE SOME EVIDENCE TO THE CONTRARY, IT SEEMS MOST PEOPLE CONSIDER THE DEATH A HOAX.
OTHERS, NOT REALIZING THE IMMEDIACY AND PERMANENCE OF DEATH, OPTED TO ATTEND HIS NEXT FUNERAL, CITING A DESIRE TO NOT FORFEIT THEIR ESTABLISHED PLANS.

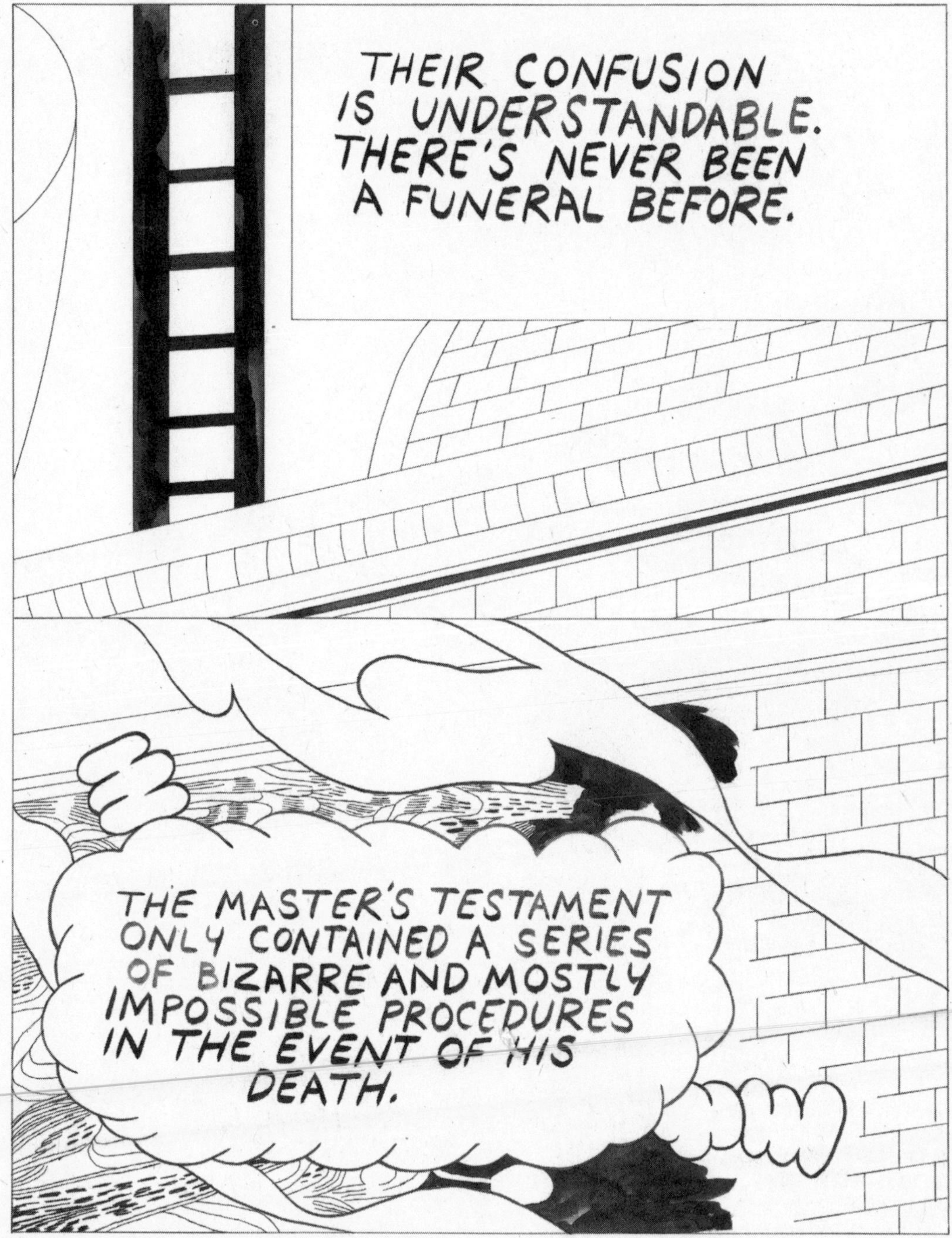
THEIR CONFUSION IS UNDERSTANDABLE. THERE'S NEVER BEEN A FUNERAL BEFORE.
THE MASTER'S TESTAMENT ONLY CONTAINED A SERIES OF BIZARRE AND MOSTLY IMPOSSIBLE PROCEDURES IN THE EVENT OF HIS DEATH.

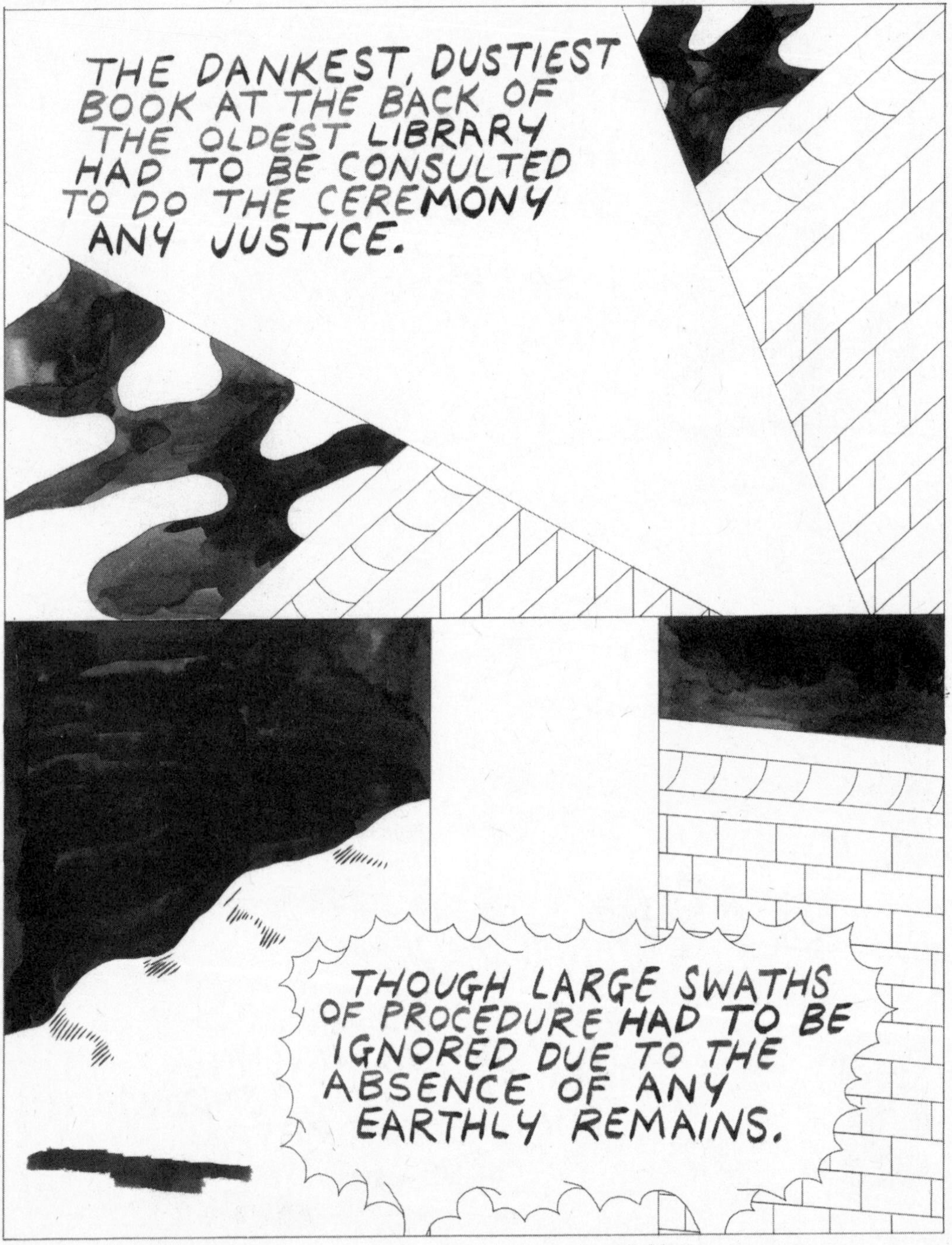
THE DANKEST, DUSTIEST BOOK AT THE BACK OF THE OLDEST LIBRARY HAD TO BE CONSULTED TO DO THE CEREMONY ANY JUSTICE.
THOUGH LARGE SWATHS OF PROCEDURE HAD TO BE IGNORED DUE TO THE ABSENCE OF ANY EARTHLY REMAINS.

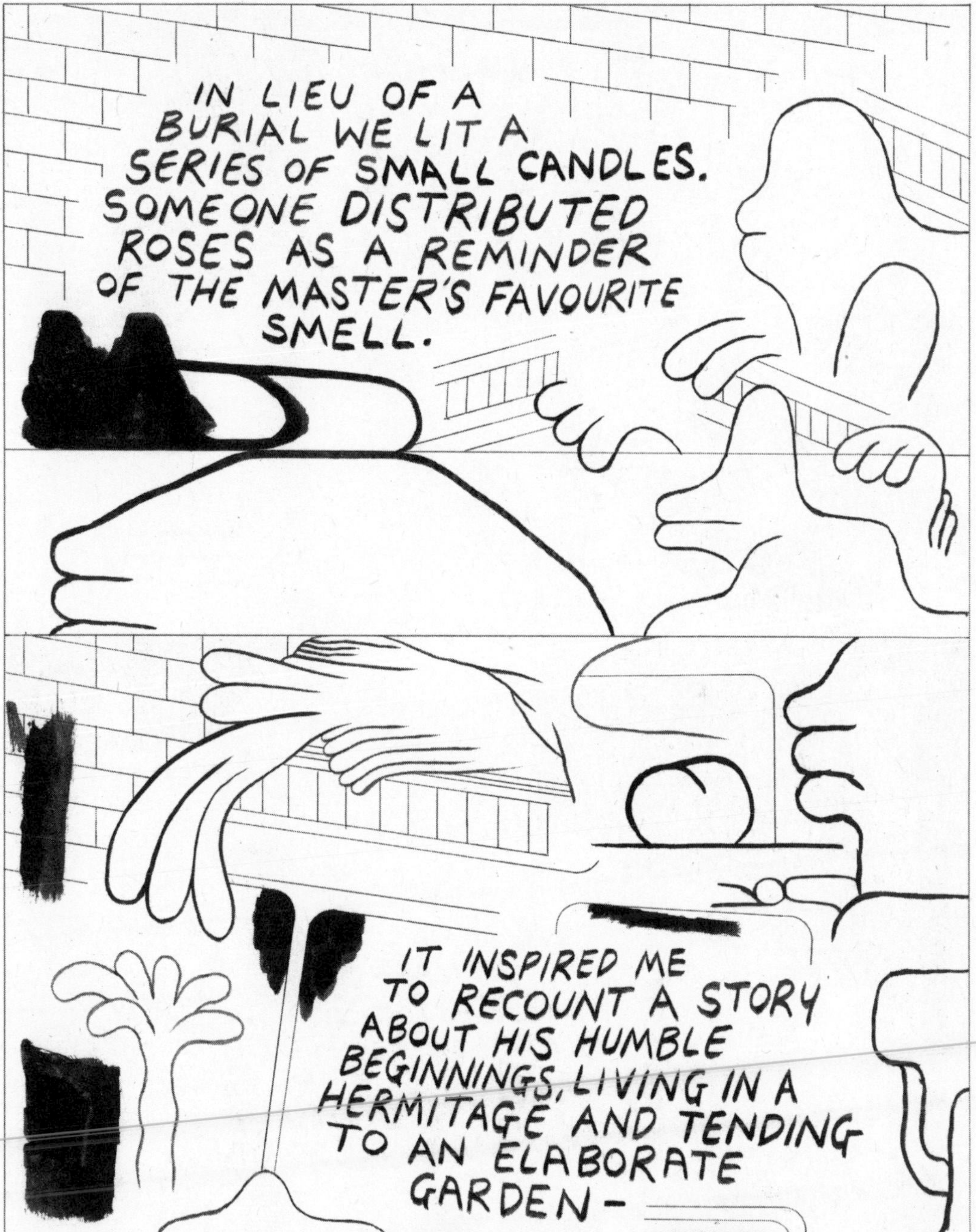
IN LIEU OF A BURIAL WE LIT A SERIES OF SMALL CANDLES. SOMEONE DISTRIBUTED ROSES AS A REMINDER OF THE MASTER'S FAVOURITE SMELL.
IT INSPIRED ME TO RECOUNT A STORY ABOUT HIS HUMBLE BEGINNINGS, LIVING IN A HERMITAGE AND TENDING TO AN ELABORATE GARDEN -

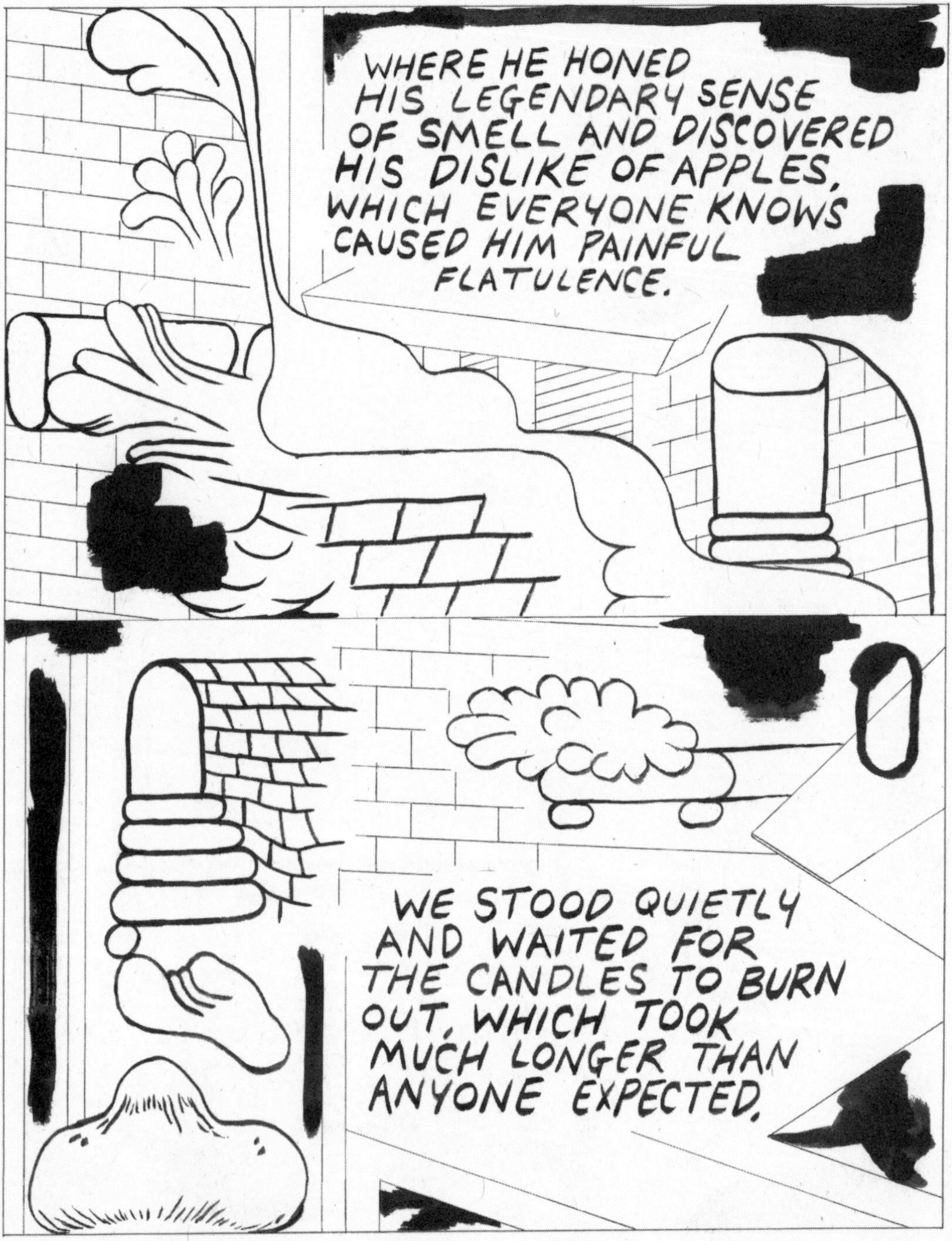
WHERE HE HONED HIS LEGENDARY SENSE OF SMELL AND DISCOVERED HIS DISLIKE OF APPLES, WHICH EVERYONE KNOWS CAUSED HIM PAINFUL FLATULENCE.
WE STOOD QUIETLY AND WAITED FOR THE CANDLES TO BURN OUT, WHICH TOOK MUCH LONGER THAN ANYONE EXPECTED.

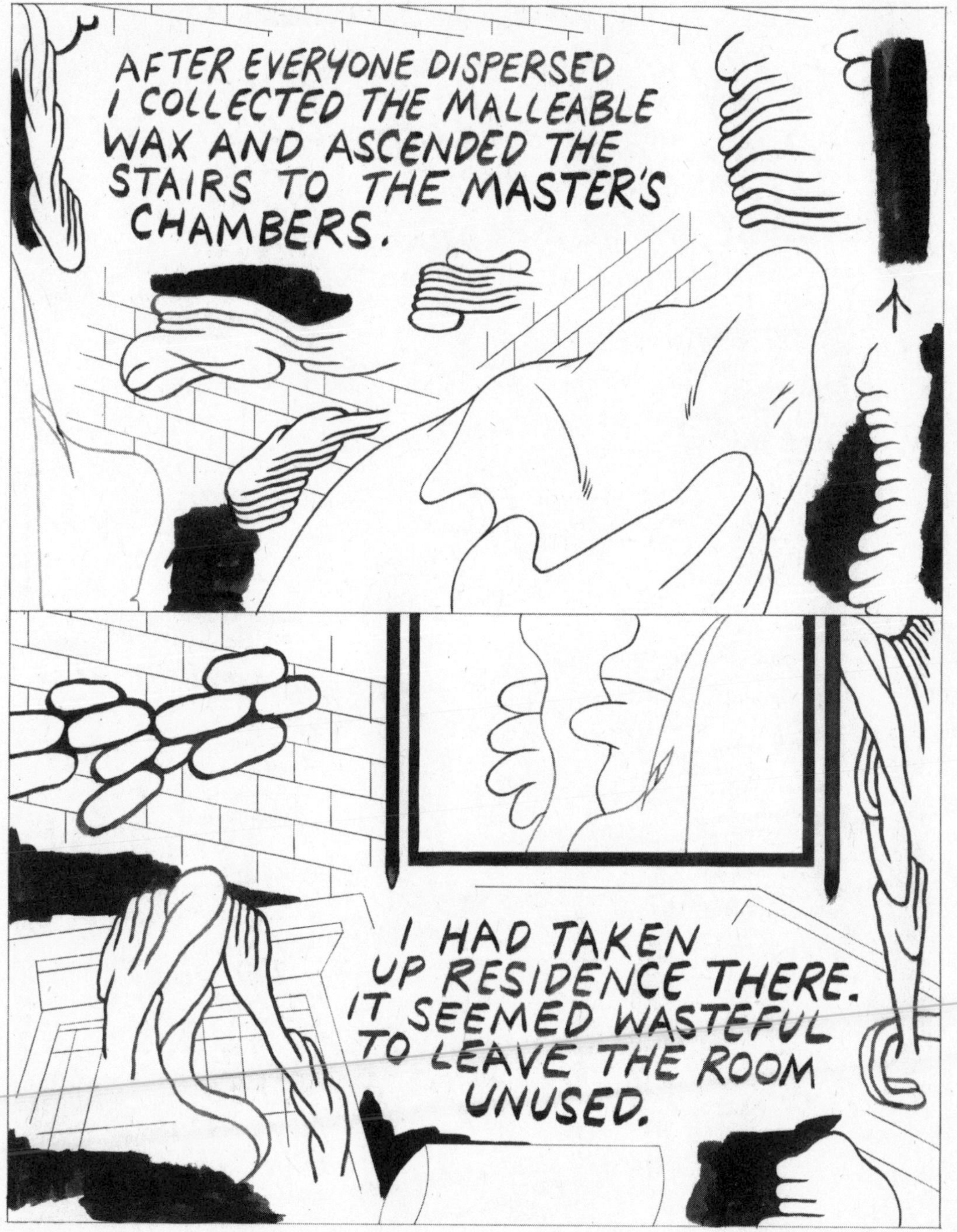
AFTER EVERYONE DISPERSED I COLLECTED THE MALLEABLE WAX AND ASCENDED THE STAIRS TO THE MASTER'S CHAMBERS.
I HAD TAKEN UP RESIDENCE THERE. IT SEEMED WASTEFUL TO LEAVE THE ROOM UNUSED.

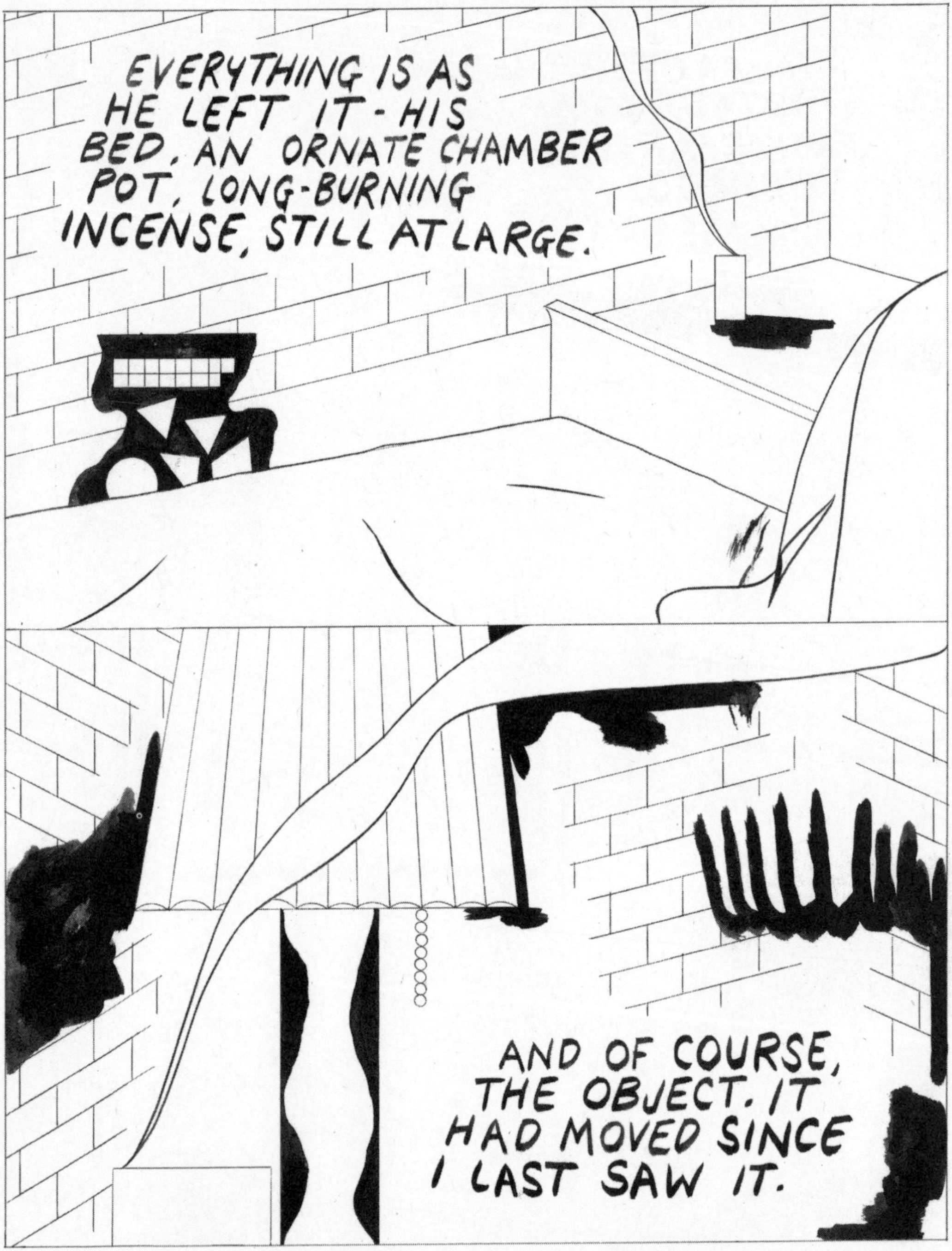
EVERYTHING IS AS HE LEFT IT - HIS BED, AN ORNATE CHAMBER POT, LONG-BURNING INCENSE, STILL AT LARGE.
AND OF COURSE, THE OBJECT. IT HAD MOVED SINCE I LAST SAW IT.

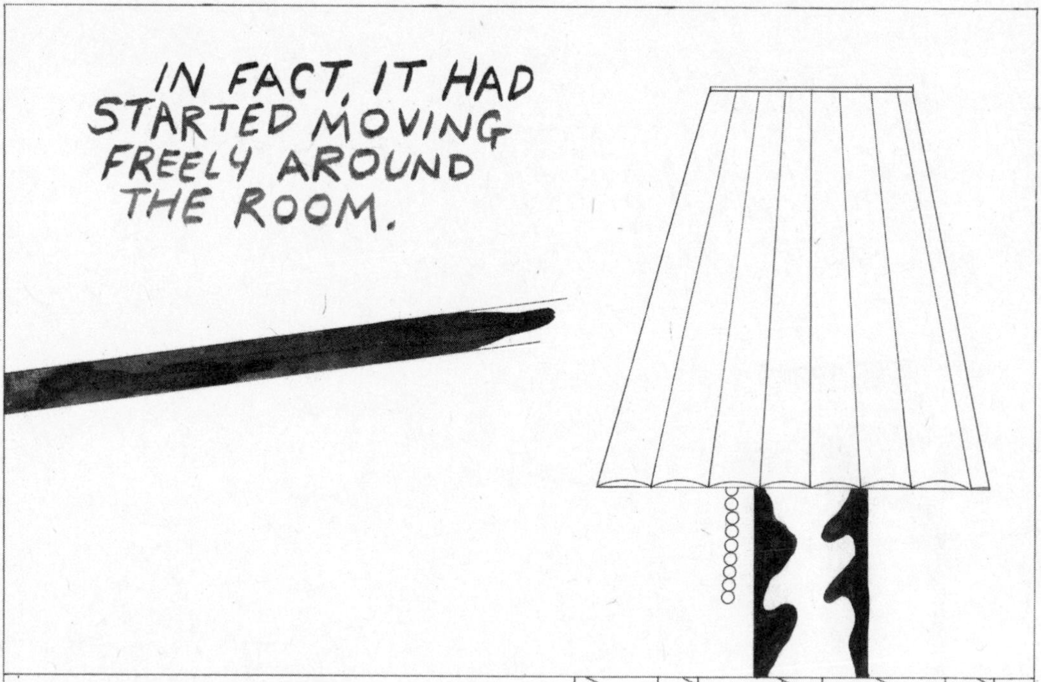
IN FACT, IT HAD STARTED MOVING FREELY AROUND THE ROOM.

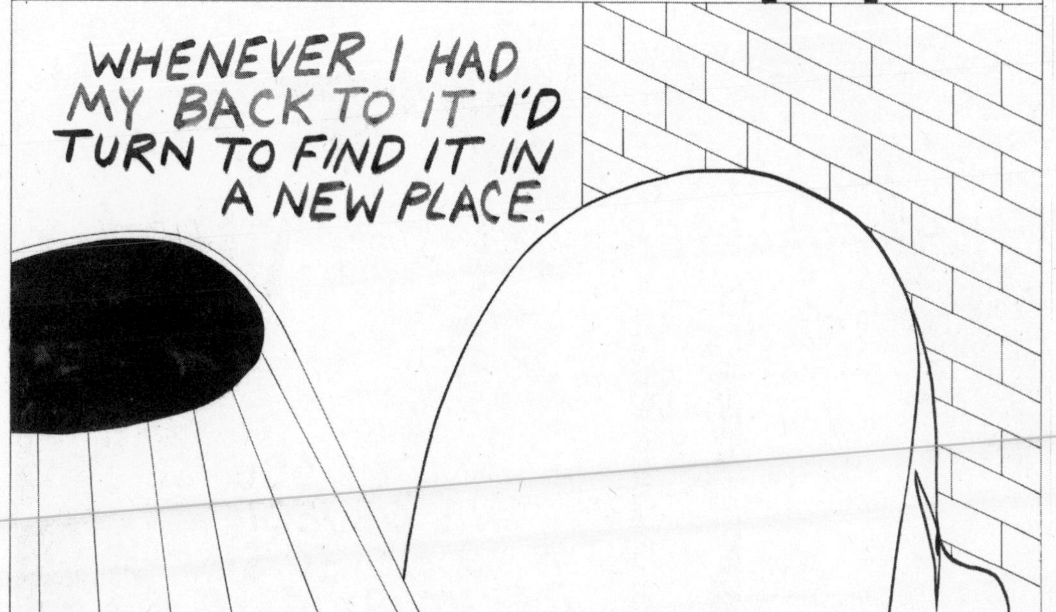
WHENEVER I HAD MY BACK TO IT I'D TURN TO FIND IT IN A NEW PLACE.

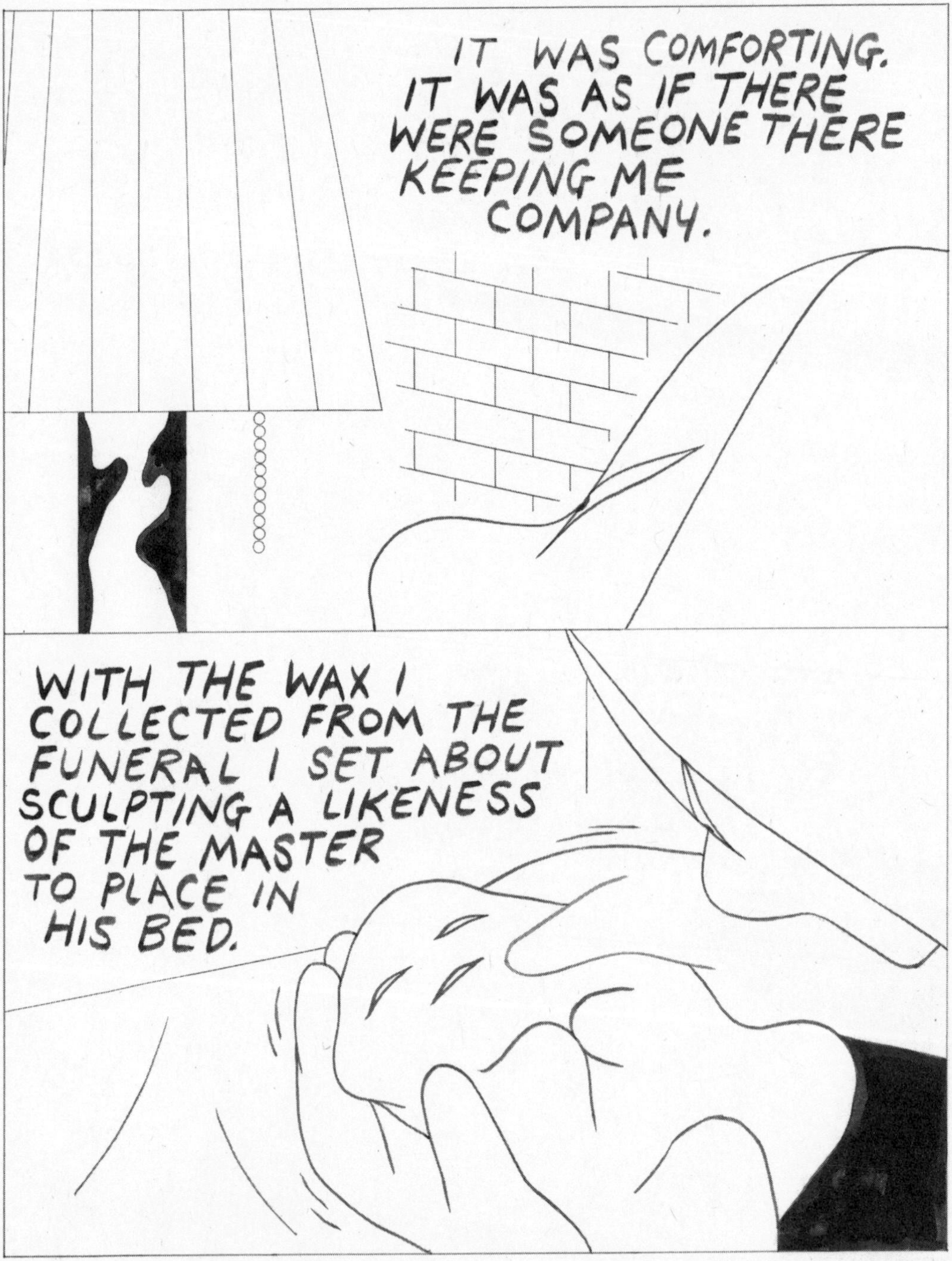
IT WAS COMFORTING. IT WAS AS IF THERE WERE SOMEONE THERE KEEPING ME COMPANY.
WITH THE WAX I COLLECTED FROM THE FUNERAL I SET ABOUT SCULPTING A LIKENESS OF THE MASTER TO PLACE IN HIS BED.

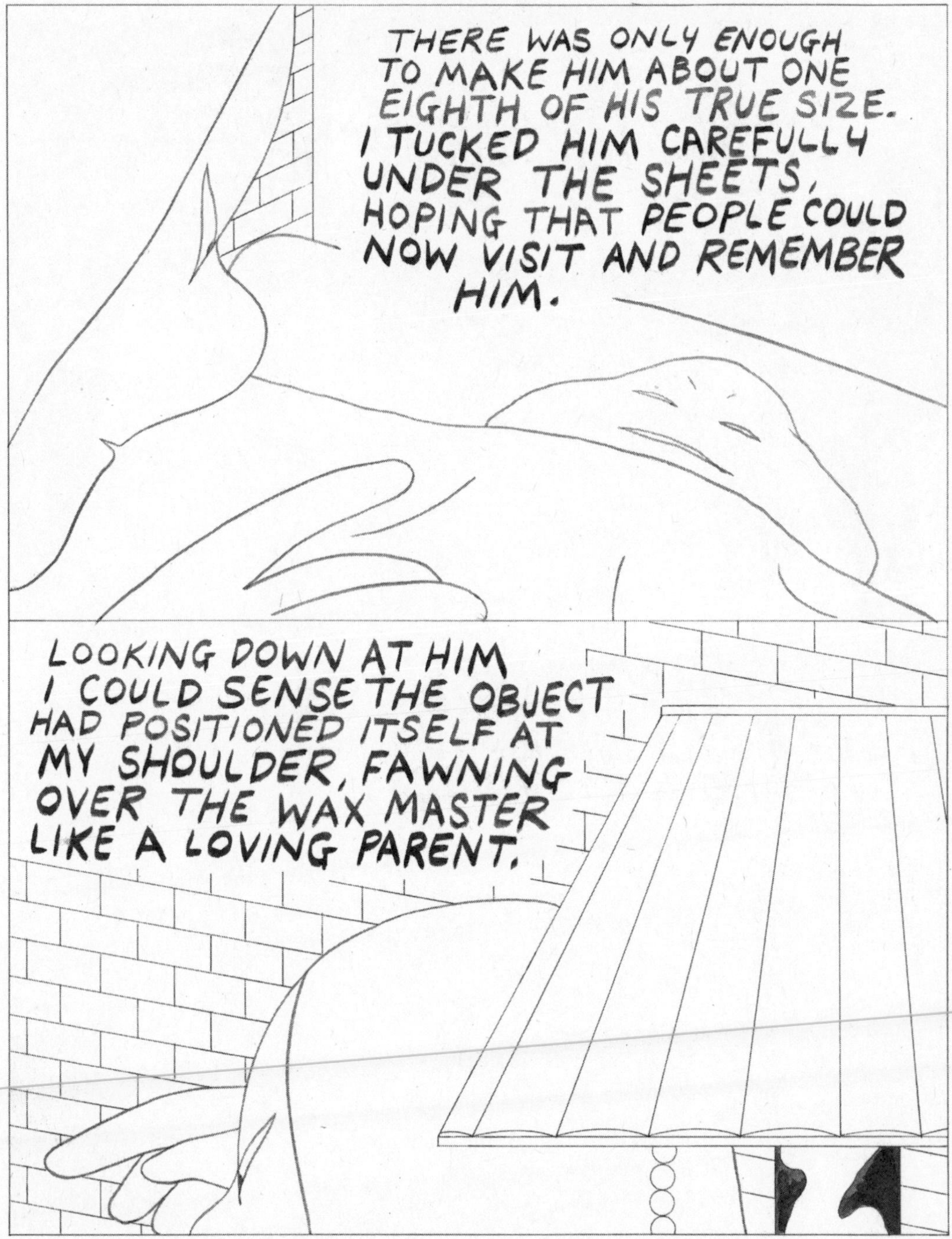
THERE WAS ONLY ENOUGH TO MAKE HIM ABOUT ONE EIGHTH OF HIS TRUE SIZE. I TUCKED HIM CAREFULLY UNDER THE SHEETS, HOPING THAT PEOPLE COULD NOW VISIT AND REMEMBER HIM.
LOOKING DOWN AT HIM I COULD SENSE THE OBJECT HAD POSITIONED ITSELF AT MY SHOULDER, FAWNING OVER THE WAX MASTER LIKE A LOVING PARENT.

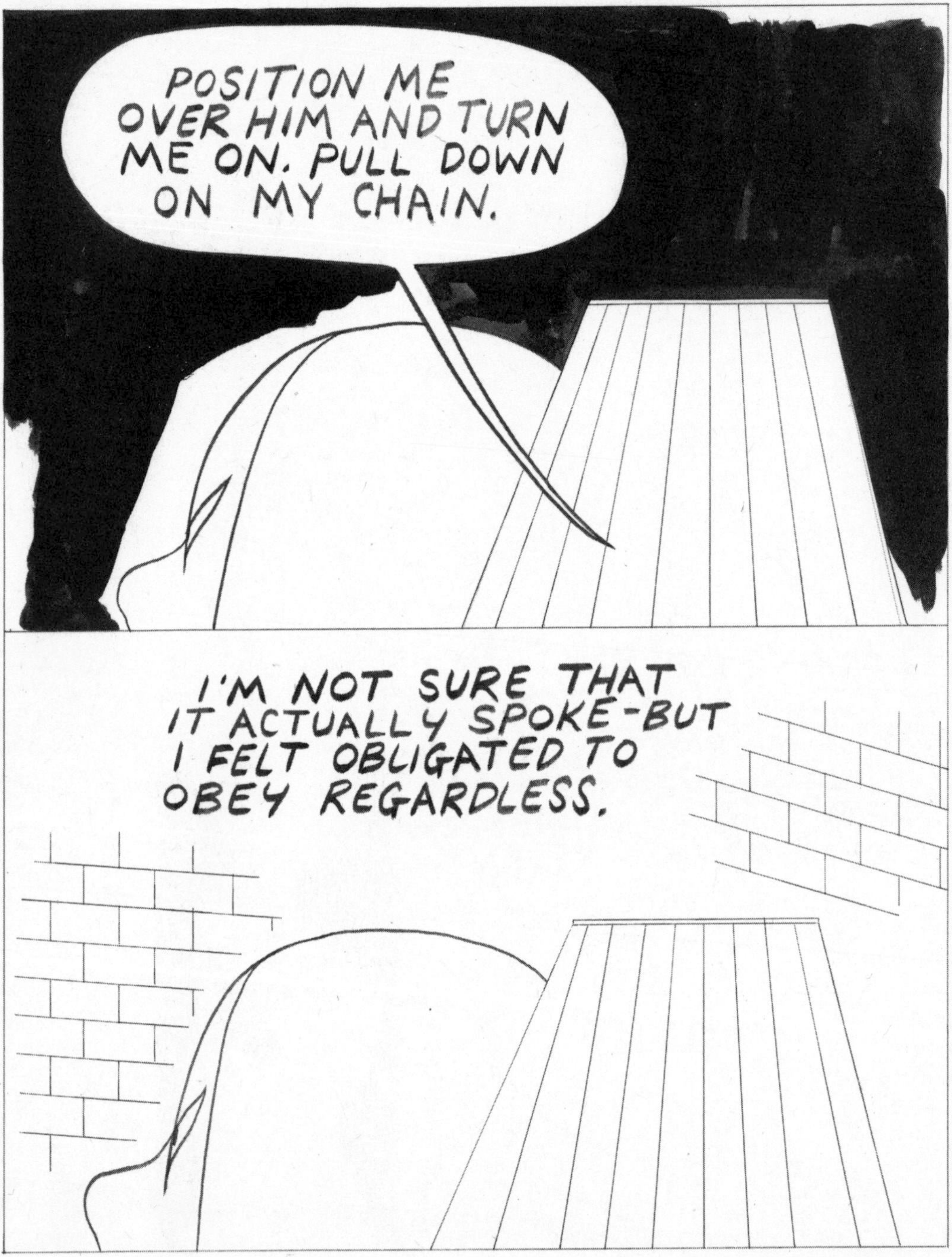
POSITION ME OVER HIM AND TURN ME ON. PULL DOWN ON MY CHAIN.
I'M NOT SURE THAT IT ACTUALLY SPOKE-BUT I FELT OBLIGATED TO OBEY REGARDLESS.

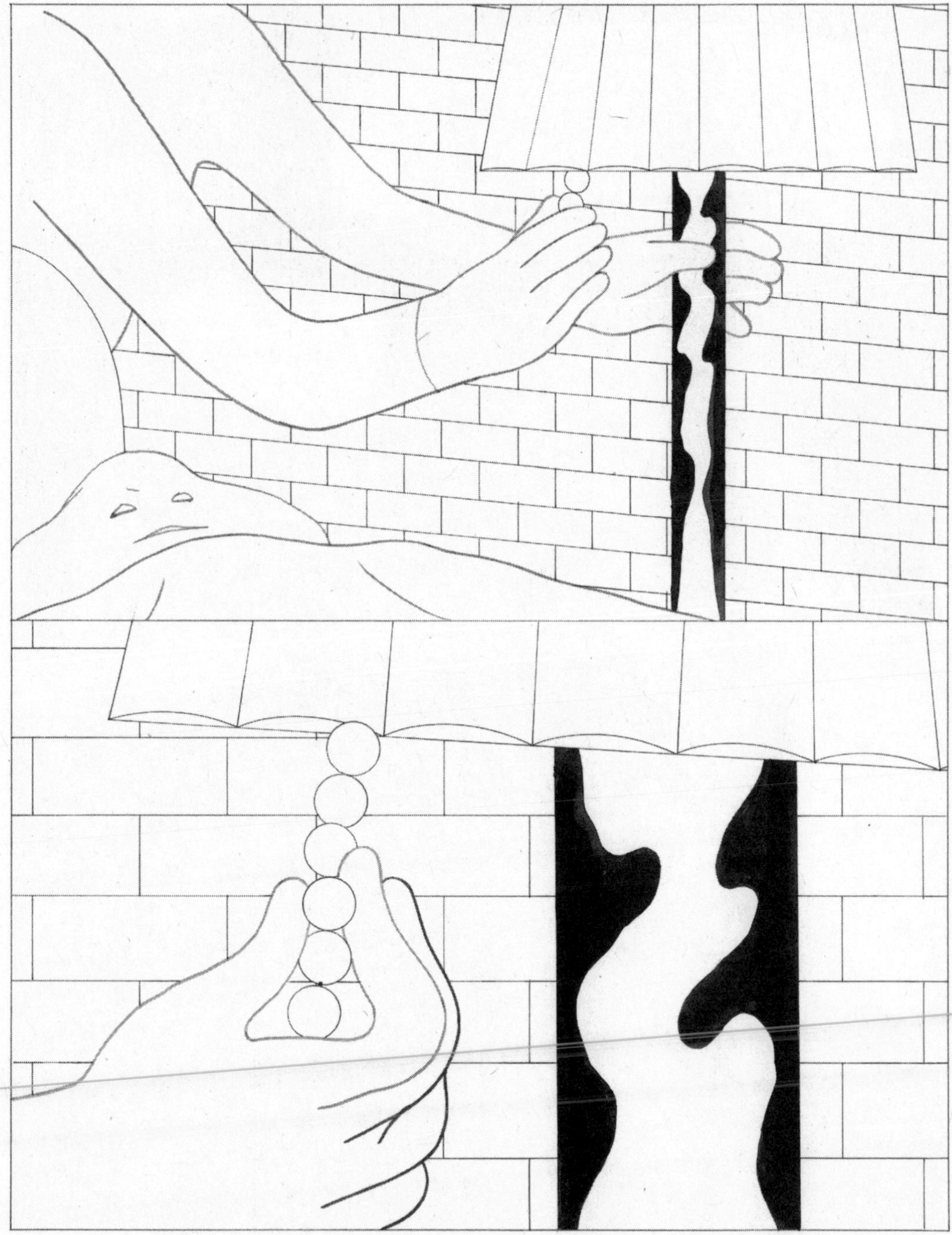

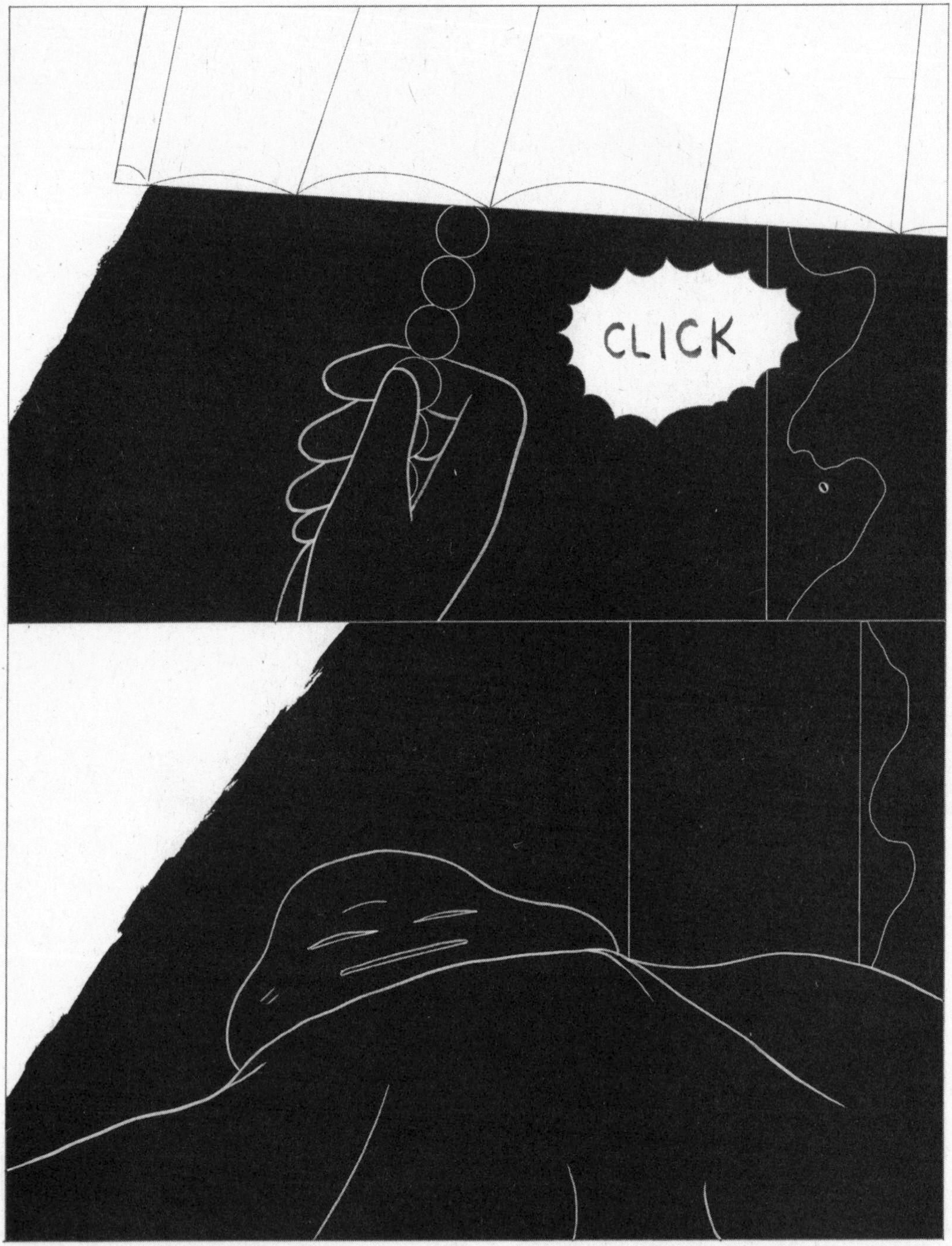
CLICK

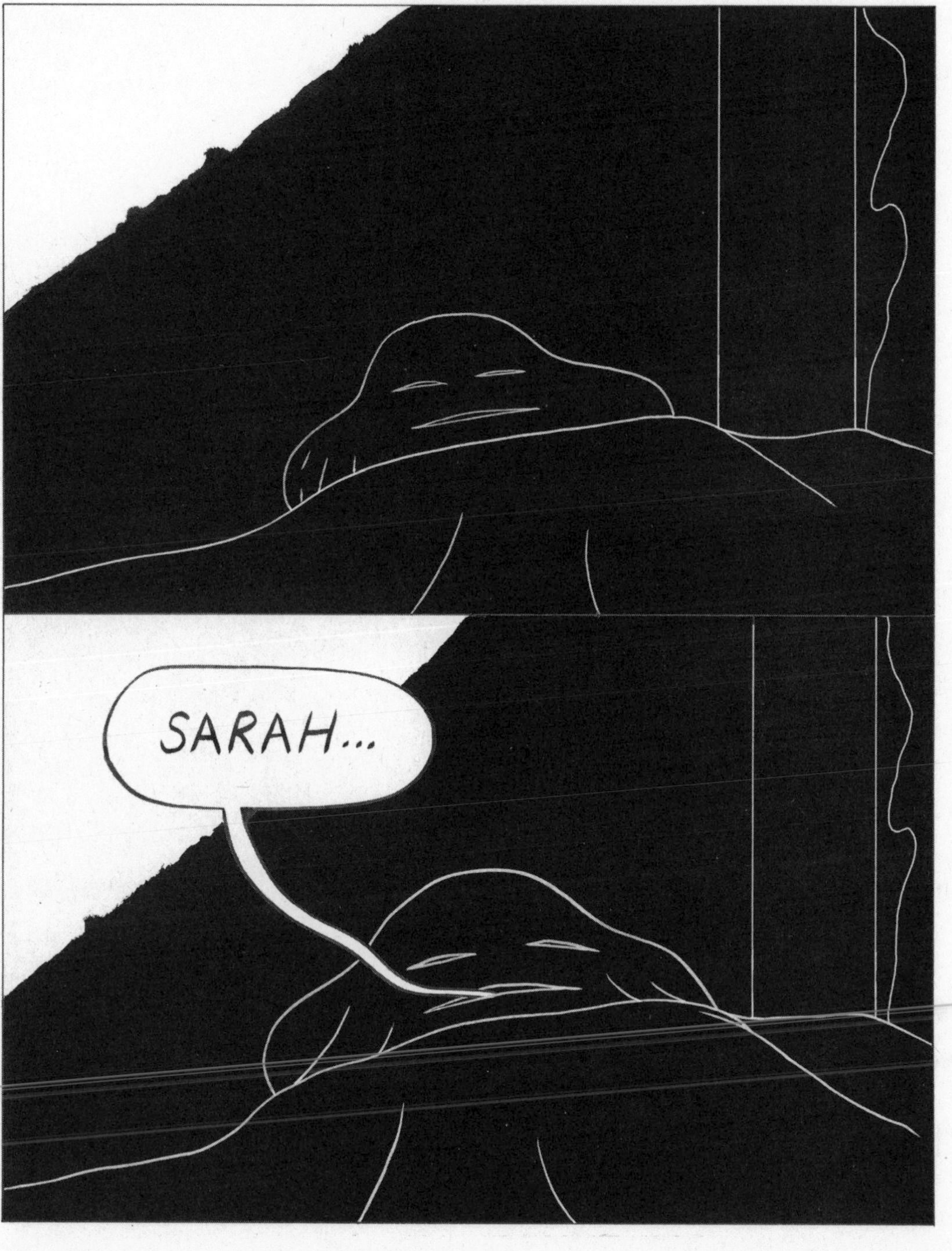
SARAH...

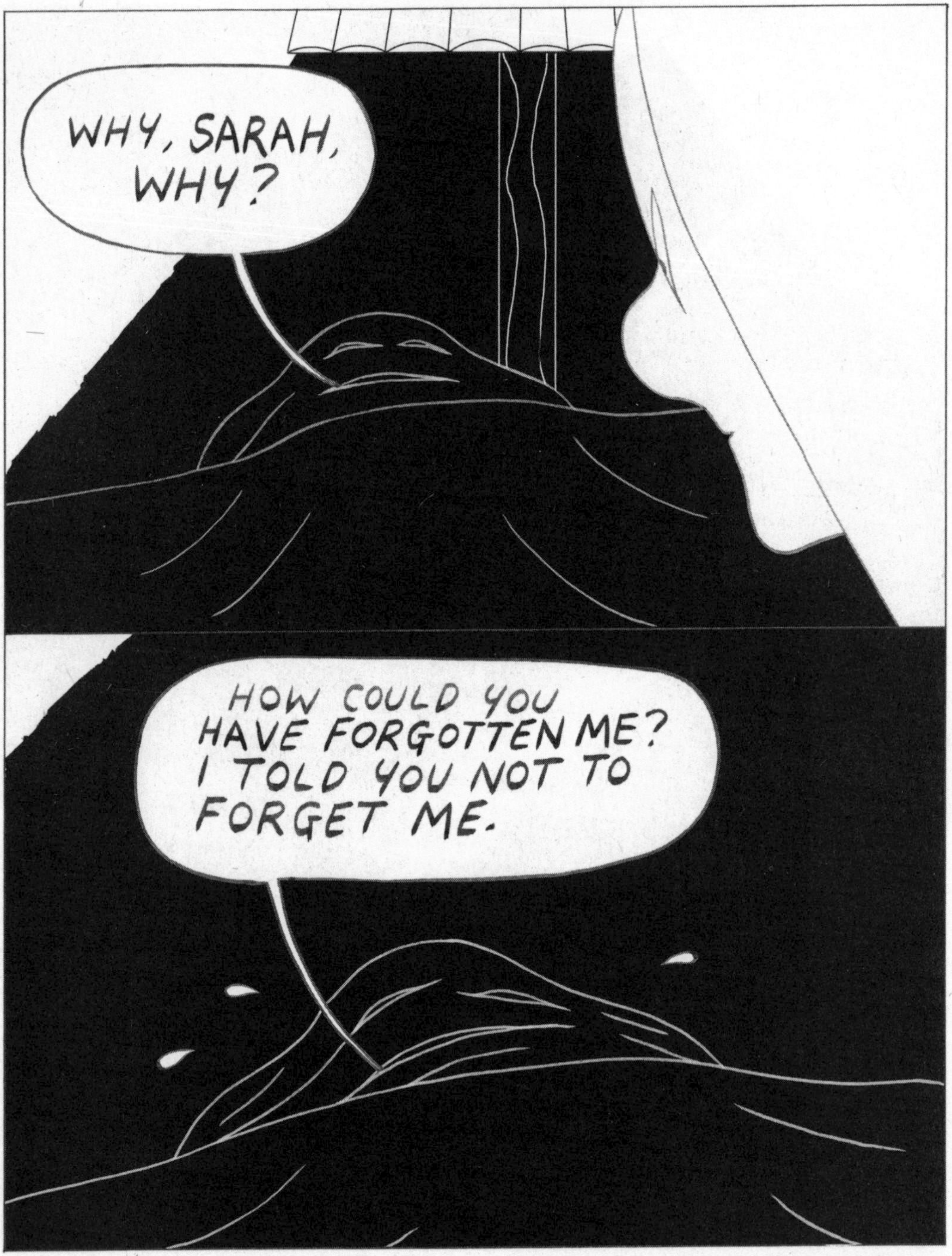
WHY, SARAH, WHY?
HOW COULD YOU HAVE FORGOTTEN ME? I TOLD YOU NOT TO FORGET ME.

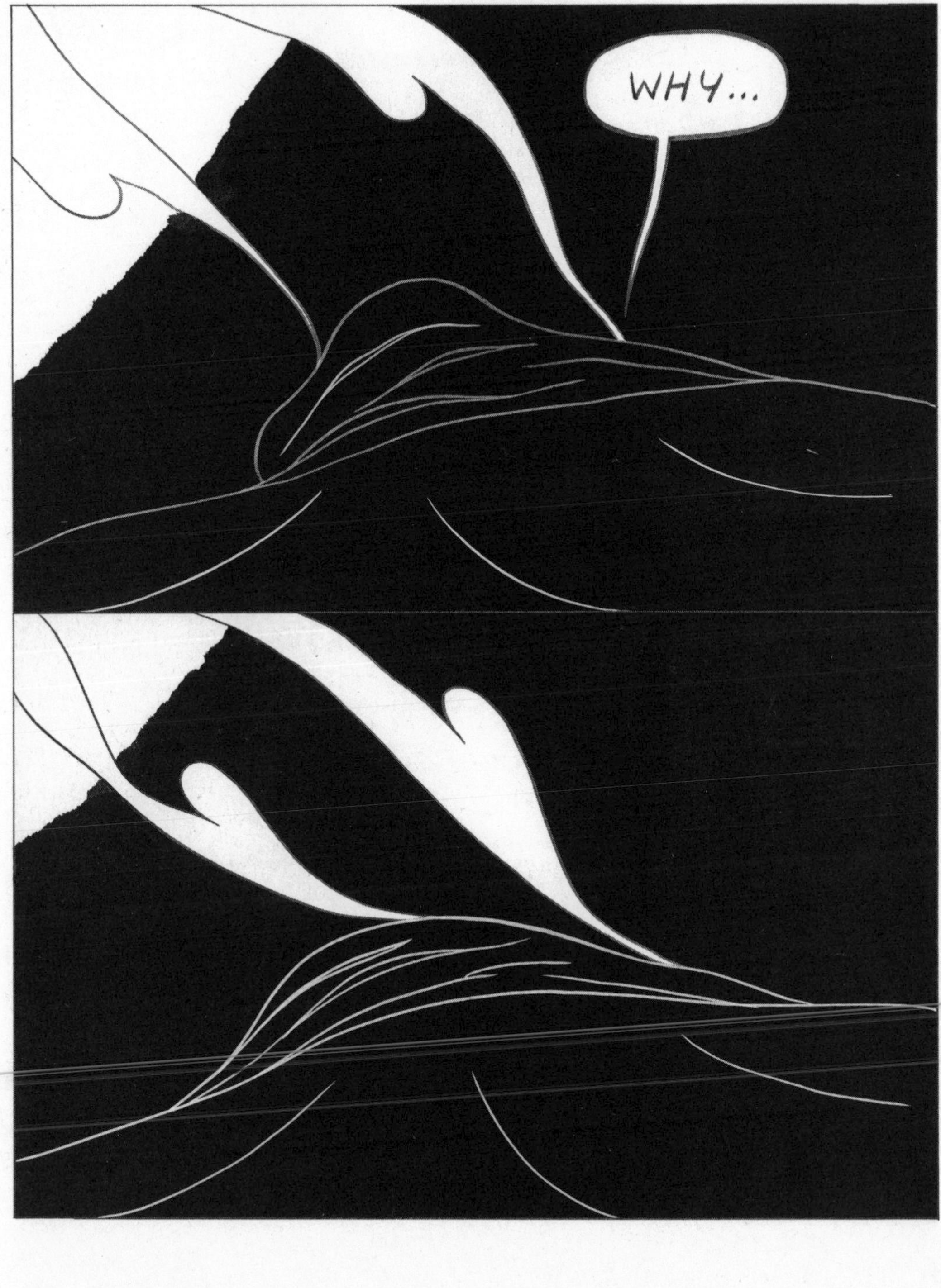
WHY...

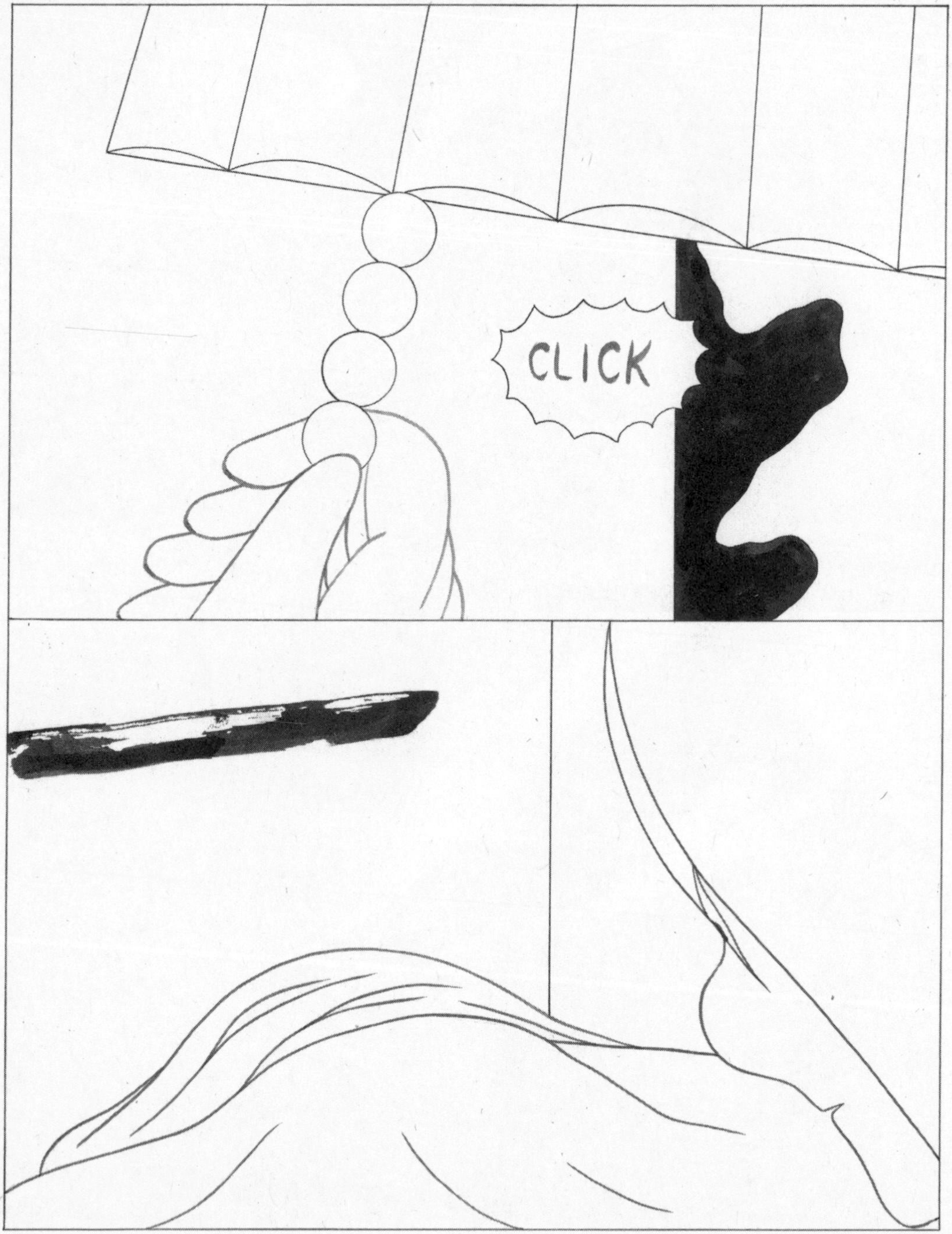
CLICK

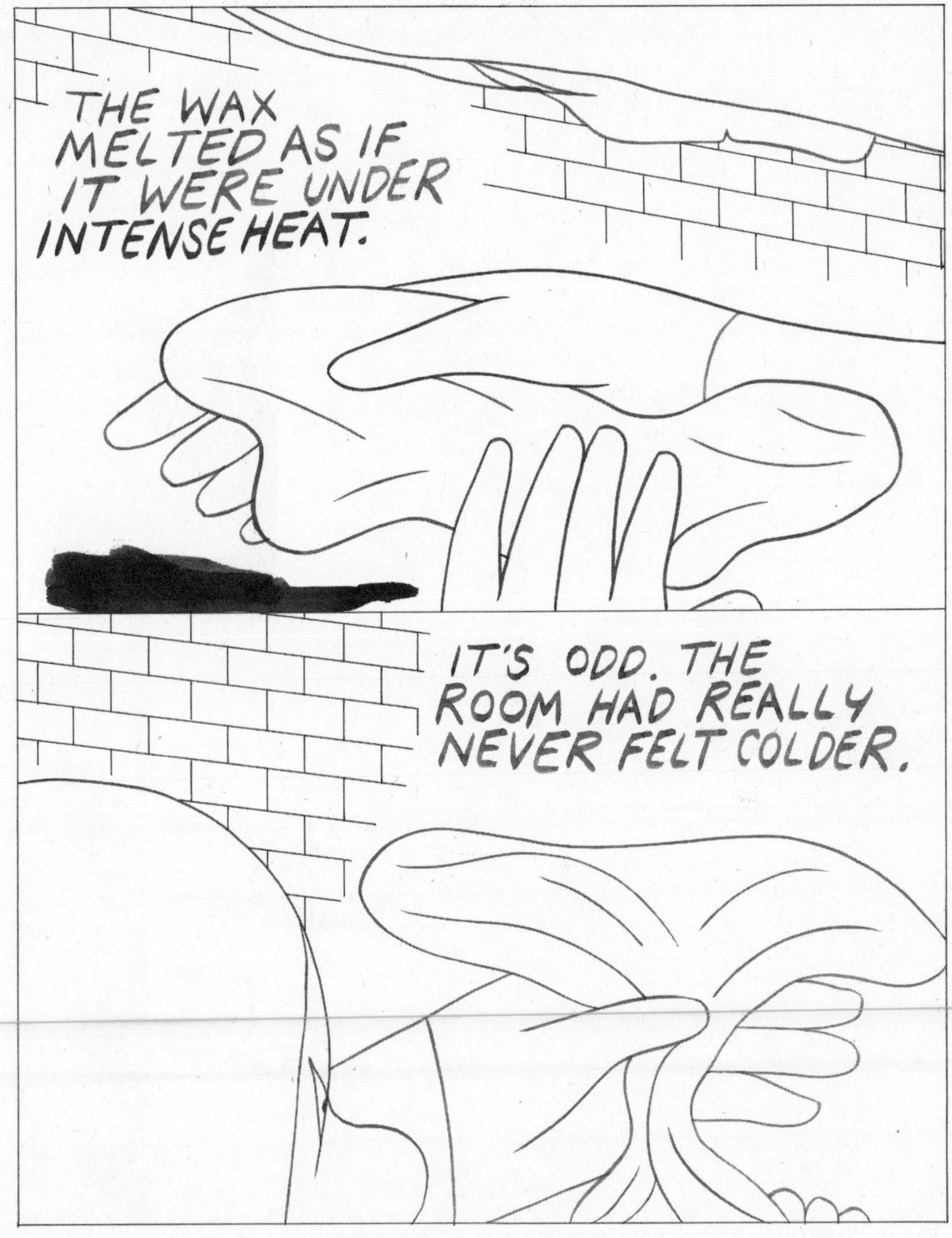
THE WAX MELTED AS IF IT WERE UNDER INTENSE HEAT.
IT'S ODD. THE ROOM HAD REALLY NEVER FELT COLDER.

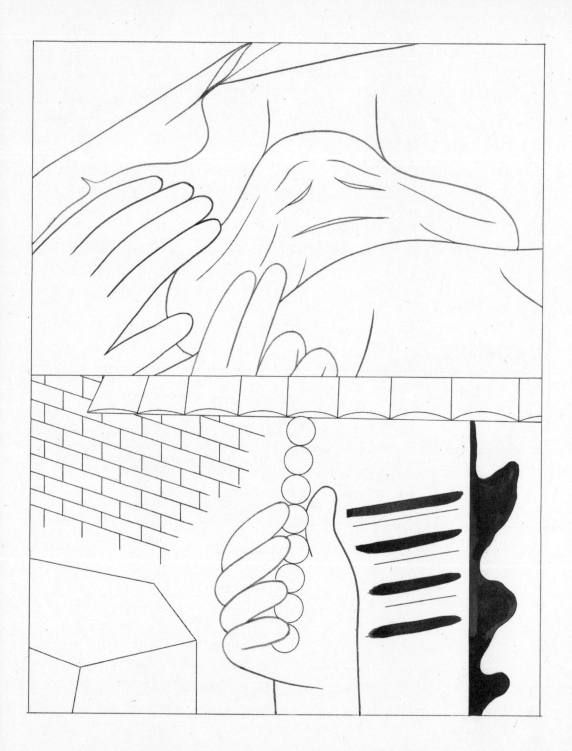

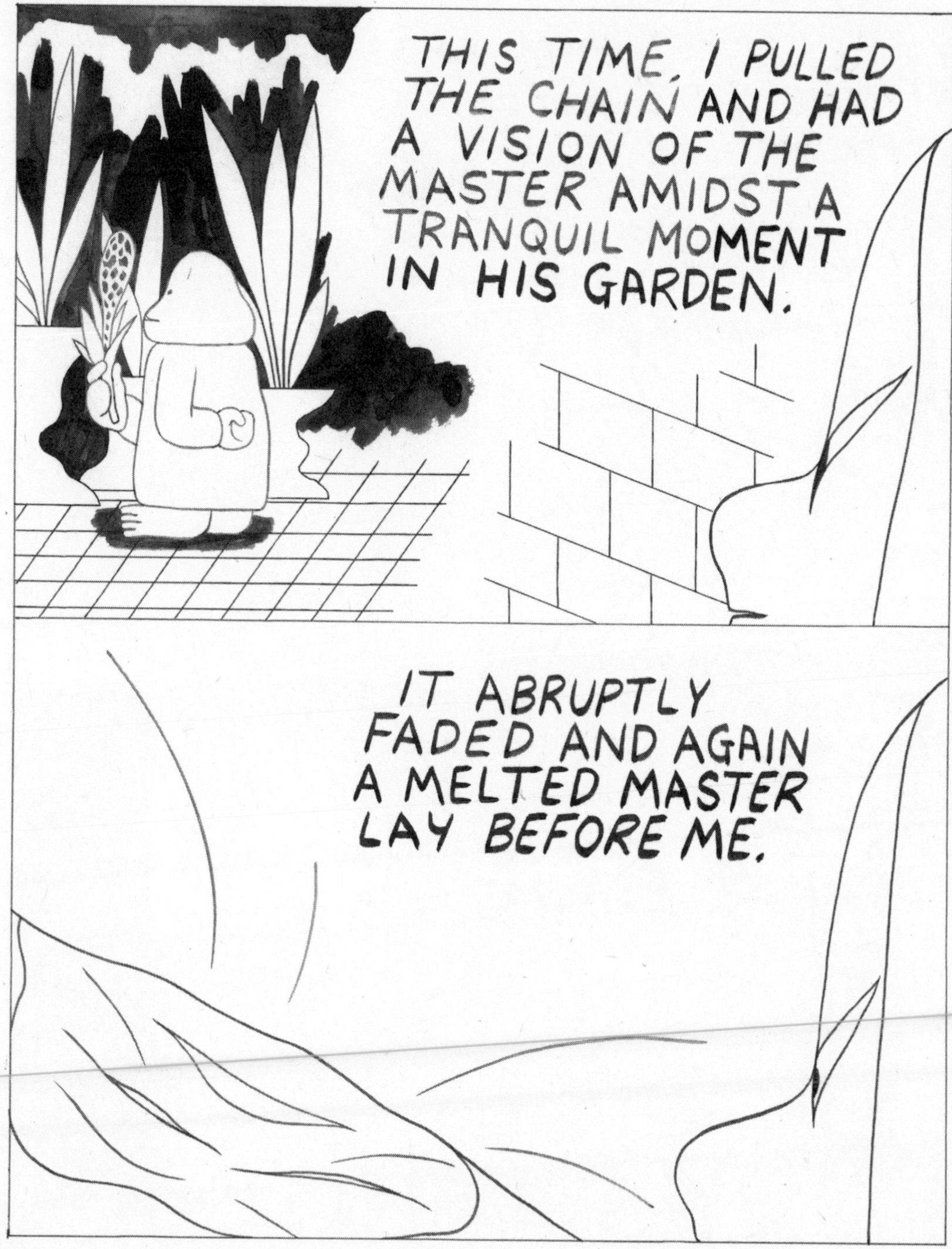
THIS TIME, I PULLED THE CHAIN AND HAD A VISION OF THE MASTER AMIDST A TRANQUIL MOMENT IN HIS GARDEN.
IT ABRUPTLY FADED AND AGAIN A MELTED MASTER LAY BEFORE ME.

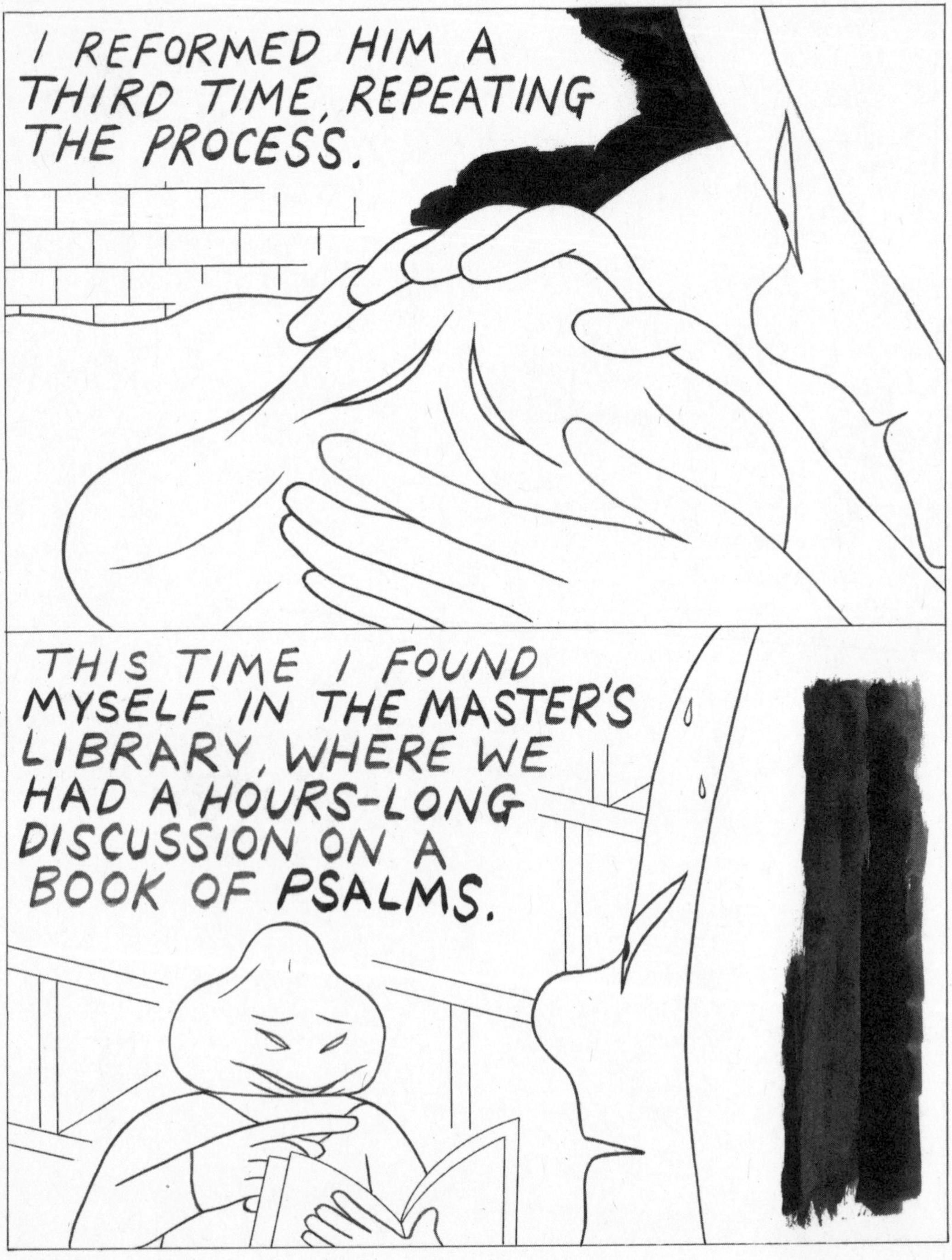
I REFORMED HIM A THIRD TIME, REPEATING THE PROCESS.
THIS TIME I FOUND MYSELF IN THE MASTER'S LIBRARY, WHERE WE HAD A HOURS-LONG DISCUSSION ON A BOOK OF PSALMS.

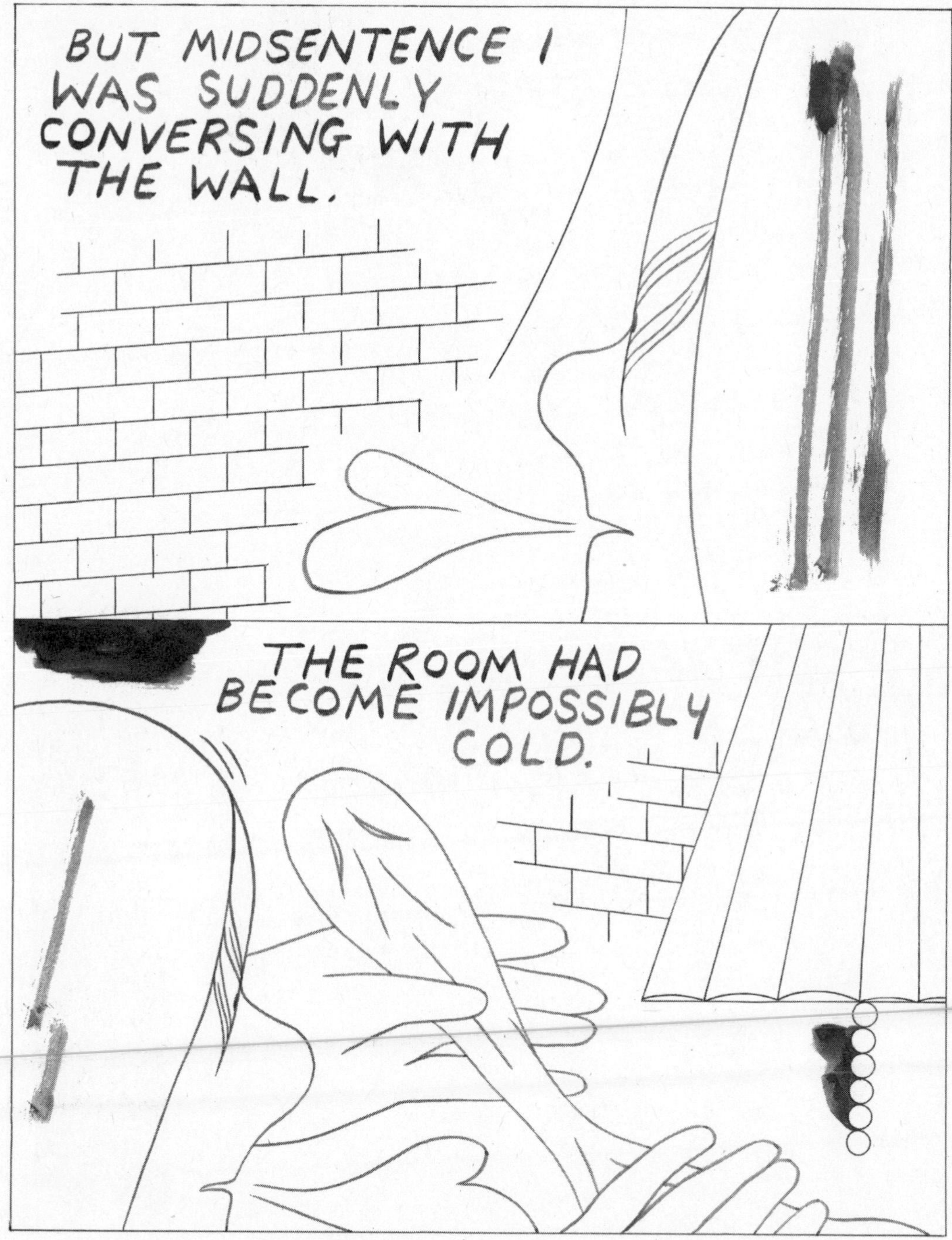
BUT MIDSENTENCE I WAS SUDDENLY CONVERSING WITH THE WALL.
THE ROOM HAD BECOME IMPOSSIBLY COLD.

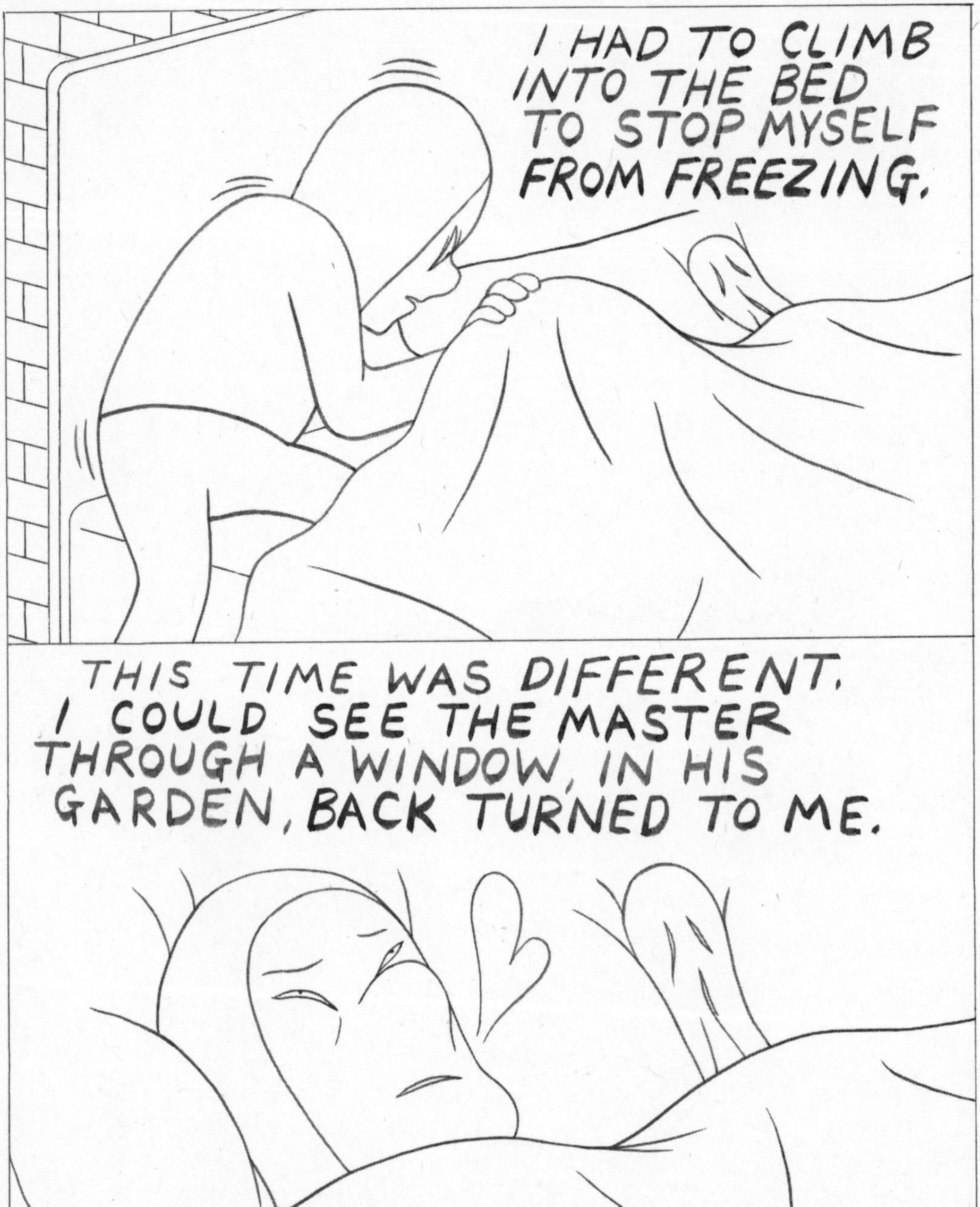
I HAD TO CLIMB INTO THE BED TO STOP MYSELF FROM FREEZING.
THIS TIME WAS DIFFERENT. I COULD SEE THE MASTER THROUGH A WINDOW, IN HIS GARDEN, BACK TURNED TO ME.

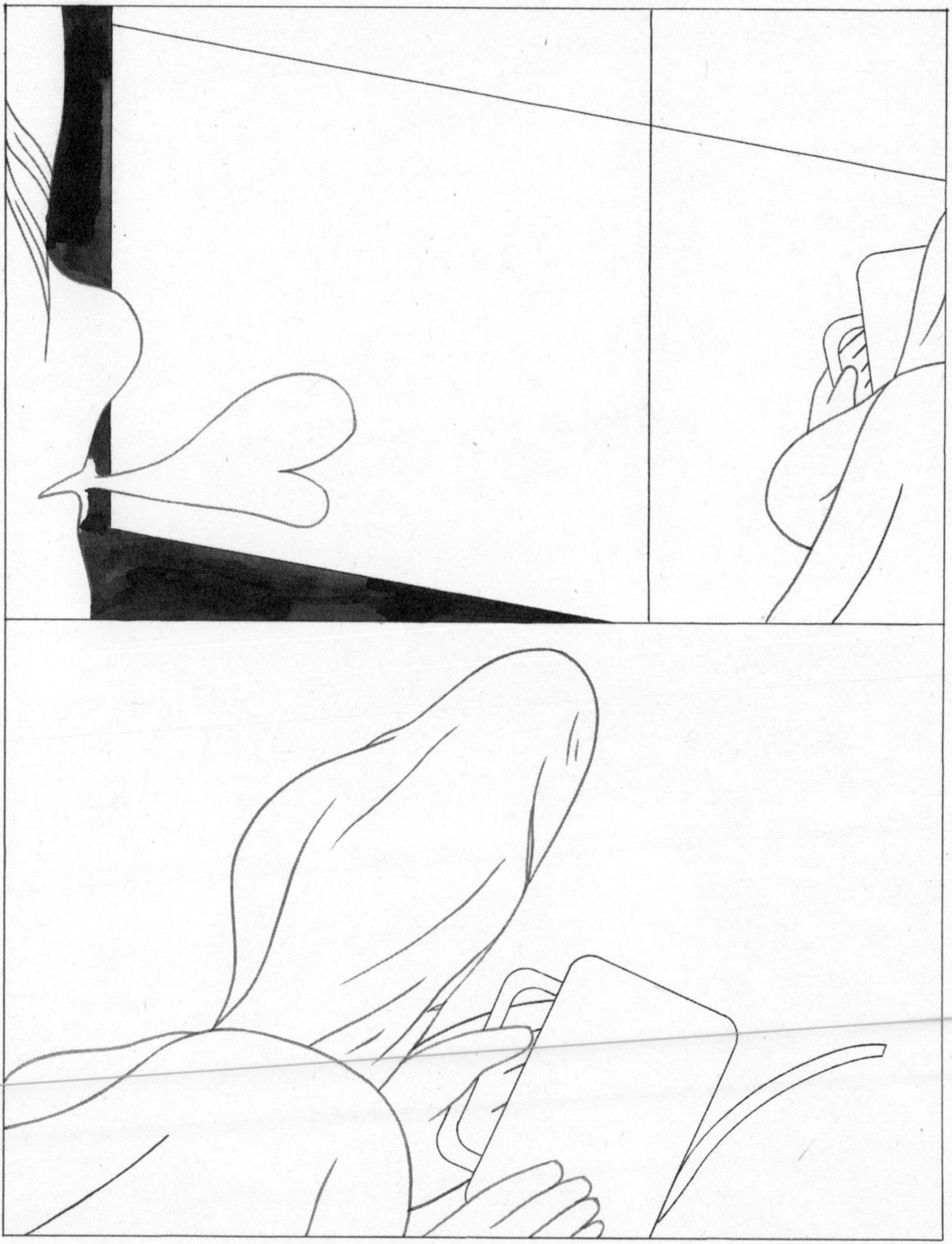

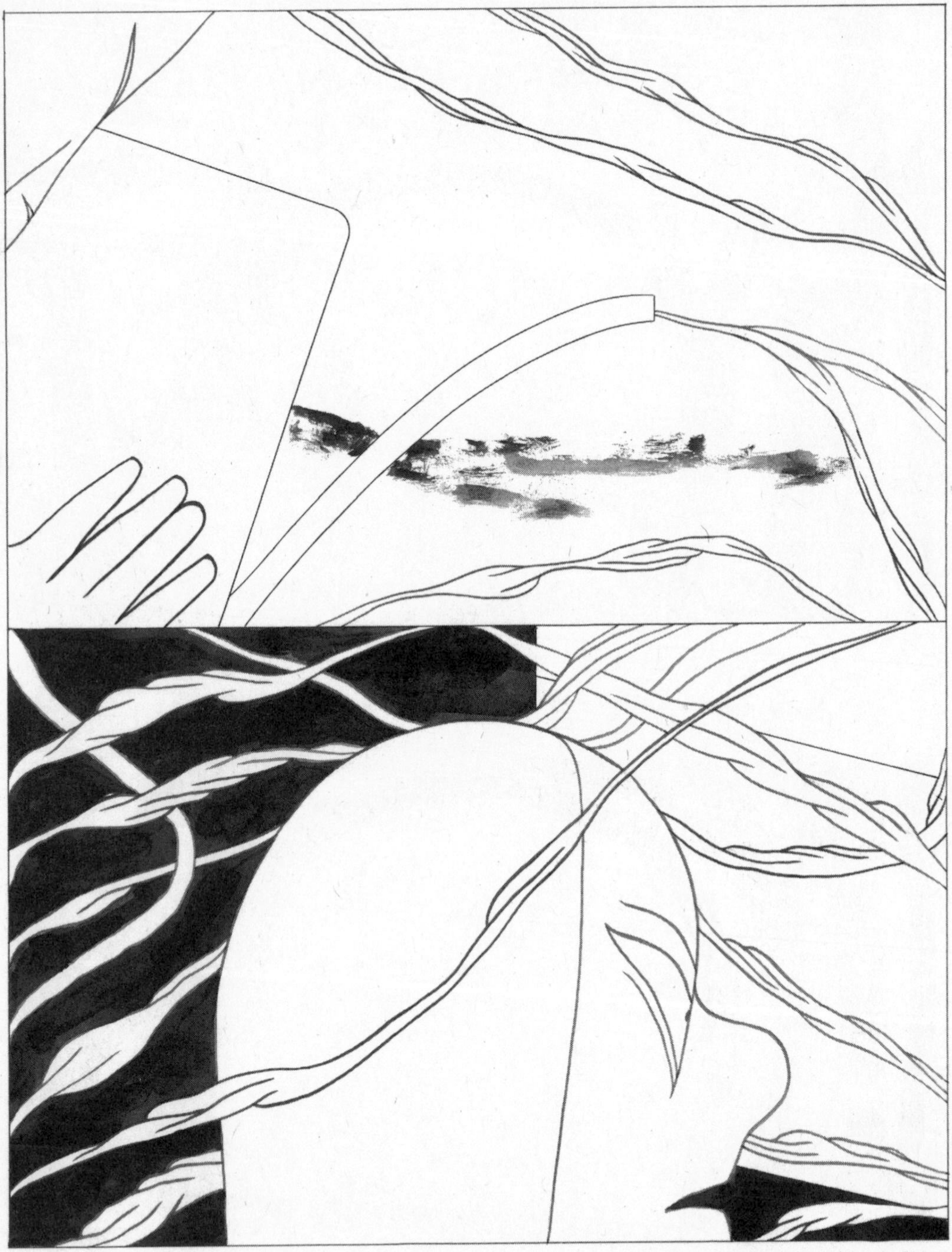

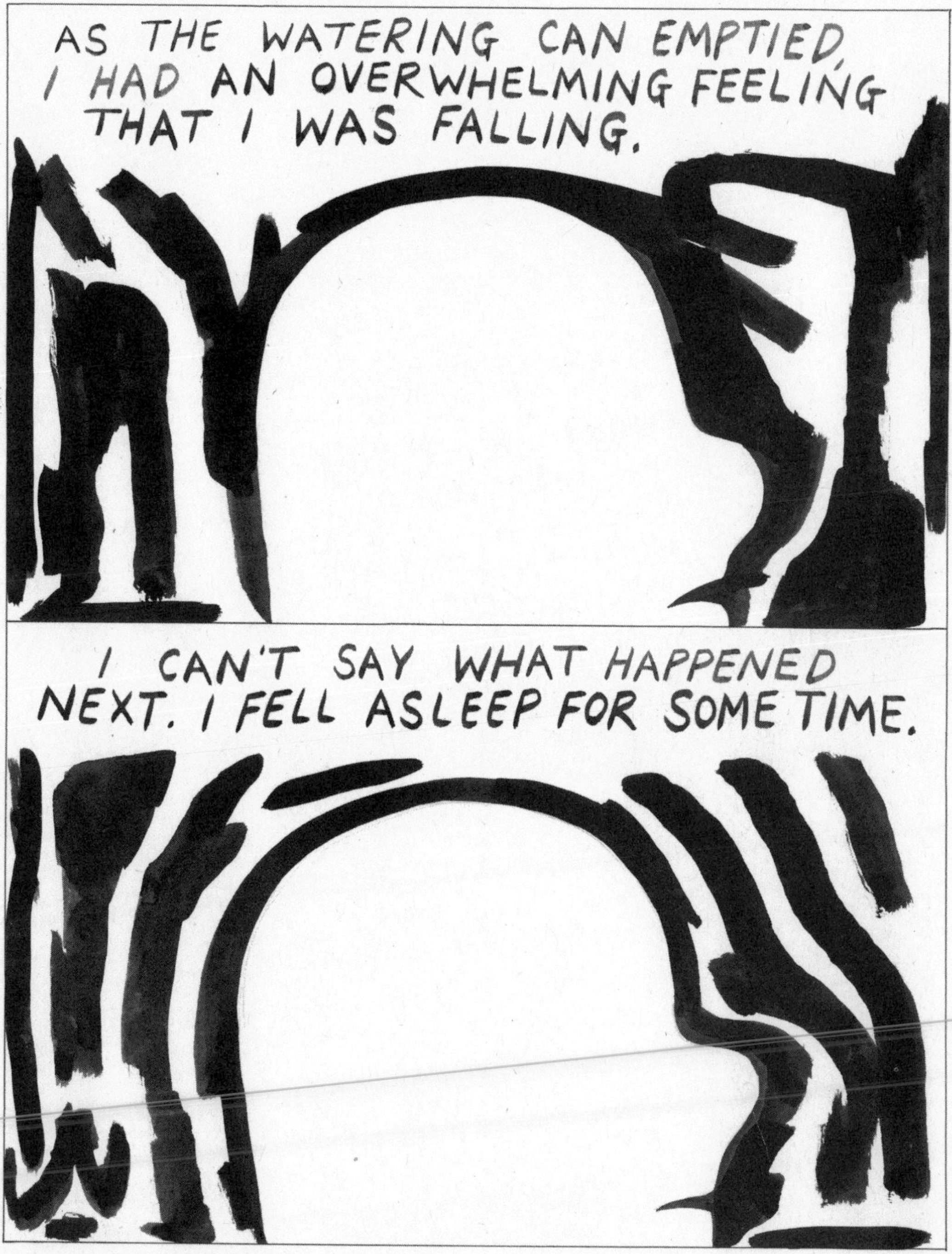
AS THE WATERING CAN EMPTIED, I HAD AN OVERWHELMING FEELING THAT I WAS FALLING.
I CAN'T SAY WHAT HAPPENED NEXT. I FELL ASLEEP FOR SOME TIME.

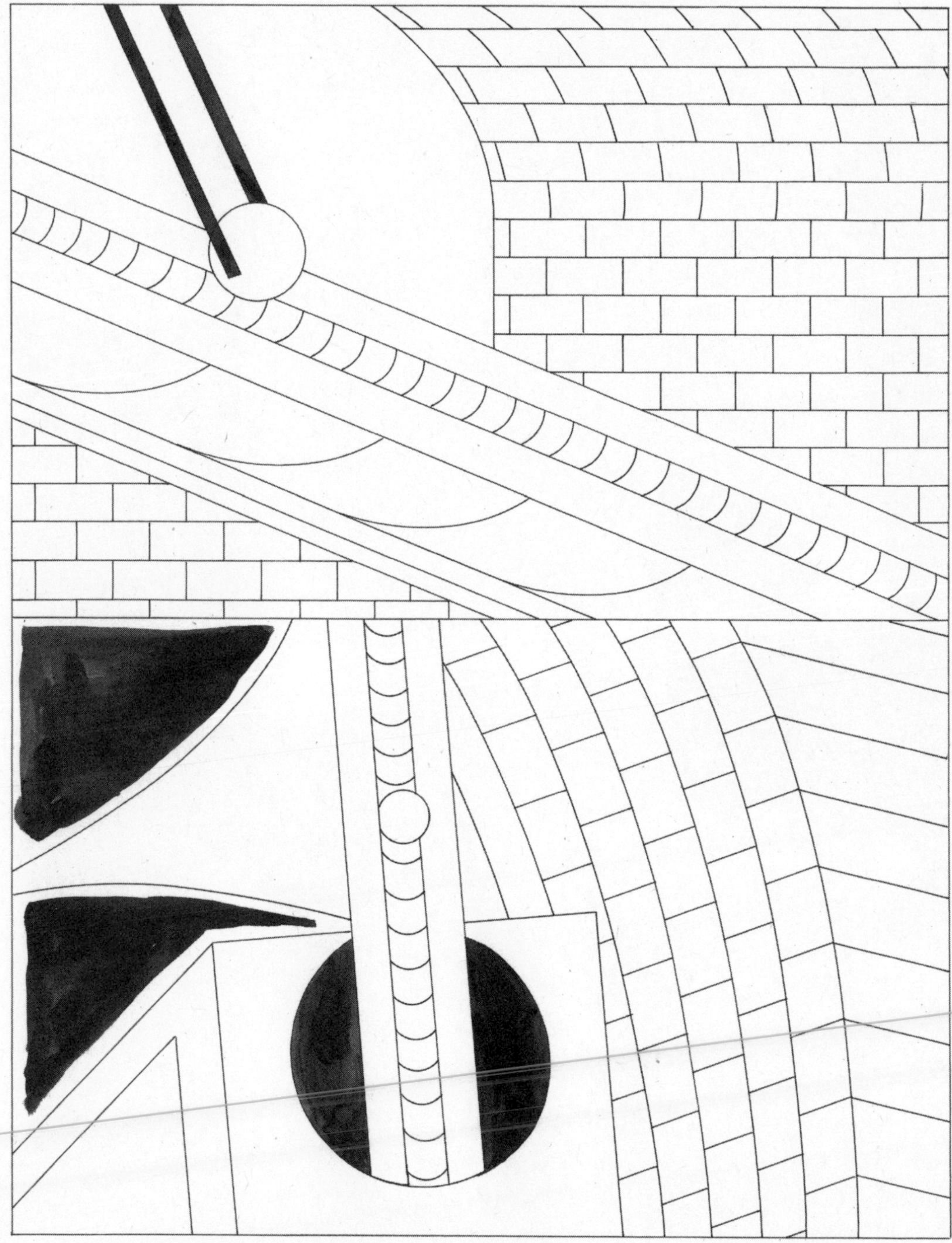

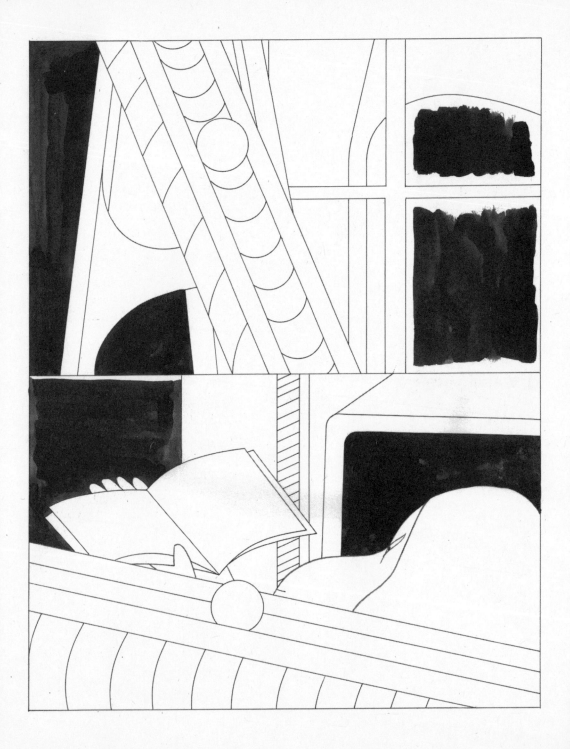

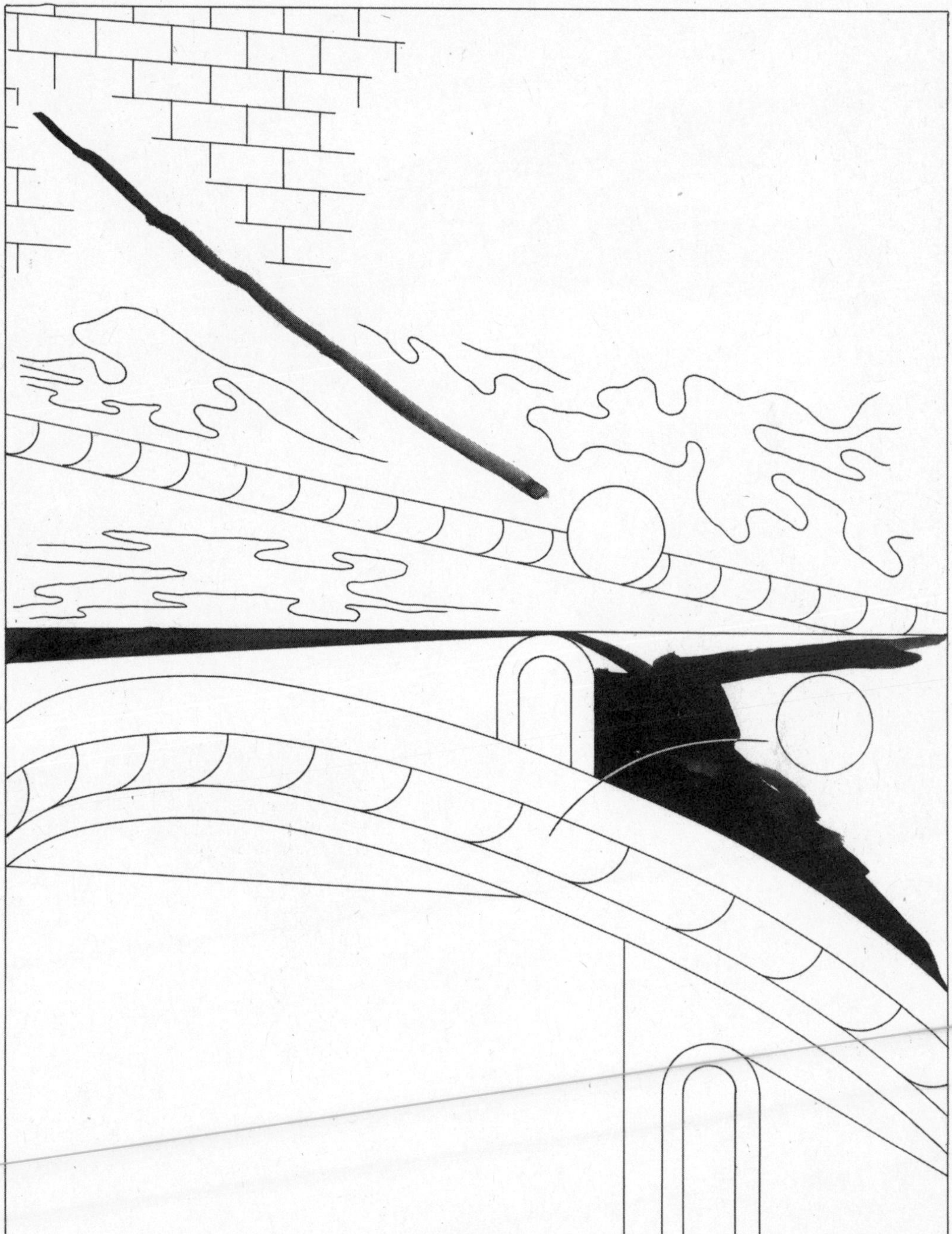

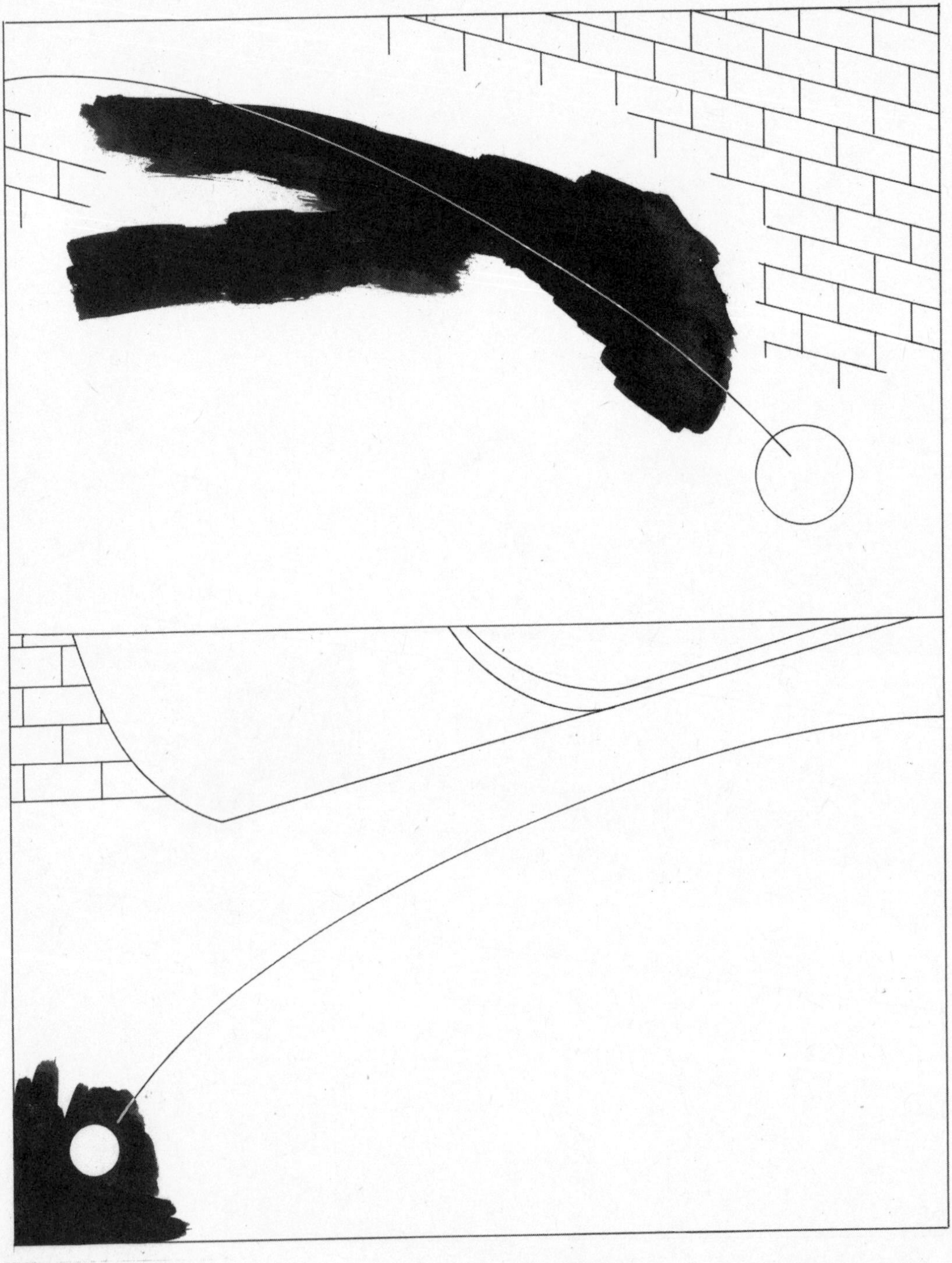

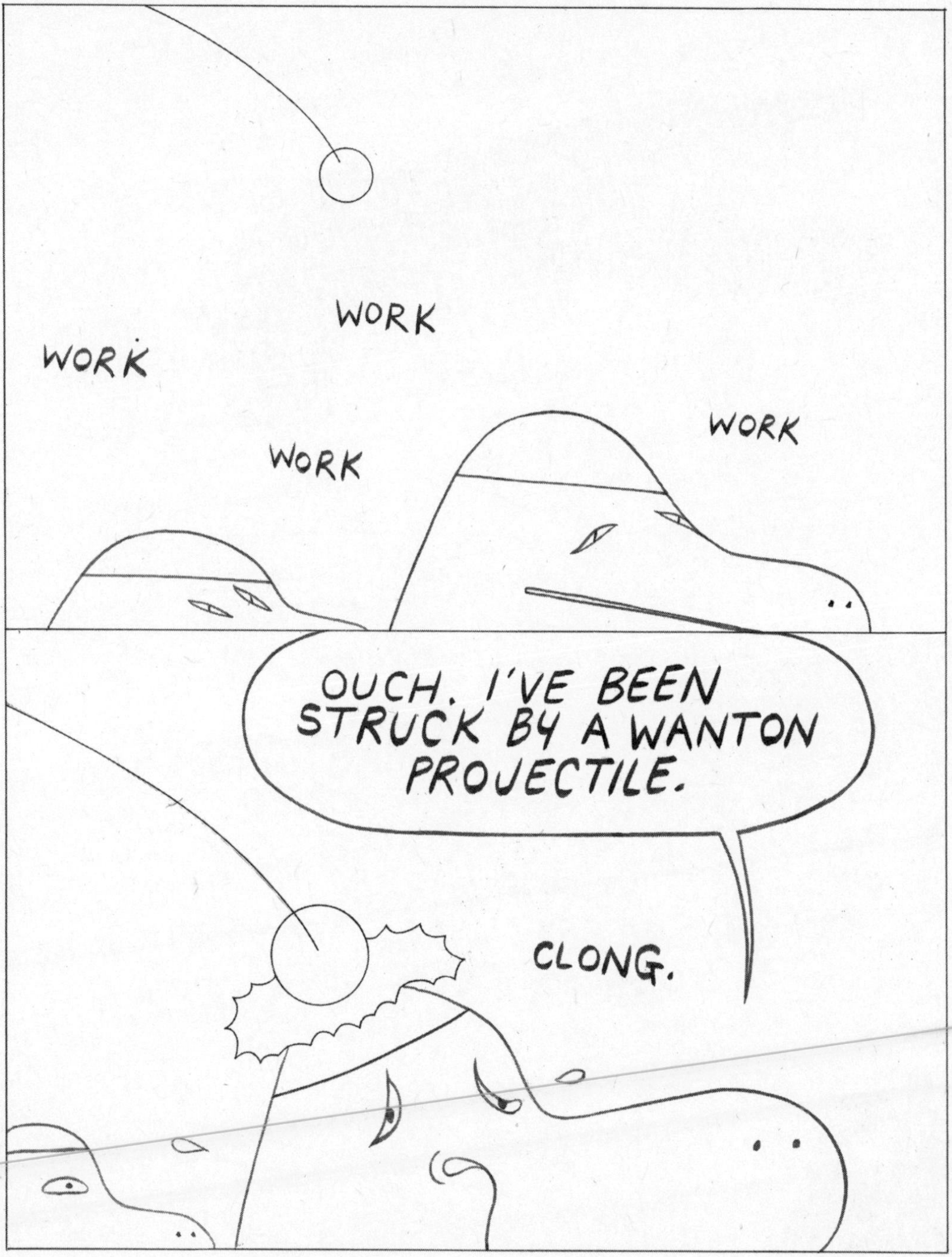
WORK
WORK
WORK
WORK
OUCH. I'VE BEEN STRUCK BY A WANTON PROJECTILE.
CLONG.

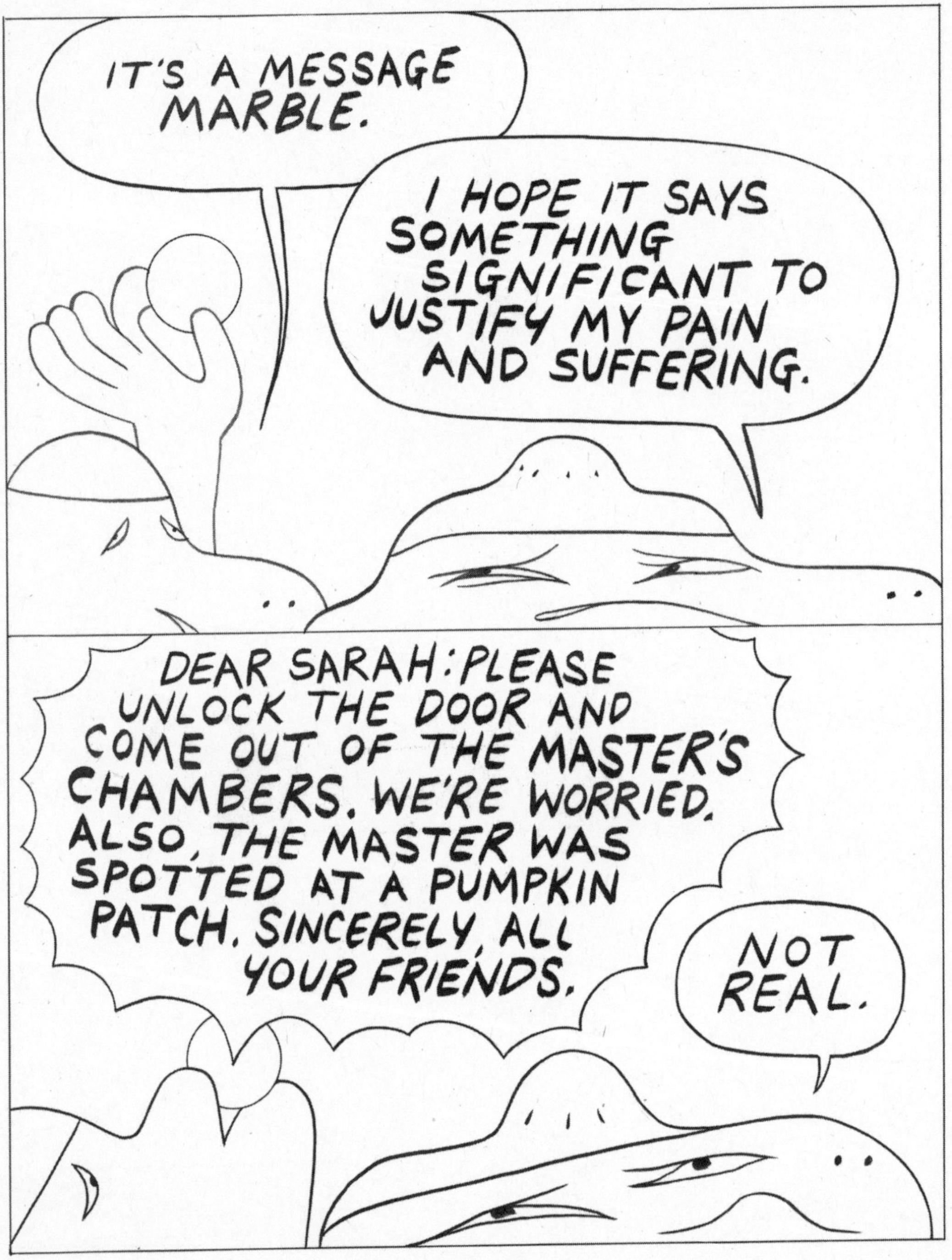
IT'S A MESSAGE MARBLE.
I HOPE IT SAYS SOMETHING SIGNIFICANT TO JUSTIFY MY PAIN AND SUFFERING.
DEAR SARAH: PLEASE UNLOCK THE DOOR AND COME OUT OF THE MASTER'S CHAMBERS. WE'RE WORRIED. ALSO, THE MASTER WAS SPOTTED AT A PUMPKIN PATCH. SINCERELY, ALL YOUR FRIENDS.
NOT REAL.

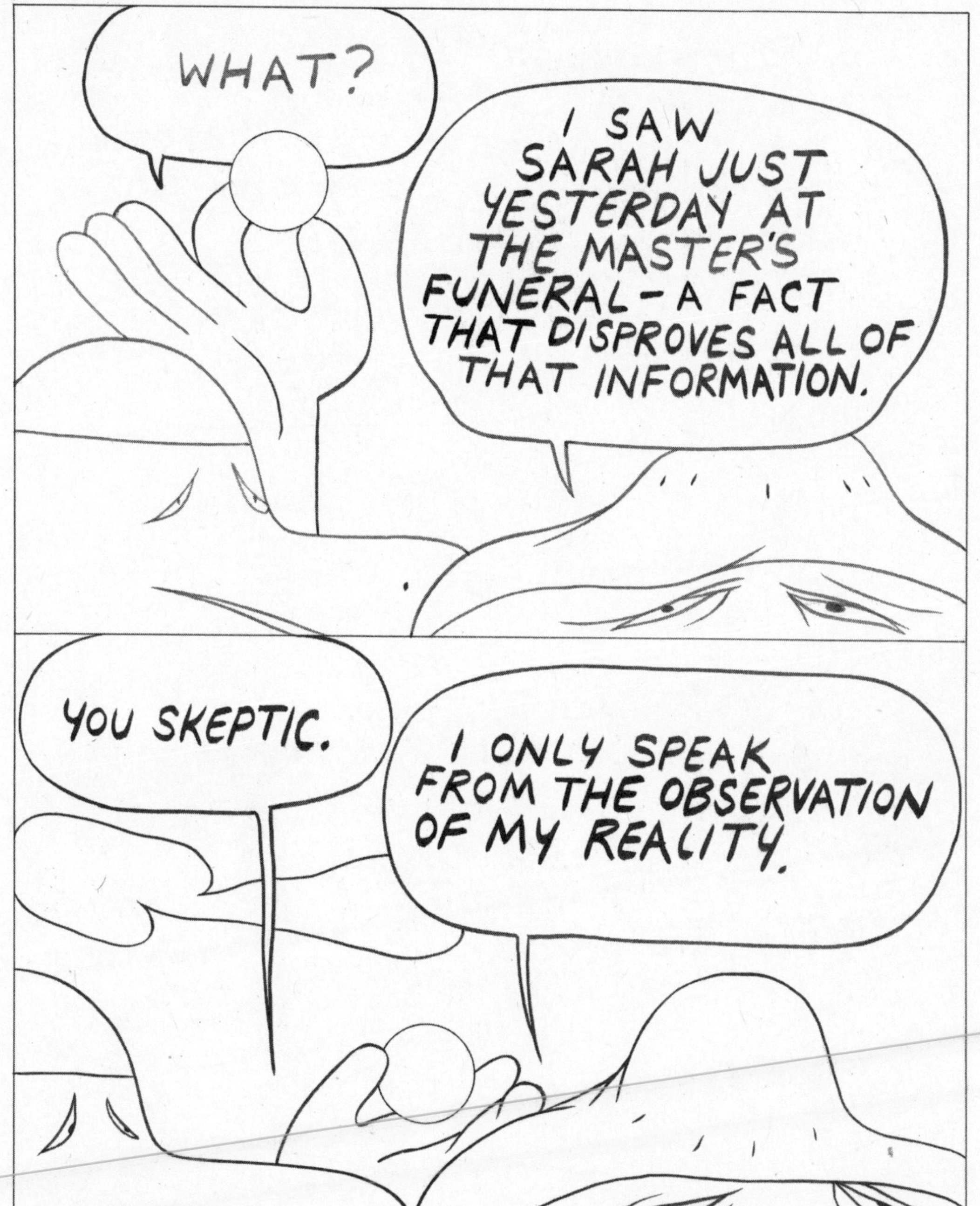
WHAT?
I SAW SARAH JUST YESTERDAY AT THE MASTER'S FUNERAL - A FACT THAT DISPROVES ALL OF THAT INFORMATION.
YOU SKEPTIC.
I ONLY SPEAK FROM THE OBSERVATION OF MY REALITY.

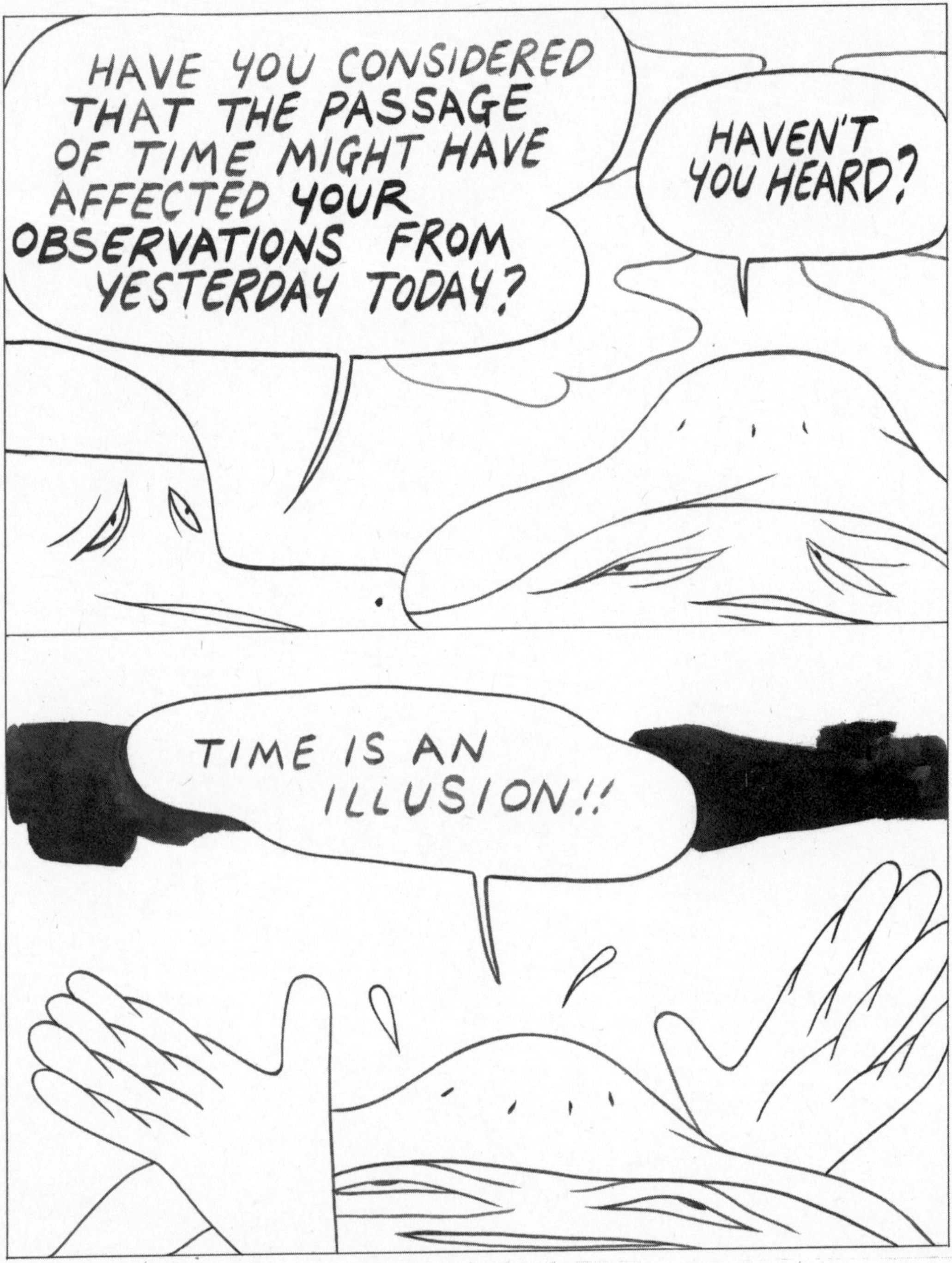
HAVE YOU CONSIDERED THAT THE PASSAGE OF TIME MIGHT HAVE AFFECTED YOUR OBSERVATIONS FROM YESTERDAY TODAY?
HAVEN'T YOU HEARD?
TIME IS AN ILLUSION!!

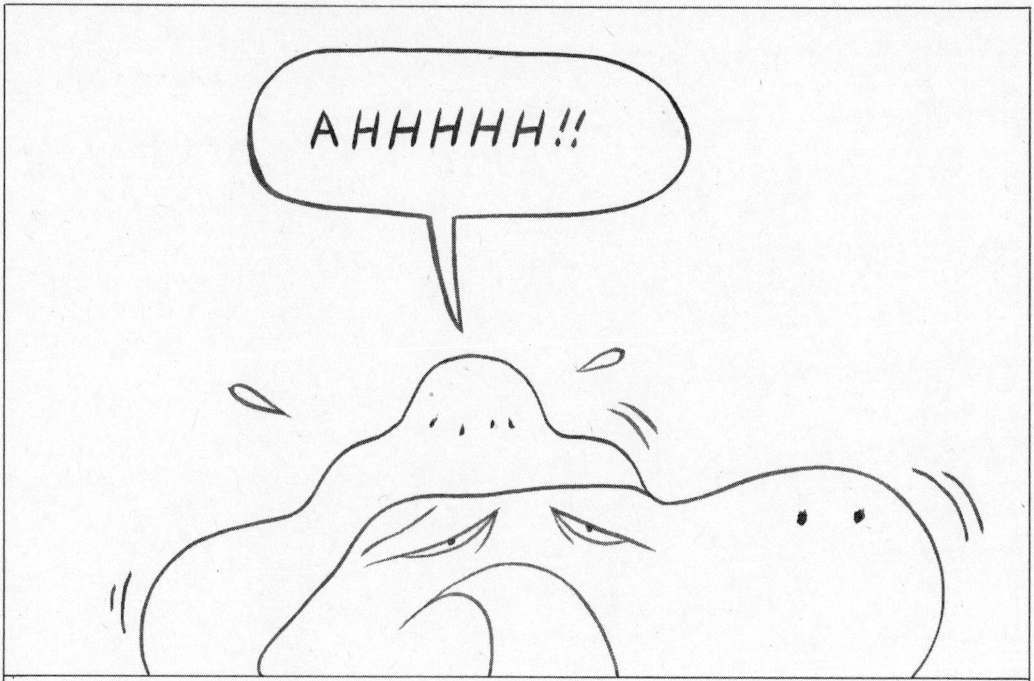
AHHHHH!!

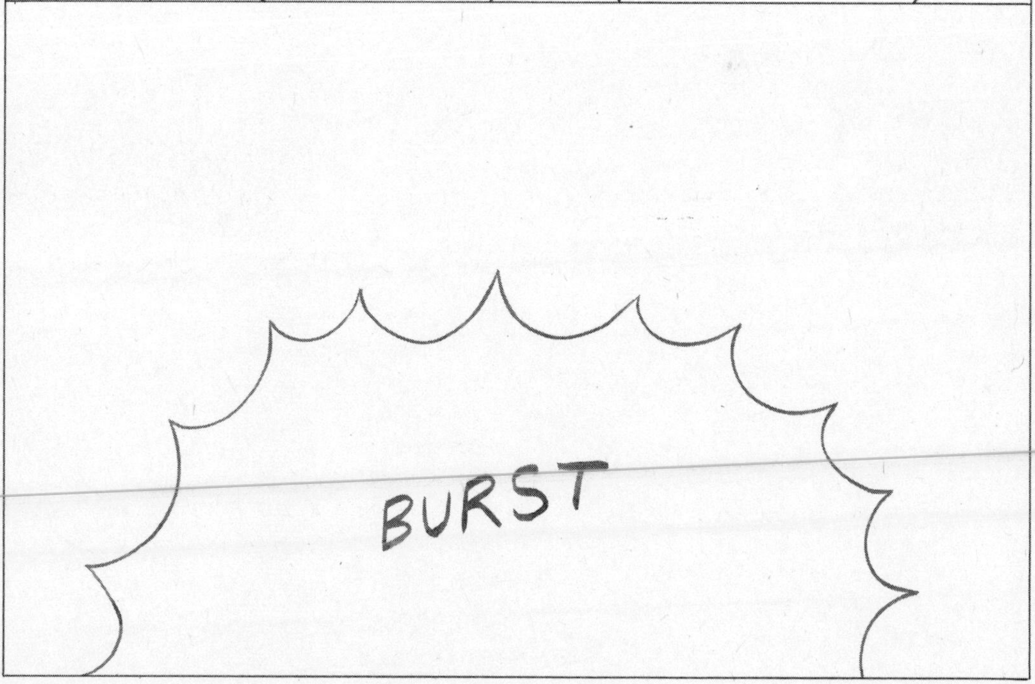
BURST

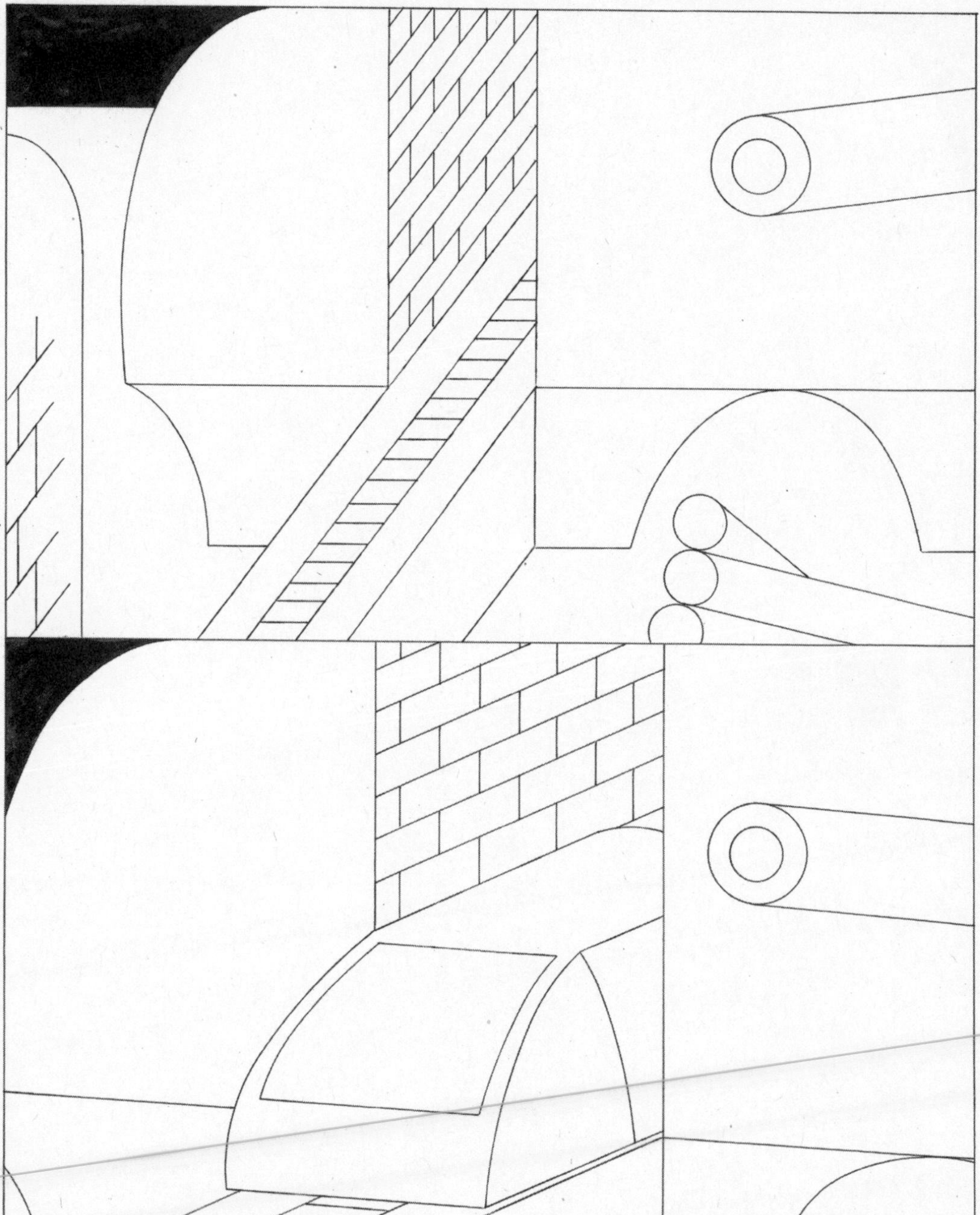

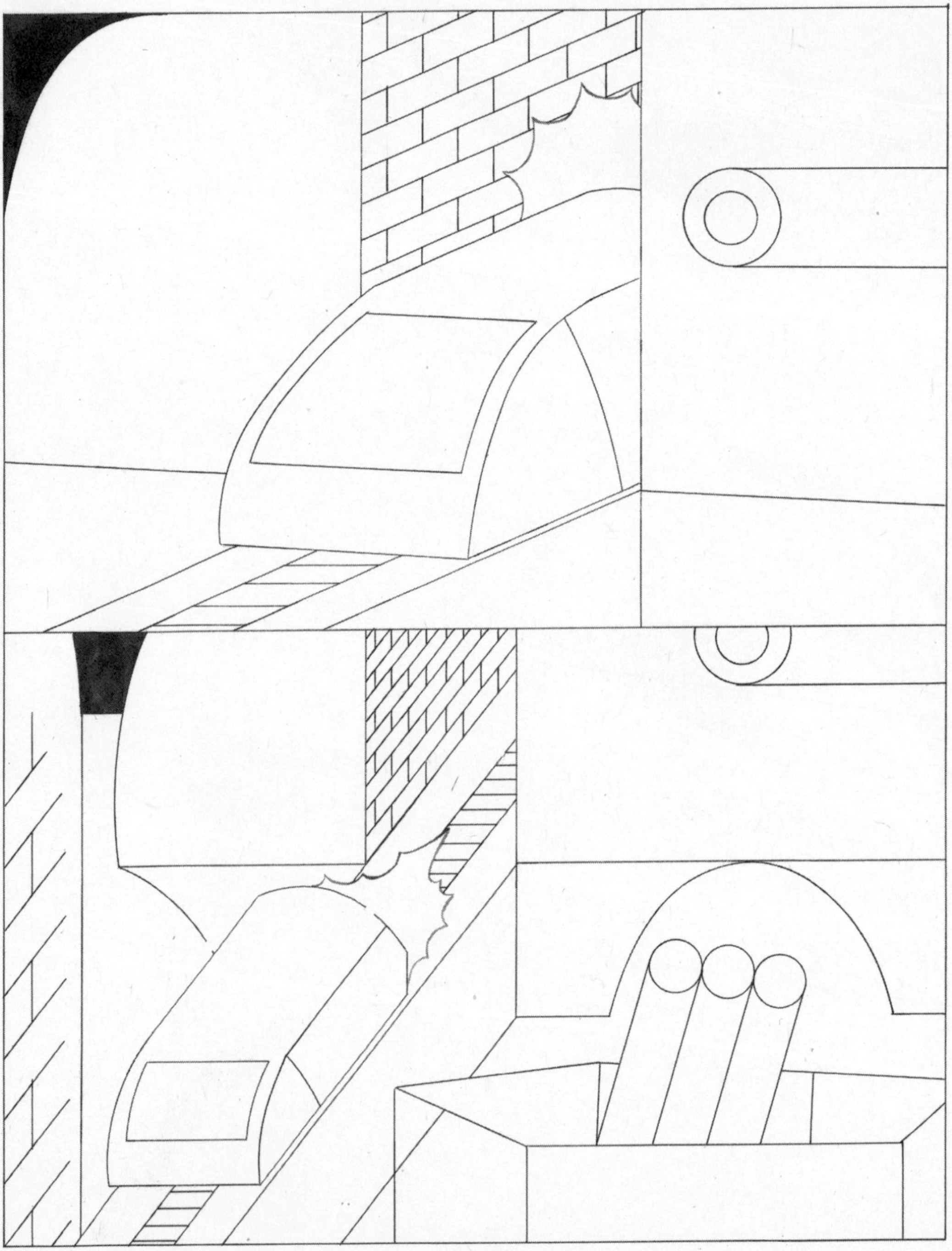

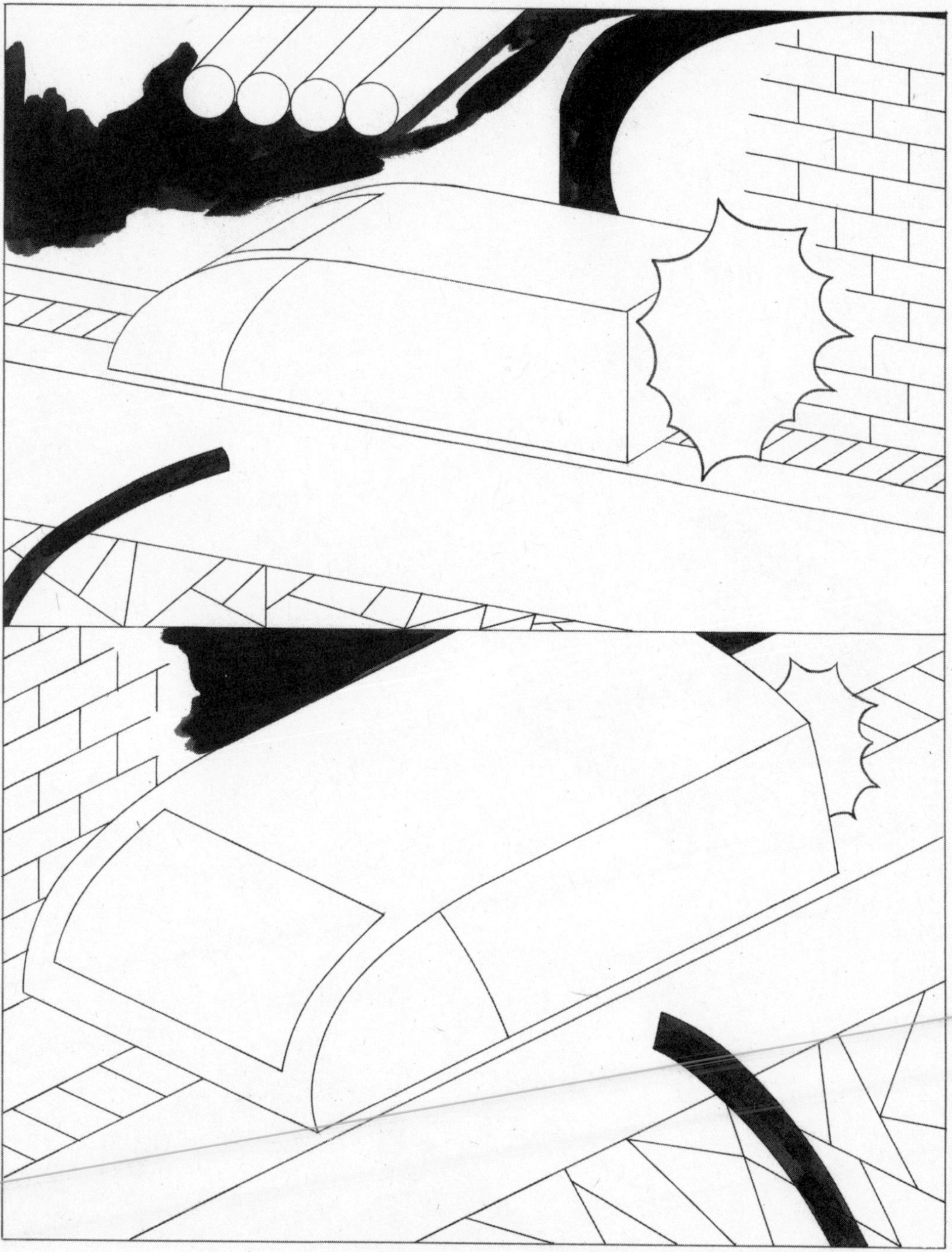

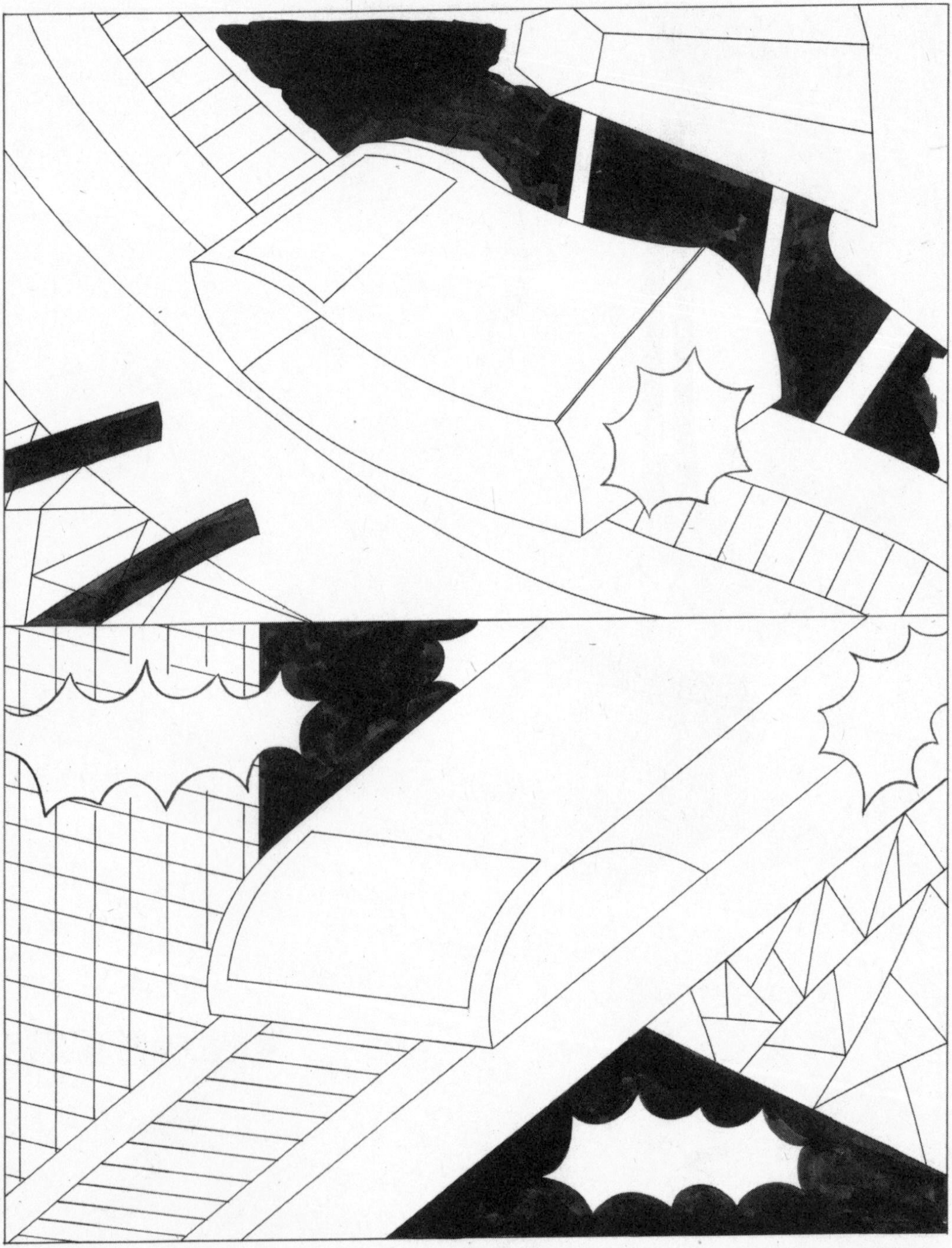

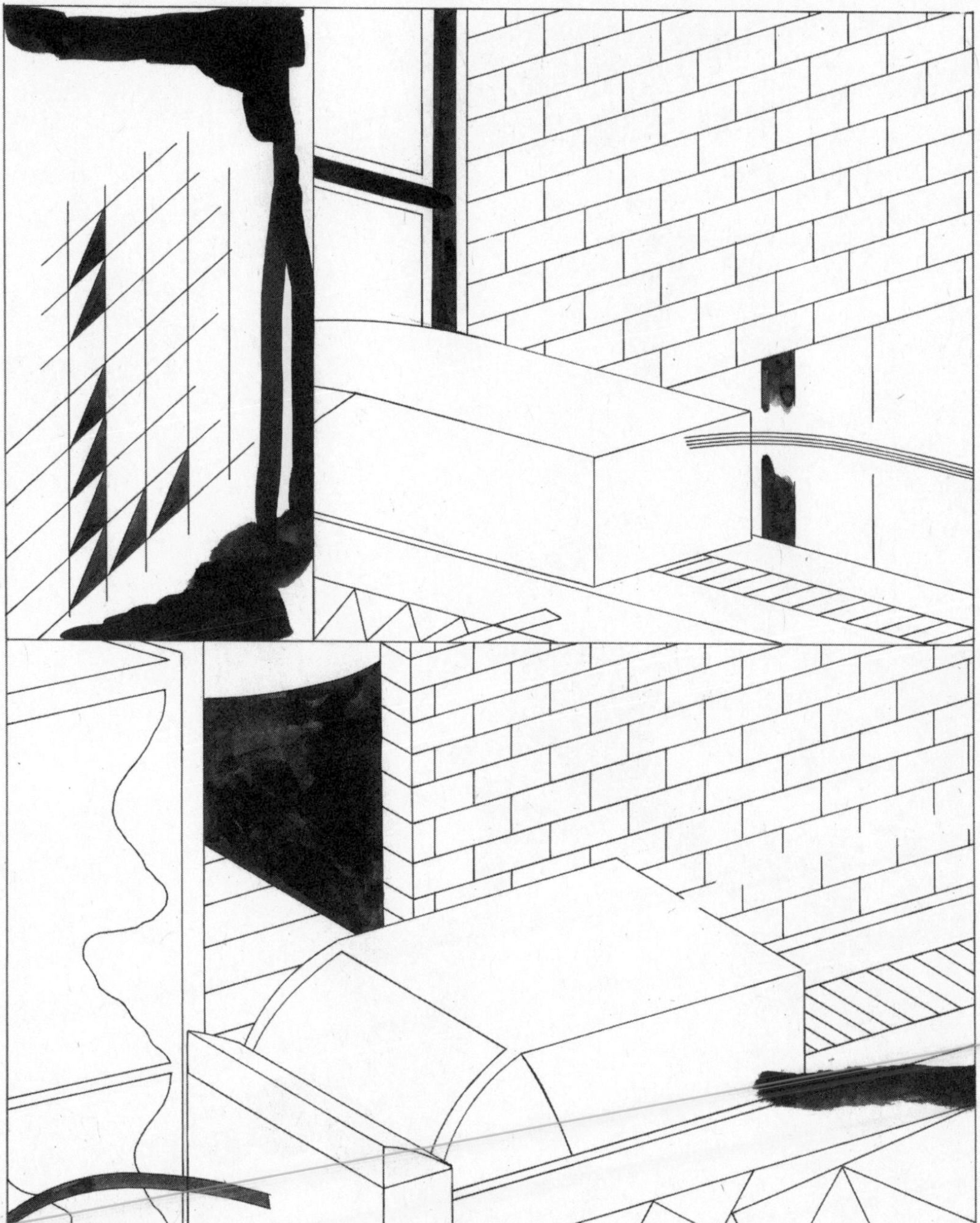

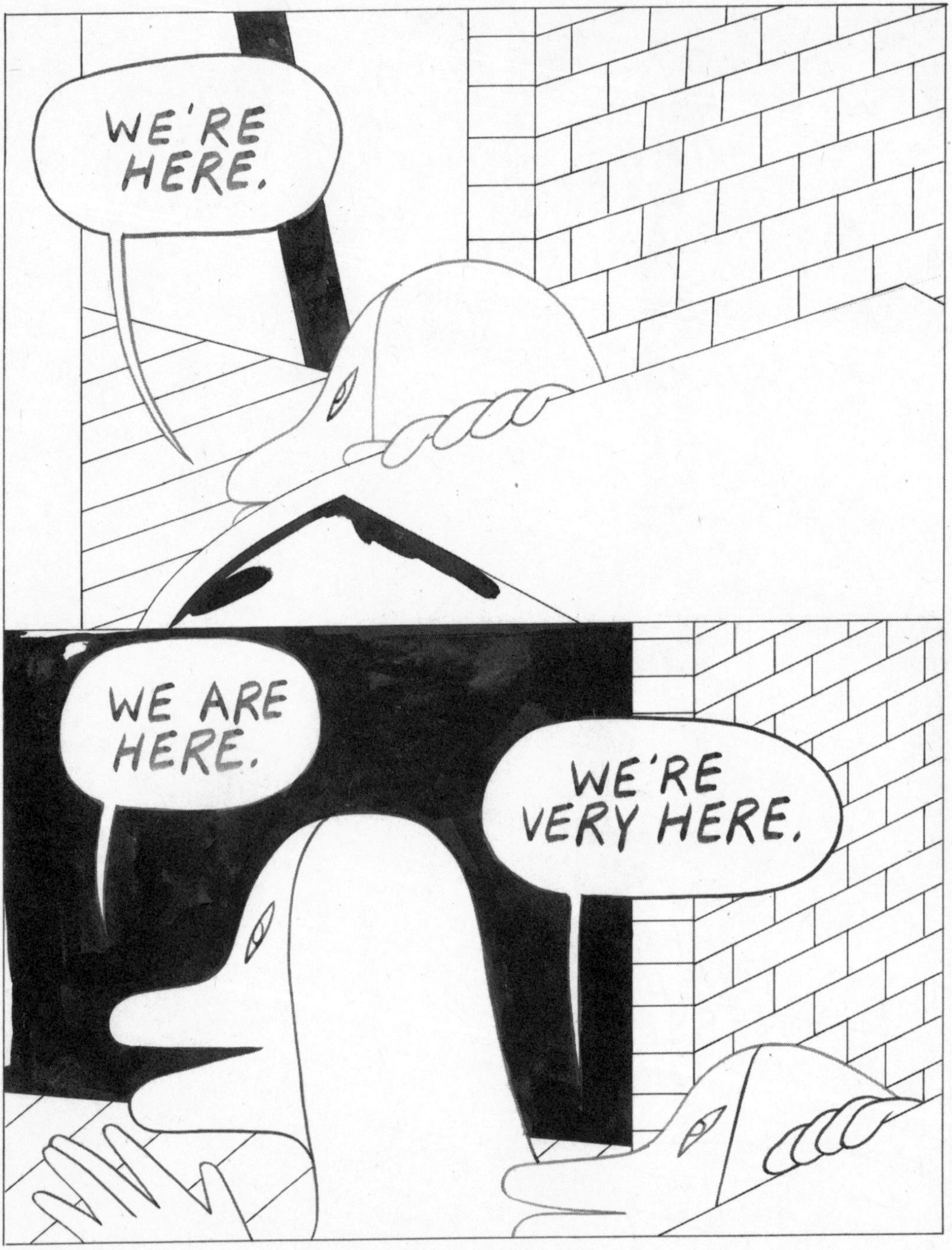
WE'RE HERE.
WE ARE HERE.
WE'RE VERY HERE.

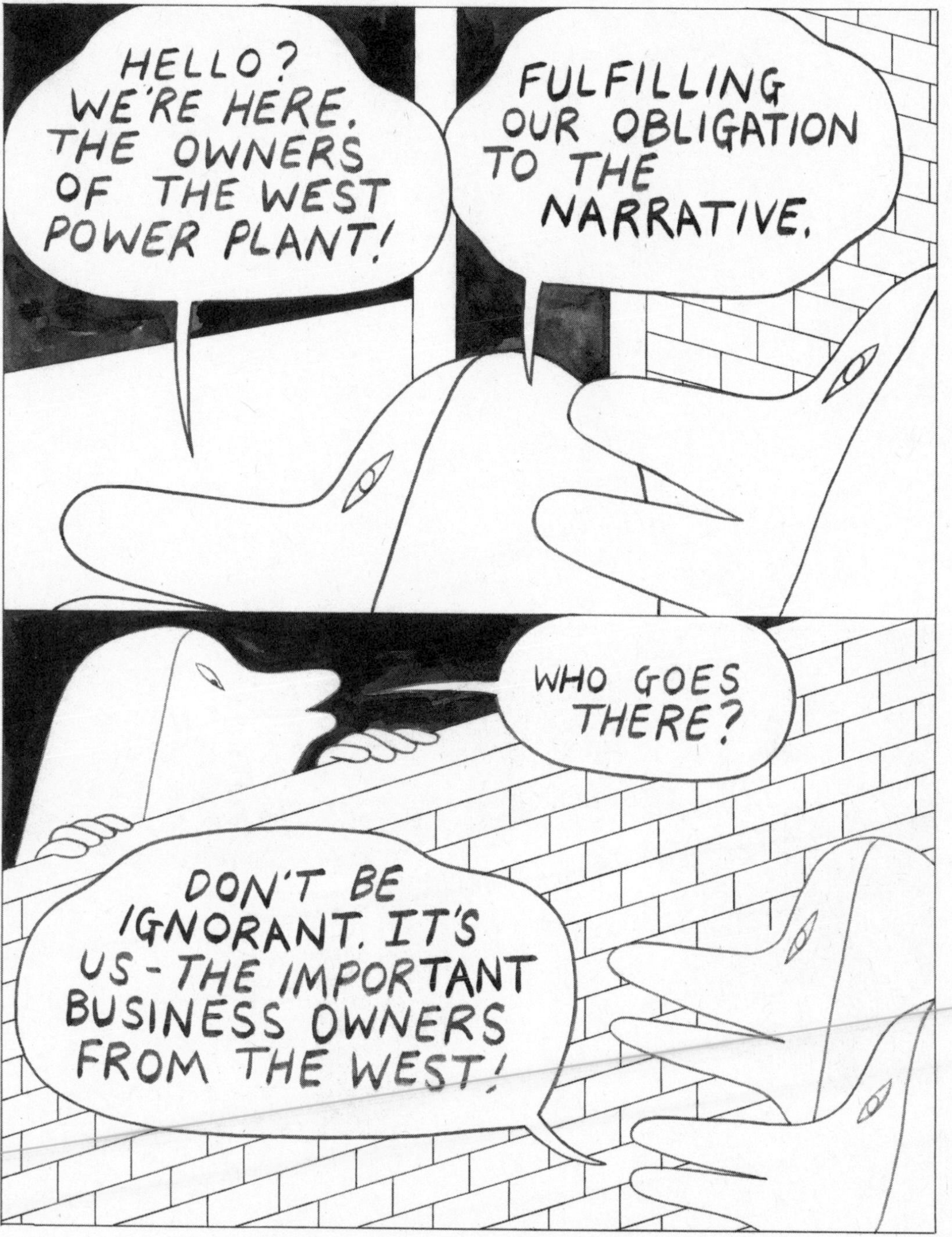
HELLO? WE'RE HERE. THE OWNERS OF THE WEST POWER PLANT!
FULFILLING OUR OBLIGATION TO THE NARRATIVE.
WHO GOES THERE?
DON'T BE IGNORANT. IT'S US - THE IMPORTANT BUSINESS OWNERS FROM THE WEST!

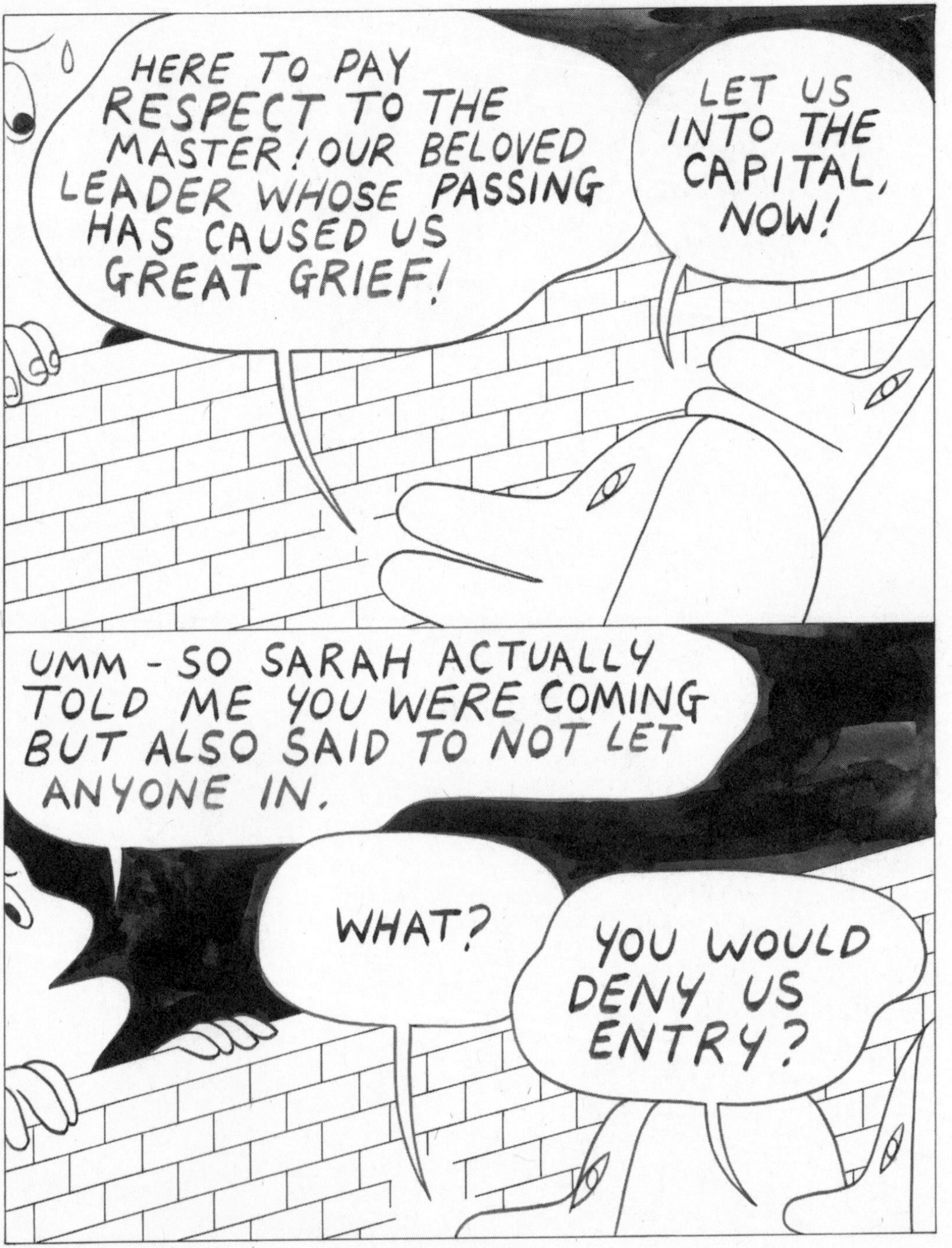
HERE TO PAY RESPECT TO THE MASTER! OUR BELOVED LEADER WHOSE PASSING HAS CAUSED US GREAT GRIEF!
LET US INTO THE CAPITAL, NOW!
UMM - SO SARAH ACTUALLY TOLD ME YOU WERE COMING BUT ALSO SAID TO NOT LET ANYONE IN.
WHAT?
YOU WOULD DENY US ENTRY?

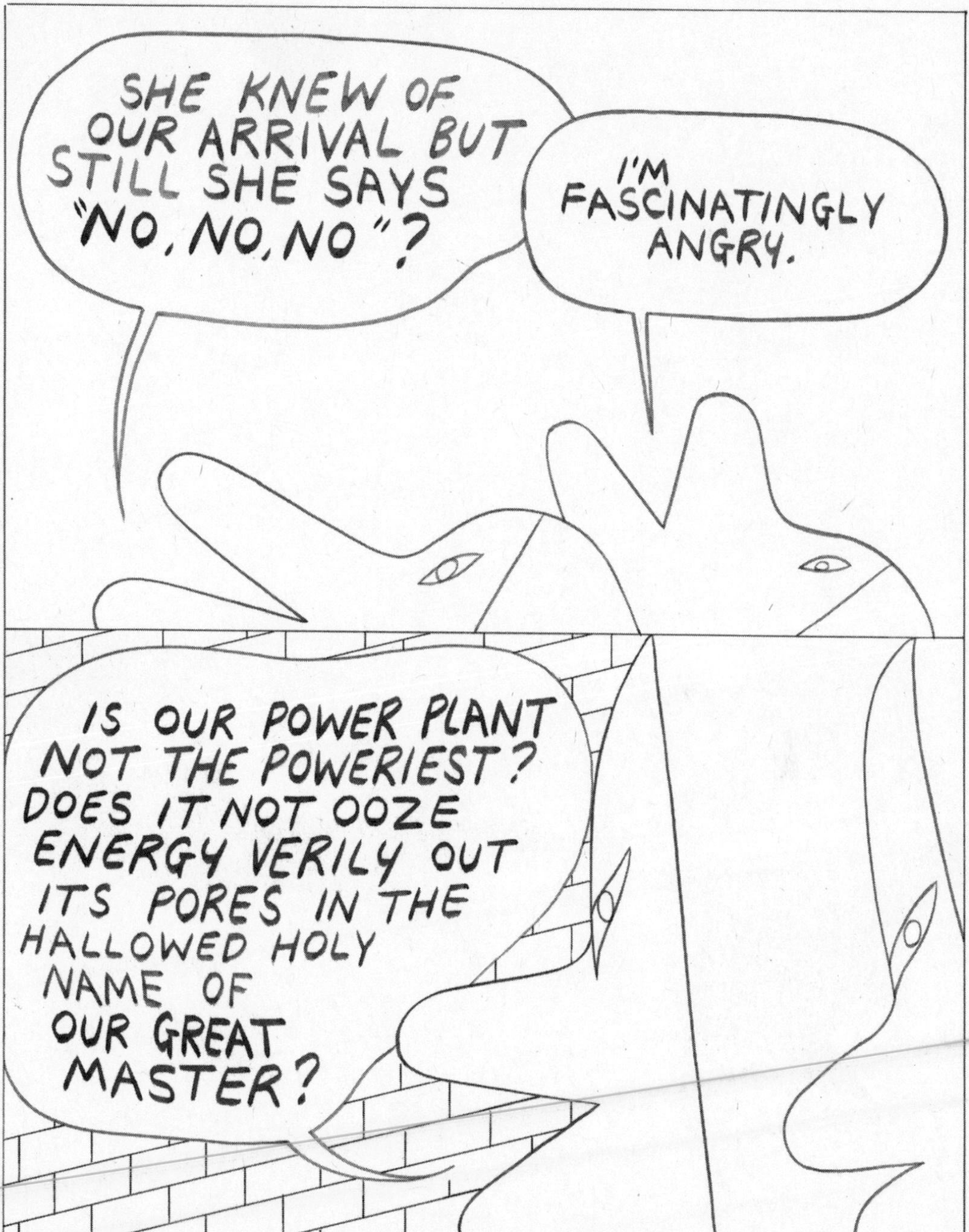
SHE KNEW OF OUR ARRIVAL BUT STILL SHE SAYS "NO, NO, NO"?
I'M FASCINATINGLY ANGRY.
IS OUR POWER PLANT NOT THE POWERIEST? DOES IT NOT OOZE ENERGY VERILY OUT ITS PORES IN THE HALLOWED HOLY NAME OF OUR GREAT MASTER?

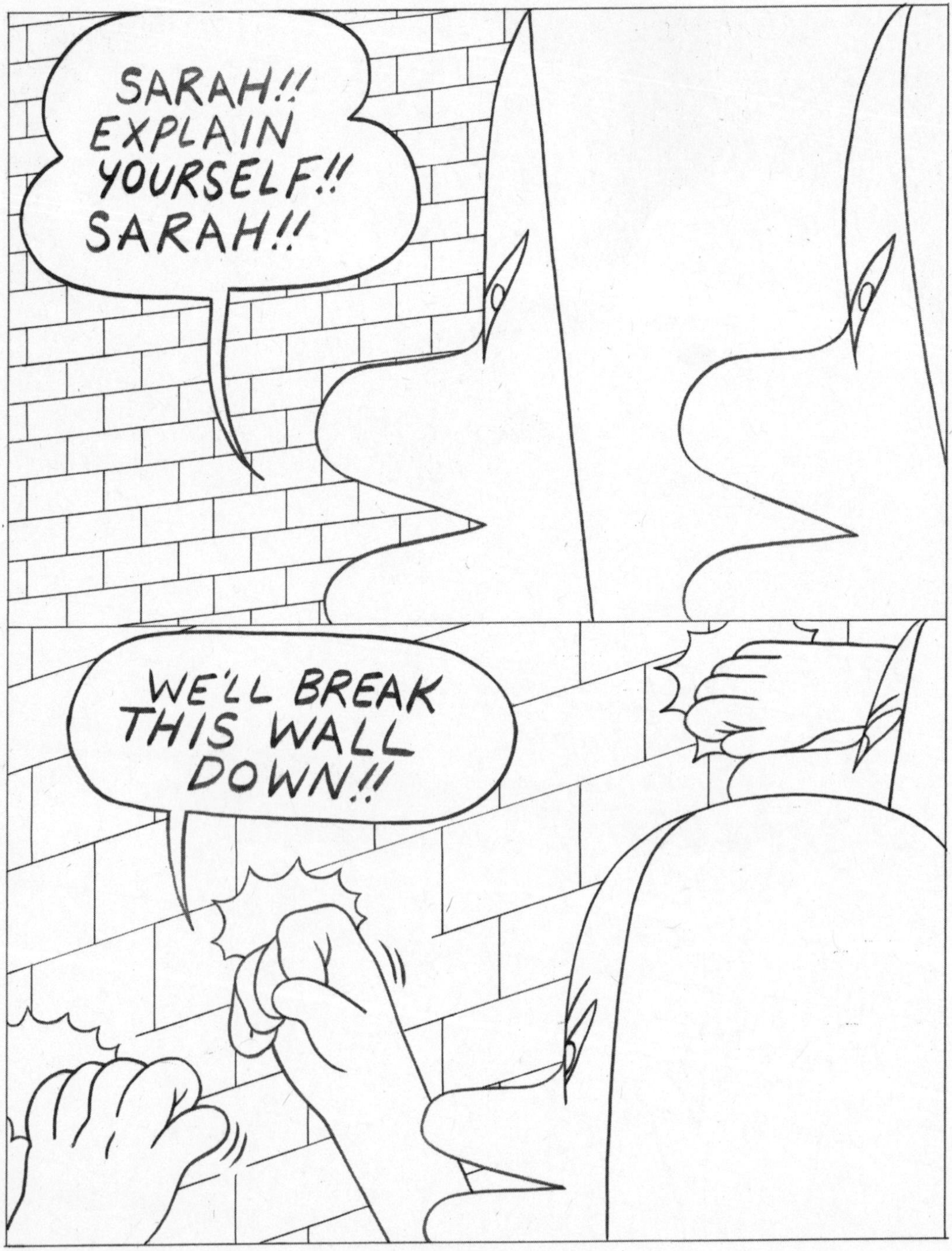
SARAH!! EXPLAIN YOURSELF!! SARAH!!
WE'LL BREAK THIS WALL DOWN!!

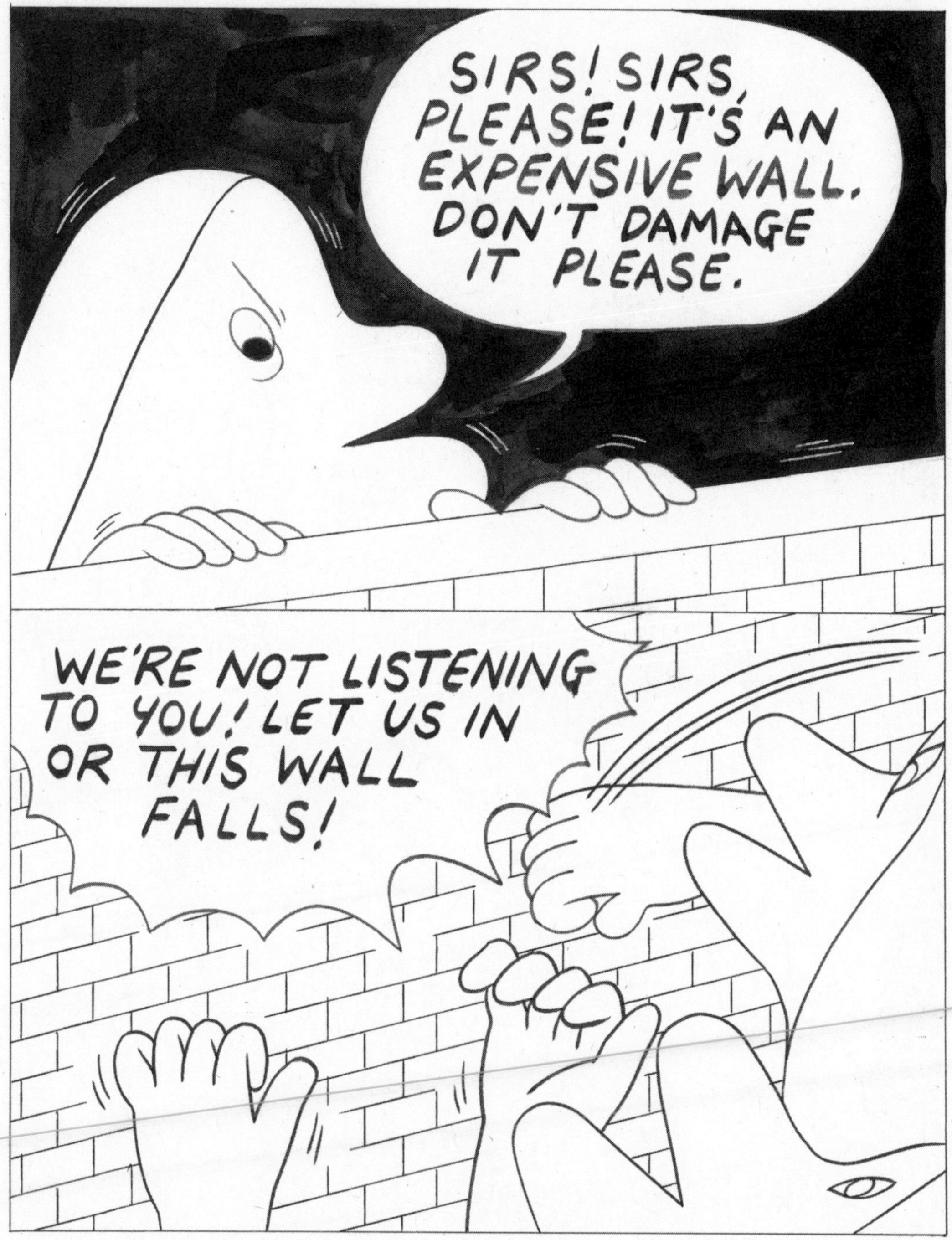
SIRS! SIRS, PLEASE! IT'S AN EXPENSIVE WALL. DON'T DAMAGE IT PLEASE.
WE'RE NOT LISTENING TO YOU! LET US IN OR THIS WALL FALLS!

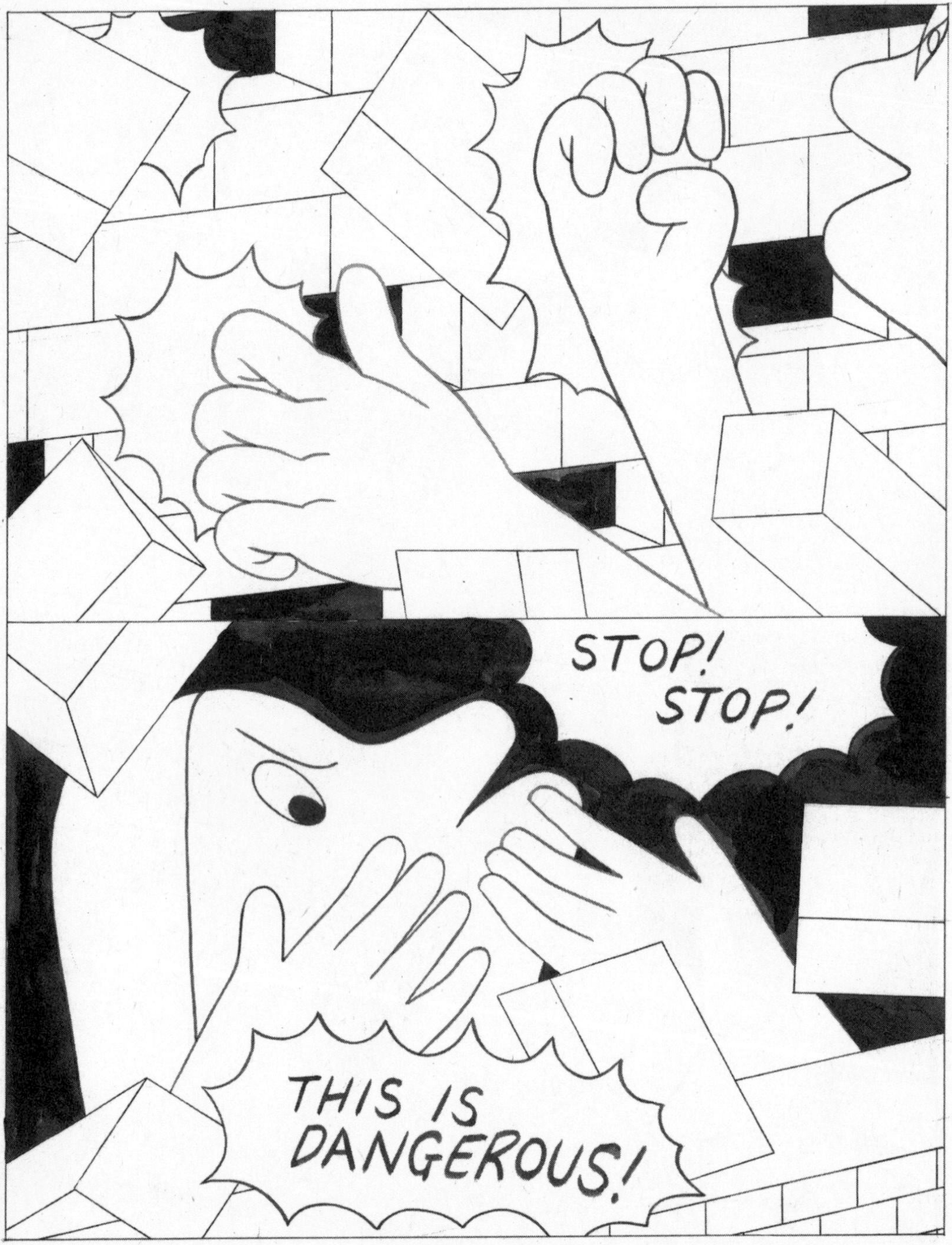
STOP! STOP!
THIS IS DANGEROUS!

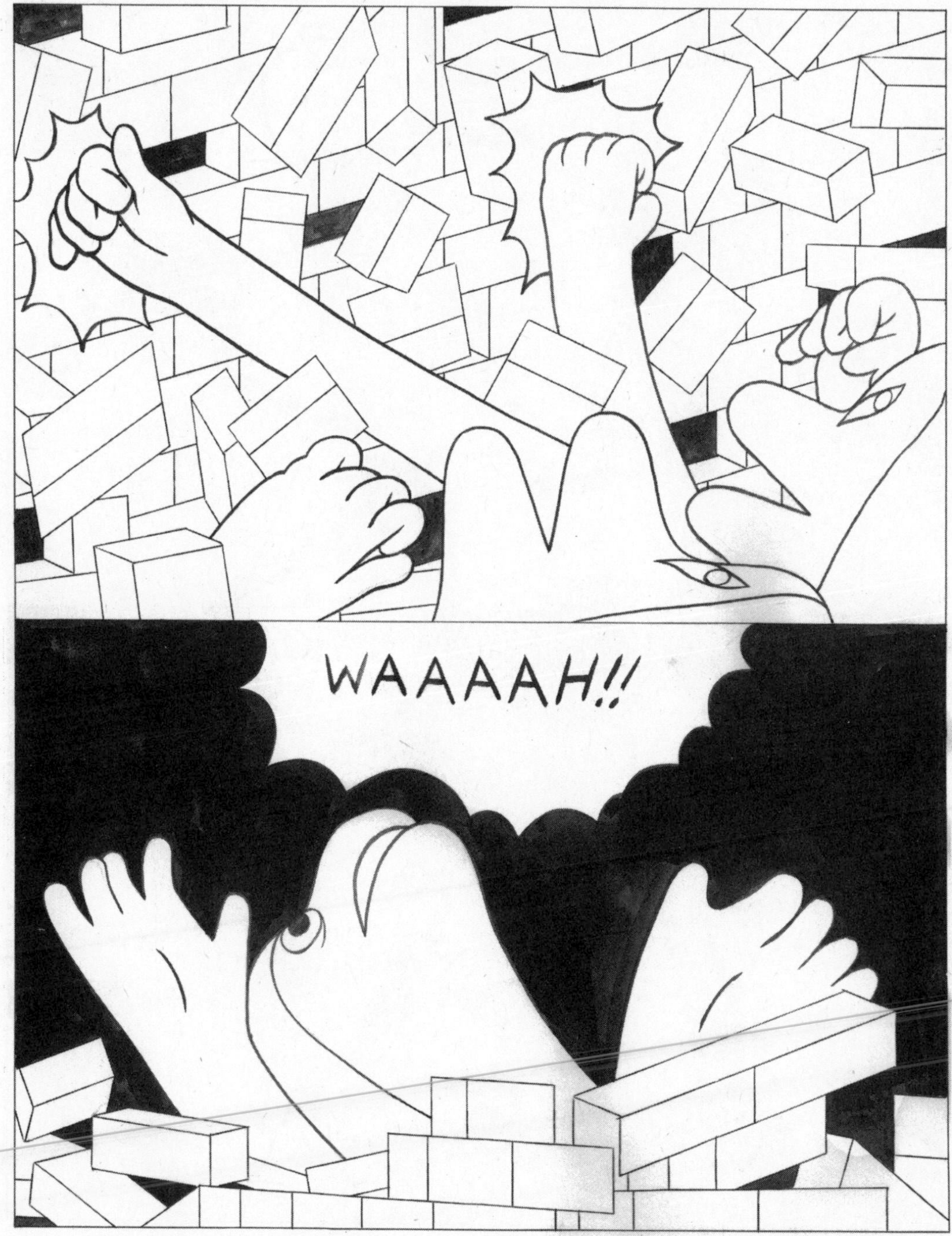
WAAAAH!!

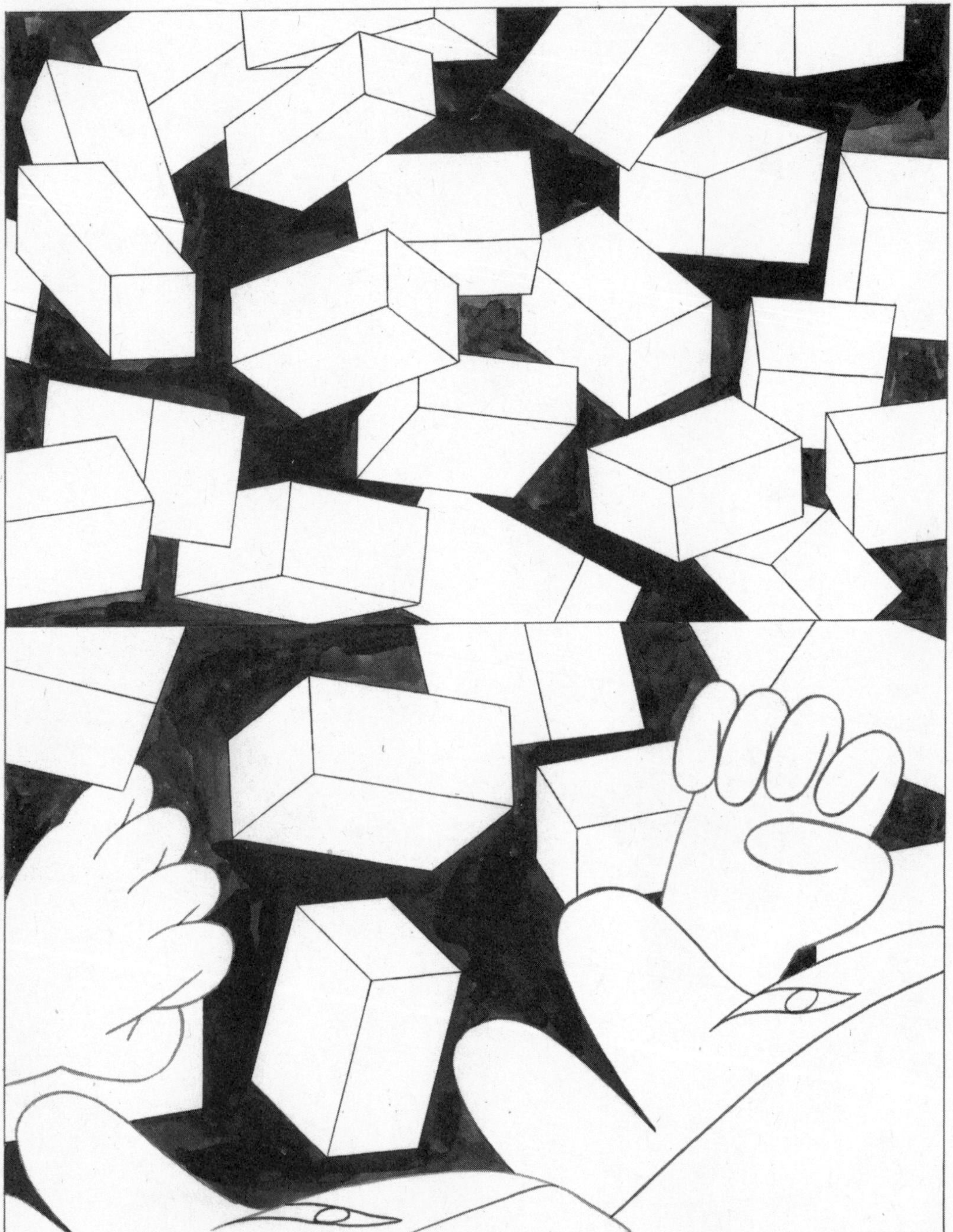

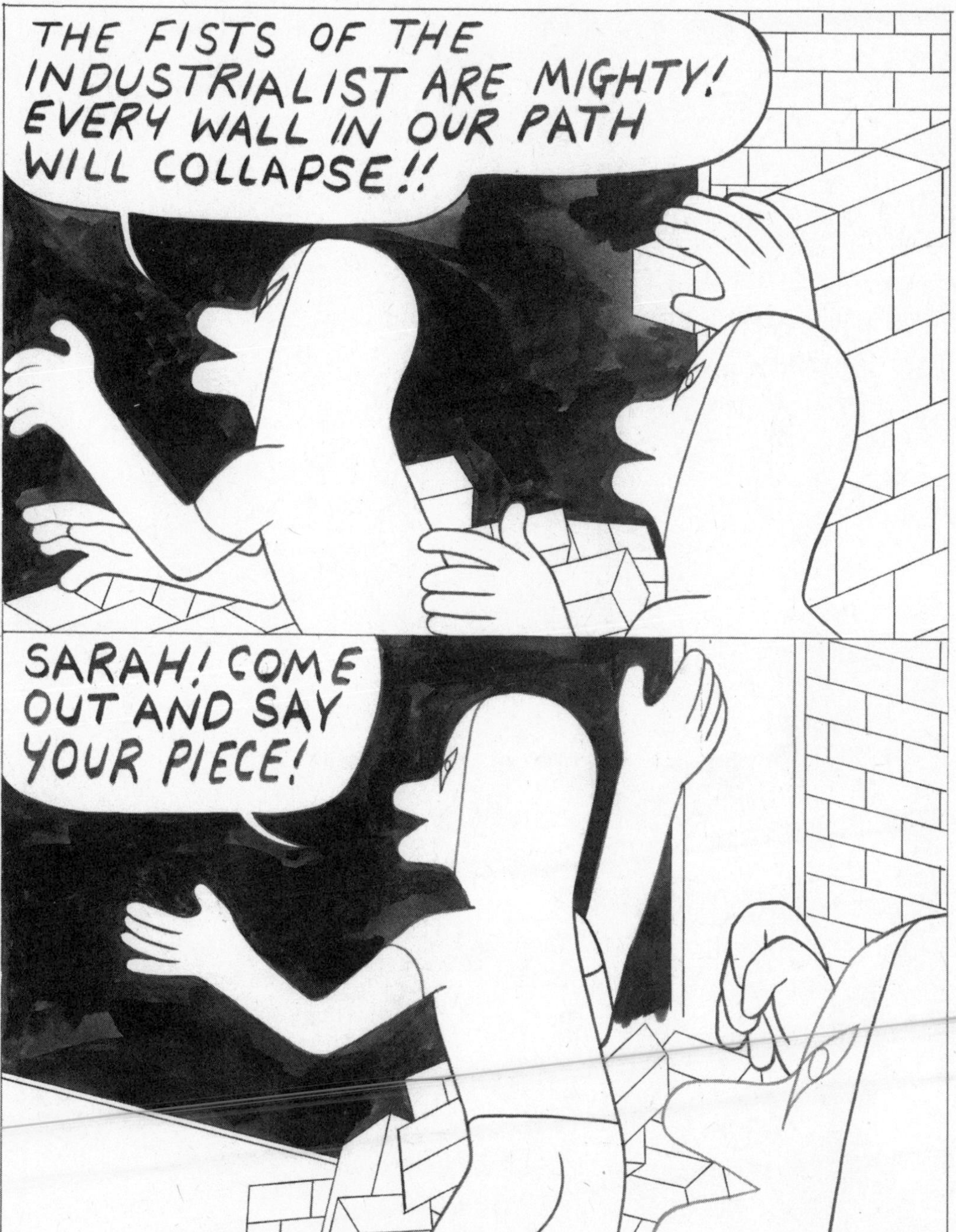
THE FISTS OF THE INDUSTRIALIST ARE MIGHTY! EVERY WALL IN OUR PATH WILL COLLAPSE!!
SARAH! COME OUT AND SAY YOUR PIECE!

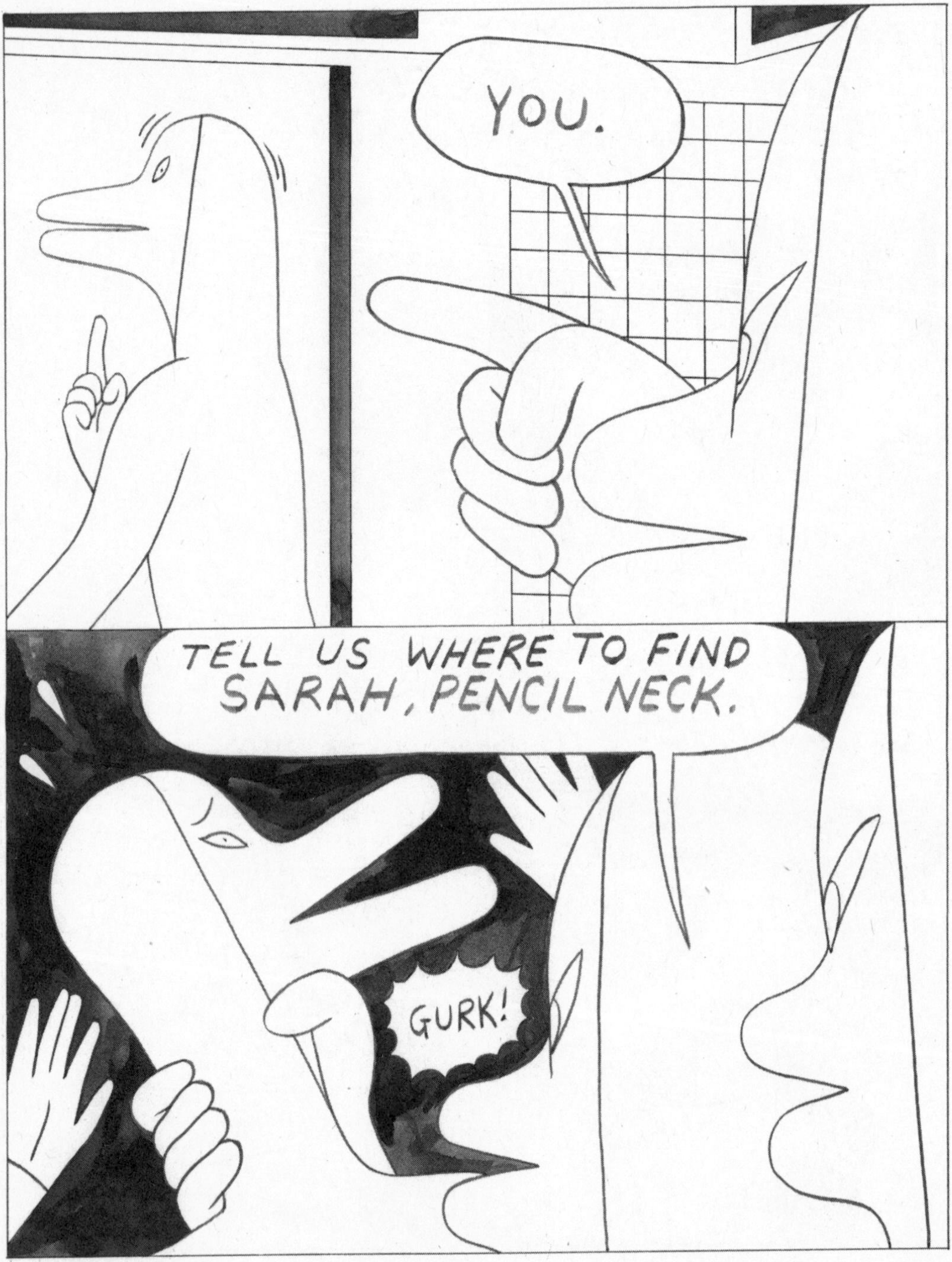
YOU.
TELL US WHERE TO FIND SARAH, PENCIL NECK.
GURK!

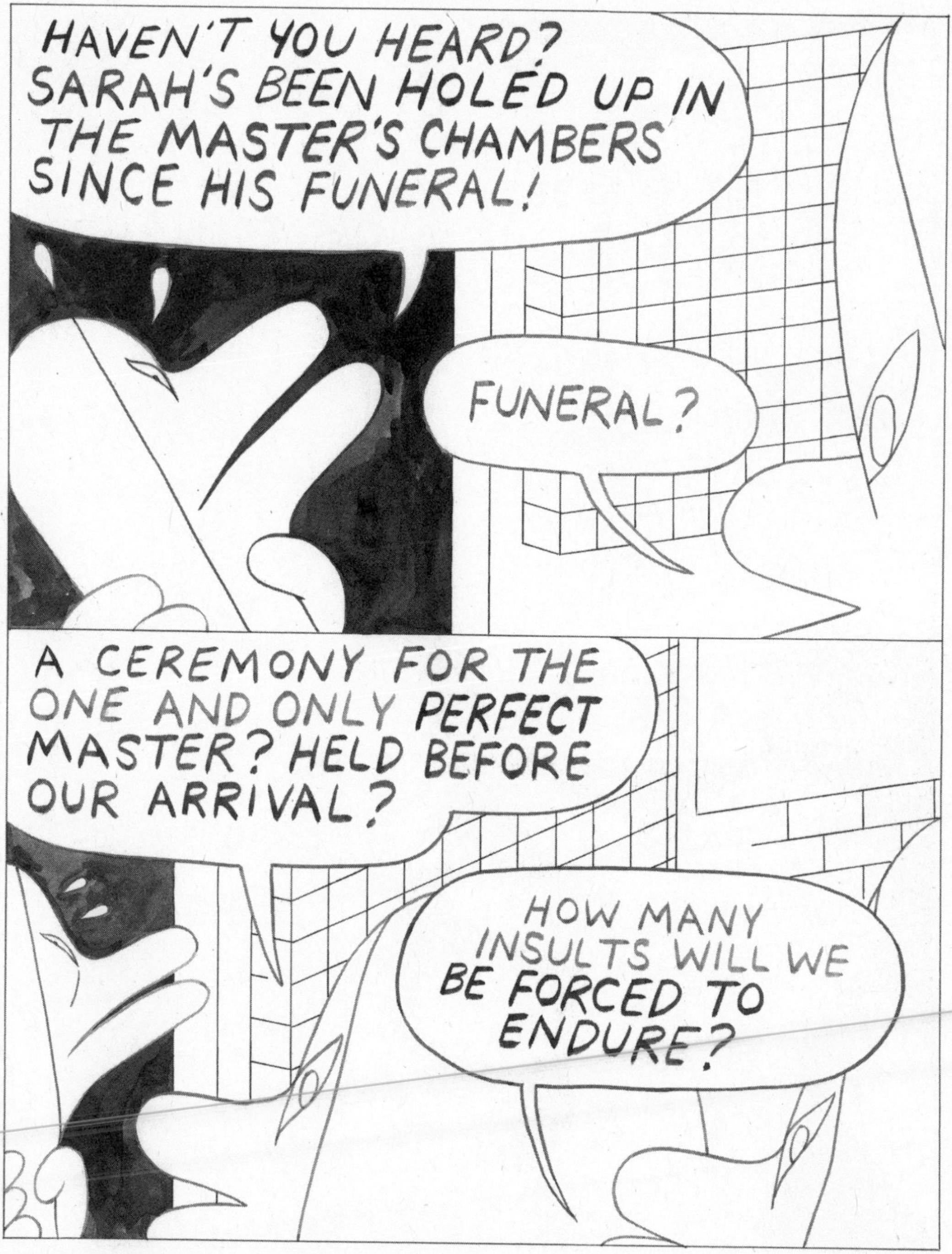
HAVEN'T YOU HEARD? SARAH'S BEEN HOLED UP IN THE MASTER'S CHAMBERS SINCE HIS FUNERAL!
FUNERAL?
A CEREMONY FOR THE ONE AND ONLY PERFECT MASTER? HELD BEFORE OUR ARRIVAL?
HOW MANY INSULTS WILL WE BE FORCED TO ENDURE?

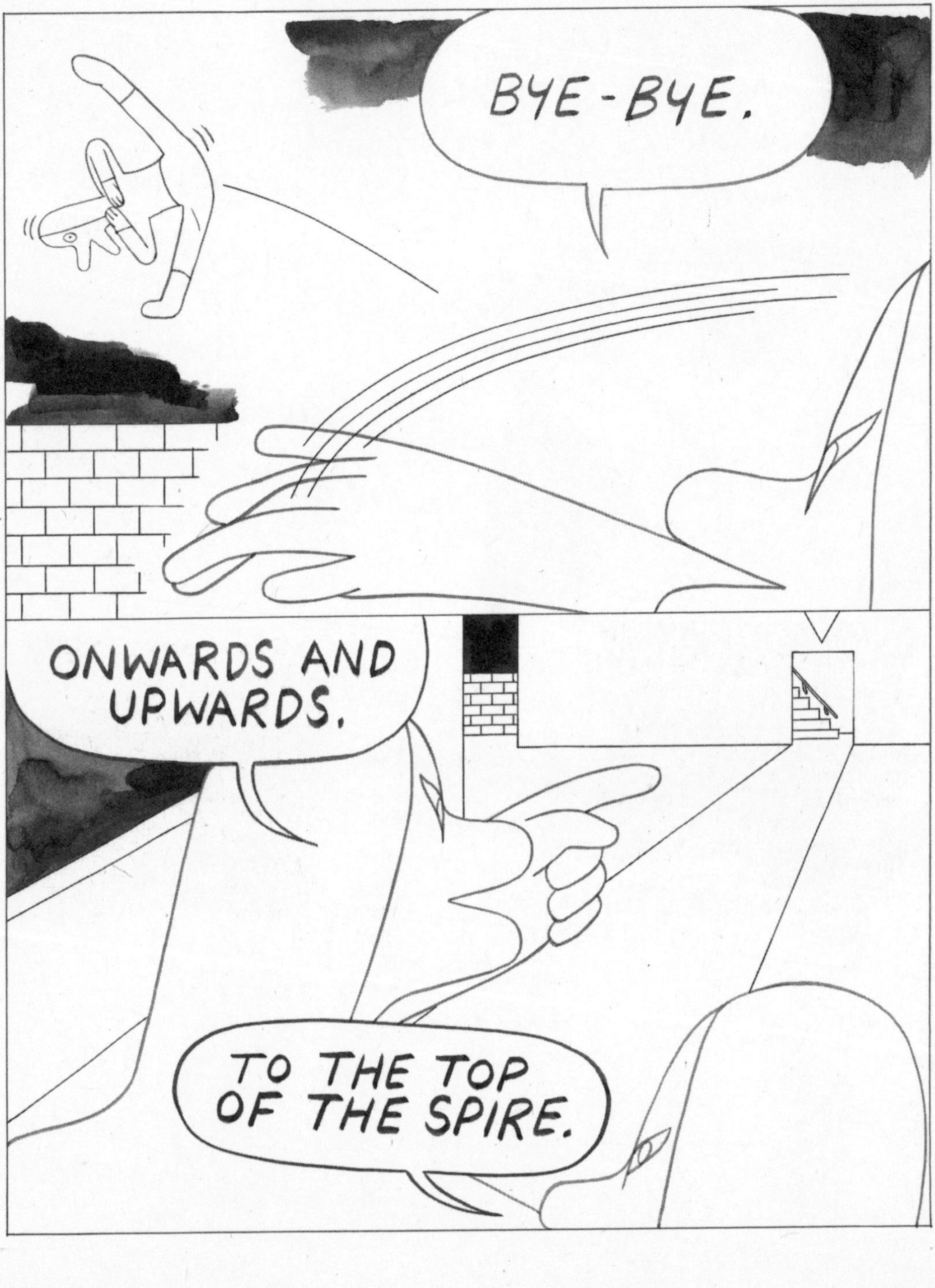
BYE-BYE.
ONWARDS AND UPWARDS.
TO THE TOP OF THE SPIRE.

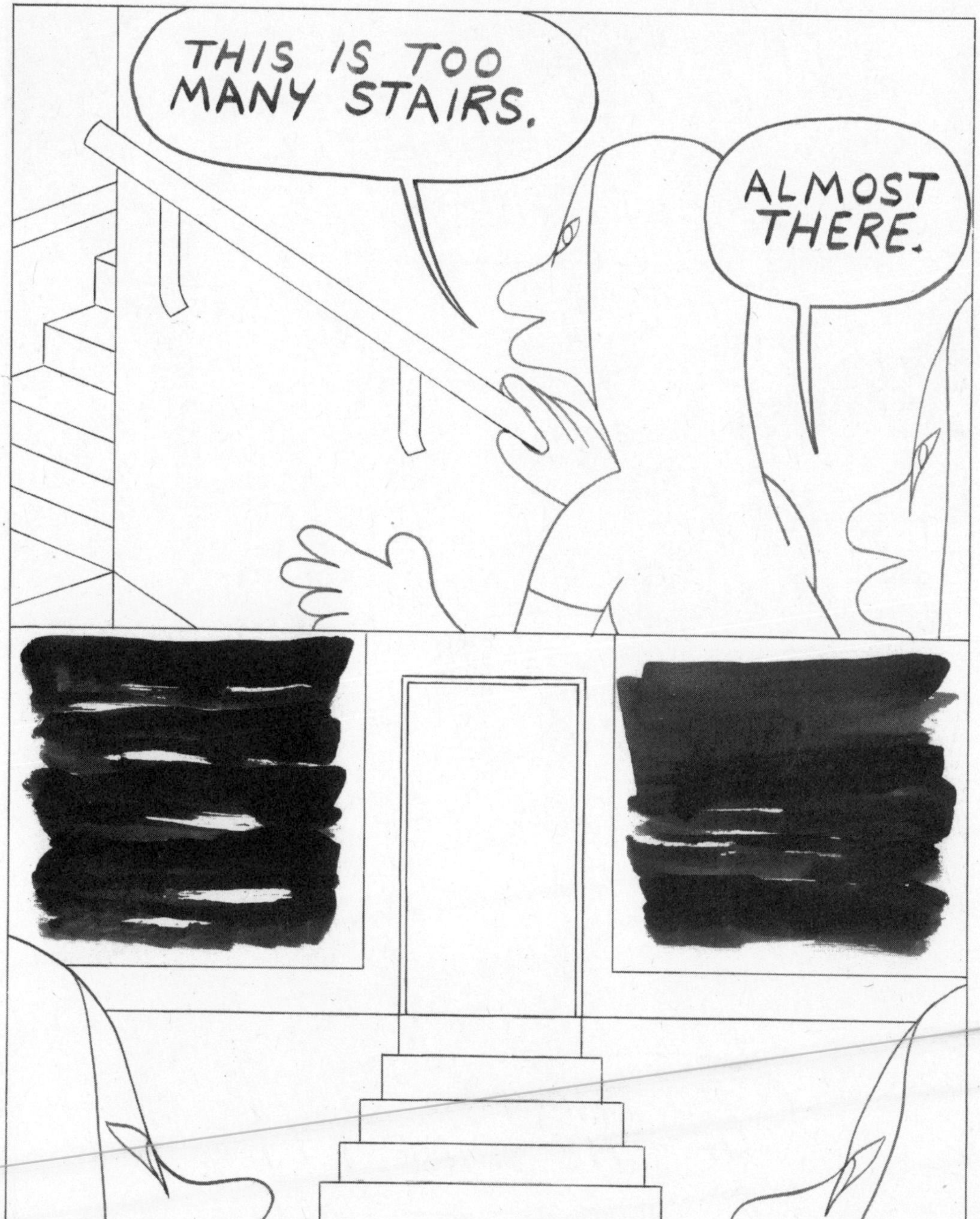
THIS IS TOO MANY STAIRS.
ALMOST THERE.

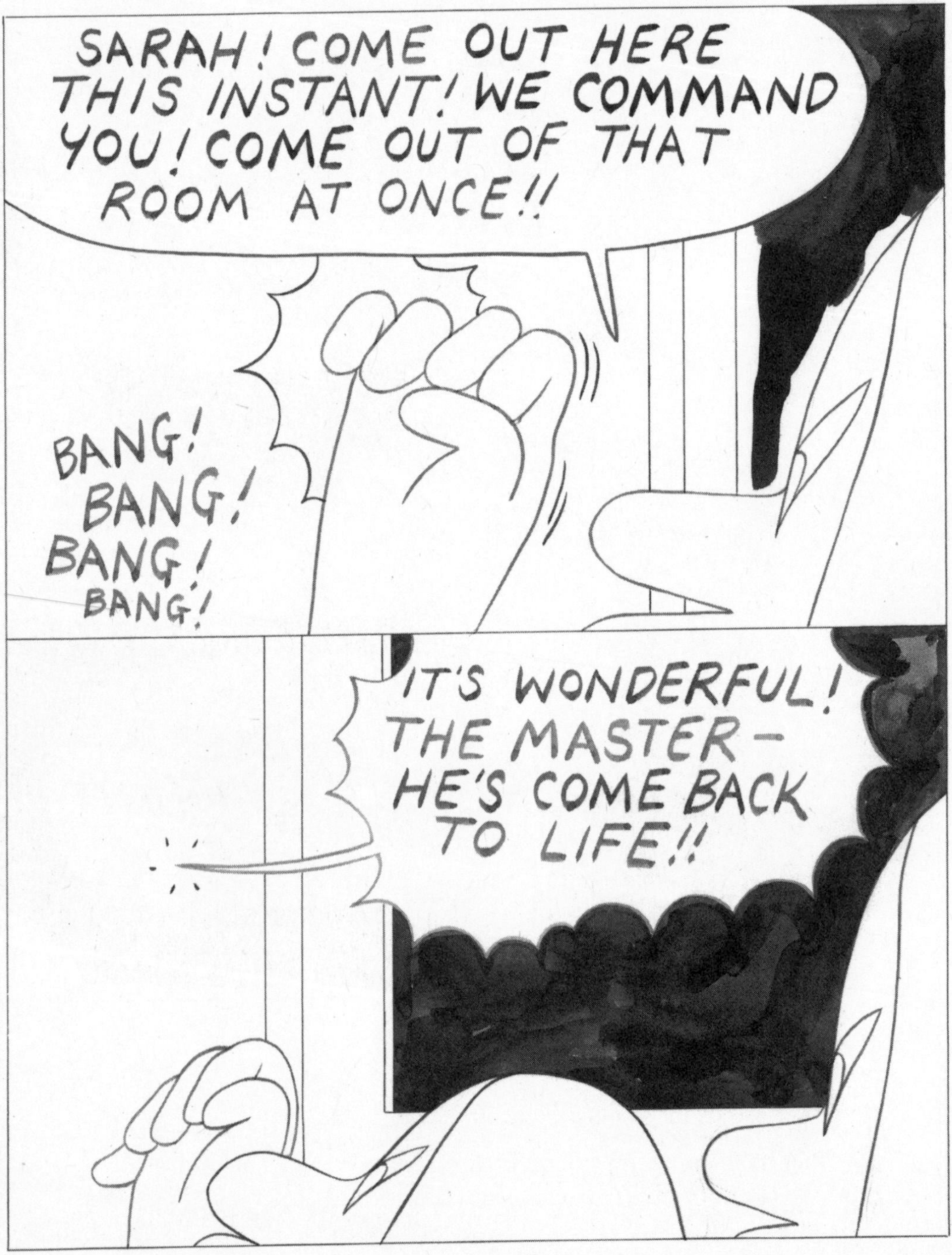SARAH! COME OUT HERE THIS INSTANT! WE COMMAND YOU! COME OUT OF THAT ROOM AT ONCE!!
BANG! BANG! BANG! BANG!
IT'S WONDERFUL! THE MASTER— HE'S COME BACK TO LIFE!!

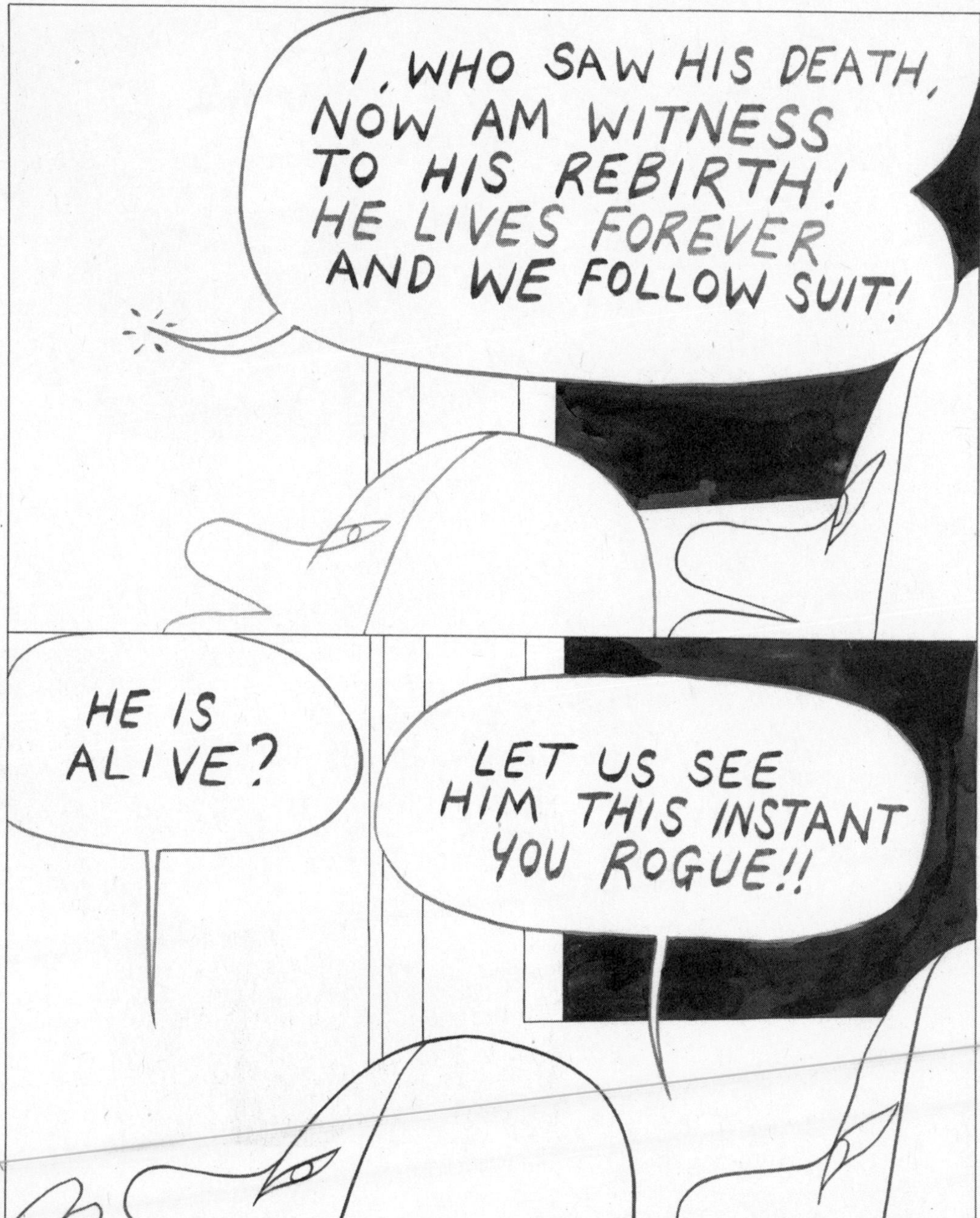
I, WHO SAW HIS DEATH, NOW AM WITNESS TO HIS REBIRTH! HE LIVES FOREVER AND WE FOLLOW SUIT!
HE IS ALIVE?
LET US SEE HIM THIS INSTANT YOU ROGUE!!

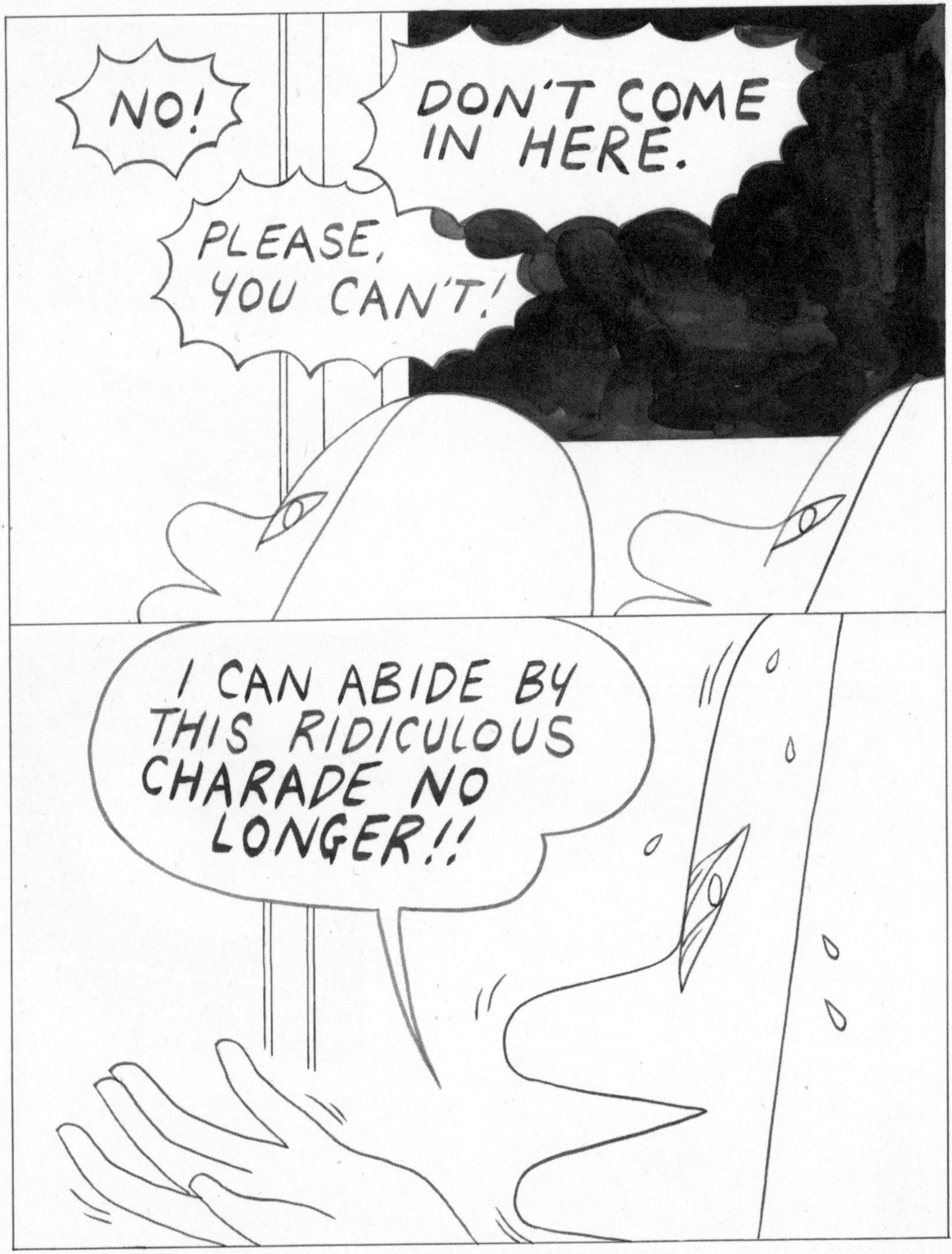
NO!
DON'T COME IN HERE.
PLEASE, YOU CAN'T!
I CAN ABIDE BY THIS RIDICULOUS CHARADE NO LONGER!!

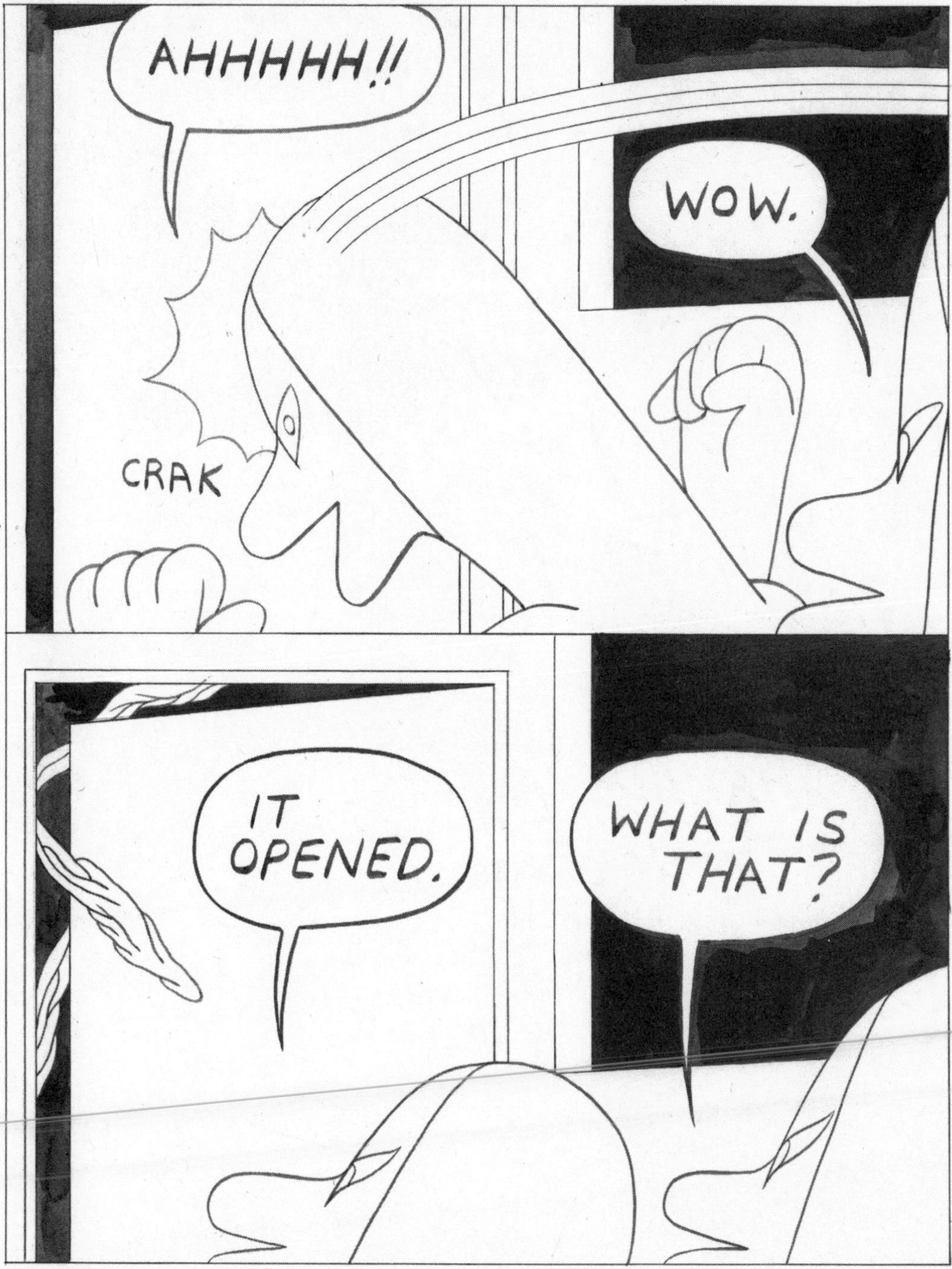
AHHHHH!!
CRAK
WOW.
IT OPENED.
WHAT IS THAT?

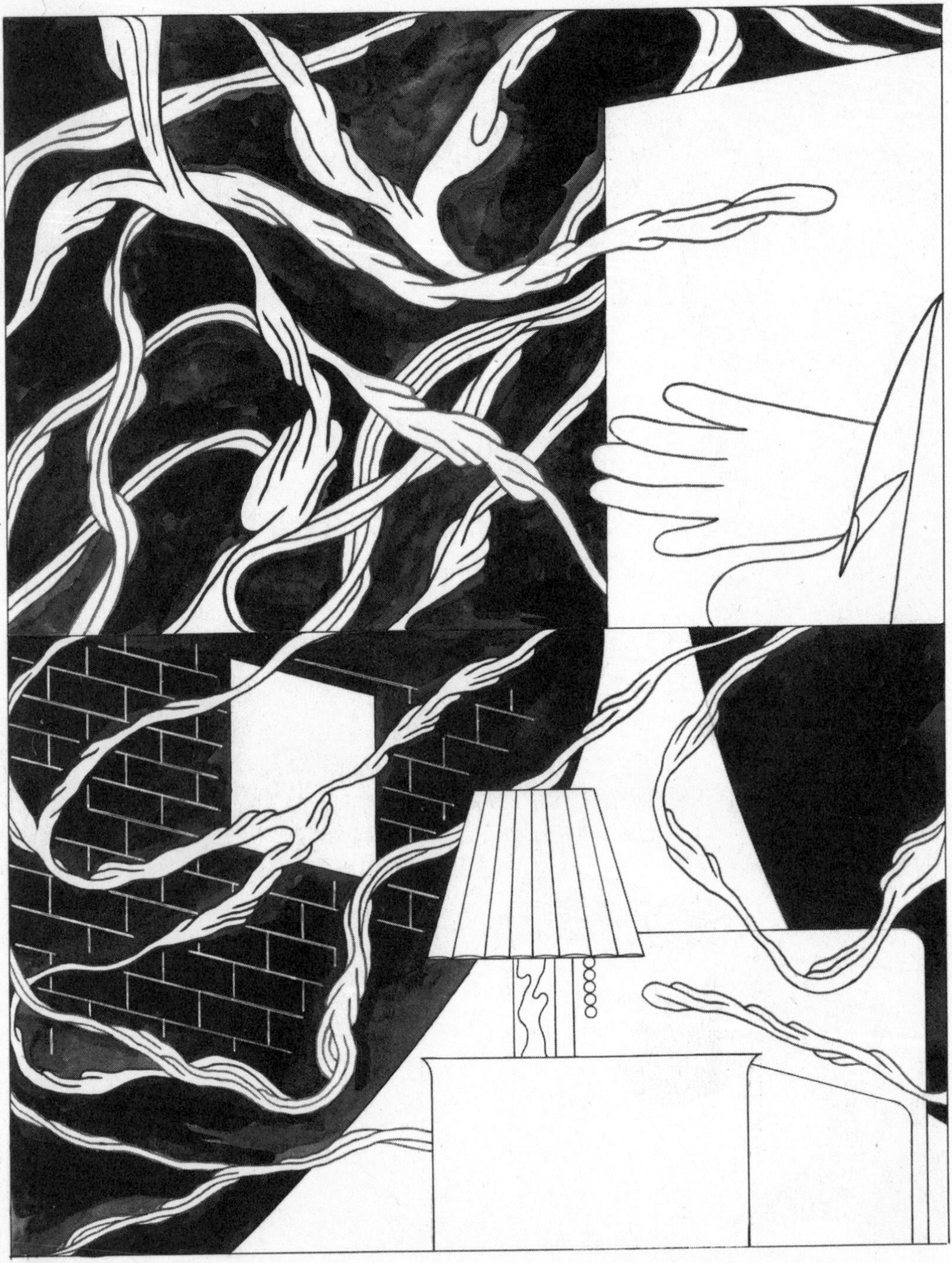

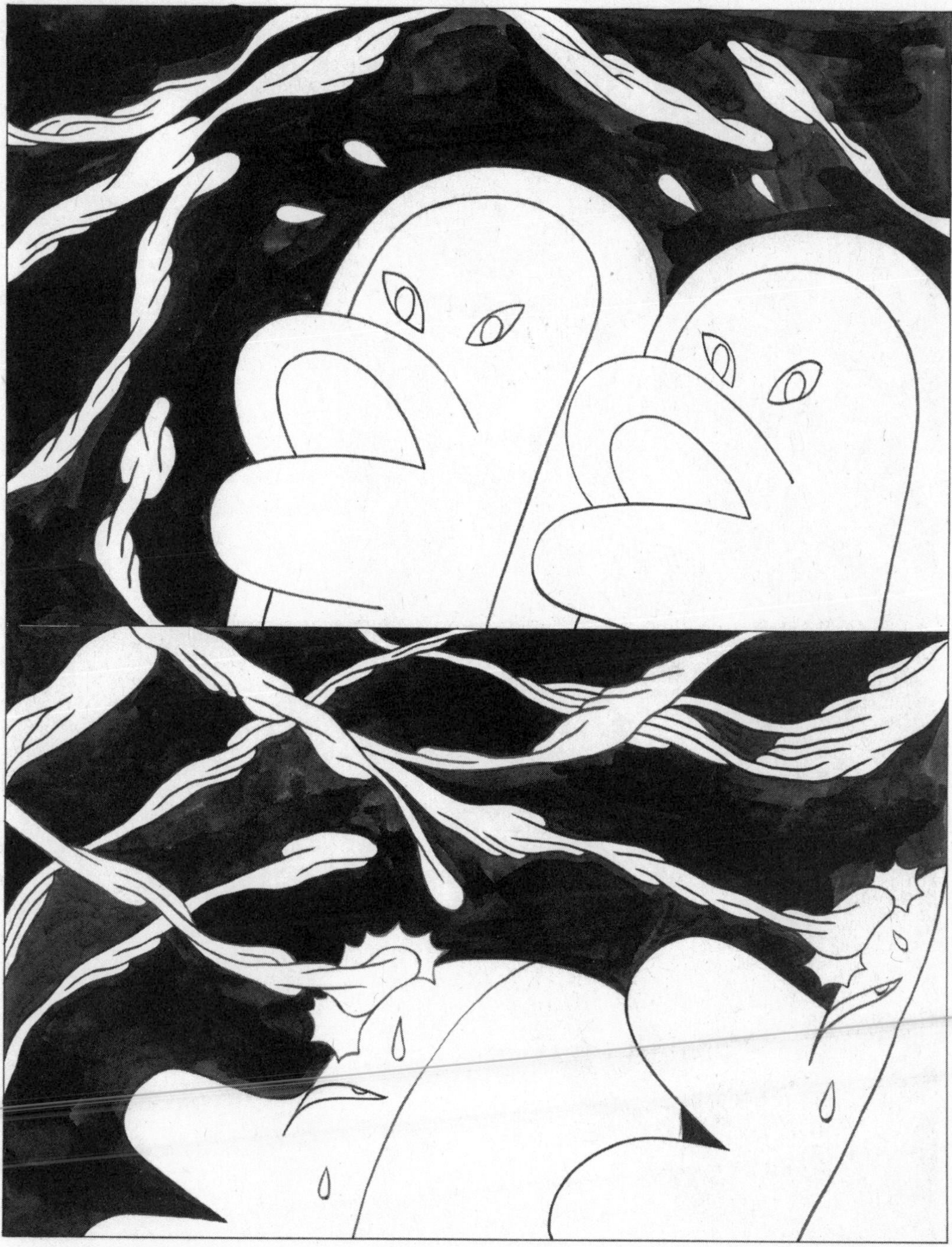

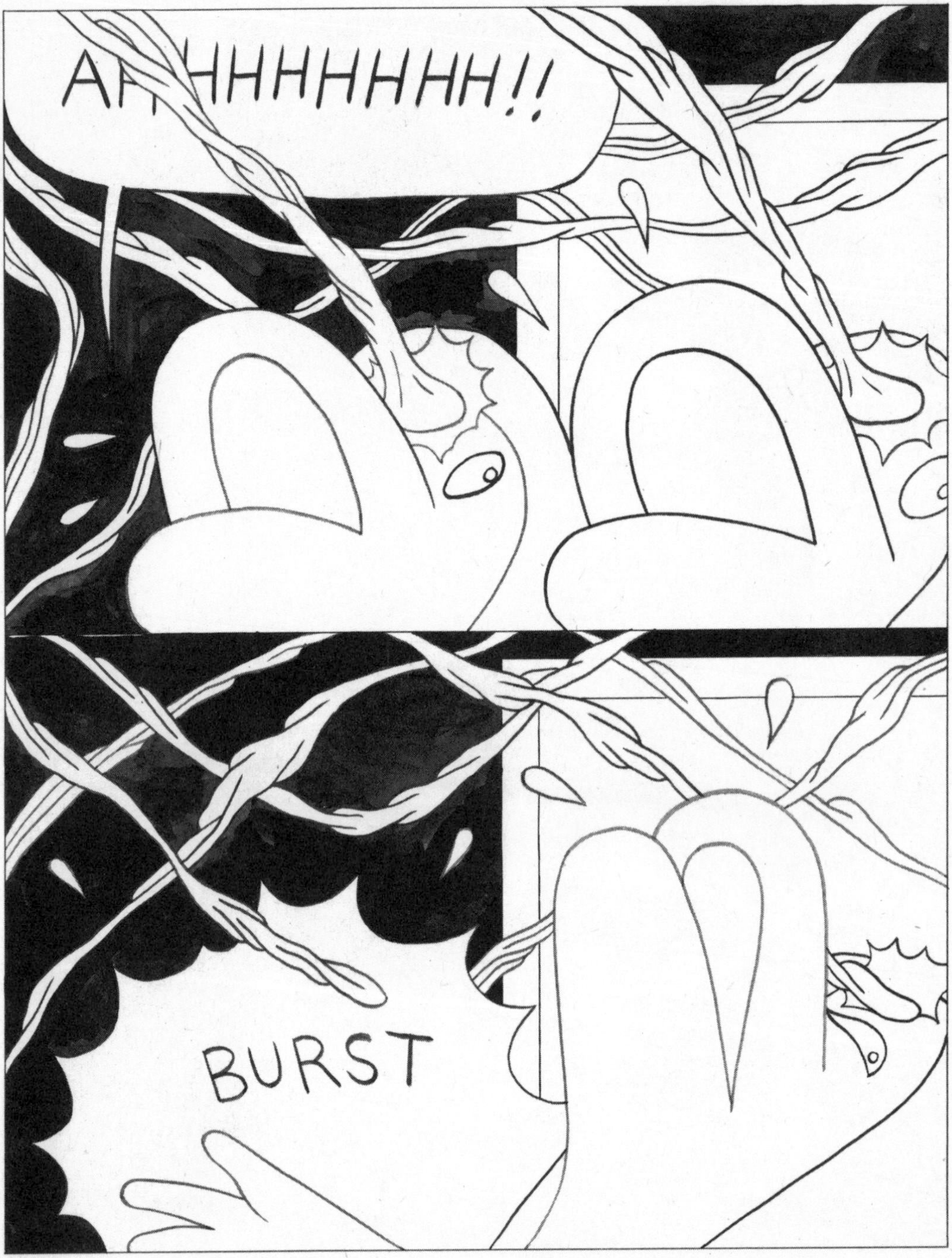
AHHHHHHHHH!!
BURST

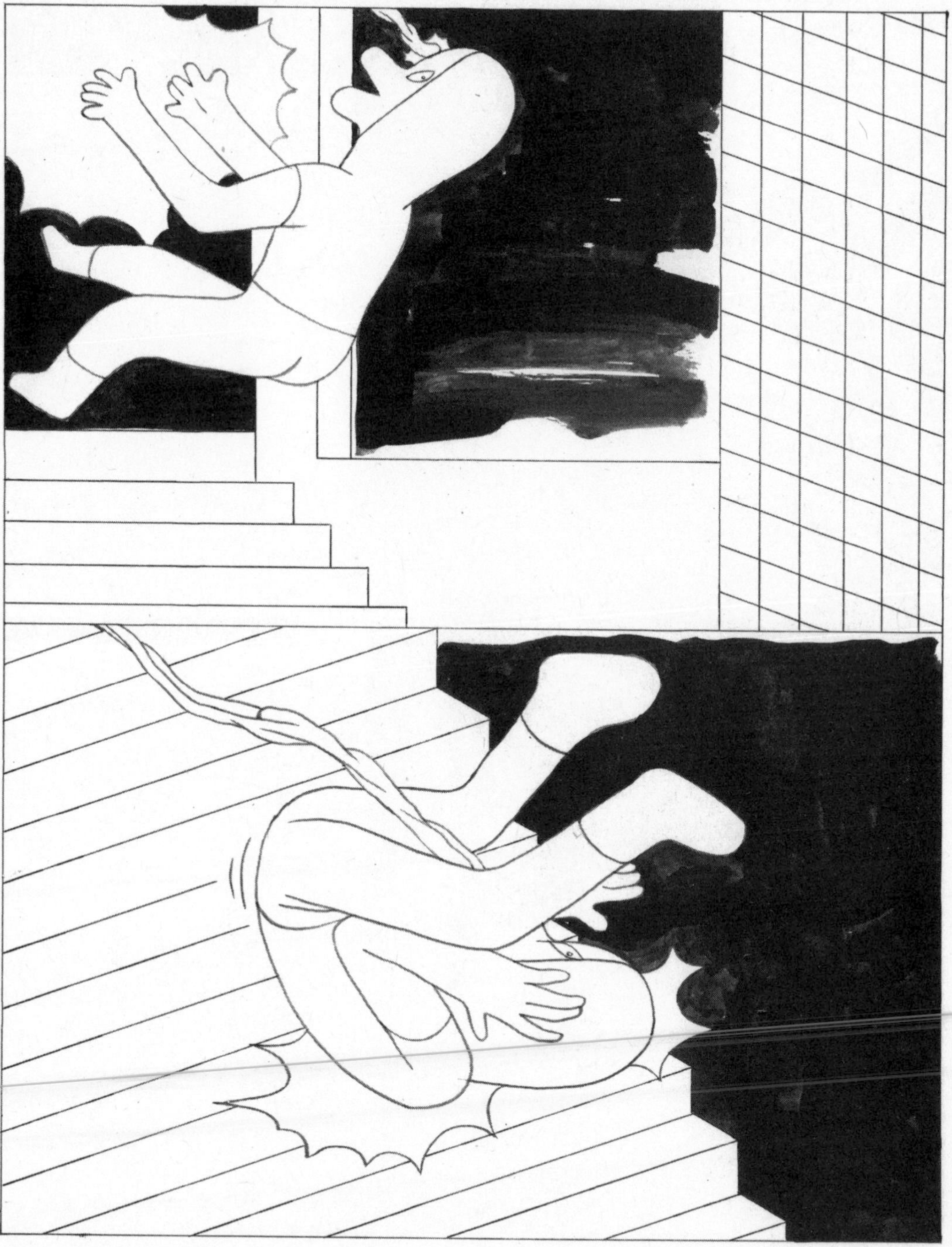

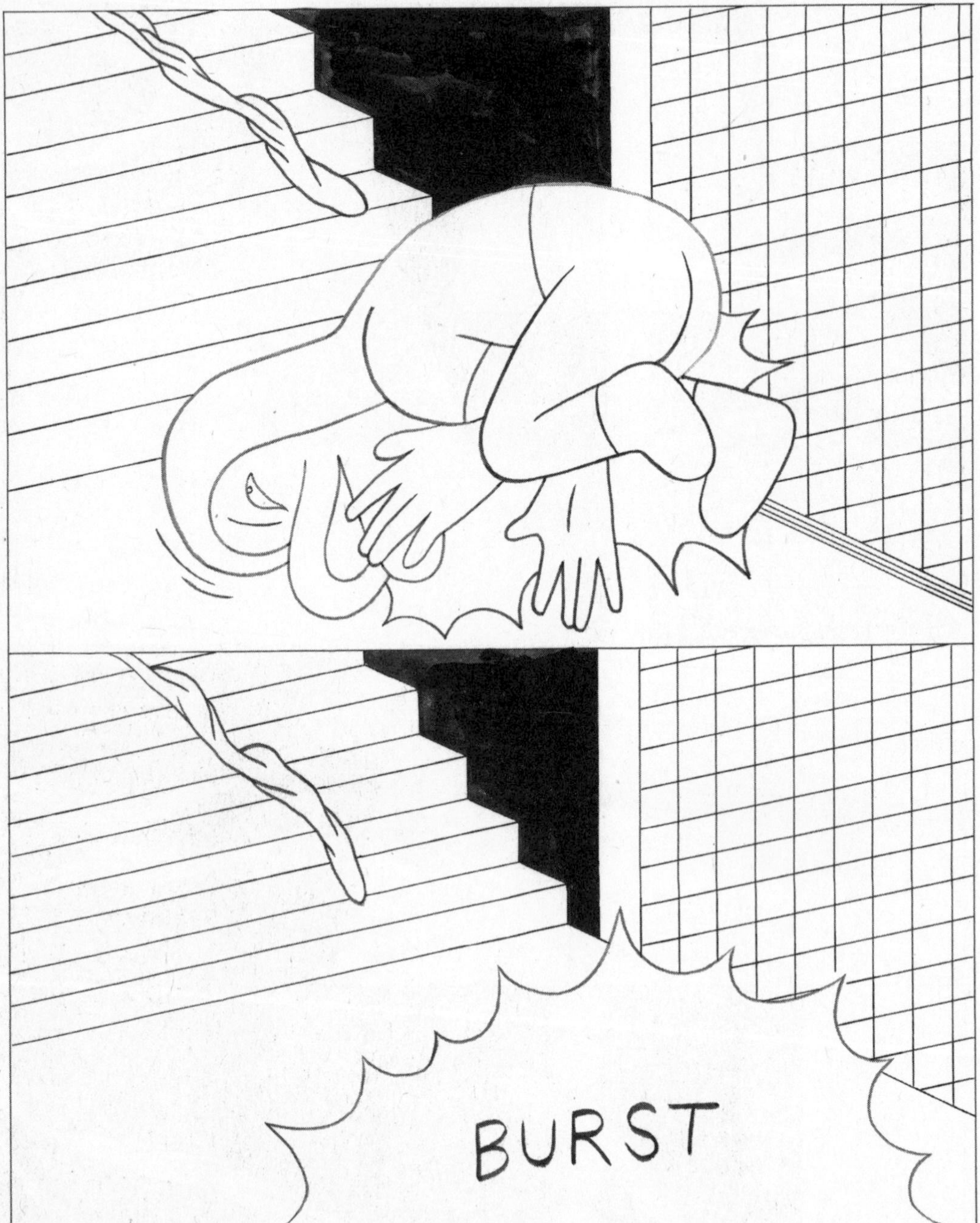
BURST

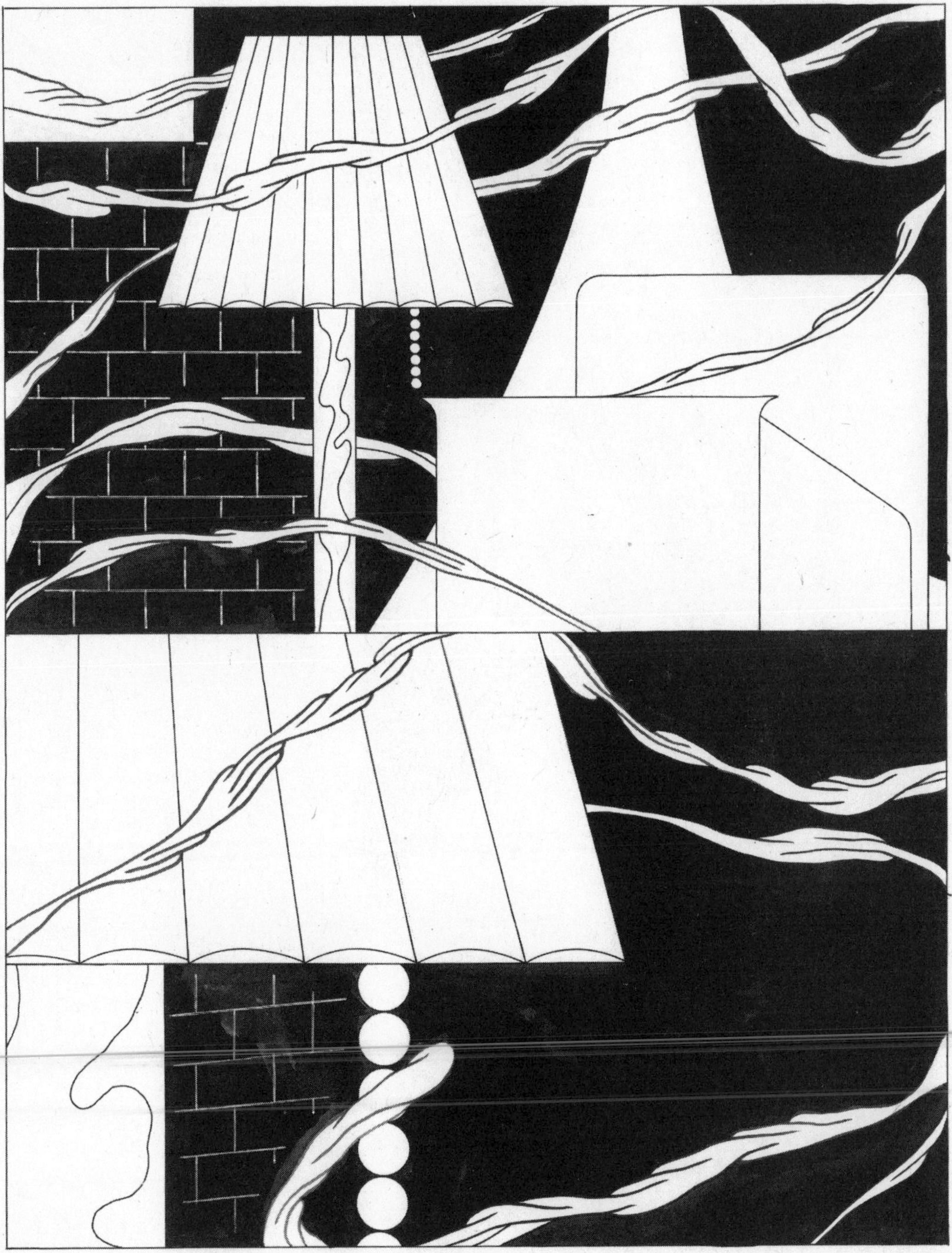

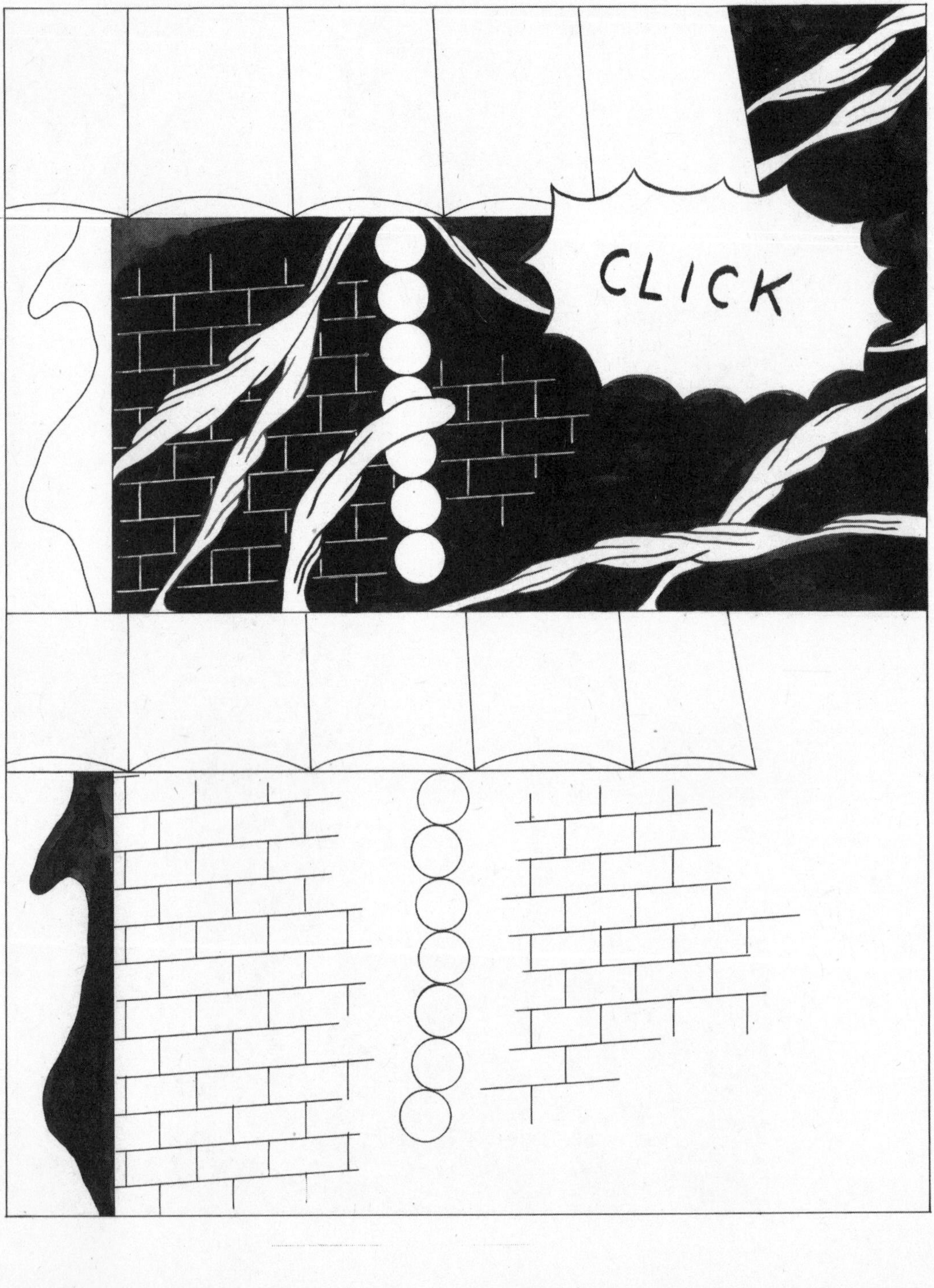
CLICK

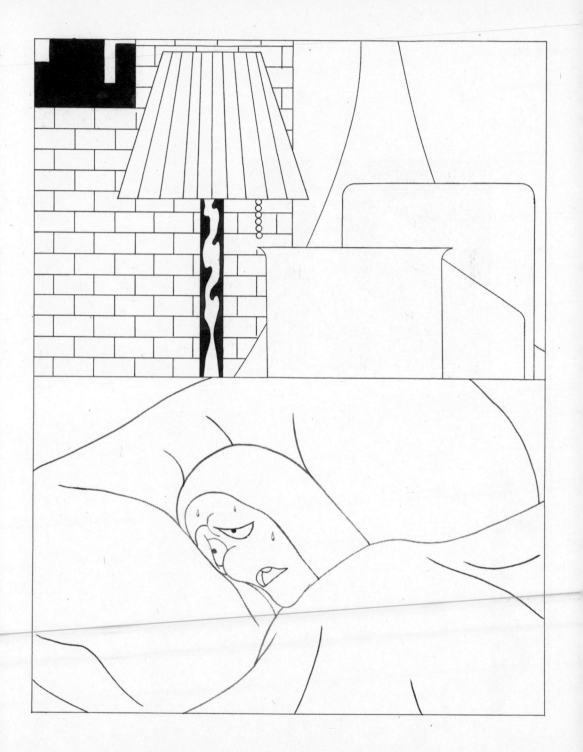

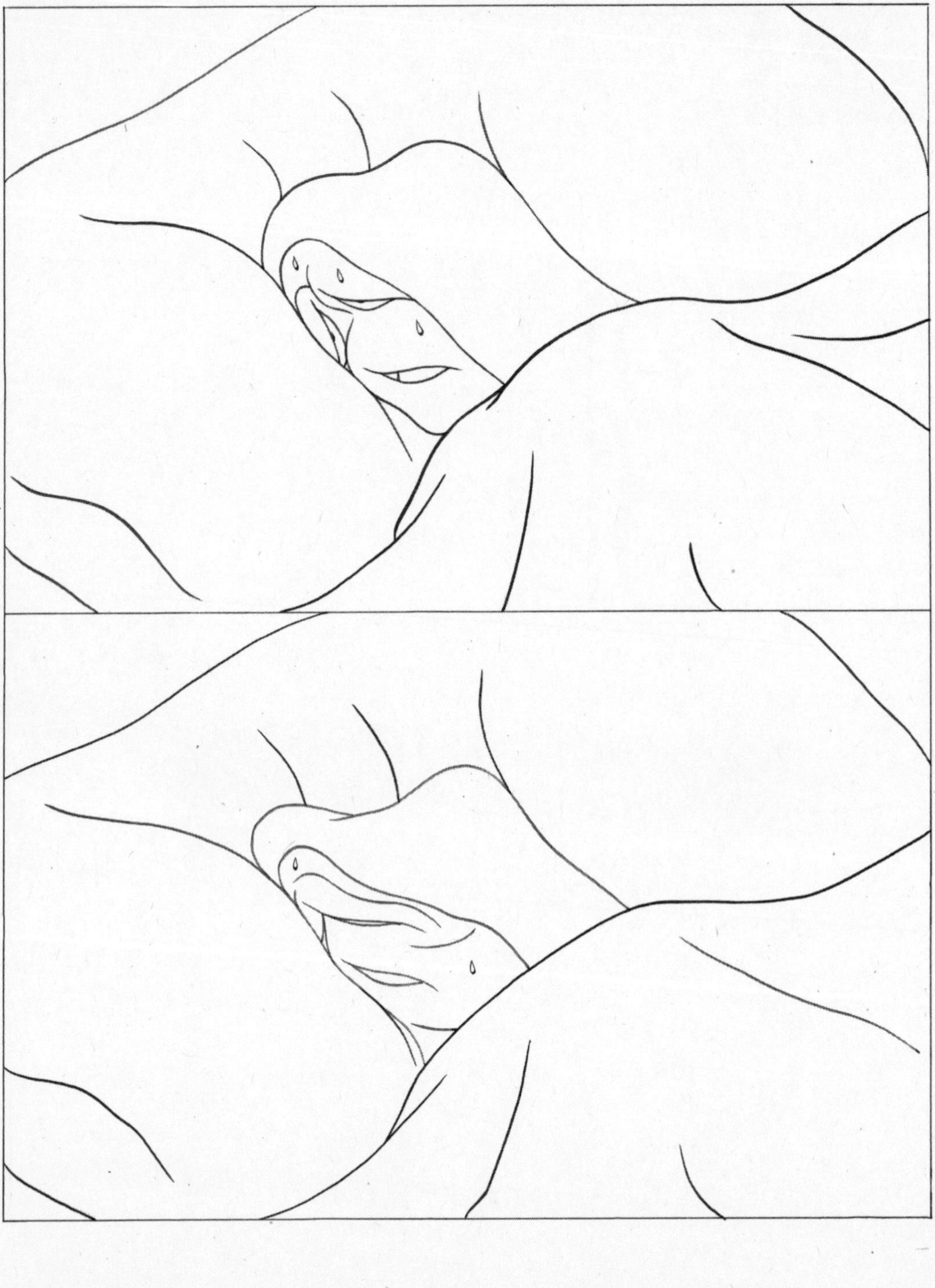

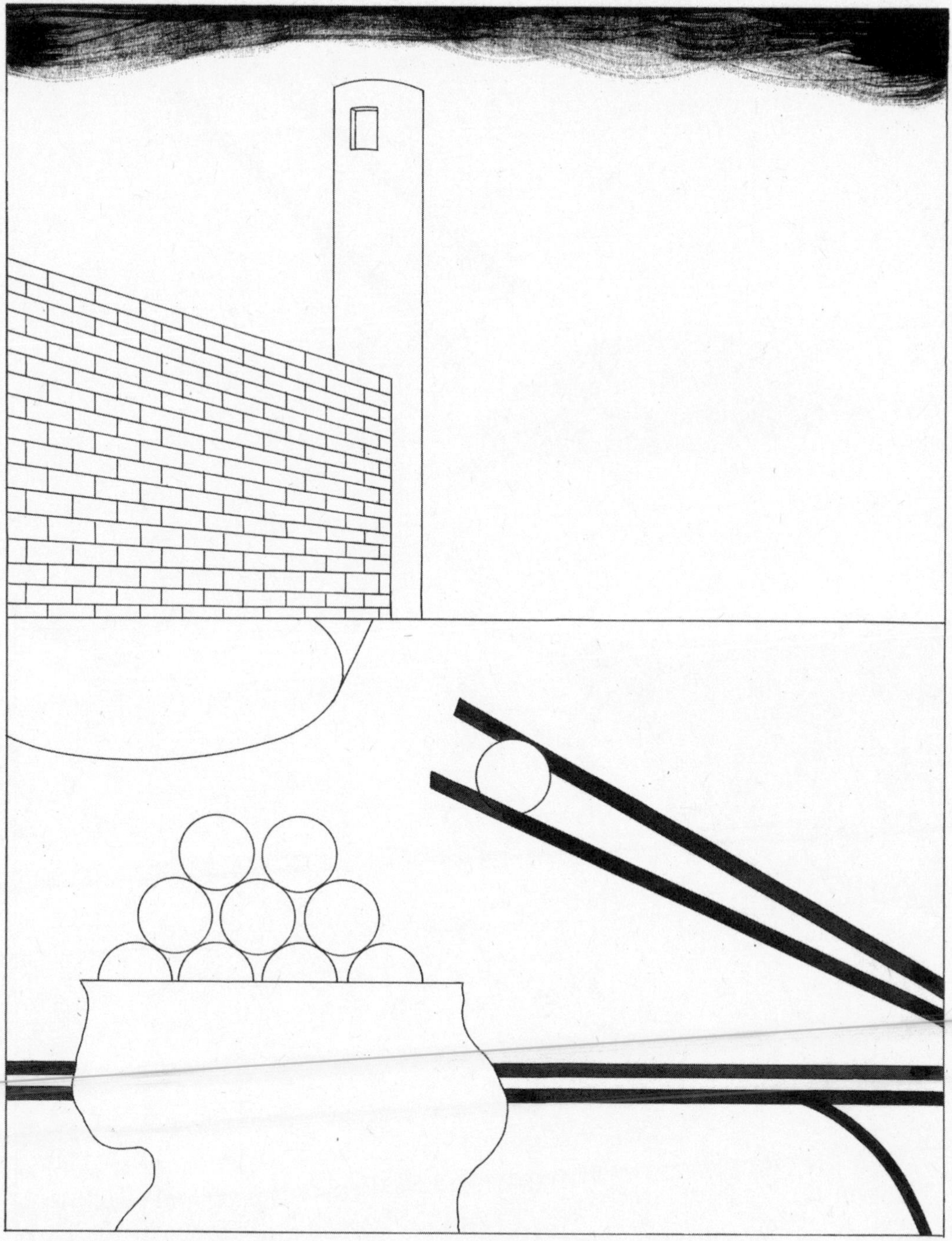

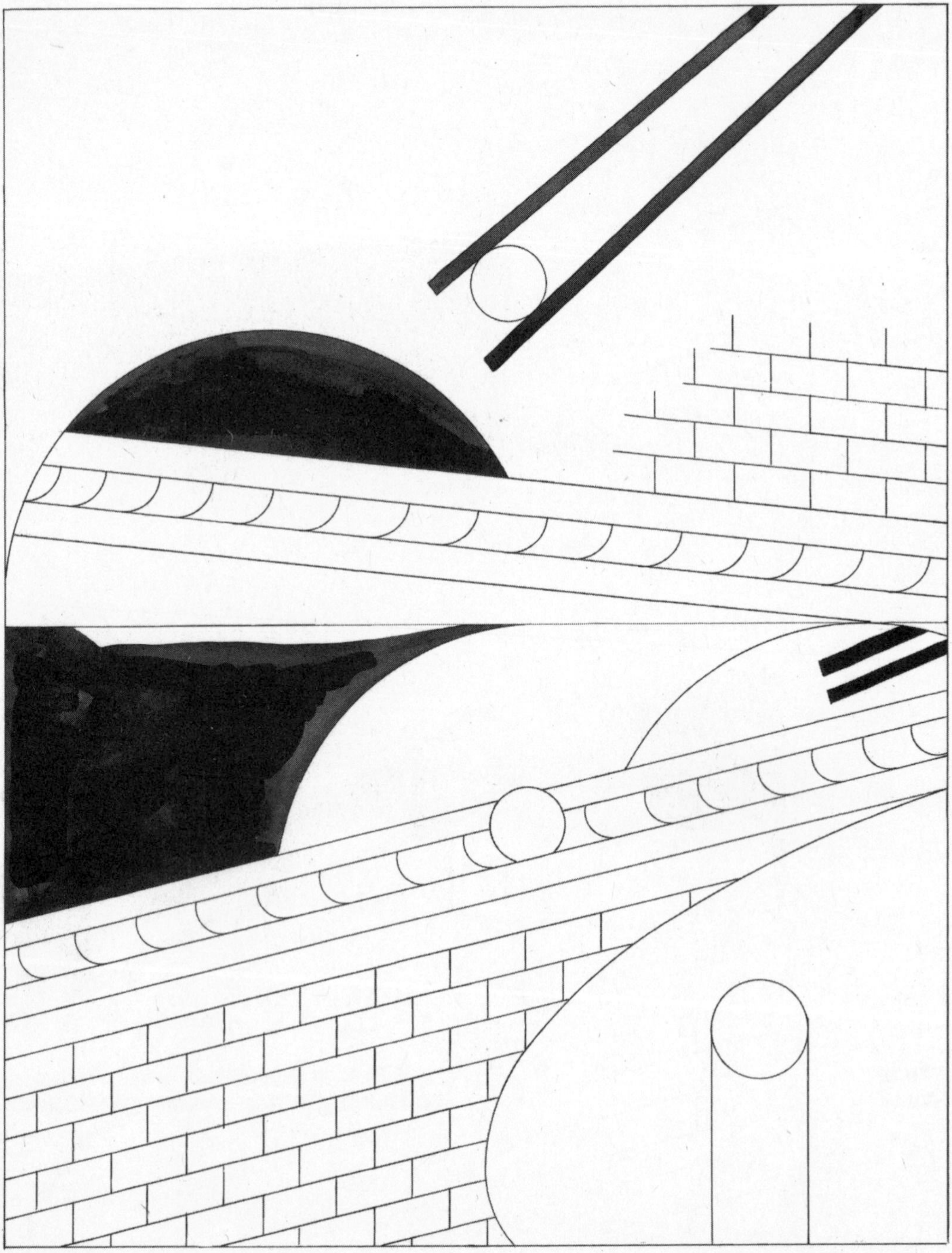

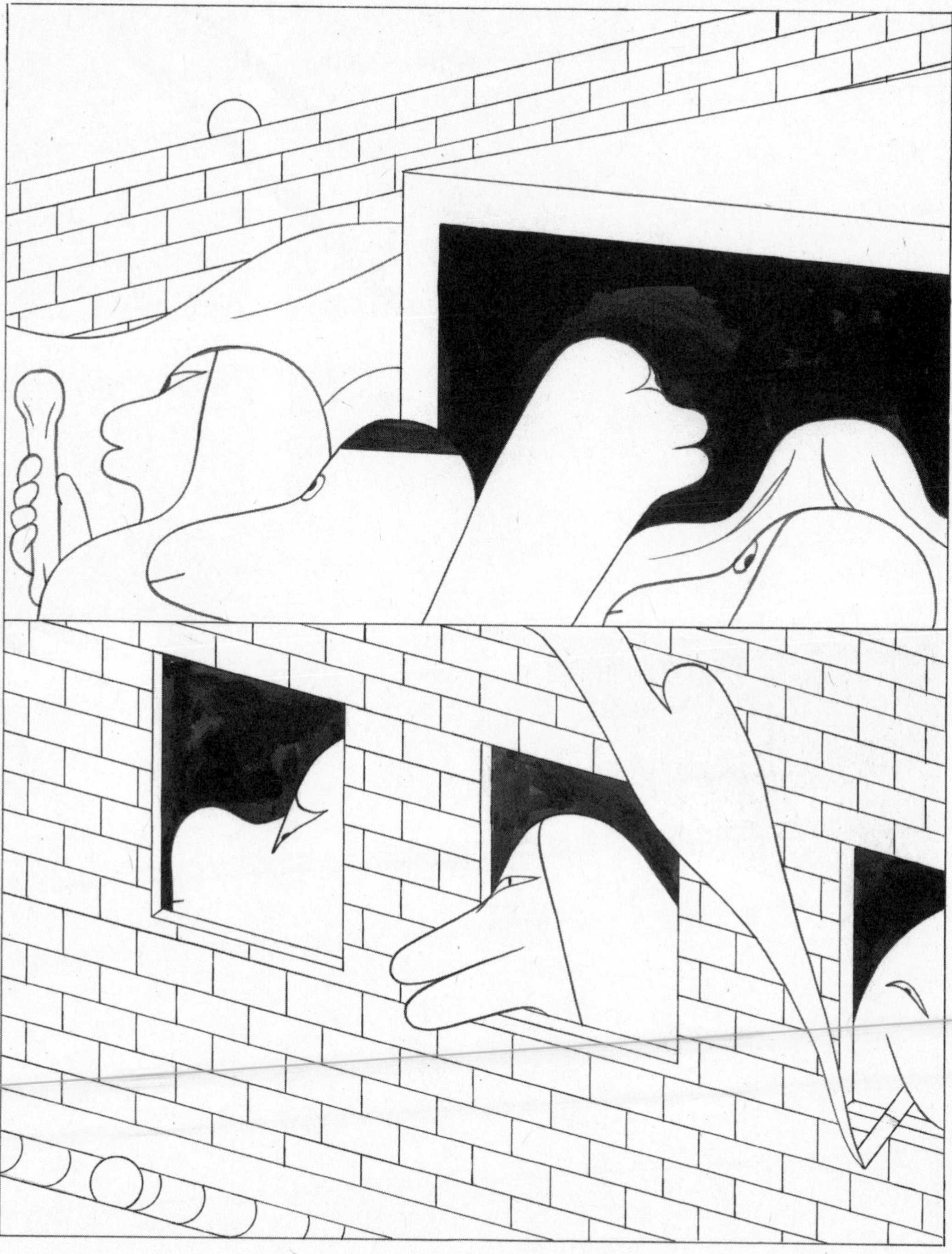

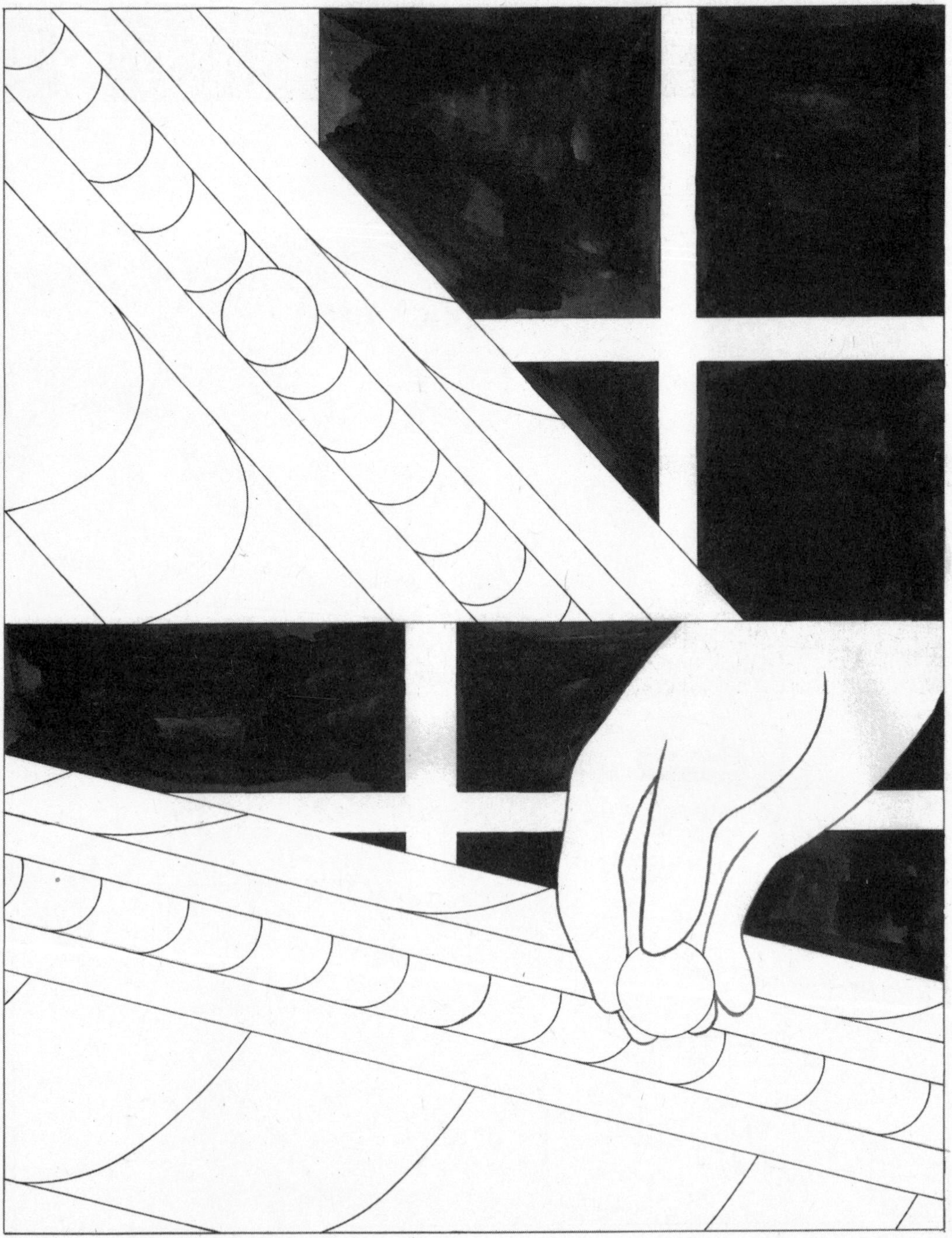

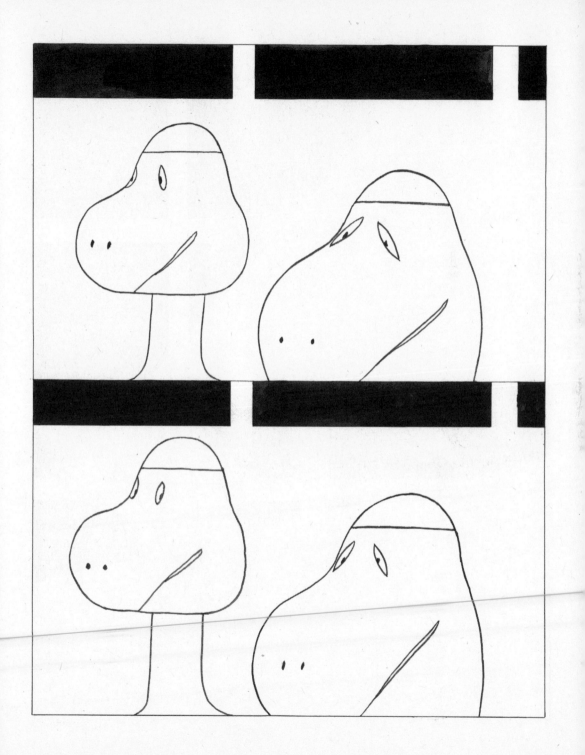

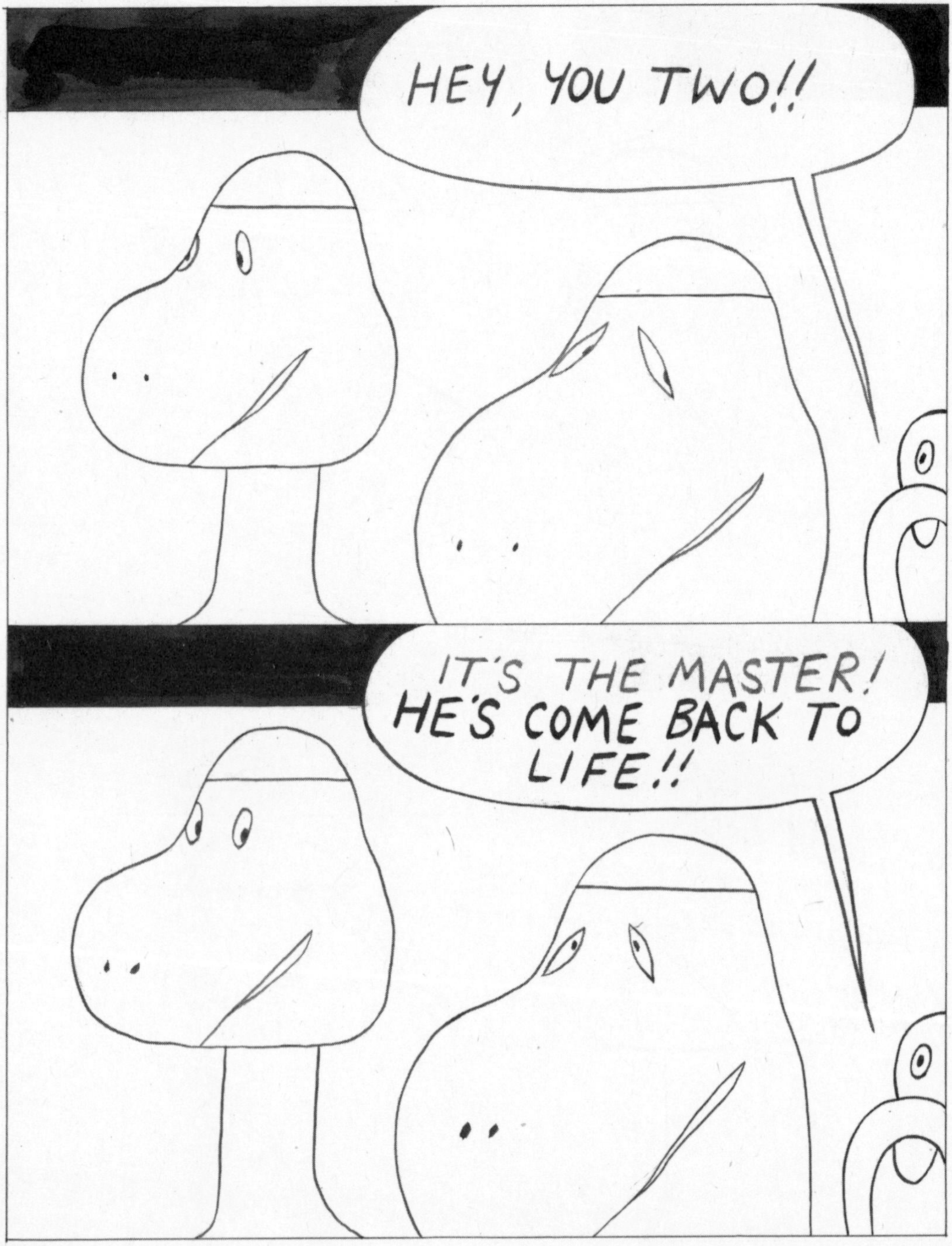
HEY, YOU TWO!!
IT'S THE MASTER! HE'S COME BACK TO LIFE!!

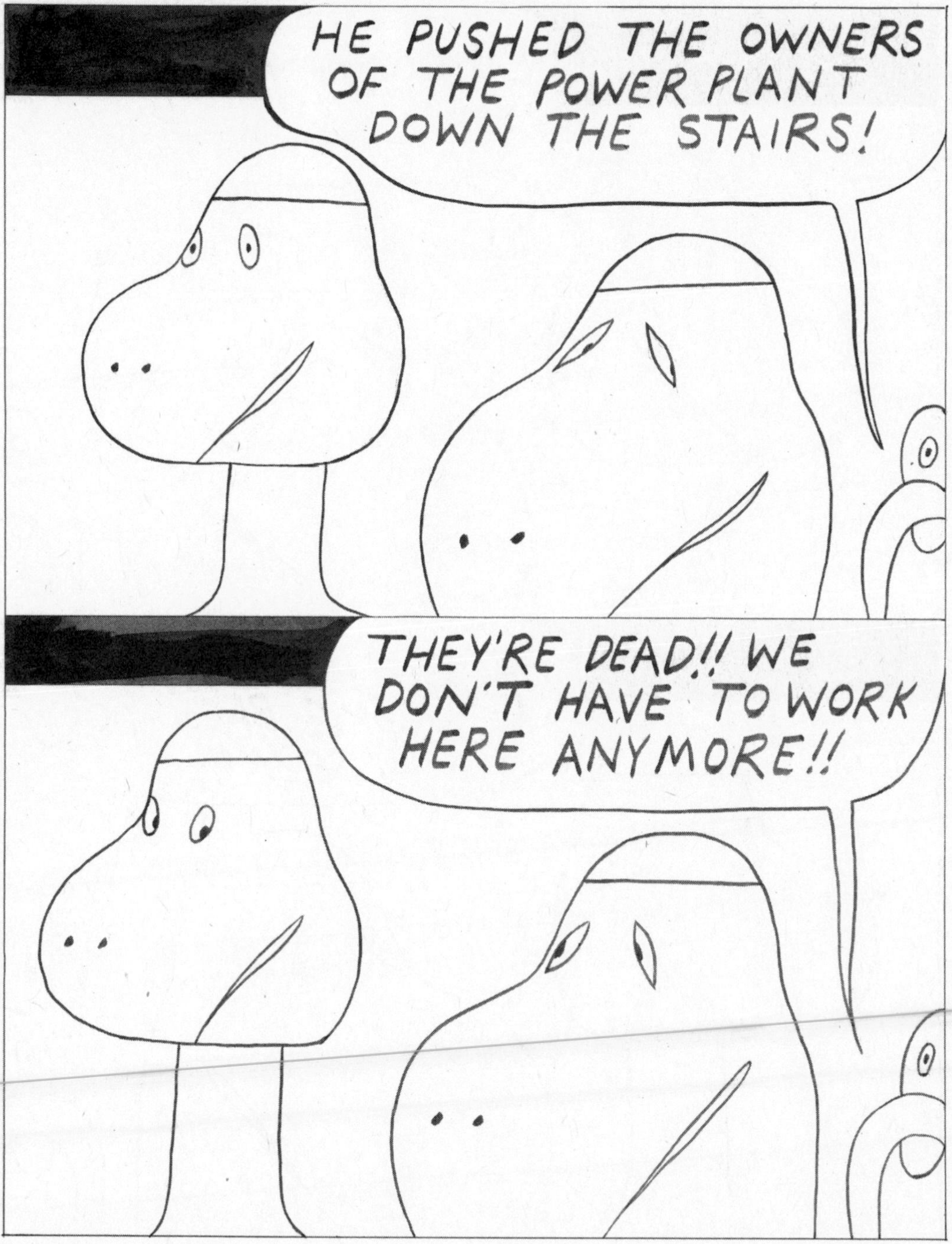
HE PUSHED THE OWNERS OF THE POWER PLANT DOWN THE STAIRS!
THEY'RE DEAD!! WE DON'T HAVE TO WORK HERE ANYMORE!!

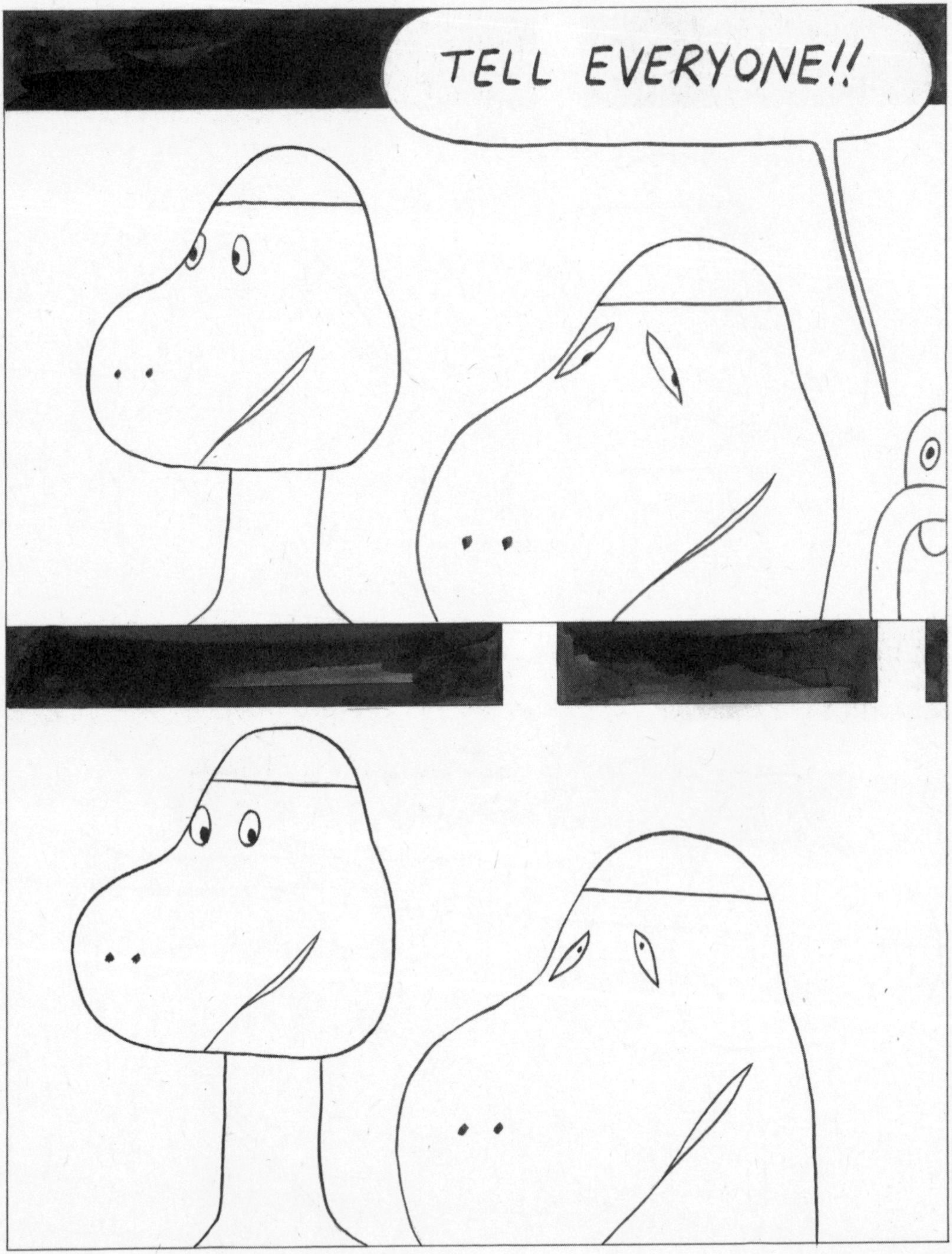
TELL EVERYONE!!

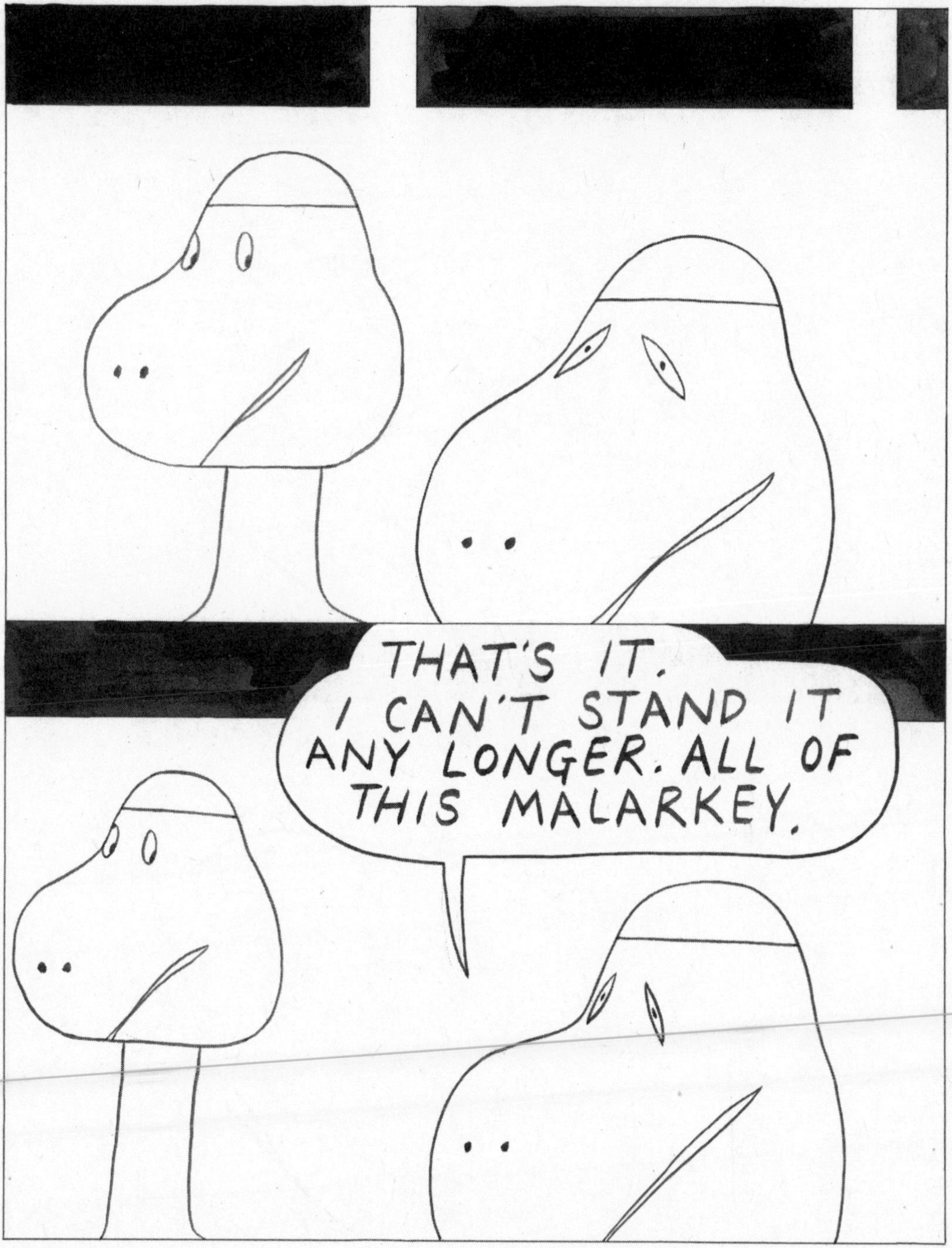
THAT'S IT. I CAN'T STAND IT ANY LONGER. ALL OF THIS MALARKEY.

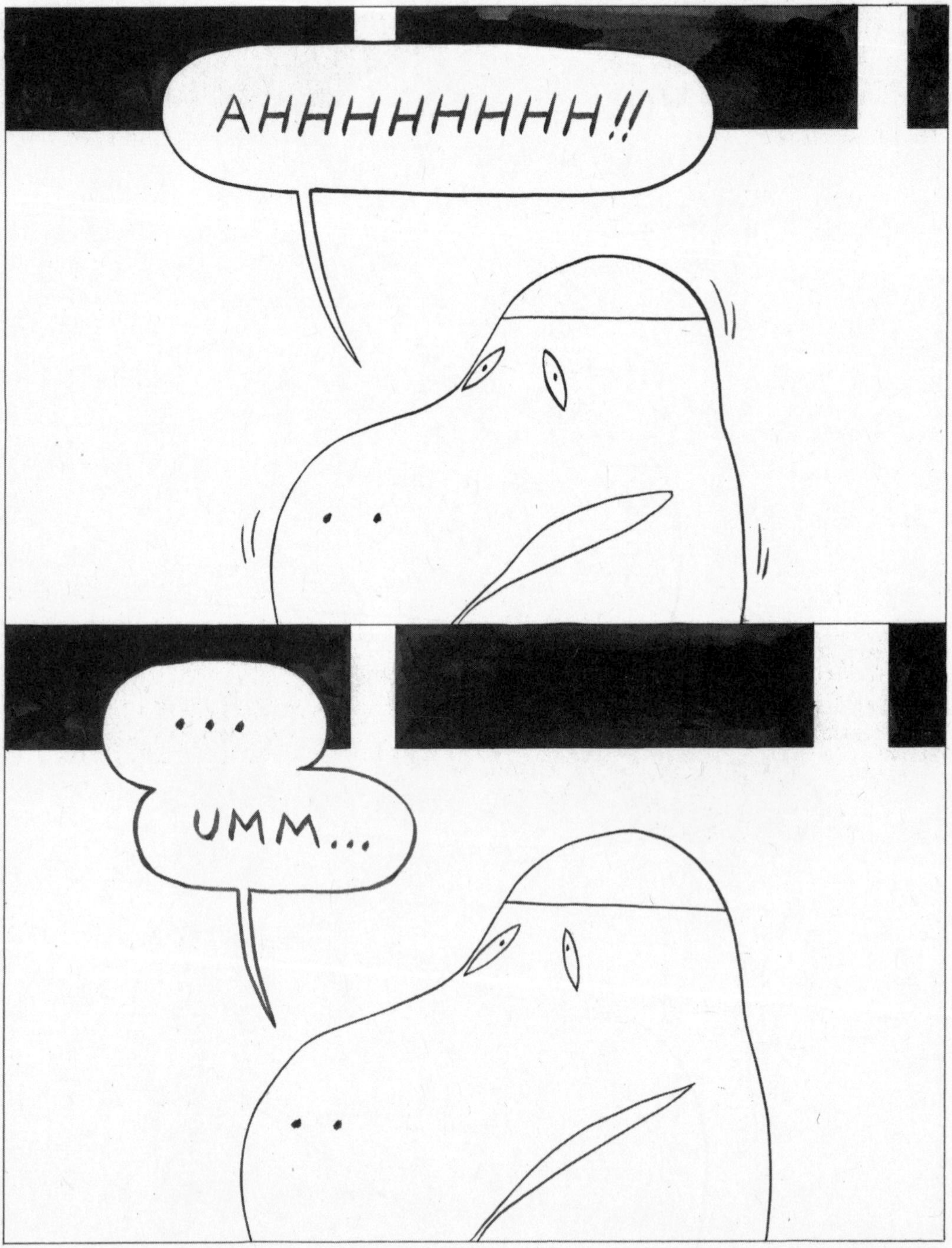
AHHHHHHHHH!!
...
UMM...

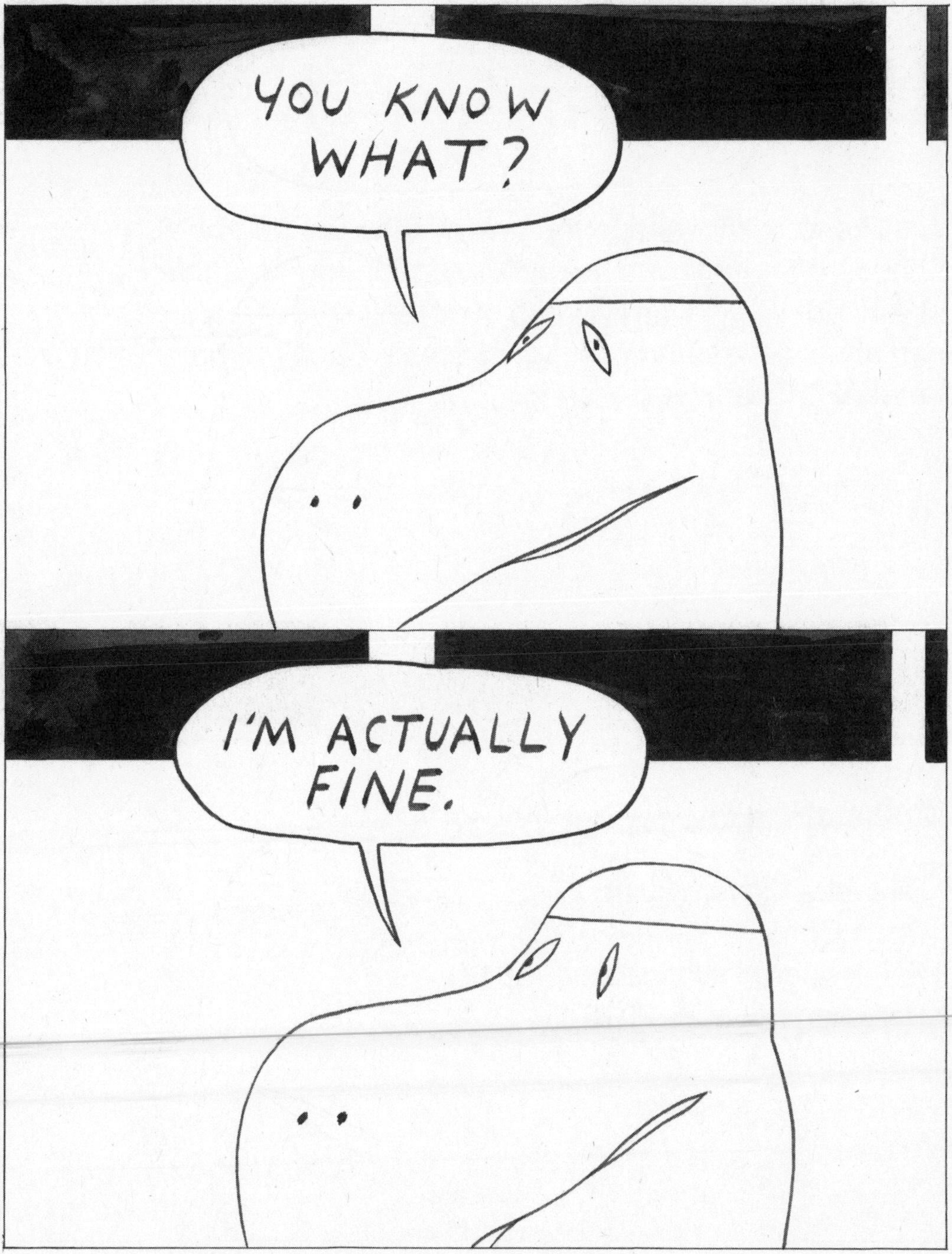
YOU KNOW WHAT?
I'M ACTUALLY FINE.

I'd like to acknowledge the unwavering support and encouragement from my publisher and friend, Annie Koyama. Working with Koyama Press over the last 10 years has been an absolute joy and privilege. I am so happy to have been a part of it. Thank you, Annie.

Other books by Patrick from Koyama Press:

Distance Mover (2014)
Don't Come in Here (2016)
Everywhere Disappeared (2017)
Roaming Foliage (2018)